MANITOBA STUDIES IN NATIV

Manitoba Studies in Native History pub   of the
historical experience of Native peoples in the western interior of North America.
The series is under the editorial direction of a board representative of the scholarly
and Native communities in Manitoba.

I *The New Peoples: Being and Becoming Métis in North America*, edited by
Jacqueline Peterson and Jennifer S.H. Brown

II *Indian-European Trade Relations in the Lower Saskatchewan River Region to
1840*, by Paul Thistle

III *"The Orders of the Dreamed": George Nelson on Cree and Northern Ojibwa
Religion and Myth, 1823*, by Jennifer S.H. Brown and Robert Brightman

IV *The Plains Cree: Trade, Diplomacy and War, 1790 to 1870*, by John S. Milloy

V *The Dakota of the Canadian Northwest: Lessons for Survival*, by Peter Douglas
Elias

VI *Aboriginal Resource Use in Canada: Historical and Legal Aspects*, edited by
Kerry Abel and Jean Friesen

VII *Severing the Ties that Bind: Government Repression of Indigenous Ceremonies
on the Prairies*, by Katherine Pettipas

VIII *The Ojibwa of Western Canada, 1780 to 1870*, by Laura Peers

The Ojibwa of Western Canada, 1780 to 1870

LAURA PEERS

THE UNIVERSITY OF MANITOBA PRESS

Printed in Canada

Printed on recycled, acid-free paper ∞

Design: Norman Schmidt

Cover/jacket illustration: Peter Rindisbacher, "Chippewa Mode of Travelling in the Spring and Summer" (courtesy West Point Museum, United States Military Academy, West Point, New York).

Canadian Cataloguing in Publication Data

Peers, Laura Lynn, 1963-
  The Ojibwa of western Canada, 1780 to 1870
  (Manitoba studies in Native history, ISSN 0826-
9416 ; 8)
  Includes bibliographical references and index.
  ISBN 0-88755-160-2 (bound) – 0-88755-636-1 (pbk.)
1. Ojibwa Indians - History. I. Title. II. Series

E99.C6P43 1994 971.2'00497 C920187-1

This series is published with the financial support of the people of Manitoba, the Honourable Harold Gilleshammer, Minister of Culture, Heritage and Citizenship. The publication of this volume was also assisted by a grant from the Canada Council.

Contents

List of Illustrations   *vii*

Preface   *ix*

Synonymy: Who Are the Western Ojibwa? A Note on Names   *xv*

1   First Steps   *3*

2   Early Expansion and Adaptation, 1780 to 1804   *27*

3   "More troublesome and daring," 1805 to 1821   *63*

4   "To take advantage of the times," 1821 to 1837   *99*

5   "Saucy & Independent," 1837 to 1857   *141*

6   "Mischiefmakers . . . [and] shrewd men," 1858 to 1870   *181*

Conclusion   *207*

Notes   *213*

References Cited   *265*

Index   *279*

Illustrations

MAPS

1. The western interior of North America *xix*
2. The Interlake and surrounding area *xx*

PHOTOGRAPHS

1. George Catlin, "The Six, Chief of the Plains Ojibwa," and "Wife of the Six" *117*
2. Western Ojibwa–style war club; found in Saskatchewan *119*
3. Peter Rindisbacher, "Winter fishing on the ice of the Assynoibain and Red River. Drawn from nature in December 1821, Manitoba" *127*
4. Peter Rindisbacher,"A savage of the Sautaux Indians on the Red River. Drawn to a twelfth part of his natural size. P. R., Manitoba, ca. 1822" *128*
5. Peter Rindisbacher, "A family from the tribe of the wild Sautaux Indians on the Red River, Manitoba, ca. 1821" *129*
6. Isobel Finlayson, "Souteaux family in the plains" *143*
7. Paul Kane, "Muck-e-too [Mukatai]," Black Powder *146*
8. Ojibwa backrest banner *147*
9. Rudolph Friedrich Kurz, "Sauteuse," western Ojibwa woman, probably from Red River *150*
10. H.L. Hime, "Birch Bark Tents, west bank of Red River, middle settlement" *182*
11. H.L. Hime "Ojibway Woman and Child" *183*
12. Western Ojibwa breechcloth design *190*
13. "Plains Cree" shirt *192*

Preface

Among the most dynamic Aboriginal peoples in western Canada today are the Ojibwa, who are known also as plains Ojibway, Saulteaux, and Bungi. The Ojibwa of the prairie provinces have played an especially vital role in the development of an Aboriginal political voice at both the provincial and federal levels of Canadian government. The former Manitoba Indian Brotherhood, and leaders such as Ovide Mercredi and Philip Fontaine, have been central to the struggles of Aboriginal people for self-determination, control of education for Native children, and the inclusion of Native rights in Canada's constitution. The pre-eminence of the Ojibwa in modern western Canada belies the fact that they are relative newcomers to the region and have occupied the parkland and prairies only since the last decades of the eighteenth century. This work traces the origins of the western Ojibwa, their adaptations to the West, and the ways in which they have coped with the many challenges they faced in the first century of their history in that region, between 1780 and 1870.

The western Ojibwa are the descendants of Ojibwa people who migrated into the West from their homes around the Great Lakes in the late eighteenth century. For them, as for all the peoples of the subarctic forests of the Canadian Shield and of the plains and parkland, this was an era of change. Between 1770 and 1870, the western Ojibwa and other peoples of the northwestern interior faced and survived waves of epidemic disease, the rise and decline of the fur trade, the depletion of game populations, the founding of non-Native settlement, the loss of tribal lands, and the Canadian government's assertion of political control over them. As a people who emerged, adapted, and survived in a climate of change, the western Ojibwa demonstrate both the effects of historic forces that acted upon Native peoples and the spirit, determination and adaptive strategies that Native people have used to cope with those forces. This study examines the emergence of the western Ojibwa within this context, seeing both the cultural changes that they chose to make and the continuity within their culture as responses to historical pressures. The origins, motivations, and development of the western Ojibwa can best be understood as the products of a creative, dynamic tension between continuity and change, between human choice and necessity, between historic forces created by humans and the environment, and between the influences of the very different ecological and cultural systems they encountered. The distinguishing hallmark of the western Ojibwa is this tension, an integration of tradition and adaptation.

Previous scholarly studies of western Ojibwa culture and history have emphasized the effects of their move from the woodlands of the Lake Superior region to the radically different western plains environment.[1] Not only was this a movement between ecological zones, but it was also a movement between what anthropologists have designated as two very different "culture areas," which corresponded with these regions. Culture areas are categories devised by anthropologists to facilitate analysis; there are many different culture areas in North America, each comprising a major ecological zone and a number of cultures that reside in that region, using many of the same resources and having many of the same cultural features or traits. The "woodlands" and "plains" culture areas have been two of the most important ones in the history of scholarship on North American Native peoples, and anthropologists developed lists of typical features (or "traits") for each early in this century. For plains peoples, these features encompassed a complex of behaviour and material culture that included "dependence on buffalo, skin tipis, use of the horse, emphasis on warfare, police forces, military societies, ritual complex including the sun dance, and distinctive geometric designs." Woodland cultures had none of these but had their own distinctive forms of housing, transportation, social organization, and decorative arts.[2]

Since earlier studies of the western Ojibwa by ethnologists Alanson Skinner, James Howard, and others were based on the culture-area theory, they focused on the changes engendered in western Ojibwa culture by their movement between different sets of resources and surrounding cultural influences, and to a certain extent on the novelty of a people moving between almost diametrically opposed anthropological categories. Thus, Alanson Skinner described the "plains Ojibway" (as contrasted to woodland Ojibwa) as being "a perhaps unparalleled example of mixed culture – almost half and half [of woodlands and plains]," and James Howard stated that they had "reoriented their culture from one suited to a lake and forest habitat to one neatly adjusted to life on the Plains," during which process crucial elements of woodlands culture "gave way" to corresponding elements of plains cultures.[3]

While these earlier studies of the western Ojibwa evaluated the presence or absence of "plains" traits among them, they lacked sufficient historical detail to reconstruct the reasons for the adoption or rejection of particular traits, the manner in which new ways of life were adopted, and the rich and complex nature of interaction between the western Ojibwa and their neighbours, especially the Cree and the Métis. Furthermore, the culture-area analysis tended to suggest that people were somehow fenced in by the limits of their culture areas, while it is evident that many western Ojibwa shifted back and forth between different ecological zones and lifestyles. The western Ojibwa were not as "neatly adjusted" as Howard believed.

By focusing closely on the details of western Ojibwa history in the crucial century of their emergence, I take a different approach from earlier studies and reach different conclusions. Clearly, the western Ojibwa made many adaptations to the new physical and human environments they encountered in the parkland and prairies, and to the changing tides of history; I examine the causes and processes of these adaptations here in detail. In addition to these changes, I examine the continuity in western Ojibwa culture, for these people maintained a vital core of the culture they brought with them to the West, which formed the basis of their identity. Though their way of life changed, in some cases drastically, they were still Ojibwa. Even those bands that adopted "plains" cultural features did so as one dons a new coat, and they retained their older, central core of identity beneath their new way of life. The western Ojibwa have much to teach us about the reality of cultural and historic adaptation, and the limits of ethnographic categories.

In examining continuity in western Ojibwa culture, I have found the concept of *ethnicity* to be useful. If the adoption of new cultural traits by the western Ojibwa was the result of new external (environmental and human) forces they encountered, the maintenance of an Ojibwa heritage rested on the internal, more intimate forces determining ethnicity. Ethnicity has been defined by Karl Barth as a personal identity that is based on a feeling of belonging to a group of people with similar lifestyles and ancestry. An ethnic group distinguishes its own members by behaviours and beliefs that the members of the group perceive as significant characteristics, values, and standards of the group. These function to sustain group identity and boundaries between members of the group (who conform to such standards) and outsiders (who do not). They include body language, clothing and decorative styles, values, reputation for certain abilities, etiquette, the group name, ascription or recognition by other peoples, widespread (although not universal) sharing of a common language, religion, artistic style, and a sense of a history, identity, way of life, and values distinct from those held by their ancestors and by neighbouring peoples.[4]

Despite these boundaries, for a multitude of reasons, the behaviour of people in one culture may come to more closely resemble that of a culture other than their own.[5] Nor do these changes necessarily lead to corresponding changes in ethnicity. An individual or a group of people may begin to dress differently, obtain their food from different sources, and move to a region never before inhabited by their people, but still identify themselves as the same people and instill a sense of heritage based on this identity in their children. This, I believe, was an important factor in the emergence of the western Ojibwa. They adopted many new behaviours ("culture traits"), and in some cases came to resemble the plains people around them, but they continued to be identified as Ojibwa and to maintain many aspects of the way of life they had brought with them into the West.

This work also differs from previous studies of the western Ojibwa in that it is primarily historical rather than ethnographic in nature, and it is based on historical documents to which Skinner, Howard, and other pioneering scholars did not have access. Documentary evidence has strengths as well as some peculiar limitations for the writing of Native history. On the one hand, the documents that I consulted – fur traders' journals and accounts, missionaries' journals and reports, explorers' and sightseers' records – yielded a rich and detailed mass of data that provide the means of reconstructing patterns of change and adaptations to specific historical events among the western Ojibwa. On the other hand, these sources must be used carefully, for they were generated by non-Native authors for particular purposes. The cultural biases of the authors, and the topical gaps created in our understanding by what they did not record, mean that the window they open on western Ojibwa life and history is narrow, and the view through it is limited and at times distorted. Traders' and missionaries' accounts tell us largely what happened around the trading posts and mission stations, and reliance on them tends to produce historical interpretations that over-emphasize the role of these institutions in Native society. The information such documents give us is not necessarily applicable to all the western Ojibwa outside these spheres of interaction. One has only to examine the rare documents produced by Native people or by those who lived with Native people for extended periods – the captivity narrative of John Tanner, for instance, who lived with an Ottawa-Ojibwa band in the West for several decades – to realize how very differently Native people saw their own lives. Eurocentric as the documents tend to be, however, they do give us a basic frame of reference – a base line for measuring change – which can be augmented and corrected with other kinds of evidence.

My own method of dealing with topical gaps and cultural bias in the data has been to use non-documentary sources, including transcribed oral history, archaeological data, and the evidence presented by material culture and photographic and art images, to fill in some of the gaps left by the archival sources, and to focus on western Ojibwa methods of coping with historical change. With this basic framework, it is possible to sift and piece together data, to compensate for a good deal of bias, and to reconstruct – albeit from an outsider's perspective – a coherent picture in which the western Ojibwa can be seen to have played an active role in coping with historical forces. I acknowledge, however, that the understanding of western Ojibwa culture and history that can be recreated from these sources is only partial, and that the perspective in this study is largely an outsider's. This study should be seen as an introduction to a people and an era in their history, and it is my hope that this work will be followed by others, by both Native and non-Native scholars.

A final word on the geographic scope of this work is in order. Although it outlines the emergence and history of the western Ojibwa as a people, it is not comprehensive. I have chosen to focus on several specific areas, leaders, and bands to make essential points about the development of this people as a whole, points that could also be applied to areas and bands not covered in the book. The groups I have focused most closely on are those that generally traded in British territory and that ultimately took treaty on the British/Canadian side of the border. This focus reflects the locations of most of the western Ojibwa bands themselves, their primary trade and political relationships with non-Natives, and the nature of the data on which the study is based. It does not do justice to the western Ojibwa (Chippewa) of Turtle Mountain and vicinity, nor to those Ontario, Minnesota, and Wisconsin peoples who moved back and forth from woodland to prairie, though it does indicate relationships among these groups. The stronger ties of these "border" bands to relatives and other peoples to the East suggest that their history would be best analysed separately, and it is hoped that the present study may contribute to the writing of such a work.

Many people have assisted me in learning and writing about the western Ojibwa, and I wish to acknowledge their contributions here. First and foremost, I would like to acknowledge the teachings and examples of the Ojibwa in Ontario and Manitoba who have helped to shape my understanding of the western Ojibwa, however incomplete that understanding may be; my limitations are no fault of theirs. My appreciation of the vitality of Ojibwa culture and history was formed while I was a student in the Department of Native Studies at Trent University from 1981 to 1985, especially by the elders and cultural-resource people who taught at the elders' conferences there and by elders with whom I worked in a number of Ojibwa and Oji-Cree communities during those years. I owe an especial debt to the late elder Fred Wheatley, who introduced me to Ojibwa language and its relationship to Ojibwa culture and history. Two courses that I taught, in 1988 and 1992, for students from the Peguis Reserve under the auspices of the University of Winnipeg, were especially enlightening for me, and I thank my students for contributing to a mutual exchange of knowledge. These and other contacts have increased my admiration for the tenacity of Ojibwa culture in its many forms. That I still have much to learn about the Ojibwa, and about the differences in our cultural perceptions, was pointed out to me most usefully by Judge C. Murray Sinclair, who read the draft manuscript of this work from an Anishinabe perspective: I thank him for bringing his knowledge and his patience to bear on this study.

The first half of this work began life as a Master's thesis in the Joint Master's Program in history at the Universities of Winnipeg and Manitoba, and I would like to acknowledge the assistance given by my thesis committee, whose perceptive questions and comments helped to refine my analysis and writing: Professors Jean Friesen, Wayne Moodie, and George Schultz. To my thesis advisor, Professor Jennifer S.H. Brown, whose fine scholarship, continuous assistance, and patience helped to shape my thinking on western Ojibwa history throughout the thesis-writing process and subsequent revisions, I would like to express my gratitude and admiration.

Those who have read my thesis will recognize that my thinking on the western Ojibwa has taken different directions since; in particular, my emphasis on continuities within western Ojibwa culture has increased greatly. This emphasis developed gradually, and it became a major theme after I encountered the work of Lauren Ritterbush on the early expansion of the Ojibwa and Ottawa into the prairies, and after comments by and conversations with Judge Murray Sinclair. I am grateful for their ideas and encouragement. My thanks, as well, to Professor Gerald Friesen, who has done much to transform an Ontarian into a scholar of western Canadian history, and whose enthusiasm and thoughtful editing encouraged me to complete the revisions to the thesis; and to Lauren Ritterbush and the anonymous manuscript readers whose comments helped to refine the final work.

I also owe sincere thanks to many other scholars who have generously shared unpublished material, research notes, and thoughts on the western Ojibwa. Mary Watrous provided crucial technical support during the initial revision stage, and Patricia Dowdall, Carol Dahlstrom, and Allison Campbell of the University of Manitoba Press were unfailingly helpful throughout the production period. Many thanks also to Victor Lytwyn for his fine cartographic work. This study could not have been conducted without the permission of the Hudson's Bay Company to research in and quote from their archives, or without financial assistance provided by a University of Manitoba Alumni Fellowship, for both of which I am grateful. Finally, I would like to thank my parents and sister for their encouragement, and especially my partner, Drew Davey, for offering me, over the entire six years during which this work was being produced, the most important support of all.

* * *

Quotations from historic documents used in this work are cited verbatim; verb tenses, capitalization, spelling and punctuation are exactly as they appear in the original.

Synonymy: Who are the Western Ojibwa?
A Note on Names

The people whom I am calling *western Ojibwa* in this book are also known in Canada as *Saulteaux* and *plains Ojibwa*, and occasionally as *Bungi*. Different parts of Canadian society know them by different names, and the names by which they refer to themselves differ from community to community. Today, in the eastern part of their territory, including the Peguis reserve and Winnipeg, many of them strongly prefer *Ojibwa* or *Anishinabeg,* while communities farther to the west prefer *plains Ojibway* or *Saulteaux.* Given the number of names for these people, it seems appropriate to discuss the origin of these different terms and the reasons for my choice in this book. I sincerely hope that persons who think of themselves as Saulteaux will not be offended by my choice of a different term to refer to their ancestors, and that they will understand the reasons for my choice.

Looking first at the origins of these terms, it is clear that the several names by which these people became known to Europeans during the early historic period are tied to the different relationships between themselves and rival European trading companies. The French who encountered the ancestors of the western Ojibwa in the Sault Ste. Marie region wrote of them as *Saulteurs* (later, the term became *Saulteaux*) and *Outchibouec* (which later became *Ojibwa* or *Chippewa*).[1] When these and neighbouring peoples became involved in the French fur trade, contact and intermarriage between them intensified as European goods were traded from band to band on a regular basis in exchange for furs collected by Native middlemen. As well, large communities composed of several Native peoples sprang up at missions and trading posts such as Sault Ste. Marie and Michilimackinac. Developments such as these may have eroded ethnic differences between small local groups, contributing to the spread of the terms *Saulteur* and *Ojibwa* to designate many formerly separate peoples who had been connected to the Outchibouec and Saulteurs by kinship, trade relationships, and probably similarity of language and other cultural practices.[2] French and Montreal-based traders referred to all these peoples as Saulteurs or Saulteaux wherever they encountered them for centuries after their first meeting at the Sault, and after the incorporation of many French-speaking employees of the North West Company into the reformed Hudson's Bay Company in 1821, the term became standard. Thus, it is necessary to bear in mind that, while most Europeans referred to Saulteaux in the West in the nineteenth century, this does not mean that the Saulteaux they spoke of had migrated directly from the Sault. The term merely recognizes a common heritage, rather than a precise place of origin.

Different names for the same people evolved in their relationship with the Hudson's Bay Company. After the Company established its bayside posts in the 1670s, some "Saulteurs" began making the long journey to trade with them at the Bay. In the 1720s and 1730s, the arrival of "Echeepoes" and "Oachiapoia Indians" at Fort Albany was noted in the journals. These terms were renderings of *ocipwe* or *Ojibwa*, the "Outchibouec" people whom the French had met almost a century earlier.[3]

Hudson's Bay Company servants also referred to the Ojibwa in terms related to fur-trade rivalry. At Fort Albany in 1733, Joseph Adams called them "the French Canada Indians" because they traded primarily with the Canadians, and James Isham referred to them in 1743 as "the Nakawawuck Indians, who border's by the Little Sea so Calld. where the french Settlement is."[4] As the frequency of contact increased between them, however, the Honourable Company's servants began using a term based on their own experiences with these Natives. "Pung'ke petun'n Enwewe son, Give me something to Eat I am a hungry or Starv'd," was the first sentence of James Isham's 1743 "Nakawawuck" vocabulary, and *pung'ke* or *bungee,* the plea for "a little bit," was the word most often heard by the traders from these people when the traders' gifts were "not adequate to their wants."[5] It was as "Bungees," then, that the ancestors of the western Ojibwa were usually referred to by Hudson's Bay Company servants – except, of course, when the Hudson's Bay Company servant had formerly been in the employ of one of the Canadian trading companies.[6] The fur traders themselves recognized the confusion over names, as shown by Alexander Henry the Younger's attempt to clarify it in his published journals: "The Ogeebois are commonly called . . . by the Canadians Saulteurs," he wrote, "and by the H.B. Co. servants Bungees."[7]

In the prairies and parklands, terms shifted with the currents of history. The early records, before 1821, speak of Saulteaux, Bungees, and Ojibwa. After 1821, the term most frequently used was *Saulteaux.* Individual men had great influence in popularizing the use of certain terms. Peter Fidler instituted the use of *Bungee* at Brandon House in 1816 when he wrote the journal there; before that, they had been called *Sotos* or *Ochippeways* in the Brandon House records. Similarly, Miles Macdonell (who had a brother, John, in the North West Company) popularized the use of *Saulteaux* in the Red River Settlement records. At the end of the period of this study, records generated by men from Ontario, who recognized the similarity between the "Saulteaux" of the West and the Ojibwa of Ontario, use the term *Ojibwa* or *Ojibway*.

For the purposes of this book, choosing a single term was most difficult. Those who have encountered my other work will note that the terms I have used have shifted over the past few years from *western Ojibwa* to *Saulteaux* and back to *western Ojibwa*. I am not trying to confuse, nor to reveal any confusion on my own part, by this vacillation. Rather, this uncertainty reflects the problems involved in linking present scholarship with historical complexity. My reasoning in choosing the term *western Ojibwa* is as follows:

Ideally, I would like to use an ethnonym, the name that a group gives itself, which often differs from the names that are given to a people by the groups around them. Unfortunately, there is not a single instance of such a term in the historic record. Even Europeans who spoke Native languages, some of whom had wives and kin from this group, invariably referred to these people as *Saulteaux* or *Bungee* or *Ojibwa*. In northwestern Ontario and southern Manitoba, the ethnonym used by the Ojibwa is *Anishinabe*, meaning "original man," or "first people." This is nowhere used in any historic document pertaining to these people in the West that I have found, however, and, while it is reasonable to assume that the people might have used this as their ethnonym, I cannot make such a leap and use this term in a book based on documentary evidence. Ethnologist James Howard claimed that the Chippewa of Turtle Mountain referred to themselves as *nakawininiok,* meaning "those who speak differently," but this is nowhere corroborated in the literature.[8]

Lacking a documented ethnonym, I was faced with a choice of one of the terms used by Europeans in the historic records to refer to this people. This choice has been influenced by my own perspective and by the strong wishes of some of the western Ojibwa to whom I have spoken. Above all, I hoped that modern Ojibwa in western Canada might identify with the people about whom I am writing. The terms that are most often heard today are *Saulteaux* and *Ojibway*; *Bungi* is used only infrequently, and therefore I chose not to use it. In making a final choice between *Saulteaux* and *Ojibway,* I was forcefully reminded by the Aboriginal reader of this manuscript that *Saulteaux* is very definitely a European word, deriving from the original French *Saulteur,* and that some contemporary Aboriginal people reject such terms. *Ojibway* is more acceptable in some communities (though not, I realize, in others), and so I have chosen to use a variant of that, which reflects my own perspective on these people as western members of the widespead Ojibwa family: hence, *western Ojibwa*.

Similar problems have emerged with the terms for the Siouan neighbours of the western Ojibwa. These peoples are generally referred to in the historic documents as *Sioux*, but sometimes instead as *Dakota* or by specific band names. Information is very limited on just who these people were and where they came from. I have chosen to use the terms found most often in the documents (*Sioux* and *Dakota*), and have quoted exact terms where these seem unusual. It is my hope that future research may clarify the identities of these people.

One of the most fascinating aspects of preparing this study has been the realization that names have power, and that in today's society band and tribal names are chosen with power in mind: political power, the power of self-determination, the power to reclaim control over the lives, destinies, and, to a certain extent, the portrayal of the heritages of Aboriginal people. In choosing the terms *western Ojibwa, Sioux,* and *Dakota,* I recognize that these names may not be acceptable to all of the descendants of the eighteenth- and nineteenth-century individuals about whom I write, or to scholars who are accustomed to different terms. In the end, the choice has been my own, and the difficulty of making it is a reflection of the rich and extremely complex history of these people.

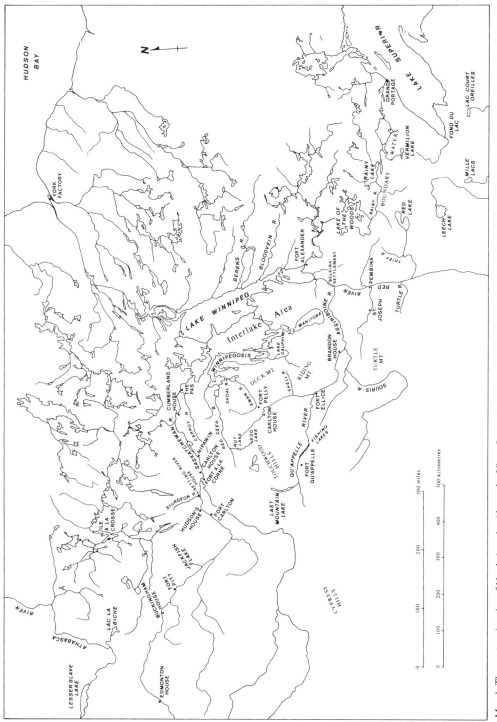

Map 1. The western interior of North America (drawn by Victor Lytwyn)

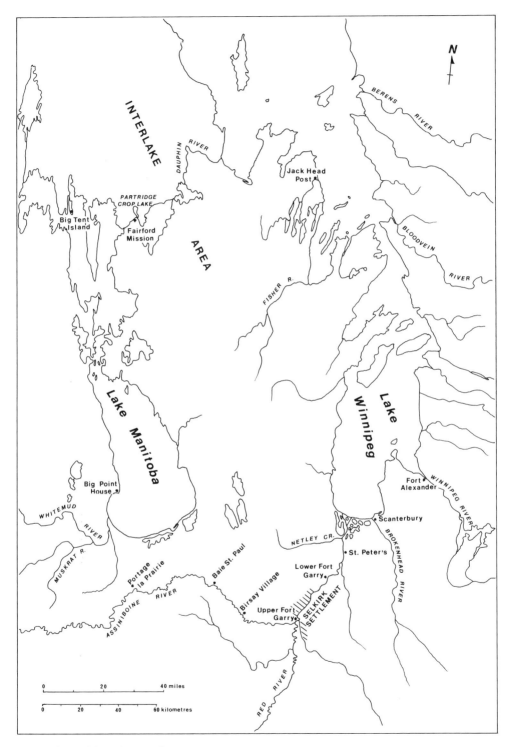

Map 2. The Interlake and surrounding area (drawn by Victor Lytwyn)

The Ojibwa of Western Canada, 1780 to 1870

First Steps

1

In the last decades of the eighteenth century, small groups of Ojibwa left their homes in the forests around western Lake Superior and began moving farther westward, into the prairies and parkland. Attracted by westward-moving trade opportunities and the chance to maintain a high quality of life – opportunities highlighted by the effects of over-hunting and smallpox in their homelands – these people spread out along the Red River, through the Interlake area, the Assiniboine and North Saskatchewan rivers, and other major water routes as far west as Edmonton House, Lesser Slave Lake, and the Columbia River. As they settled into these new regions, their way of life changed – subtly in some cases, dramatically in others. Despite their adaptations to the West, though, the identity of the western Ojibwa continued to be founded firmly on their eastern heritage.

The western Ojibwa came into being as the result of complex processes set in motion by the evolving fur trade. They were, however, neither "pawns in the trade,"[1] as one scholar has accused their ancestors of being, nor direct products of it. Their emergence, and their strategies for coping with the problems and taking advantage of the opportunities created by the fur trade, exemplifies the interrelationships between human choice and the forceful currents of history. Still, it was the fur trade that provided the particular conditions that fostered the emergence of the western Ojibwa, and its history is closely connected to their own.

By the late eighteenth century, Ojibwa villages encircled western Lake Superior at prominent sturgeon fisheries and trade centres such as Grand Portage, Chequemegon, and Ontonagan River. Others were scattered throughout the forests to the west, along what is now known as the Boundary Waters – Vermilion Lake, Rainy Lake, Rainy River, Lake of the Woods – as well as a few to the west of the western tip of Lake Superior, including Milles Lacs, Leech Lake, and Red Lake (Minnesota). It was from these areas, and to a lesser extent from the region east of

Lake Winnipeg and the central Great Lakes region of Michilimackinac / Sault Ste. Marie, that the Ojibwa moved into the West.[2]

Despite the fact that they became – and, centuries later, remain – strongholds of Ojibwa culture, scholars are uncertain about just when some of these communities were first occupied by the Ojibwa. The history of the entire region north and west of Lake Superior in the century before the beginning of the Ojibwa move into the prairies is poorly documented. This is especially true for the Boundary Waters communities around Rainy Lake, which were major points of origin for the western Ojibwa, where, according to the rather scanty records, the Ojibwa appeared only some time in the fifty years before some of them decided to move farther west. There are two schools of thought about the length of the Ojibwa occupation of this region: one that the Ojibwa moved into it from farther south and east during the eighteenth century, and the other that only the name, *Ojibwa,* dispersed to Algonquian-speaking groups that were already resident in the area. As with other aspects of Ojibwa history, this background to the emergence of the western Ojibwa is tangled with the development of the fur trade and, ultimately, with the very reasons for Native participation in the trade.

The concept of an Ojibwa migration into the western Lake Superior region is suggested by the earliest historical records. The first observations of the area west of Lake Superior and along the Boundary Waters were made by Jacques de Noyons in 1688 and by La Vérendrye and his sons between 1728 and 1757, all of whom stated that the Native inhabitants of that region were Cree, Assiniboine, and Monsoni, and none of whom mentioned Ojibwa as residing in this area. The only groups readily identifiable as Ojibwa were "Saulteurs," said to be located on the shore of Lake Superior at the Kaministikwia River by 1718, and the "Ouace," believed to be an Ojibwa clan group, at the same location by 1730.[3] The first references to Ojibwa residing permanently in the Boundary Waters region do not occur until 1767.[4] Trader Alexander Henry the Elder, passing through the region in 1775, mentioned Ojibwa villages at Lac la Croix, Rainy Lake, and Rainy River. He also mentioned that there had "formerly" been a larger Ojibwa population along this route but that attacks by the Sioux had greatly diminished the Ojibwa presence there. It is impossible to know for certain the accuracy of this statement, though he may have been referring to the Ojibwa encountered by Carver in 1767.[5] On the basis of these few pieces of data, and a good deal of negative evidence, ethnohistorians have generally concluded that the Ojibwa were not present in the area north or west of Lake Superior until the mid-1700s, and that they solidified their presence in the region only after the Cree and Assiniboine residents moved westward onto the plains themselves, thus creating a "vacuum." The standard explanation for the Cree and Assiniboine movement west is that they had lost their profitable positions as middlemen in the fur trade when inland western posts were established, and they moved westward to become fur trappers and, later, bison hunters and provisioners for the western fur trade.[6]

There are a number of serious problems with these hypotheses. The idea that the Ojibwa filled a "vacuum" created by westward-moving Cree and Assiniboine has several flaws, not least of which is the implied simplicity of the process. At the very least, the Ojibwa would surely have coexisted with the other groups. Nor is the notion of a Cree and Assiniboine migration completely accepted. Ethnohistorian Dale Russell points out that there is no evidence to suggest that all the Cree and Assiniboine moved west at this time; the documents either never mention such a mass movement at all, or else they report garbled second- or third-hand information. On the other hand, La Vérendrye and others do describe the replacement of Cree and Assiniboine by Ojibwa in the Boundary Waters region in the mid-eighteenth century. One factor that may be obscuring our understanding of this process is the effect of the westward progression of Europeans on our knowledge of Native group locations: were the Native people really moving west, or did they only appear to as Europeans themselves penetrated the interior and encountered them farther westward?[7]

Another set of difficulties arises when one considers the question of group names. In asking when the Ojibwa first occupied this region, one assumes that the term *Ojibwa* was an ethnonym that referred to a discrete group in the seventeenth and eighteenth centuries, the same group to which it refers today. This is by no means a certainty. The name *Ojibwa* emerged out of a welter of names for smaller groups in the early seventeeth-century records and may have continued to be applied to other, related, groups in the eighteenth. It may not have been Ojibwa people who moved into northern Ontario and the area west of Lake Superior but rather the name *Ojibwa*, which came to apply to many groups already resident there.[8]

Given these problems of interpretation, and the lack of solid evidence, it is unclear exactly how and when communities such as Rainy Lake, Lake of the Woods, and others in the Boundary Waters region became "Ojibwa" communities, or how and when the people who were consistently identified as "Ojibwa" who moved westward from these communities emerged. All we do know is that some time between the 1730s and the mid-1760s, people identified as Ojibwa began to occupy Rainy Lake, Lake of the Woods, and much of what is now northern Ontario. By 1775, when Alexander Henry the Elder travelled along the Rainy River, the Ojibwa were so established there that they were charging tolls to traders "on account of the ability they [the Ojibwa] possessed to put a stop to all trade with the interior."[9] By the late 1770s, Ojibwa settlements were scattered throughout northern Ontario, circled Lake Superior, and were also to be found inland at Mille Lacs, Lac Court Oreille, Lac du Flambeau, and other locations.[10]

As the Ojibwa moved westward from Lake Superior into the Boundary Waters, the upper Mississippi drainage, and the upper Red River drainage, they came into conflict with the Dakota. This region offered an abundance of furs, large game, fish, and other resources, but much of it was either held or contested by the eastern Dakota. Ojibwa-Dakota relations fluctuated between periods of alliance and periods of enmity in the seventeenth and eighteenth centuries but became increasingly strained in the mid-eighteenth as the Ojibwa pushed into the Boundary Waters region and farther west and south. According to historical geographer Gary Doige, in the middle decades of the 1700s the Dakota "made major inroads among the Ojibway to the west of Lake Superior, and had thinned their ranks as far west as Lake of the Woods."[11] The conflict caused by the initial westward expansion of the Ojibwa had several results. Ojibwa north and south of Lake Superior began fighting together against the Dakota, with whom the southern bands had earlier been allied. By the late 1700s, the Ojibwa also succeeded in securing possession of the disputed lands west of Lake Superior, and began to look even farther west.[12]

Given the difficulty that the Ojibwa had in establishing settlements within what was traditionally Dakota territory, considerable debate has focused on Ojibwa motives for moving into the region. As Doige has noted, the new settlements were subject to Sioux attacks and were maintained only at the cost of lives. The Dakota objected fiercely enough to the presence of the Ojibwa that the Ojibwa population was "thinned" from the Boundary Waters all the way south to the upper Mississippi. The "debatable zone," or "contested zone" as it is known, between the Ojibwa and the Dakota is generally defined more narrowly, but it is important to recognize that Ojibwa in the entire region west of Lake Superior, including the Boundary Waters, were affected by the conflict. As well, the conflict over this region is related to the motivations for the later migration of some Ojibwa farther west into the prairie and parkland, and is therefore germane to the background of the western Ojibwa. In both cases, some scholars have concluded that movement into new regions reflected a serious need for fresh fur and game supplies to support an Ojibwa population that was dependent on the fur trade. This was how pioneer ethnohistorian Harold Hickerson interpreted the Ojibwa move into the debatable zone west of Lake Superior. According to Hickerson, Ojibwa who were dependent on European trade goods for hunting and daily life, and on deer for subsistence, were forced to wage war with the Dakota and drive them westward past the debatable zone in order to gain control of the deer and fur resources in that zone.[13]

Recent re-evaluations of Ojibwa and Dakota histories have pointed out several flaws in Hickerson's theory.[14] Most importantly, the Ojibwa were not as dependent on deer as was once thought. New data indicate that they had a well-balanced seasonal harvesting round that emphasized wild rice and fish. Deer was valued but was not so crucial that war would have been waged to protect access to deer populations. In fact, as scholar Thomas Vennum has recently observed, the debatable zone contained some of the best wild-rice stands in the region, and skirmishes were particularly likely there because both groups not only continued to harvest rice in close proximity to each other but also knew the locations of their enemies' rice stands.[15] Hickerson's theory is also weakened by the fact that the Ojibwa did not completely succeed in driving the Dakota westward out of the region. Some Dakota had begun shifting to the West by the late 1730s, well before Ojibwa movement into the region, and their own oral tradition emphatically denies that they were "driven" westward by their enemies.[16]

The resources of the debatable zone were certainly attractive to the Ojibwa. They offered fruitful subsistence and trade and the chance to readily maintain a high quality of life – but not merely, as Hickerson maintained, a final opportunity for a desperate people to survive. In addition, the Ojibwa were taking advantage of the effects of increased trade rivalry between French and British traders after the end of the French and Indian War in 1760. This rivalry gave Ojibwa groups even more incentive to enter and trap the richer areas to the west and southwest of Lake Superior and to control major trade routes such as the Boundary Waters. For the Dakota, the desire to maintain control over fur-rich lands arose not out of technological dependence on European goods but in order to be able to accumulate trade goods with which to finance the purchase of horses – and thus their transition to the plains and a position of relative independence vis-à-vis the fur trade – from other Native groups.[17]

As well, the debatable zone was also attractive to Ojibwa warriors precisely because it was debated. In addition to game, furs, rice, and fish, and the profits to be gained from controlling traders' access to the region, the debatable zone offered the opportunity to harass a traditional enemy. Their desire to occupy the disputed territory, then, was not only over access to furs and game but also to fulfill personal and group desires for revenge and status – reasons as valid to them as economic and technological ones have been to non-Native, twentieth-century scholars.

In the end, the villages established on the borders of and within the debatable zone were stepping stones in the continued westward movement of the Ojibwa, and the reasons for Ojibwa exploitation of this region were similar to their reasons for exploring the area west of Red River. These motives were far more complex than the simple idea that the Ojibwa were forced to move west because of their dependence on the fur trade, although the fur trade was certainly the most important reason for these events. Understanding this seeming paradox is crucial to an understanding of Ojibwa history generally, and requires further consideration.

THE FUR TRADE AND THE OJIBWA

In the many questions that surround the Ojibwa occupation of their historic Boundary Waters and western Lake Superior communities, one thing is clear: the fur trade played a crucial role in the birth and history of these communities and in the decision of some Ojibwa to continue moving west, into the parkland and prairies, in the last decades of the eighteenth century. Given the importance of the fur trade in Ojibwa history, one might well ask how it became so, and why, indeed, they entered it in the first place. These questions revolve around the central issue of whether the western Ojibwa and their ancestors were dependent on the fur trade, and whether the western Ojibwa emerged because they were under the control of fur traders and because their ancestors were forced to move west in search of fresh fur stocks after those closer to their homes became depleted. This is the argument that has generally been given for the origins of the western Ojibwa; however, while there is some truth in it, it is simplistic.[18] Other factors, including the motivations and goals of Native people who participated in the fur trade, need to be considered. In addition, some thought needs to be given to what the term *dependence* really means, and whether Native peoples saw their participation in (and dependence upon, if such it was) the fur trade in the same manner as have non-Native fur traders and scholars.

We cannot assume that Native people regarded the fur trade in the same manner as Europeans, or that they traded for the same reasons. To begin with, the fur trade was not a novel concept to the Ojibwa, whose ancestors participated in a continent-wide prehistoric trading network.[19] It was no great leap for this existing system to expand to include Europeans and their goods, and thus to some extent they viewed the fur trade in the same manner as they viewed the older trade, and they participated in it for many of the same reasons. Furthermore, Native people engaged in trade not only to obtain goods but also for political reasons: to create and sustain alliances and friendly relations among tribes.[20] Given the extraordinarily direct relationship between trade and politics in the early-seventeenth-century Great Lakes region – a relationship that resulted in the dispersal of the Huron confederacy and the waves of change that this generated around the Great Lakes – Ojibwa leaders may well have felt it expedient to participate in the fur trade and thus cultivate European allies.

Trade was also stimulated by reasons related to the practice of reciprocity and the ethic of sharing among Native societies. Native people were expected to share possessions and food with friends and kin, with the expectation that something given would be matched by a return gift (not necessarily of the same item) in the future: a form of barter and a means of maintaining social relations at the same time. A great deal of social pressure was exerted on people to share. Hoarding or refusing to share was regarded as shameful, while the ability to provide (and thus to give) generous amounts of food, hides, and other materials to share was highly valued and conferred prestige. Ojibwa hunters who prided themselves on their ability to supply large numbers of highly desired furs to the traders may also have been priding themselves on their ability to obtain trade goods for their bands.[21] In short, the European concept of trading as an economic exchange is a much narrower one than that which would have been held by seventeenth-century Ojibwa, for whom it was also a political and social obligation and a tool for enhancing prestige.

As well, some European goods appealed to Native groups on grounds other than technical practicality. Many of the most popular trade items could be considered purely non-functional and decorative from a European perspective: glass beads, vermilion paint, and shiny metal jewellery. To Native people, however, these items had significant spiritual and social meanings, which made them desirable. In a cross-cultural exchange, trade goods may mean different things to each side.

In attempting to understand how Native people regarded these trade items, we should note first that much of what circulated in the pre-historic trade included light-coloured, reflective, and red materials such as shell, crystalline stone (mica, quartzite, and exotic flint), and copper. Early references to the use of these materials in northeastern North America indicate that they were associated with the forces of life and well-being, and items made from them carried connotations of supernatural power.[22] Such items were often used in healing and divination ceremonies or worn to lend their protective powers to the wearer. Their association with life-giving powers gave such materials and objects made from them the promise of "long life, . . . well-being, . . . and success, particularly in . . . hunting and fishing, warfare, and courtship."[23] Personal decoration using such objects had special significance in this context. According to curator Ruth Phillips, "Rich dress was valued throughout the Great Lakes; . . . a display of richly decorated clothing was a further mark of the successful hunter and warrior, a success which . . . could only have been achieved with the help of a personal manito [guardian spirit]." Personal decoration was not simply a display of material wealth, then, but a statement and mark of respect for spiritual assistance and guidance.[24] Using materials that had connotations of sacred power for personal decoration, both of the body and of one's clothing, would thus have elevated these materials and decorations far beyond the status of ornamental "baubles."

Scholar George Hammell notes that the same associations held true for European items made of similar colours and textures as their Native analogues.[25] European trade goods such as brass and trade-silver ornaments, wampum and glass beads, metal goods, and red cloth were therefore desirable for the powers they connoted, rather than solely for their decorative appeal. Certainly, the popularity of certain colours of cloth and beads – red cloth, sky-blue beads – and items such as mirrors and (shiny) trade-silver jewellery suggests that to Native eyes these items resonated with such meanings and powers. Thus, vermilion paint, obtained from traders, was used in the same ceremonial manner as Native-harvested red ochre, and red cloth became a favourite item to sacrifice to powerful beings. John Long, who traded with Ojibwa north of Lake Superior in the 1770s, gave their term for glass trade beads as *mannetoo menance*, or spirit berries.[26] That these special objects were available locally and readily after the advent of the fur trade made them especially desirable.

At least in part, then, Ojibwa were drawn into the fur trade because it and European trade goods corresponded with existing aspects of Ojibwa culture and not necessarily because they were overwhelmed by a novel technology. As Chippewa author Gerald Vizenor has reminded us, Ojibwa identity, history, and motives have always been tied to the sacred.[27] But if these points of intercultural "fit" stimulated a desire to participate in the fur trade, was this desire to trade ultimately overwhelmed by a need to trade? Did they become dependent on the trade? And was the emergence of the western Ojibwa the result of a dependence that led them ever farther afield in quest of furs to support themselves?

Fur traders – and, later, scholars who drew uncritically on traders' works – have argued that Native people became involved in the fur trade because they desired European trade goods, which were technologically superior to their own stone knives, clay pots, and other tools. As the fur trade progressed and stocks of large game were depleted, Native people began to need larger amounts of trade cloth in lieu of leather for clothing. As well, Natives and traders (and, later, scholars) alike claimed that Native people quickly forgot how to produce their aboriginal tools and weapons, which had been replaced by European trade goods that became necessary for survival: "Within a decade of their becoming acquainted with European goods, tribe after tribe became utterly dependent on regular European supplies. The bow and arrow went out of use, and the Indian starved if he did not own a serviceable gun, power and shot."[28]

Recently dubbed the "cultural amnesia" argument, such statements focus on what was perceived (by Europeans) as the poverty of Native people and their inability to sustain a decent standard of living without European goods, and on the hardships that Native people supposedly underwent when they were deprived of these goods or of the means of obtaining them. Furthermore, the standard argument goes, the amount of time Native people began devoting within their seasonal round to trapping limited the amount of time they could spend hunting, and this, combined with the decline of large game, made them reliant on trade blankets, cloth, and handouts of food from trappers. All these factors supposedly caused

Native people to become wholly dependent on European goods and on trapping for furs to obtain them, creating an escalating cycle of desperation.[29] As noted recently by Shepard Krech III, these ideas have been accepted and have become pervasive in the literature on Native people without a consensus on the actual definition of the concept of "dependence."[30] Clearly, it is a concept that requires defining and greater caution in its application to Native cultures.

Rebuttals to the "cultural amnesia" argument have focused on the need to see such statements in context. Traders, missionaries, government officials, and early historians all tended to assume the superiority of their own culture and technology and saw Native peoples as impoverished without it. To them, an Ojibwa hunter might be "poor" without a gun, even though he had a bow. This was compounded by the strategies of Native people themselves: as Paul Thistle points out, the "cultural amnesia" idea was used by Natives as a ploy to arouse traders' sympathy and increase their generosity. "Pity us, we are poor; you have guns, while we have not; how are we to live?" they might have said – a reference, of course, to the ethic of sharing with those who have less, and an attempt to indoctrinate the trader into this ethic.

The question of whether Aboriginal people found European trade goods to be superior to their own material culture has been reassessed in the past few years, with some surprising results. Researchers point out that European goods were not always superior; some European items were less suited to the North American climate than their Native counterparts.[31] True, metal kettles and blades wore better than their bark or skin and stone equivalents in Native society, but one has only to think of the many items of Native material culture adopted by fur traders and other European inhabitants of North America to realize that European goods were not always so useful to Native people. Skin footwear, for instance, was far more practical for Native lifestyles and the North American climate than were European shoes.

Most interestingly, recent work indicates that firearms – long held by many scholars to be the most crucial link between Native people and the fur trade, and necessary for the very survival of Native people, particularly in the subarctic environment where hunting of nonherding big game was an important part of Native subsistence – may not, in fact, have been as important as once believed.[32] In reassessing this argument, scholars have pointed out that, while guns did offer greater range (an advantage in stalking wary animals), they were also prone to breaking, and they required powder and shot, which was heavy and neither readily transportable nor continually available. Between breakage and absence from sources of shot and powder, Native families might have been without the use of guns for months at a time. Nor were guns necessary for killing small animals, for which clubs, snares, and deadfalls were used quite successfully.[33] Bows continued to be used well into the nineteenth century. Peter Rindisbacher, who painted detailed and accurate images of the Ojibwa around Red River in the 1820s, portrayed both men and boys with bows in several of his paintings. In many families, the transition from bows to guns continued to occur in every generation: boys used bows until they could afford to purchase a gun.[34] Thus, guns may have been useful for killing large game, as a mark of becoming an adult hunter (particularly a successful fur trapper), but were not strictly necessary to survival.[35]

It is important to bear in mind that European technology was incorporated into Ojibwa life and that it did not simply displace existing elements of Ojibwa technology and culture. In analysing the Bellamy site, a 1790s Ojibwa camp, archaeologists concluded that, while "European goods had been fully integrated into an Ojibwa way of life" by that date, "the ethnohistoric and archaeological data suggest that these items were not altering an Ojibwa world view or way of life." Similarly, in an article examining the prehistoric development of the inland shore fisheries of the northern Great Lakes, ethnohistorian Charles Cleland noted that "increased efficiency of technology . . . does not necessarily imply the simple replacement of less efficient implements by more efficient ones. For the case in point, the accommodation of new implements into a preexisting technological complex produces a technology that becomes more efficient as it becomes more diversified." Both these ideas are relevant to the question of the attraction of European trade goods to the Ojibwa and their ancestors.[36]

Despite the fact that European trade goods were associated with Native equivalents, were sometimes given uniquely Native meanings, and were used in much the same manner as their aboriginal analogues, they introduced two significant changes into Native societies. The first of these has to do with the manner in which trade goods enhanced Native concepts of wealth and well-being. Many Ojibwa saw the trade as a source of prestige; they were able to supply desirable furs and gained status from both traders and their kin as the result of this ability. This was reinforced by the fact that trade goods such as silver ornaments, scarlet cloth, wampum, and alcohol held connotations of power and spiritual wealth. The assignment of Native meaning to these new objects allowed Native peoples to retain their world view, culture, and identity in the face of drastic change, but it also wrought a powerful link between Native peoples and trade goods.

Similarly, the creation of "trading captains" and the adoption of customs such as the wearing of chief's coats and special hats (top hats with trade-silver bands) by Native leaders – some of whom were appointed by European traders rather than being acknowledged by their bands – is an indication of the degree to which Native concepts of prestige, rank, and social structure came to be bound up with the trade. Native-made versions of such coats, with painted leather and quilled epaulet decorations, were being worn in northern Ontario by the last quarter of the eightccnth century. While Native peoples re-interpreted such marks of status, the integration of trade goods and trading roles into the social and religious systems of Native cultures bound Native people to the trade as firmly as the "need" for powder and shot did.[37]

The second type of change that the fur trade introduced involved the social and economic relations that came into play to obtain trade goods. This type of change is not yet well understood.[38] Aboriginally, for example, women made their own birchbark, clay, or skin cooking vessels. In the fur-trade era, they generally obtained metal kettles from their male relatives. Women did process the furs to make them fit for trade, and a few women trapped and traded for their own supplies, but in general the use of trade items caused them to become reliant on others for basic household goods. The precise changes that such shifts caused in family, gender, and intra-band relations need to be studied more carefully. Related changes may well have been caused by the loss of knowledgeable elders and the depopulation caused by epidemics, leading to changed family structures, socialization processes, and age-sex roles. The loss of working members of a family who made the family's storage and cooking vessels, to give one example, may have made it advantageous for the remaining members to use manufactured kettles, or cloth for garments instead of labour-intensive tanned hides and furs.

The relationship between Native peoples and the fur trade also changed over time. If at first the fur trade merely intensified existing aspects of Native culture, did these later lead to cumulative, disruptive changes? How much was the seasonal round altered to meet the desire for furs and trade goods? Researchers have arrived at widely differing answers to such questions; the debate is by no means over, and our understanding is as yet only partial. We need, as well, to understand how the reactions of particular bands in different eras and conditions varied in response to the fur trade. Conditions that might have induced reliance on the fur trade were not uniform over time, nor were the responses of Native people universal.[39]

Dependence, therefore, is a simple term for a complex series of changes and choices that enmeshed Native peoples in the fur trade. The Ojibwa, like other Native peoples, chose to participate in the fur trade at this level for their own ends – even if some of those motivations and goals were products of cultural changes set in motion by the fur trade itself: they had made them their own. During the eighteenth century this choice brought but few penalties; their involvement in the fur trade resulted in cultural change on many levels, but rarely cultural damage. But as fur-trade competition escalated, the effects of epidemic disease and alcohol use mounted, and the trade itself waned, the western Ojibwa were forced to use their utmost ingenuity to maintain control over their personal and corporate autonomy and to maintain their standard of living. I would argue that they were largely successful in doing so for much of the nineteenth century, even if their strategies for continued autonomy did include reliance on the fur trade and traders. True dependence came with the reserve era, when the loss of land and resources, personal freedom, political autonomy, and cultural self-determination compounded the changes that participation in the fur trade had wrought in Native societies.

In answer to the question of whether the Ojibwa moved west because they were "dependent" on the fur trade, then, one can reply that the Ojibwa were intertwined with the fur trade, were changed by it, and were to some degree reliant on it; but they were also stimulated by the aspects of it that resonated with their own goals and perceptions of the world. The expansion of the fur trade into the West was for the Ojibwa an opportunity, not a desperate attempt to sustain themselves. For those who chose to pursue that opportunity, the next several decades would prove an exciting and vital period for Ojibwa in the parkland and prairies.

OJIBWA MIGRATION INTO
THE PRAIRIES AND PARKLANDS, 1770 TO 1790

Why did some Ojibwa move west? What factors in addition to the historical currents of the era led – or compelled – them to leave their homes? What did they hope to find in the parklands and prairies?

The foregoing discussion of the nature of Ojibwa participation in the fur trade becomes especially relevant when considering Ojibwa motives for moving into the West, for the earliest and most common explanation for their migration has been that the North West Company "introduced some of the Saulteaux as trappers and hunters" during a period of intense fur-trade competition in the 1780s and 1790s.[40] Hudson's Bay Company trader Peter Fidler stated that Ojibwa were "introduced [into the West] by the North West Company about the year 1797; . . . they was induced by the Reports of the Canadians that Beaver abounded here."[41] Explorers Lewis and Clark and trader-historian Alexander Ross also offered this explanation in the nineteenth century.[42] Twentieth-century scholars have offered a similar explanation. While downplaying the idea that Ojibwa were directly contracted by traders, they have emphasized the notion of Ojibwa dependence on the fur trade and their need for fresh beaver stocks. Harold Hickerson emphasized the "need" for richer beaver areas as the prime motivation for the Ojibwa expansion into the middle Red River area.[43] There is, of course, a good deal of truth to these explanations. The Ojibwa did come west about the same time as the advent of intense fur-trade competition there; they realized that the centre and progress of the fur trade was moving westward in the late eighteenth century and moved to take advantage of the trend. Caught up in the expansion of the fur trade and in the westward-moving human current that this created, but prevented by the "debatable zone" from fully exploiting the transitional parkland-prairie region east of Red River and north of the upper Mississippi, some Ojibwa took an easier path and expanded north and west around it, into the lower Red River area and beyond to the Assiniboine River. The early western Ojibwa also concentrated on trapping large numbers of beaver, so that it may well have seemed that they had been brought in by one company to exhaust new areas. Too, many of them did trade almost exclusively with Canadian traders; friendships and kin ties existed between Ojibwa and Canadians; and some Ojibwa, such as those who traded with Nor'Wester George Nelson between 1807 and 1812, sought out the same trader at different posts. Rival Hudson's Bay Company traders quite naturally got the impression that Ojibwa bands accompanied Canadian traders, and the Canadians probably played up this image to their rivals. Gertrude Nicks has speculated that William Tomison, a Hudson's Bay Company trader on the Saskatchewan River in 1801-02, "may have been deliberately misled into believing that (the Iroquois and other eastern groups) . . . were under contract."[44]

Despite the beliefs of the fur traders, however, there is little evidence of "moving arrangements" or actual contracts made between traders and specific Ojibwa men or families. This differs from the records on Iroquois men who were engaged by Montreal fur companies for service in the western fur trade, for whom actual contracts do exist. Far from having any arrangements with the Ojibwa he traded with, Alexander Henry the Younger, a North West Company trader whose journals are an important primary source for the Ojibwa expansion, had great difficulty in getting the Ojibwa to go where he wanted them to.[45] He did arrange for some Red Lake Ojibwa to trap near Red River, but not until about 1800 – nearly two decades after the first records of Ojibwa in the West. The Ojibwa-Ottawa group with which the White captive John Tanner lived travelled to Red River to visit relatives rather than at the request of any trader, and they were strikingly autonomous in their relations with traders; they did, however, choose to come west in the early 1790s, about the same time as Henry and trader Charles Jean Baptiste Chaboillez, as well as many other traders.[46] Henry and Chaboillez, whose journals are also an important source for these early years, worked with bands that had considerable familiarity with the Red River valley, indicating either that they had used the area on their own before the arrival of traders in the area or that they had simply followed earlier traders there.

I have found just two mentions of any arrangements made to bring Ojibwa people to the West. The first is a note in the Edmonton House journal for August 1795 indicating that a group of Ottawa (closely allied with Ojibwa in the region) "with many more came to the red River last autumn with the new company"; the second is the proposal made by explorer-trader David Thompson in the fall of

1800, who asked permission of the Piegan to bring Ojibwa and Iroquois to hunt furs in the foothills.[47] These dates are both rather late in the expansion of the Ojibwa, though it seems that a few bands, at least, actually did accompany North West Company traders into the West. John Tanner also makes an oblique reference to traders' involvement in this westward movement, stating that when his family first travelled from the Michilimackinac region to Red River they put their baggage on a trader's ship bound for Grand Portage.[48] The traders' role in the movement of the Ojibwa may, as Nicks suggests, "have involved some public relations work in the West, and help with transportation, but stopped short of actual contracts."[49] It also seems likely that some of the Ojibwa who came west did so in company with Métis and freemen relatives who had short-term contracts, rather than being formally contracted themselves.

The idea that the North West Company "introduced" the Ojibwa to the West is connected to the close relations between the Ojibwa and French Canadian fur-trade employees, often mentioned in works dealing with Ojibwa history and movements. The relationship between the two peoples stems from their association in the central and western Great Lakes during the seventeenth and eighteenth centuries. As Peter Fidler expressed it, the Ojibwa were "from their infancy acquainted with the Canadians as they come from towards their Country, which makes them so much attached to them." Similarly, John Tanner noted that one Canadian company was called "The Chippeway Frenchmen."[50] The Ojibwa enthusiasm for the French was based on the impression they left during the exuberant beginnings of the fur trade: "The days of the French domination were the Augustan era of the fur trade, and beavers were so plenty and the profits arising from the trade were so large, that the French traders readily afforded to give large presents of their coveted commodities, their beloved tobacco and fire-water to the Indians."[51]

This passage by mixed-blood historian William Warren, written in the 1850s from information gathered from his Ojibwa relatives, indicates the degree to which Warren's people mythologized their relationship with Canadian traders. This is not to demean the many genuine relationships that existed between Ojibwa and Canadians. In situations of trade competition, though, the Ojibwa readily embellished and capitalized on these relationships by presenting an exaggerated image of Canadian generosity and goodwill to Hudson's Bay Company traders in an attempt to benefit from heightened trade competition (just as Hudson's Bay Company traders may have overemphasized the effects of kin and other ties between Ojibwa and Canadians to excuse their poor fur returns). Ojibwa manipulation of European traders by such means places a different perspective on the claim of earlier scholars that the Ojibwa moved west because they were "pawns in the [fur] trade," completely at the beck and call of powerful traders.[52]

Another statement made by several traders to explain the westward movement of the Ojibwa was that they had come in search of more abundant game and fur supplies. David Thompson and Alexander Mackenzie, among others, asserted that the forests around the west end of Lake Superior from Lake of the Woods south to Red Lake and inland to Fond du Lac and Grand Portage were seriously depleted of animal resources, especially beaver and large game, by the 1790s. Thompson met several Ojibwa at the North West Company post at Swan River in 1798 who had left "their own countries," which were "exhausted of the Beaver and the Deer." The following year he travelled east of Red River and noted with astonishment: "Since we left the Red River . . . we have not seen the track of a Deer, or the vestige of a Beaver. . . . The Indians we met with all appeared very poor."[53] Similarly, trader John McKay recorded in his journal in 1793 that Ojibwa from the Rainy River area told him that "the land [there] was in a manner ruined" for hunting and that some from the region had "gone to the red river, a place more suitable For the support of their families."[54]

These statements are not easily interpreted. Mackenzie's and Thompson's specific emphasis on beaver and large game reveals their own standards of plenty. Fur traders were especially prone to emphasizing the availability of beaver and of large game, which fuelled the fur trade. In the absence of game, Native people stopped hunting furs and concentrated solely on subsistence. Large game was also a much-desired food among the Ojibwa, especially the men, for whom maturity and success were defined in part by the ability to catch large game consistently. Both traders and Natives were liable to complain of "starvation" in the absence of large game, but, as Mary Black-Rogers has pointed out, this term often meant only that there was no large game and was used even when other sources of food were available.[55] Nutritionally, game was important in the Ojibwa diet, but it was only one of several major resources. The Ojibwa had a well-integrated seasonal round and were capable of anticipating and compensating for all but the worst ecological fluctuations. It is thus somewhat difficult to believe that the Ojibwa were as impoverished and starving as Mackenzie claimed they were, especially given the abundance of alternate resources. For instance, the bands that Thompson saw near Red Lake (Minnesota) in May 1798 had no ducks but did have sufficient sugar and rice, a not-unusual diet for the season.[56] And, while Mackenzie claimed that Ojibwa in the area just east of Lake of the Woods "could hardly find subsistence, game having become so scarce, that they depended . . . for food upon fish, and wild rice," the extremely high productivity of some of the fisheries and rice lakes in that area makes it difficult to believe the first part of his statement.[57]

However well they were able to cope with change, the Ojibwa may have perceived the depletion of game and beaver as a threat (especially to their potential profits in the fur trade) and a deprivation. Certainly, it would seem from the traders' statements that the region between Red River and Lake Superior and around the northwestern end of Lake Superior in the late eighteenth century (particularly along major trade and transportation routes), was partially – to seriously – depleted of large game and beaver, but not of fish or small game. Given the broad base and flexibility of the Ojibwa subsistence cycle, this evidence suggests that the Ojibwa could, in fact, have lived fairly well in the region. Many who stayed there evidently did. Others were drawn to the West by reports of more abundant resources there. Alexander Mackenzie noted in 1789 that the Red River valley was "covered with herds of buffalo and the elk; . . . the whole country is well wooded, level, abounding in beaver, bears, moose-deer, fallow-deer, &c."[58] Nor'Wester John Macdonell gave a similar description of the area just a few years later, in 1795: "Buffalo, Elk, Moose deer, Caberie and Fowl of all kinds . . . abound in this country. . . . The country is so plentiful that the Canoes have always either fresh meat or Fowl for their kettles."[59]

Thus, the Ojibwa came west with the fur trade, into the fur- and resource-rich Red River valley and beyond. The earlier Cree inhabitants of this region had done little to deplete its fur resources, for they were middlemen rather than trappers. As skilled trappers, the Ojibwa saw great potential in the region even though it had been occupied for some time by other peoples.[60]

Certainly, the traders extolled the virtues of the West and may have encouraged the Ojibwa to explore it and to patronize their new trading posts along its waterways. This was the heyday of the fur trade, an era in which rising competition made the trade profitable and flattering for Native people. Too, the fur trade had permeated deeply into Ojibwa culture by the late 1700s, and trade goods had already fitted smoothly into their social structure and their daily chores. Given all these intertwined motivations, some of the Ojibwa chose to move westward in order to maintain a position of power in the expanding trade. But their decision to move west may have had one final, terrible impetus: the smallpox epidemic of 1780 to 1782.

SMALLPOX, 1780 TO 1782

In addition to the westward evolution of the fur trade, the effects of the smallpox epidemic of 1780 to 1782 provided compelling reasons for some Ojibwa to move away from their homes into the prairies and parklands. The smallpox epidemic devastated the Native populations of the Great Lakes and the Northwest. As reported by David Thompson, the epidemic spread from the south to the Sioux and Ojibwa, then to the Missouri area, and then to the Cree, Assiniboine, and other plains tribes.[61] Several decades after the epidemic, a tribal historian consulted by William Warren told him that the disease had been caught by a party of Cree,

Assiniboine, and Ojibwa warriors who raided an infected Gros Ventre camp on the Missouri.[62] Whether this version of the story is true or not is impossible to say, but Warren's source does ring true in one respect: according to him, most of the party died on the journey home, and the others scattered in horror, contributing to the spread of the disease. Mortality varied among the infected populations. William Tomison, then at Cumberland House, reported that at least two-thirds of the Cree died (sixty-six percent), and Edward Umfreville believed that only one in fifty had survived (ninety-eight percent).[63] Warren states that a large Cree village at Netley Creek was entirely depopulated, giving it the name Dead River, and Henry noted the presence of huge graves at the junction of the Red and the Assiniboine rivers where "hundreds of men, women, and children," probably Cree and Assiniboine, who had died in the epidemic were buried.[64] These figures are entirely consistent with other data on major smallpox epidemics among unvaccinated Native North American populations, which suggest a fifty- to seventy-percent (although sometimes as high as ninety-eight percent) mortality rate. Data on one later epidemic, however, suggest that not all communities would have been affected uniformly: some would have been virtually untouched, remaining isolated from the disease, while others would have been virtually destroyed.[65]

The spread and effects of the epidemic are less well-documented for the Ojibwa. No Ojibwa are mentioned in accounts of the epidemic west of Red River. Matthew Cocking wrote from York Factory in August 1782 that the disease was then "raging among our poor Pungee Deer Hunters of whom almost every one that has been seized with it have died."[66] The "Pungees" were, presumably, the Ojibwa of northwestern Ontario who traded with the Hudson's Bay Company at the Bay. Natives around Lake Nipigon and Sturgeon Lake in northern Ontario were also hard hit; one survivor reported in the spring of 1783 that, of two "tribes" (presumably groups of extended families) that had lived about Sturgeon Lake, "not more than 2 or 3 children are alive."[67] Further south, "smallpox hit the Ojibwa in their villages in present Wisconsin and Minnesota. As Indians left their own villages and moved to other settlements, the disease spread to Grand Portage . . . then through the boundary waters region to Rainy River and Lake of the Woods. At the same time, it was carried to Sandy Lake and Leech Lake at the head of the Mississippi River."[68] Canadian trader J.B. Cadotte reported in June 1783 that "all the Indians from Fond du Lac, Rainy Lake, Sandy Lake, and surrounding places are dead from smallpox." A Hudson's Bay Company trader at Gloucester House corroborated this, noting in June 1782 that "there is a great Mortality among the Indians and . . . most of the Indians in and Near the Raney Lake is dead and . . . the Assineybois Country is almost Depopulated."[69] While Cadotte's statement may have been an exaggeration, the two statements together give an indication of the terrible mortality caused by the disease. J.B. Perrault, another trader, stated that mortality was not very high at Leech Lake; Warren speculated that the epidemic died out there.[70] These meagre data suggest that the area from northwestern Ontario to Fond du Lac probably experienced a fifty- to seventy-percent death rate, while that at Leech Lake and possibly other villages southwest of Fond du Lac was below fifty percent. A few, more isolated, communities may have had lower or negligible death rates. While it cannot be said with absolute certainty, it is likely that between half and three-quarters of the Ojibwa living west and north of Grand Portage perished between 1780 and 1783.[71]

Epidemics are triply fatal to hunting-and-gathering societies. Besides their extremely high mortality rates, the terrible fear and despair they created caused other deaths. Recalling a later epidemic, trader George Nelson wrote of survivors committing suicide in despair at being left alone and of healthy individuals helping sick relatives to die sooner. Nelson claimed that "these acts of their despair, probably carried off more than the disease itself." In 1781, William Tomison at York Factory noted, similarly, that "many put an end to their own existence to end the pain, and others for grief at the loss of their families."[72] The smallpox epidemic also left survivors vulnerable to the crucial problems caused by a greatly reduced labour force. In a hunting-and-gathering society in which each person made a significant contribution to the subsistence and well-being of the group, the death of a single hunter or female worker could be a threat to the survival of an entire extended family.

This problem would have been emphasized by the common response of families to isolate themselves in an attempt to avoid the disease. With few members to hunt or gather food or to provide water and basic nursing, many deaths occurred during and after the epidemic from complications induced by malnutrition and dehydration. When people were in such a weakened state, secondary infections were more apt to kill, and these were often brought on or worsened by the lack of appropriate medical techniques to deal with the new illnesses. Sweatbaths followed by plunging in cold water, a common curing technique among Native societies, often brought on fatal pneumonia and cardiac arrest when the patient was weakened by smallpox and malnutrition.[73] Finally, the epidemics had profound social consequences. A number of deaths in a closely knit group would have disrupted the normal pattern of social relationships: parents lost children, children lost grandparents or other elders who functioned as teachers, and if individuals with powerful guardian spirits died there might be no one to plead for supernatural assistance.[74]

A common response to such problems is the amalgamation of survivors from different families, clans, areas, and even ethnic groups into social units of the "right" size. This allowed survivors to continue using familiar group-hunting techniques and to defend their territories against enemies. Similarly, a "marriage boom" followed the 1918 influenza epidemic in northern Manitoba; researcher Ann Herring has suggested that "this may have been especially important in a fur trade economy where the division of labour along sex lines and the cooperation of a network of kin is vital to its success."[75] Such responses must have been partly responsible for the formation of mixed Ottawa-Ojibwa groups in the 1780s and 1790s such as John Tanner's family. It also validates accounts of Ojibwa being invited to move west into depopulated Cree and Assiniboine lands. As an old Red River settler understood it,

About the year 1780, smallpox overtook them, and decimated them fearfully. Thereafter . . . the Saulteaux left the forests . . . and entered on the plains of Red River. . . . The Saulteaux found the Assiniboines and the Crees encamped at the Pembina Mountain, . . . and after smoking and feasting for two or three days, the children of the forest were formally invited to dwell on the plains – to eat out of the same dish, to warm themselves at the same fire, and to make common cause with them against their enemies the Sioux. . . . "Your presence," they said, "will remove the cloud of sorrow that is in our minds and strengthen us against our enemies."[76]

One final connection between the smallpox epidemic and the emergence of the western Ojibwa lies in the loss of property due to the hasty abandonment of infected camps and by the practices of including trade goods in burials, of making large sacrifices of goods to the spirits in an attempt to escape the disease, and of giving away the property of the dead. As well, the fur trade dropped sharply throughout the Northwest for several years during and immediately after the smallpox epidemic, thus limiting Native peoples' access to trade goods.[77] These circumstances would have caused many of the Ojibwa to have been quite poor in trade goods when the epidemic subsided. The resulting shortage would have been made more acute by the need of a reduced labour force for efficient tools such as kettles and axes. Perhaps the aggressive trapping and the showiness that characterized the early western Ojibwa were as much attempts at restoring a feeling of normality to life as they were the means of sustaining life. As David Thompson commented, "despair and despondency had to give way to active hunting both for provisions, clothing and all the necessaries of life; for in their sickness, as usual, they had offered almost every thing they had to the Good Spirit and to the Bad, to preserve their lives, and were in a manner destitute of everything."[78] To the Ojibwa, the West offered a chance to begin again in a new and promising area that would supply "all the necessaries of life" without the reminder of so many deaths.

LATE-EIGHTEENTH-CENTURY OJIBWA LIFE

The Ojibwa who moved west brought with them a culture that had evolved for thousands of years in response to changing environmental conditions and human relationships, modified somewhat by over a century of participation in the fur trade in the forested regions around Lake Superior. Communities in different ecological regions took advantage of the specific resources available to them, creating several ways of life that were variations on a common cultural theme. The following summary of late-eighteenth-century Ojibwa life focuses most closely on the Boundary Waters communities from which many migrated west, to give a sense of the cultural and environmental context from which the western Ojibwa emerged.

For an Ojibwa in the late eighteenth century, the most important social and economic unit was the extended family. This was composed of several close relatives and their spouses, children, and other kin: often an older hunter, his wife, and one or more of their married children with his or her family, or two adult brothers and their families. The number and composition of the group was subject to change as a result of marriage, death, or personal conflict. In times of need, people unrelated by blood or marriage would be incorporated into the "family." The size of the group ranged from about six to a dozen people. When all but the smallest children assisted with the necessary tasks, this number was large enough to perform daily chores but small enough not to exhaust local resources too quickly. This unit has also been referred to as the "tent bandlet" and the "local group."[79] As accounts by Alexander Henry the Elder and John Tanner indicate, it was this group, more than any other, in which the individual's life experiences and identity were centred.

In most regions, every Ojibwa also belonged to a patrilineal clan or descent group that was named after a totemic animal.[80] Members of each group considered themselves to be close relatives, even though they might live hundreds of miles apart. An Ojibwa meeting another person belonging to his clan would treat the person as a brother or sister and offer any assistance possible. Clan members chose spouses from a different clan, so that every extended family consisted of members of at least two clans (that of the senior male, and that of his wife). In times of need, they could "claim kin" with another member of either group for assistance.

In early spring, several extended families travelled by snowshoe and toboggan from their winter hunting grounds and gathered in a sugar bush to make maple sugar.[81] While there they ate a great deal of the sugar, supplemented by small game, caches of meat, and wild rice gathered the previous summer. During this period the women were usually responsible for the sugar production, and the men might leave for several days to trap for furs. When the sugar run ended, people from many sugaring camps gathered at nearby sturgeon-fishing sites. Sturgeon was an extremely important food for the Ojibwa, especially in the Boundary Waters area.

During the annual three- to four-week spawning run, thousands of sturgeon weighing an average of twenty-five pounds each might be caught at numerous weirs along the Rainy River and at the mouths of other rivers around Lake Superior. Excess sturgeon was processed by the women into a type of pemmican made of dried, pounded sturgeon and sturgeon oil; the oil was also stored separately in "jars" of fish skin.[82]

Gatherings lasting for a month and ranging in size from several hundred to over a thousand people are recorded at the sturgeon weirs, making sturgeon fishing a regional social gathering as well as a subsistence activity. The large fishing groups built villages at the weirs consisting of dozens of dome-shaped wigwams made of birchbark or rush mats over a framework of poles. Each of these structures sheltered an extended family. They were built by the women, who also erected drying frames outside the lodge for game, fish, and other meat being processed. The families who gathered at these sites traded information about the availability of game and other resources in various localities, and they made decisions such as whether to accept invitations to join war parties and where each family should spend the next winter. When the Ojibwa started migrating into the West, the size and composition of the parties were probably also determined by this group.[83]

In the Boundary Waters and other regions, spring trade occurred during or just after these gatherings, when the men made a visit to one of the local posts. In some areas, traders established their posts right next to the spring villages or sent men to the villages to trade. Often Ojibwa from several villages would meet at the posts, where, besides trading, they made and renewed social acquaintances and discussed political alliances and enmities, recent Sioux attacks, and the state of the trade. Group religious ceremonies such as the Midewiwin were also held during these gatherings. While older, experienced members of most extended families conducted divinatory ("conjuring" or Shaking Tent ceremony) and seasonal thanksgiving ceremonies for their own families, the Midewiwin was performed only at large gatherings and by initiated members.

The origins of the Midewiwin ceremony have long been debated by scholars: some maintain that it was a post-contact development in Ojibwa culture, stimulated by certain features of European belief and organization. Aboriginal people maintain that it is much older than this, however, and recent re-assessment of the post-contact origin argument tends to support the Aboriginal view.[84] Certainly, by the late eighteenth century the ceremony was well established and played an important role in Ojibwa culture. The Midewiwin has been described by its practitioners as a life-giving ceremony: it was performed to cure serious illnesses, and its teachings helped the people to live properly so as to obtain success and health in life and to prepare for the afterlife. The Midewiwin ceremony included the retelling of Ojibwa history and origin stories, which contained lessons on the "right" way to live. Men and women who were initiated into the Midewiwin regarded themselves as relatives even if they came from different clans, families, and areas, and because of this the Midewiwin reinforced social ties among these groups and spread a common body of traditions to people who were usually isolated from each other.[85]

The spring-fishing gathering was the largest gathering of Ojibwa, although they recognized that their population extended beyond those present. While European documents often use the words *nation* and *tribe* to describe this largest category of membership, these are European terms, and they differ greatly in meaning from the words that might have been used by Native people to describe this larger category.[86] Unlike the European idea of a "nation," for instance, the Ojibwa had no formal political institutions linking their scattered villages. Peace treaties made between the Ojibwa and the Dakota were frequently broken by bands that had not been present at the negotiations or that felt that their interests had not been served by the treaty. Similar problems exist with the term *tribe*, which implies uniformity of language and culture, for the Ojibwa spoke (and still speak) many different dialects and used local resources very differently across their vast territory. The Ojibwa concept of their people as a whole seems to have been closer to the idea of ethnicity: the perception of an individual *being* Ojibwa, something that depended to a great extent on personal identity, kinship, and upbringing. The idea of kinship, kin-based groups such as clans, and wide-reaching kin networks may more closely reflect Ojibwa concepts of inter-band and inter-village relationships than the political, hierarchical concepts embodied in the European concept of "nation."

After the spring gathering, the Ojibwa dispersed for the summer. Some families travelled to visit relatives at other villages. Fishing, berry picking, and some hunting sustained the people until the end of the summer, when they once again began gathering to hunt migrating wildfowl and to harvest wild rice.[87] Wild rice was a crucial resource in the Boundary Waters, where families harvested five to twenty-five bushels each, much of which was stored for winter use and trading. In late July 1775, Alexander Henry the Elder was able to purchase about 100 bushels of rice from the previous year's crop, from a village of only about 100 persons at Lake of the Woods.[88]

Another trip to the trading post would usually be made in the autumn to obtain goods necessary for the winter hunting and trapping season, and the people would take advantage of the autumn whitefish run. Individual extended families then left the gathering and moved into the forest. Once they arrived at their winter hunting grounds, a fall hunt was made to take a number of fat deer, moose, or bear; this meat, the amount of small game such as raccoons that they were able to obtain during the winter, and the size of the caches of stored foods, determined the amount of time the Ojibwa spent trapping, rather than hunting for food, over the winter. Towards spring, several families came together for a final, intensive period of trapping, after which the combined group would join other families in the sugar bush again.[89]

The Ojibwa seasonal round was not simply a movement of humans over a natural landscape. As did other Native peoples, the Ojibwa moved within a world that was at once spiritual and physical. A decision to move camp might be made because the weather was favourable, but the favourable weather was controlled by supernatural beings, and occasionally a person with the ability to communicate with those beings had to call on them for assistance. The forest, streams, and lakes were alive with supernatural "persons" and powers, all of whom had to be treated with respect to prevent misfortune, accident, and illness from befalling the human persons who moved among them.

Sent out into the forest to meet these beings and beg for their assistance during life, young men and women acquired "guardians" from among them who bestowed protective power, the ability to ask for help from the guardian in times of need, and objects of power that embodied these gifts. Some were given extraordinary powers by the spirit-beings: the power to diagnose and cure certain illnesses, to predict the future, to change the weather, to call the game. Making use of such a gift required the observance of great respect towards the guardian at all times to maintain the relationship between them, and a ceremony in which the human called on his or her guardian for the power to perform the function.

The spiritual nature of the Ojibwa world could be seen plainly in the objects they used every day. Knife handles were sometimes carved into animal forms; birchbark storage vessels, made by women, the gatherers, were decorated with plant designs. Thunderbirds adorned cradleboards, that their life-giving powers might be extended to the infant. Painting and quillwork on the webbing of snowshoes prevented malignant spirits from harming the wearer. In ceremonial objects, the connection between humans and the supernatural was even plainer. Images of powerful underwater beings and sky beings decorated ritual pouches and pipestems. The materials from which objects were made also signified power relationships with supernatural beings. Animal skin, wood, and birchbark were symbols of human relationships with the animate beings who had animal and tree forms. When formed into ordinary objects, these materials did not lose their powers; thus, snowshoes and canoes are animate objects in Ojibwa language.[90] By the time the Ojibwa began moving into the parkland and prairie, they had begun to fashion much of their clothing from European cloth using their own, older patterns. Moccasins they retained as more practical than European shoes, but leggings, breechcloths, shirts, and sidefold dresses were made of wool or cotton with ribbon and beadwork trim. These innovations were thoroughly integrated into an Ojibwa world view; the favourite colour for wool clothing, red (a continuation of the earlier custom of painting with red ochre on leather garments), expressed relationships with life-giving spirit forces, and the curvilinear outlined designs of the beadwork and ribbonwork on these garments remained tied to the animate natural-spiritual world they had always known.[91]

This was the way of life that the first Ojibwa who ventured west carried with them. Although many elements in this lifestyle would be changed by the new ecological and social environments in the prairies and parkland, much also would prove adaptable and functional. And despite all the changes that the western Ojibwa wound undergo, the culture they brought with them continued to form the core of their identity for the next century.

Early Expansion and Adaptation, 1780 to 1804

2

Between 1780 and 1804, Ojibwa families spread throughout the West and began adapting to the different peoples and environments they found there. Within this period, the entry of the North West Company and the XY Company into the West and an epidemic that affected the beaver population about the turn of the century proved to be major events in the development of the western fur trade and the lives of those Native people who participated in it. For the emergent western Ojibwa, the period between 1780 and approximately 1800 was marked by expansion, while 1800 to 1804 saw the first signs of their real adaptation to the West.

Tracing the first movements of the Ojibwa into the West is made difficult by the nature of the available documentary sources, all of which are fur-trade records. This bias may contribute to an over-emphasis on the fur trade within Ojibwa life at this time; we might do well to remember that, although the fur trade was important to the Ojibwa mentioned in its records, it may not have been as central to their lives as it seems.

The fur-trade records pose other, special problems for reconstructing this era in western Ojibwa life. Journals covering a number of consecutive trading seasons at a single post are generally not available, and the opening, closing, and re-opening of early inland western trading posts generated records that tell us more about the evolution of fur trade companies than about the emergence of the Ojibwa. Further complicating the picture is the fact that many early western Ojibwa were strongly attached to Canadian traders and had very little to do with the Hudson's Bay Company. This means that the Hudson's Bay Company journals, which are in some cases the only records available, reveal only a fraction of Ojibwa life in the West. Given these various limitations, we must acknowledge that the documentary record offers only a narrow window on western Ojibwa life at this time, though the picture seen through this window is rich.

What evidence there is for this early period indicates that Ojibwa people did not move westward in an organized, large-scale exodus. Rather, the "migration" was a process of extended-family visits to relatives, of invitations to live with more westerly groups, and of travelling in both directions many times. Information given by Ojibwa people at Berens River, on the east side of Lake Winnipeg, to anthropologist A.I. Hallowell in the 1930s suggests that similar complex, overlapping, back-and-forth movements brought their ancestors from several points in Northern Ontario in the eighteenth and early nineteenth centuries.[1] These early journeys were voyages of exploration and were followed for several decades by what Harold Hickerson has called a pattern of seasonal "commuting"; that is, the Ojibwa set out from their eastern villages or from Great Lakes trade gatherings in late summer, spent the autumn and winter in the West, and returned east in late spring. This pattern is well documented among the Ojibwa from Red Lake, Leech Lake, and Rainy Lake by the 1790s, and had probably been occurring long before. These families spent part of the autumn and winter near Red River to hunt bison and trade, but many returned to their villages for the sugaring season.[2] For them it was a short journey to the parklands and prairies of Red River, and they made it part of their annual cycle of movement. Other "commutes" might have been even shorter, as in the case of Ojibwa from northwestern Ontario who travelled expressly to trade at Cumberland House or at the mouth of the Red River in the 1770s. For those few families who came from the south shore of Lake Superior or the Michilimackinac region, though, a considerable journey was involved, and the journey may not have been made every year.[3]

In studying the development of an Ojibwa band at Pembina on the Red River, ethnohistorian Harold Hickerson attributed their seasonal migration to a lack in the West of hard-maple trees from which sugar could be made, and to a similar lack of wild rice and fish, on which the Ojibwa in the Great Lakes and Boundary Waters regions relied for food.[4] Recent analyses of Ojibwa subsistence in the Red River valley have shown Hickerson's conclusion to be simplistic. In fact, the Ojibwa had access to all these resources. The wooded banks of rivers and isolated stands of timber in the Red River region, for instance, were essentially "islands" of familiar resources within the less-familiar prairie region, so that the Ojibwa were not completely cut off from their familiar environment and resources.[5] This suggests that resources were not the only tie that bound the Ojibwa to their eastern villages.

Some bands, of course, did return east to tap sugar maples. Ojibwa also had two other means of obtaining sugar in the West. A good deal of sugar was traded to posts along the Red and Assiniboine rivers in most years, some of which came directly from the Red Lake and Boundary Waters regions. Sugar was also produced in the West (despite the lack of sugar maples) from box elder (Manitoba maple, *Acer negundo*) trees, and there are many references to sugar production in the West throughout the historic period.[6] Fish were also plentiful in the major rivers and lakes of the West and were a staple food there. Ojibwa always harvested sturgeon during the spring run, whitefish in the autumn run, and they took other species in nets below the ice in winter. There was no lack of this resource, and no need to return east to obtain it.[7]

Wild rice was not found west of Red River, though, and many Ojibwa families may have continued to "commute" solely to obtain it. As ethnohistorian Tim Holzkamm has recently noted, a supply of wild rice, which was a storable high-carbohydrate food, was an important addition to a winter diet of lean meat. It helped to provide the energy and stored food to allow time to be spent hunting for furs, rather than for food.[8] Rice was found in some areas along the Red River and the Interlake district and was introduced to a few small lakes along the lower Assiniboine River soon after 1800, and some Ojibwa bands turned to bison, prairie turnips, and cultivated crops as substitutes after that date. Until these became established alternatives, though, Ojibwa families who were accustomed to relying on rice had to obtain theirs either by trade or by travelling east to the rice fields.[9] Since Ojibwa canoe brigades were reported in the Lake Winnipeg and Forks area carrying large quantities of rice well after the turn of the century, there is evidence that some bands continued to "commute" to obtain wild rice.[10]

Food resources were certainly not the only tie between the early western Ojibwa and their Great Lakes and Boundary Waters roots, however. There were less tangible but equally important social and emotional ties. Although such personal links are not documented in the written record, they are suggested by the different kinds and lengths of "commutes" and the fact that some bands began living year-round in the West well before others. It seems likely that many "commutes" were made for social reasons. Ojibwa who spent time in the West returned home to reaffirm personal relationships and visit villages and sacred places that were the touchstones of their identity. For all the early western Ojibwa, commuting ended only when they began to form their most important social networks in the West and when their experiences in the West began to form as important a part of their identities as their personal ties to the East. Even then, visiting between eastern and western kin continued, and the western Ojibwa have never forgotten their origins and heritage.

The problematic nature of the available documents makes it extremely difficult to pinpoint the exact year or even decade of the movement of Ojibwa people into the West. Ojibwa from Lake of the Woods, Rainy Lake, Leech Lake, and Milles Lacs must surely have hunted bison on the parkland fringe from the very births of those communities, as they were recorded doing later in the eighteenth century. Ojibwa may also have travelled to the great trade fairs at the Mandan-

Hidatsa villages on the Missouri River by the mid-1700s, for fragments of birchbark vessels with curvilinear incised decorations typical of Algonquian work have been found in excavations there dating from that period.[11] Of the very few records from the early French trade in the West, none mentions Ojibwa or people whom we can identify as Ojibwa. Nor do any of the few British fur traders who travelled west of Lake Winnipeg or Red River before 1770 mention meeting Ojibwa, though, according to ethnohistorian Dale Russell, other sources suggest that several bands of "Mantawapowa" people encountered at Dauphin Lake by William Tomison in 1769 were Ojibwa.[12]

The first definite mention of Ojibwa west of Red River or Lake Winnipeg is found in a Cumberland House journal entry for 6 January 1778, which describes "an old Bungee Leader and Family belonging to York Fort."[13] This hunter had already been at York Factory the previous spring "for necessaries." At Cumberland, he traded his fall hunt with the Canadians and was apparently trying to get more credit from the Hudson's Bay Company. The man's connection to York Factory and the Cumberland area suggests that he was from the Canadian Shield region just east of Lake Winnipeg, one of the "poor Pungee deer hunters" who would be devastated by smallpox in a few years. By the late 1770s, Ojibwa residing in that region began to be affected by fur-trade competition in the interior and stopped journeying to Hudson Bay to trade. The man's visit to Cumberland House may well have been an experiment with the more immediately competitive situation there.[14]

To a canoe-oriented people, the Winnipeg River, the Manitoba lakes and the rivers that surrounded them were highways rather than barriers to movement. With no physical barrier, and no enemies in that direction, families from the east side of Lake Winnipeg may have customarily harvested resources on the western or southern shores long before 1780. By the 1770s, canoes from the Berens River area were travelling to the mouth of the Red River to trade, as after 1800, Ojibwa from the east side of the lake definitely travelled to posts in the Interlake region.[15] Not far west of Cumberland House, a band of Ojibwa was trading at Sturgeon River and Hudson's House (on the north Saskatchewan River near the later Carlton House) in 1779. Ojibwa at Berens River also informed anthropologist A.I. Hallowell in the 1930s that some of their ancestors had resided west of Lake Winnipeg in the 1770s.[16]

Sources are equally meagre for the 1780s. Ojibwa were encountered northeast of Cumberland House in the summers of 1781 and 1782, and they were said to reside in the Interlake by 1782. In early 1783, William Tomison reported that Ojibwa were again trading near Hudson's House.[17] The early westward movement of Ojibwa from northern Ontario was probably encouraged by the capture and destruction of York Factory by the French in 1782 and the effects of the smallpox epidemic, followed by the failure of the Hudson's Bay Company supply ship to arrive in 1783.[18] Ojibwa also entered the West from areas farther to the south during this decade. Alexander Mackenzie reported that "Algonquins from the country between the Red River and Lake Superior" (the Boundary Waters?) were frequenting trading posts around Lake Winnipeg by the winter of 1789-90. He noted, though, that these people were not "fixed inhabitants" of that area, implying that they were as yet seasonal commuters.[19]

A much clearer picture of Ojibwa movements emerges with the expansion of the network of inland posts in the 1790s and the proliferation of post journals after this time. Once again, it is sometimes uncertain whether these sources were for the first time recording the presence of Ojibwa who were already resident in the West, or whether the most rapid Ojibwa migration occurred at the same time as this period of intense development of the western fur trade.

Large numbers of Ojibwa began trading at posts throughout the Northwest by the late 1790s. They spread out across an enormous territory: beginning at Fort Alexander at the mouth of the Winnipeg River and other posts along the east shore of Lake Winnipeg; up the Red River to slightly past Pembina and west to Turtle Mountain and the Hair Hills; throughout the Interlake district; along the Assiniboine River past Brandon House, Shell River, Dauphin River, and Red Deer River; along the Qu'Appelle River; north and immediately west of Lake Winnipegosis; and along the North Saskatchewan as far as Edmonton House and Lac la Biche.[20] They were also present in larger numbers than before and are noted as travelling in groups of seven to more than forty canoes (about forty to 100 or more persons).[21]

Some of these people came west with Ottawa relatives. The Ottawa, whose homelands lay around Lakes Michigan and Huron, were known for their spirit of enterprise; the Ojibwa name for them, *odawag*, means "trading people."[22] The Great Lakes Ojibwa had lived in close contact with the Ottawa, traded with them at European posts such as Michilimackinac, and established villages with them in the seventeenth and eighteenth centuries. John Tanner's narrative reveals something of Ojibwa-Ottawa relationships and their role in Ojibwa migration. Tanner came west with his adoptive family after his Ottawa mother, Netnokwa, decided to visit her husband's family. Her Ojibwa husband, Taw-ga-we-ninne, was described as being "of Red River," near the Forks, making him one of the first western Ojibwa. In company with a number of other Ottawa, including a prominent man from the village of L'Arbre Croche, Netnokwa and her family travelled to the forks of the Red and Assiniboine rivers in the 1790s, where they "found great numbers of Ojibbeways and Ottawaws encamped."[23] While much of Tanner's narrative deals with a mostly Ottawa family, the similarities of their culture to that of the Ojibwa and the frequency of his contacts with Ojibwa in the West make it a most useful source for reconstructing the emergence of the western Ojibwa.

Other Ottawa groups are known to have wintered with or near Ojibwa in the vicinities of Edmonton House and Brandon House during the winter of 1795-96, where they brought in good returns of beaver.[24] Henry noted a number of instances in which he found Ojibwa camped with Ottawa, and at Lac la Biche during the winter of 1799-1800, eleven Ottawa and five Ojibwa men and their families wintered together at the mouth of the Slave Indian River, visited the posts together, and apparently hunted together.[25] Despite Henry's claim that the Ottawa had "no inclination to intermarry with the Saulteurs," then, there is evidence at least for the existence of mixed camps (and, in all likelihood, more widespread intermarriage than that of Netnokwa and Taw-gaw-we-ninne) among the early Ottawa and Ojibwa in the West just as there had been in the Great Lakes. Such cooperation and assistance from venturesome kin may well have encouraged those Ojibwa who first explored the West to remain there, or to return for more than one winter.[26]

As they spread across the West, the Ojibwa quickly became known as consistently productive trappers of beaver. In fact, traders tended to note the presence of Ojibwa near a post for this very reason, such as the one who wrote that "14 Canoes of Lake le pluis Indians arrived on their passage to the Red River; . . . they are most of them prime Hunters."[27] In one instance, an Ojibwa encountered by Duncan McGillivray near Nipawin in the fall of 1794 insisted on accompanying the trader despite warnings of danger (presumably from the Blackfoot, who were then hostile to the Ojibwas' Cree allies) because "he supposes [our wintering ground] to be a good Beaver Country."[28] Large returns, of fifty to several hundred prime beaver from a single extended family, were frequently made throughout the entire Northwest from Pembina to Edmonton House between 1780 and 1805.[29]

The plentiful supply of beaver enabled the Ojibwa to share in the general affluence that marked the early western fur trade. They demanded not only basic goods such as knives, kettles, guns, and ammunition in exchange for their furs, but also liquor and decorative items such as wampum beads, red cloth, silver jewellery, and bone and glass beads.[30] William Tomison, a Hudson's Bay Company trader at Fort Edmonton, noted on 27 March 1798 that "the Bungee Indians traded 45 B[eave]r 20 of which was for silver work they wanted Wampum v.[ery] much which I was sorry to inform there was none." Similarly, at Brandon House in 1794, the Ottawa, like the Ojibwa, were "much in want of Wampum beads, silver works and steel traps," and Chaboillez noted in 1797 that he had to bring silver jewellery from Pembina to another post at the junction of the Red and Forest rivers to replenish the supply there.[31] This desire for silver jewellery was unparalleled among the peoples of the northwestern prairies and parklands. Alexander Henry once compared another style of headgear to the effect made by "a Saulteur head covered with silver brooches," suggesting that such a style was common among the western Ojibwa.[32] David Thompson also recalled that during this period the Ojibwa and Ottawa in the West "were rich, the Women and Children, as well as the Men, were covered with silver brooches, Ear Rings, Wampum, Beads and other trinkets. Their mantles were of fine scarlet cloth and all was finery and dress."[33] John Tanner also mentioned that his family was "rather wealthy" when speaking of his silver ornaments, blankets, clothing, and other possessions.[34] Another trader at a post on Lake Winnipeg stated in 1797 that his trade was virtually at a standstill because he had no more cloth or blankets. A few years earlier, the Cumberland House trader fumed that the Bungees there would "not trade any thing for their Furrs but cloth and guns. As for all other articles they look for to be given them."[35] Rather than being an indication of the depletion of large game, as it may have been decades later, the Ojibwa desire for cloth was at this time a mark of their ability to indulge their decorative tastes and their desire for prestige and ritual goods within the expanding wealth complex. As curator David Penney has recently stated, "Possession of products of European manufacture, particularly those employed in fashion such as manufactured textiles . . . and ornaments of silver, communicated high social standing among Indians active within the fur trade system. Fur trade wealth had social meaning primarily when worn as part of an ensemble of clothing. . . . The indigenous fashion system . . . valued dress as a means for displaying symbols representing acknowledged social standing."[36] The fur trade had earlier triggered such dual social and material desires among the Ojibwa. Judging by their material affluence at this time, the early western Ojibwa who participated so fully in the fur trade clearly enjoyed their ability to satisfy such desires.

The Ojibwa were quite aware of the demand for the prime beaver they supplied. Adding to the ready availability of goods that could be acquired by trapping, traders in competitive situations gave out substantial amounts of goods as gifts in an attempt to prevent the Indians' hunts from going to the competition. Some ammunition, tobacco, and alcohol were supplied gratis as part of the trading ceremony, and gifts of cloth, knives, gun flints, awls, needles, net thread, and vermilion were also made during this period. Indians were also given large amounts of goods on "debt" (or credit) as the traders called it, in anticipation of receiving the group's next lot of furs. Both Chaboillez and his successor, Henry, gave from twenty to twenty-five skins' worth of credit as well as a gift that generally comprised some ammunition, an awl, some needles and thread, some twine for making fish nets, some vermilion paint, and tobacco. One Hudson's Bay Company trader noted that because of Canadian competition he had outfitted the Indians with whom he traded "with a Part of every article of Tradeing Goods in the Company's warehouse as presents & as much Debt as they would take."[37]

Traders hoped that such tactics would instill the European concept of economic debt and obligation in the Natives. The Ojibwa, on the other hand, had their own ideas about what constituted debt and obligation and what the acceptable ways of meeting those demands were. They also, like many other Native peoples engaged in the fur trade, interpreted the practice of gift giving and the giving of "debt" (or credit) differently from the way Europeans did. For some Ojibwa, presents and debt implied the mutual gift giving that was part of their kinship relations and, by extension, of their political alliances. Such relationships involved an obligation to trade that was socially and spiritually, rather than economically, motivated, and were more reciprocal and egalitarian than the hierarchical European conceptual relationship of lender and debtor. Gift giving and debt could also be regarded as indications of the Ojibwas' desirability to traders, as a confirmation of their prestige, and as a way of obtaining more trade goods. This encouraged some Ojibwa to take advantage of the competitive situation and trade with several companies, by taking debt at one post and later taking their furs to the opposition. A few used their reputations as excellent beaver hunters to play opposing traders off against each other and thus increase the amount of presents and debts they were given.[38]

These strategies were not unique to the Ojibwa of this era. They are related to Aboriginal peoples' reasons for participation in the trade, and have provoked scholarly discussions about whether Indians traded primarily to create and sustain political and social relationships, or whether they sought, as Europeans would, to accumulate property and maximize profits from the trade.[39] It may be useful to examine these attitudes to trade as they were demonstrated by the early western Ojibwa in this period of intense fur-trade competition. The Ojibwa used both strategies at various times, reminding us that as well as being an exchange of goods, the fur trade involved peoples with very different cultures, agendas, and expectations.

Looking at the first of these two basic patterns of behaviour, we can see that trade had both social and political dimensions for the Ojibwa. Trade was conducted with allies and not with enemies, and alliances were sealed with ceremonial exchanges of goods. Many Ojibwa remained loyal to a single trader or company for long periods of time and took pride in maintaining such relationships: "The Bunges . . . always Pay with Great Honor their Debts," one trader noted of such families.[40] These alliances and long-term relationships were frequently cast in a kinship or familial tone by the Ojibwa, an indication that for them trade was not simply an economic exchange. Relationships based on the metaphor of family implied a close degree of kinship and corresponding obligations, and they carried the expectation basic to Ojibwa society that kin should provide for one another. Thus, Native "kin" should provide furs to their trader "relative," and he should reciprocate by giving trade goods to his "relatives." Similarly, in Ojibwa thought, the fortunate were obligated to share with the less fortunate, and they therefore encouraged "adopted" traders to "take pity" on their "poor younger brothers" with generous gifts and plenty of goods on debt. Terms such as "brother" and "father," which were chosen and used deliberately by Native people in addressing Europeans, had specific meanings and expectations.[41] These connotations – the responsibility of parents to nurture their children, and the independence and equality of siblings – presumably carried as much weight as the trader's term *debt*, which similarly implied obligation by the debtor to the trader. Such relationships were of value during periods of food shortage and other short-term crises: traders were far more willing to advance food and trade goods to Indians with whom they maintained longstanding relations than they were to those who were known to slip their debts. Conversely, traders themselves benefitted during periods of scarcity by having Native relatives willing to assist them in finding and sharing food.

Social and kinship relations between traders and Ojibwa were established by marriage as well as by trade in the Northwest, as they were throughout the whole North American fur trade. Henry the Younger noted that the Ojibwa he traded with along Red River were "very officious in wishing to provide me with a wife."[42] Their motives for doing so lay in the desire to create a permanent link between themselves and the trader (and, by extension, with his "kin," or company), to ensure that they would always have access to trade goods and favourable terms in trading. The implied social obligations that were normally part of the son-in-law/father-in-law relationship were an added benefit to the band. It was Ojibwa custom that after marriage the groom lived with his wife's family for at least a year, hunting and trapping (and providing goods for) his in-laws. European trader sons-in-law were also expected to contribute to the well-being of their Ojibwa in-laws. Not all Europeans who married into Ojibwa bands conformed to these expectations, but some did in various ways. Henry, for instance, provided ammunition and goods to avenge the murder of his wife's parents.[43]

Fur-trade marriages were usually prompted and arranged by trading captains or other leading men who wished to cement their relationship with the trader. Marriages were initiated by traders, too, to ensure a productive band's loyalty to a particular post. This is not to say that the Indian women involved in these relationships were pawns of such schemes for power and profit. As historian Sylvia Van Kirk has documented, women "had a vested interest in promoting cordial relations with the whites" to maintain supplies of labour-saving trade goods such as steel needles and kettles, and some women preferred the life they had as wives of White men.[44] Women themselves could initiate marriage, as Henry discovered at Park River when "Liard's daughter took possession of [his] room and the devil could not have got her out."[45] These women played crucial roles in maintaining relationships between their families and their trader husbands, often for extended periods, mediating, translating, coping with crises and cross-cultural misunderstandings, and providing necessary country skills for their husbands. At its best, the custom of fur-trade marriages embodied the intertwined social and economic dimensions of the fur trade and gave women added prestige and power within their families as the wives or potential wives of such wealthy sons-in-law. During the period of most intense fur-trade competition around the turn of the century, however, Indian women were sometimes abused by traders who formed liaisons of convenience, for reasons of trade only, and who abandoned them or gave them to another trader when they were posted elsewhere.

In addition to marriage, both traders and Indians could establish kinship relationships by the giving of gifts. Not surprisingly, this practice paralleled the use of gifts in Ojibwa adoption ceremonies. Thus, in 1797, one Ojibwa formally transferred his allegiance from the North West Company to the Hudson's Bay Company at Brandon House by exchanging twenty beaver pelts for two guns and a small keg of brandy after smoking a pipe and having a drink with the Hudson's Bay Company.[46] Just as traders hoped to instill concepts of economic debt and obligation in their Indians when they gave credit, so do some Ojibwa seem to have hoped to instill in European traders the concept of social obligations when they formally exchanged gifts. Nor'Wester George Nelson was addressed as "my son" by Ayagon, an Ojibwa leader with whom he dealt in the Dauphin River area between 1808 and 1811. Ayagon did act in a fatherly manner towards Nelson, applying his herbal remedies to Nelson's medical problems and teaching him a great deal about Ojibwa culture. As well, he was instrumental in getting his relatives to trade their furs with Nelson. In return for his assistance and for his family's furs, Ayagon expected to be well recompensed and maintained in his rank as leader: to be treated with respect, as a father should be treated. That Ayagon made this quite clear is indicated by Nelson's habit of referring to him as "My Lord."[47]

As well as giving the basic "gratuities" to each Indian who received credits, traders made larger annual presents to their more influential and productive hunters. Alexander Henry described one such presentation in 1800: "Everything being ready, I gave Tabashaw, Maymiutch, and Vieux Collier each some clothing and other articles, as follows: A scarlet laced coat; a laced hat; a red round feather; a white linen shirt; a pair of leggings; a breech clout; a flag; one fathom of tobacco, and a nine-gallon keg of rum. Among the others I divided three kegs of mixed liquor . . . and four fathoms of tobacco."[48] Tanner's description of his adoptive mother's annual trade ceremony is similar: "After we had completed our trade, the old woman took ten fine beaver skins and presented them to the trader. In return for this accustomed present, she was in the habit of receiving every year a chief's dress and ornaments, and a ten gallon keg of spirits."[49] Some of the annual gifts to these "chiefs," or trading captains, were redistributed by the captain amongst his band, further raising his status and helping to ensure his loyalty to the trader who "clothed" him. As George Nelson reminded one of the Ojibwa men he clothed, "It was given him . . . as a mark of his being a great man so that the others might look upon him as such also."[50] Whether these gifts actually did make others look upon trading captains as great men is worth considering.

The institution of the trading captain and the ready acceptance of the symbols of that office – the chief's red or blue stroud military-style coat, the top hat with feather plumes, and the flag – as prestige items among Native people, provides an excellent example of the complexity of the changes amongst Native cultures engendered by the fur trade. On the one hand, the clothing and gifts given to trading captains conformed to some extent to Native aesthetics and social structures (the feather headdress, worn by men of status, translated into the trading captain's plumed, silver-banded top hat) and clearly stimulated the creativity of Native women: witness the development of quilled hide coats cut and decorated to resemble European military dress, right down to the quilled epaulets. A number of such coats exist in museum collections and are attributed to the area north and west of the Great Lakes from the 1780s on. By the 1820s they were in use at Red River, Leech Lake, and throughout the Northwest, suggesting that Ojibwa who moved west brought their value system with them.[51] On the other hand, such acceptance speaks of the fur trade's role in the development of a spiralling wealth and status complex among Native peoples, and the tensions thus engendered between the desire to own such signs of affluence and the moral imperative to share and to gain status by giving.

Further complicating these tensions was the fact that traders deliberately used these goods to manipulate Aboriginal social and political structures for their own purposes by appointing trading captains rather than recognizing leaders acclaimed by the bands, and by promising the chief's outfits to productive hunters. While scholars have begun to re-assess the status of trading captains, arguing that their influence existed only at the trading post, David Penney has noted that chief's coats and cloth clothing functioned as powerful symbols of affluence, status, and well-being among Native people in the fur trade.[52] Finally, while they themselves emphasized the social and political dimensions that trade had for them, Native people in the fur trade were trading to obtain goods rather than simply to create and sustain relationships. No matter which strategy Native people adopted with their traders, it is clear that the ties that bound them to the fur trade were many, interwoven in complex patterns, and not entirely economic in nature.

In contrast to "clothed" chiefs such as Ayagon, many Ojibwa trappers and their families chose not to tie themselves so closely to one trader or company. The advantages offered by the competitive situation were plain: it was far more convenient to trade with the nearest post than to travel for days to reach a particular trader, and it was also possible to obtain twice as many goods by taking debt at one house and trading furs at the other (although this could not be repeated often with impunity), or by making promises to both traders. As early as 1793, Ojibwa trading at Brandon House were branded as "the most Rascals in the Country" for this practice. Just four years later at the same post, James Sutherland complained that the Ojibwa there "seldom winter two years in one place, which gives them many an opportunity of cheating those from whom they take debt." To be fair, Ojibwa mobility during the 1790s was partly due to their relative newness to the region, and Sutherland's irritation with them was tempered by his observation that "whoever has the luck to get their trade generally gets a good one, as they hunt nothing but Beaver."[53] It was also sometimes necessary for Indians to go to both agents in order to obtain specific goods. One frustrated Hudson's Bay Company trader complained of a shortage of steel traps and silver jewellery, saying, "An Indian who otherwise would never Trade a skin with [the Canadians] must do it for these articles."[54] The practice of sending runners from the posts to the Indians' tents to trade en derouine also ensured that convenience and the desire for a steady supply of goods often won out over loyalty.[55]

It is clear, then, that some of the early western Ojibwa wanted more goods, better terms, and convenience. For these bands, ideas about trade either overrode or were unconnected to their concepts of kinship and family responsibilities. However, trading was for many Ojibwa clearly connected with their own concepts of gift exchange and kinship responsibilities. Ethnohistorians Bruce White and Bruce Trigger have each pointed out that "profit" may have taken many forms, not simply that of financial gains, and that Native people who adhered to traditional patterns of gift exchange in the fur trade may also have been gaining social benefits, political influence, and economic security by doing so. "The real question," according to Trigger, "is not whether individual [Native] traders sought . . . profits but why they did so and what they did with their gains." The giving-away of trade goods to maintain one's status as a elder, or in expectation of having them returned (reciprocated) at a later date, were types of profit and storage as valid as the accumulation and hoarding of trade goods, a practice that was considered miserly by the Ojibwa.[56]

In the end, the choice between loyalty and "freelancing" was made by each family and probably depended a great deal on the needs and desires of individuals and on current trade conditions (economic, ecological, and social) at the local level. Nor should we fail to place such strategies, and the prominence that the fur-trade records give them, back into Ojibwa context. Their strategies for dealing with fur traders were worked out, and sometimes changed, within the broader cycles of the year, of food harvests, and of the growth and decline of individual families and bands.

EARLY ADAPTATION: 1797 TO 1804

After a decade and a half of seasonal migration and tentative expansion, a new and more permanent Ojibwa adaptation to the West began to emerge in the mid-1790s. This change was fostered by the increasing association between the Ojibwa and their plains allies and by slightly weakening ties with their former villages: the results of a decision, conscious or not, that the West was indeed home for these families. Ojibwa in the West were also affected during the 1790s and afterwards by the decline of beaver, heightened competition in the fur trade, and more frequent Sioux attacks. Beginning in 1797, the beaver population upon which the Ojibwa relied for the fur trade dropped sharply as a result of an epidemic that killed beaver across the entire Northwest.[57] Compounded by intensive trapping, the beaver epidemic gave one of the first warnings that the former plenty of the West would not last forever.

Given the degree to which the Ojibwa relied on the beaver for their material prosperity, the epidemic might have been a disaster. Fortunately, its effects were lessened by an increase in fur-trade rivalry. The competition that had arisen between the Hudson's Bay Company and the North West Company in the 1780s and 1790s was spurred to new heights by the entry of the XY Company to the West in 1798, just prior to the drop in the beaver population. The increasing lengths to which Europeans resorted to obtain the Indians' furs during the six-year life of the new company ensured the ready and continued availability of trade goods to the Ojibwa even after the beaver epidemic. Such was the case with those taking advantage of the competitive situation around the Hudson's Bay Company's Winnipeg River post in the fall of 1800. "16 Sept.: 7 Canoes of Indians came down 6 of whom went to the other house. 17 Sept.: Indians still drinking, the Quantity of Liquor and Goods they are getting for Nothing is Astonishing."[58] Under this pressure, traders became even more willing to collect furs and trade at the Indians' tents, and the yearly gifts to trading captains and their wives and followers continued.[59] Competition also caused traders to become more protective of "their" beaver hunters, to the point that, in 1799, Hudson's Bay Company men at Edmonton House accompanied an Ottawa-Ojibwa group to the Indians' wintering grounds, presumably to prevent a rival company from taking them elsewhere.[60]

Increasing European competition for their furs strengthened the power of the western Ojibwa in their relations with the traders, for they knew they could obtain goods virtually wherever and whenever they desired. The Hudson's Bay Company trader at Brandon House, facing great competition from two rival houses in the fall of 1801, noted on 23 December that two Indians who had left the fort were not likely to return, despite the quantity of brandy given them. Similarly, Alexander Henry fumed when an Ojibwa band refused to move to a richer trapping area:

"The Indians [were] so obstinately bent on remaining at this place, where I was assured there were very few beavers." Earlier, he had observed of this same group that "they were independent of us, and vigorous measures could have availed nothing."[61] The Ojibwa were fully aware of their power in the trade, as is illustrated by incidents such as the one that occurred at Brandon House in November 1798. On that occasion, a band approached the two rival posts, which were close together, and sent several people into each house to ask traders to go to their tents and collect furs. The outcome of this simultaneous request, of course, was that men from the two companies were forced to race in the middle of the night in a competition to see who got the furs. The Ojibwa must have known that this would happen, leading one to wonder whether they set the whole thing up as entertainment.[62]

Some bands made even more "insolent" demands of the traders. Henry and his men felt obliged to build blockhouses at the Pembina River post in 1803, and, as he said, "We pretend it is on account of the Sioux, but I apprehend much less danger from them than from the Saulteurs, who are getting numerous, and at times insolent." The following year, he faced an open confrontation: "Indians very troublesome, threatening to level my fort to the ground . . . I perceived they were bent on murdering some of us and then pillaging."[63] When he was harassed by another group of Ojibwa, one Hudson's Bay Company trader "was obliged to threaten to take all their guns from them and throw them in to the river as they threatened to fire on us."[64]

The extra credit, presents, and bribes that the Ojibwa received during this period meant that they did not need to trade as many beaver, a factor that acted to lower beaver returns for some Ojibwa bands perhaps as much as the beaver epidemic did. According to Victor Lytwyn, at the height of the fur trade in the Little North, east of Lake Winnipeg, traders at one post were giving 4.6 made beaver (MB) in liquor and gifts to Indians for every single MB worth of furs they received, a not-unusual ratio for highly competitive situations. Lytwyn's research also demonstrates that, as competition escalated in this region, returns plummeted.[65] The intensity of the competition and its effects on both Native trappers and European traders was evident as early as 1793-94 on the Assiniboine River where, it was reported, "the Indians will not hunt, as they can get plenty now between so many houses; . . . on this river at present there is nine settlements." Peter Fidler lamented a similar situation at Lac la Biche in 1799: "There is so many different oppositions that the Indians are supplied by one & another for nothing – and they have very little occasion to kill furrs – while the petty companys keeps them in any kind they ask for." Henry also wrote that, during this period, "every man who killed a few skins was considered a chief and treated accordingly; there was scarcely a common buck to be seen; all wore scarlet coats, had large kegs and flasks, and nothing was purchased by them but silver works, strouds and blankets. Every other article was either let go on debt and never paid for, or given gratis on request."[66] Traders' comments such as this should be taken with a grain of salt, since they are so clearly coloured by self-interest. Nor were the aggressive incidents and hard bargaining necessarily caused by economic factors. Social relations between traders and Indians, European treatment of Indian wives, and, by 1800, the heightened wealth and status complex among Natives involved in the fur trade and tensions arising from competitive tactics used by European traders, may all have been part of the motivations behind such manipulative and occasionally hostile behaviour. Still, these comments suggest the considerable power of Native consumers and trappers at this time, and the frantic effort expended by rival trading companies to gain Ojibwa furs.

If the fight for furs brought an extra measure of prosperity and autonomy to Native people, it also brought problems. Fur traders' determination to succeed in highly competitive situations led in some cases to threats and acts of violence against Native hunters. Like Fidler's lament about Indians being supplied by the "different oppositions," reports of traders' aggressive behaviour towards Indians were often made by their rivals and therefore may sometimes have been exaggerated. Not all were, though, and it is clear that traders did sometimes resort to force to obtain furs, as in the seizure of 500 MB in furs from Ojibwa by the Canadians opposing Edmonton House in 1798, or the actions of a Canadian trader at Lac la Biche in 1799: "as soon as [the Ojibwa] came near the shore – all the Canadians ran into the water and took every thing from [them] . . . by force."[67] Other traders made threats. One "Mr. McKay" (possibly William McKay, a North West Company trader) notified the Indians around the south end of Lake Winnipeg in 1800 that if any of them were to land at the rival Hudson's Bay Company post, he would "either shoot or hang him," and, at Lac la Biche, Ojibwa hunters were forced to go to the Hudson's Bay Company post "slyly at midnight" to trade.[68] Not surprisingly, even the legendary loyalty of the Ojibwa to Canadian traders began to wear thin in response to the Ojibwas' growing sense of power and to harassment by traders caught up in rivalry.

Far worse than the hostilities that competition engendered between Natives and traders were the effects of the use of alcohol as a weapon in the fur-trade war. More than other European trade goods, alcohol proved to be a double-edged sword for the Ojibwa. On the one hand, alcohol was readily incorporated into Ojibwa culture in several ways. For whatever reason it initially appealed to them, alcohol had by the late eighteenth century come to symbolize and be termed by Native people "mother's milk, the gift that more than any other signified the concern of a parent for her child and the loyalty of a child for his mother." In relations between traders and Indians, alcohol thus connoted the fictive kin relationship between them that obliged the trader to share generously and the Indians to be loyal with their hunts. It may not simply have been the desire to become intoxicated that made the Ojibwa who traded with Henry anxious to taste the "new milk" in the autumn of 1802.[69]

Alcohol was incorporated into Ojibwa culture in other significant ways as well. By the 1790s, Ojibwa families had evolved a tradition of having drinking parties at the trading posts when they took debt in the fall and often again in the spring. Furthermore, alcohol, like other trade goods, had become connected to Ojibwa social structure and religion. As was the case with silver jewellery, red cloth, beads, and other "luxury" items, the ability to obtain alcohol became tied to a wealth complex as well as to traditional means of obtaining social prestige by giving away goods and food, and was thus part of the overall elaboration of Native cultures that occurred during the fur-trade era. Henry noted that, during this competitive era, the Ojibwa "all wore scarlet Coats, [and] had large kegs and flasks." The link between alcohol, prestige, and leadership was also made clear by Tanner, who recalled that, when Netnokwa participated in the semi-annual drinking parties at the posts, "It was her habit, whenever she drank, to make drunk all the Indians about her, at least as far as her means would extend."[70] Alcohol had also become an accepted item for use in religious offerings; Henry recorded several instances of Ojibwa asking for alcohol for funerals and for feasts when bears were killed.[71] This liquor may have been sacrificed (poured into a fire or on the ground) rather than consumed, but the documentary references suggest that this trade good, like others, had woven its way into the very fabric of Ojibwa life.

The use of alcohol in Native cultural activities, and the assignment of Native meanings to this new substance, rapidly became a problem for Native people as fur-trade competition escalated. Around Nipawin in 1794-95 there were several small posts opposing the Hudson's Bay Company, with "no less than six Interpreters, of the Southern and Bungee Languages . . . who are continually running about with Liquor &c, when anything is to be got," and in 1802, one Hudson's Bay Company trader claimed that the Canadians at Sturgeon River were keeping the Indians there so drunk that they were often unable to hunt and were building up debts. Native people did, of course, request alcohol of their own accord; it was among the most popular of the trade goods desired by the Ojibwa, to the point that on a journey from Osnaburgh House to Dauphin River in 1795, another Hudson's Bay Company trader was accosted by six canoes full of Indians (probably Ojibwa, given the locality) who threw the tobacco he gave them into the river when they saw he had no liquor for them.[72] Ultimately, alcohol proved to be addictive and terribly damaging to Native people. The semi-annual drinking parties may have been conducted in a traditional Native manner and for traditional ends, but they also resulted in injuries and deaths. Henry noted several deaths and innumerable serious injuries as a result of fights that occurred during drinking parties among the Ojibwa who traded with him. Henry did not always face serious or immediate local competition; the injury and casualty rates in situations in which Indians were pressured to drink, or were even more readily supplied with alcohol, were in all likelihood much higher.

The use of alcohol in competitive trade situations provides a striking example of the ambiguous role that European trade goods played in Aboriginal cultures. Where some trade goods reinforced and elaborated many aspects of Aboriginal cultures, others caused rapid cultural change and damage. Some trade goods did both. The destructive nature of fur-trade drinking parties – even when these were conducted as redistribution events or ceremonies – hints at great stresses generated by the fur trade and at cultural changes resulting from participation in the fur trade.

These stresses were also expressed in a myriad of nativistic and prophetic movements that flowed in waves across the Northwest between 1760 and 1860.[73] One of the earliest recorded of such incidents was a dream that Tabashaw, leader of a band that traded with Henry, related to him in 1801. Incorporating a number of Christian concepts in a Native framework, Tabashaw's dream visitor gave him "a writing, by virtue of which he could procure whatever he wanted." Tabashaw interpreted his dream to mean that "he was independent of everybody, [and] . . . had a secret power of making rum, iron arrows, etc."[74] Tabashaw's "secret" reveals tensions felt by many Aboriginal people who participated in the fur trade: the desire for material goods versus the dependence on European traders to obtain them, and a feeling of powerlessness in the face of European control over trade goods.

Pressure from traders caused further difficulties for the Ojibwa by encouraging them to venture farther south along the Red River, into the area that was used by both Sioux and Ojibwa as a war road. In the 1790s, the Red River and its tributaries beginning just south of the Assiniboine River were considered unsafe by Ojibwa.[75] Ojibwa trapping beaver in this "no-man's land" were in constant fear of Sioux attacks but did so to reap the rewards offered by the increasingly competitive fur trade. In the process, they provoked raids, and warfare became a yearly, predictable, and continuous state. This had significant effects on the emerging western Ojibwa by strengthening their relations with the Cree and Assiniboine, who had sporadically opposed the Sioux since the early 1700s. Alexander Henry recorded mixed-group war parties ranging in size from fifty to 300 warriors setting out against the Sioux in 1800, 1801, 1802, twice in 1804, and once in 1805, and there were probably at least as many parties that set out unrecorded by European observers.[76]

Warfare led to contacts among women, children, and elders as well as warriors, since non-combatants from several groups often gathered at trading posts for safety while their men were away at war. During times of peace, different peoples met during the fall and spring gatherings at trading houses. Brandon House, for example, was "swarming with Indians of all descriptions" in late April 1805.[77] Continuing inter-tribal trade also afforded opportunities for contacts. Henry recorded Ojibwa camping and trading with Assiniboine and Cree people in the Pembina Mountains and Hair Hills regions around 1800, and there were presumably many other such gatherings at which non-Native observers were not present.[78] Ojibwa sometimes pitched their tents with those of Cree families in winter, especially when it was necessary to hunt bison; John Tanner's family spent parts of three winters around the turn of the century camping with Cree families, and he commented that many Ojibwa and Cree lived together as well as with the Assiniboine.[79] Tanner referred to one Cree group with whom his family camped as "our friends," and mentioned their generosity when his own family was short of food. As well, some of these new-found friends were literally made "part of the family" through the creation of fictive kin relationships. Of a Muskego who befriended his family when they were in need, Tanner said that if any of his own family "were now, after so many years, to meet one of [his family], . . . he would call him 'brother' and treat him as such."[80] Marriage also established kin ties. Henry mentioned an Assiniboine who arrived at his post with "a young Saulteur . . . who, having been married to an Assiniboine woman, was perfectly well acquainted with their language."[81]

Ojibwa-Cree relations were generally closer than those between Ojibwa and Assiniboine. Tanner said of the Cree, "These peoples are the relations of the Ojibbeways," but he also mentioned the "habitually unfriendly feeling which exists between the Ojibbeways for the [Assiniboines]" that was borne out by his own experiences. Ojibwa-Assiniboine uneasiness deteriorated into hostility along the Red River during the summer of 1801, and three years later Lewis and Clark claimed there was a "partial war" between Ojibwa and Assiniboines.[82] The cause of this hostility is uncertain. Hickerson suggested that it stemmed from increasing Ojibwa use and subsequent depletion of game and fur resources that the Assiniboines felt to be theirs.[83] Increasing Ojibwa reliance on bison after 1800 may have provoked it, but given the lack of such conflicts elsewhere it may also have been based on interpersonal or social conflict. Whatever its cause, the tensions did not keep the Assiniboine from participating in mixed-group war parties with the Ojibwa, nor did they interfere with Ojibwa-Cree relationships.[84]

The development of such generally positive relations helped to ensure that the expansion of the Ojibwa into the West was not seriously challenged by peoples already there. Some quarrels did occur, of course, such as those between the Ojibwa and the Assiniboine, and John Tanner was denounced as being "a stranger . . . and one of many who have come from a distant country to feed yourself."[85] But for the most part, the peoples into whose territories the Ojibwa moved, and whose resources the Ojibwa used, made no objection to their presence. Several factors supported this acceptance. Kinship ties and lasting friendships among families of different ethnic groups, as noted above, helped to keep inter-group conflict to a minimum during the westward expansion of the Ojibwa.[86] As with marriages to traders, inter-group marriages played a crucial role in maintaining these ties, for after marriage one partner lived with the spouse's family. Men often lived with their wives' relatives for several years after the marriage but then took their wives back to their own people. Learning a new language and living amongst people whose customs were often very different from their own must have been a daunting life change for these spouses. Those who did so, together with their children, became vital links between the different peoples of the West.[87]

In addition, the presence of Ojibwa in the West was not generally contested because they usually did not compete directly for resources with established local groups. When they entered the West, the Ojibwa harvested beaver and game such as moose, which many of the Cree and Assiniboine, who were adopting a horse-and-bison economy, were no longer hunting intensively. And while Ojibwa did not always use different ecological zones regularly on a seasonal basis, as other tribes did (which might have allowed them to avoid conflict by alternating the use of certain areas with other groups), their bands were generally small and moved frequently so that they did not exhaust all local resources on which other groups might depend.[88] It would not be not until well after the turn of the century that competition over food resources, especially bison, provoked serious and prolonged conflict among the peoples of the parklands and plains.

Historical biographer Hugh Dempsey has suggested another, less economically oriented, reason for the ready acceptance of Ojibwa in the West that was connected to Native cosmology and to the way in which the Ojibwa were seen by other Native groups.[89] Like Native peoples across the continent, the Ojibwa lived in a world in which ordinary reality was permeated by the supernatural. Objects of power and relationships with supernatural beings were necessary to find game, maintain good health, and have success in war. Conversely, in this world view, the failure to accord the proper respect and ceremonies to the spirits of guardian animals and of game killed led to starvation, illness, and misfortune. The Ojibwa were often distinguished from and by the peoples around them by a reputation of having especially potent and dangerous supernatural powers and protection. It is unclear how this reputation arose, although it may have been connected to the presence of the Midewiwin ceremony among the Ojibwa, and to the magical "killing" and "resurrection" of participants in that ceremony.

Whatever the origins of this reputation, by the 1790s it was a factor in relationships between the Ojibwa and other peoples in the parklands and prairies. David Thompson noted in 1798 that, "Of all the Natives, these people are the most superstitious, they may be accounted the religionists of the North," and John Macdonell noted similarly that "Almost every great man or chief among the Indians [of Red River, i.e., the Ojibwa] is likewise a Juggler or doctor of physic [shaman]." More than any other Native group in the West, the Ojibwa were noted in the post journals as "conjuring and feasting," a trait that became more pronounced after they began celebrating the Midewiwin in the West.[90] Spring and autumn trade gatherings, attended by many Native groups, became the focus for Ojibwa religious ceremonies including the Midewiwin, Wabano, and Shaking Tent ceremonies.[91] Some Ojibwa made use of their reputation and powers in their relations with other groups: in 1799, Peter Fidler found himself unable to persuade any of the Indians around Bolsover House, at Meadow Lake, to guide him to Lac la Biche, "because all the Indians in this quarter are frightened of the Bungees [there]."[92] It is possible, of course, that they were afraid of a physical rather than a supernatural threat. Still, the Ojibwa maintained their reputation for having strong supernatural powers even in their close friendships with the Cree and Assiniboine. Ojibwa were trading "medicines" with the Assiniboine in the fall of 1801, for example, and at the same time the Cree were trading medicines that came from the Lake Superior region and had thus presumably been obtained from the Ojibwa.[93] In some instances, then, established Native groups may not have challenged incoming Ojibwa for fear of the potential consequences. This reputation functioned to maintain a boundary between Ojibwa and other ethnic groups, and therefore it played a role in maintaining Ojibwa identity and heritage in their new territories.[94]

Relations between the Ojibwa and other western groups were strengthened by Ojibwa participation in the Cree-Assiniboine trade at the Mandan villages and in the problems arising from it between 1795 and 1805. By the 1790s, the Mandan-Hidatsa had become the most important suppliers of horses and corn (an important, portable, easily stored staple food for nomadic tribes) to the peoples of the northeastern plains.[95] Before the mid-1790s, the Cree and Assiniboine were also major suppliers of goods. European trade goods from the Red and Assiniboine rivers (and, earlier, from Hudson Bay), which they traded to the Mandan. For several decades this system worked well. European goods passed south through the Mandan-Hidatsa, and corn and horses passed north to the Cree and Assiniboine. It is quite likely that the Ojibwa, too, were visiting the great trade fair, either for pleasure and fancy craftwork brought by the Crow and other western tribes, or for corn before they began growing their own.

To the plains Cree and Assiniboine, Mandan corn was far less important than Mandan horses. Horses were not easily come by, though; the Mandan were shrewd traders and demanded high prices for them. The Cree and Assiniboine could meet these prices as long as they remained the primary suppliers of European goods to the Mandan, but once Europeans established direct trading relations with the

Mandan in the mid-1790s, the balance of this trade relationship was upset. The Mandan continued to supply horses and other goods to the Cree and Assiniboine, but at a much higher price since they maintained their monopoly while the Cree and Assiniboine lost theirs.[96]

According to historian John Milloy, the resultant inability of the Cree and Assiniboine to pay Mandan horse prices led to poor relations between the Cree and the Mandan in the mid-1790s. Some Ojibwa participated in attacks on the Mandan during this period. The Brandon House journal noted in 1795, for instance, that "11 Crees and Soeties came here going to war against ye Mandalls."[97] The plains groups could not risk having their horse supply cut off in retaliation for such actions, however, and this, as well as increasing Sioux hostility to all four groups, resulted in the temporary restoration of peace to the alliance by 1800. Later in the decade, John Tanner learned of a war party involving "the Assiniboines and Crees, and all the Indians of this part of the country, with whom the Mandans had made peace," being invited by the Mandan to make war on the Minnetaree (Gros Ventres).[98]

While peace was restored for a short time, the Cree monopoly over European goods was not, and so the problem of horse prices remained. One of the Cree solutions to this problem may have been to re-sell (at even higher prices) some of the expensive horses to the Ojibwa, who were the only people in the West who did not have horses. This theory is supported only by indirect evidence; still, the first eyewitness reports of Ojibwa possession of horses in the West do date from around 1800, when the Mandan horse supply had been re-established, and the Cree were encountering problems paying for their horses. Alexander Henry noted that Ojibwa along the Red River had no horses before that time. Indeed, one Ojibwa whom he surprised near Thief River nearly fled on seeing Henry on horseback, "as he knew of no person who had horses in this part of the country but the enemy."[99] A few other Ojibwa living along the Assiniboine River did have horses by 1800. One band from the Assiniboine River with horses joined the Ojibwa trading with Henry, and apparently used their horses to hunt bison en route.[100]

Whether these early horses were obtained from Cree or Assiniboine allies is unknown, but the timing is suggestive. Ojibwa are known to have visited the Mandan villages in company with Cree and Assiniboine in 1805, by which time they were almost certainly either trading for horses themselves or assisting their allies to do so.[101] What little evidence does exist about the source of the first horses owned by Ojibwa in the West indicates that they were being acquired from the Cree and Assiniboine and by raiding. In addition to the horses that Henry noted that Ojibwa were trading from the Assiniboine for medicine, some were obtained by trading from the Cree in the Hair Hills in the winter of 1802. Tanner and Charlo (one of the Ojibwa who traded with Henry) both obtained horses by raiding around

1800.[102] Although the Ojibwa remained "horse-poor" for many years, the number of horses they possessed increased steadily. By 1804, one Ojibwa band of sixty-five people had ten horses.[103]

The reasons for the adoption of the horse by some Ojibwa at this time are not as obvious as they might at first seem. Hickerson believed that this development stemmed from "a need for mobility in warfare and for transport," but both of these reasons are complex.[104] Although horses were an efficient means of transportation, Ojibwa in the West continued to live along the wooded shores of rivers and lakes for the greater part of the year: an environment to which canoes, rather than horses, were more suitable, and in fact canoes remained their standard means of transportation. Rather than turning to horses when birchbark was difficult to find, skin canoes were substituted, at least for short trips.[105] And, while horses made the bison hunt more efficient, allowing hunters to travel greater distances in search of herds and women to transport larger quantities of meat, Ojibwa were commonly hunting bison without the aid of horses well before 1800. Given the fact that that they remained horse-poor for several decades, they evidently continued to hunt on foot or with only a few horses. As Tanner recalled of one winter, "Buffalos were so numerous . . . that I often killed them with a bow and arrow, though I hunted them on foot, and with no other aid than that of dogs well trained." The anger of Ojibwa hunters at the Métis, who drove the bison far from Red River during their mounted hunts in 1817, also confirms the continuation of this practice.[106] Nor did all of the Ojibwa adopt horses at the same time, or incorporate them into their lifestyles in the same manner or to the same extent. From what we can reconstruct from the documents, Ojibwa along the Red and Assiniboine rivers seem to have had horses about a decade earlier than Ojibwa west of the Assiniboine, and were the first to value horses highly enough to begin stealing them.[107]

The other reason that has been given for the adoption of horses by the Ojibwa is that they needed horses to defend themselves from the mounted Sioux. As one Ojibwa told David Thompson, the problem was: "We being foot men, they could get to windward of us, and set fire to the grass; When we marched for the Woods, they would be there before us . . . and under cover fire on us." Alexander Mackenzie was of a similar belief, that, if the Ojibwa continued "to venture out of the woods, which form their only protection, they will soon be extirpated."[108] Mounted Sioux attacks were particularly dangerous for Ojibwa camps without horses. Henry's Ojibwa in-laws were killed in such a situation when "the Sioux gained the advantage by circling them and cutting off their retreat."[109] The Dakota themselves had a different perspective on this inequality, however. As late as the 1830s, they said that the Ojibways had greatly the advantage over them [in warfare], because they could float down the current of the Mississippi, bringing plenty of provisions in their canoes, and being fresh and fit for action on their arrival. On the other hand, they were obliged, when invading the Ojibway country, to make long and toilsome marches on foot, carrying their weapons and provisions, and were exhausted when they most needed to be rested and refreshed.[110]

Many Ojibwa attacks were made on foot, in which case they would have lost these advantages, but this quotation does demonstrate that they were not entirely power-less against the Sioux without horses.

In addition to these differing perspectives of the Ojibwa and the Dakota, it should be noted that for horses to have provided effective defense against mounted Sioux attacks, nearly every individual in the band would have required a mount, either for the use of the warriors or for the escape of women, children, and the elderly. This was certainly not the case, however. By 1798, Ojibwa just east of Red River had "no Horses, and only Dogs for winter," and as late as 1815 – by which time the Ojibwa were firmly established in the West, not driven back by Sioux attacks – the number of horses to Ojibwa in the Assiniboine and Red River area was only one per tent, while there was an average of eleven persons, including three warriors, per tent. Nor were horses entirely necessary even for long-distance war parties, as Hickerson has suggested. Even mixed-group war parties in the Red River area were not fully mounted by 1805, yet they stepped up rather than de-sisted from raids against the Sioux. In 1804, 300 Ojibwa and Assiniboine left Pembina to go against the Sioux, yet only half of these were mounted.[111]

Because of these inconsistencies, Hickerson's belief that the emergence and survival of the western Ojibwa was dependent upon their acquisition of horses cannot be correct. Ojibwa people occupied the West for several decades, and formed deep attachments to their new lands, before they adopted horses in a wide-spread manner. Nor were they "extirpated" by their enemies without them. Thus, while some Ojibwa undoubtedly obtained horses for practical reasons (for use as beasts of burden and for long-distance travelling across the plains), others did not feel obliged to do so.

For those who did acquire horses, social as well as practical factors were an issue. Many of the Ojibwa who had horses at an early period seem also to have spent more time with Cree and Métis friends and relatives. The band that Henry observed leaving Pembina for the Hair Hills in 1804 was one such group; they possessed ten horses.[112] Intermarriage and other contacts exposed the Ojibwa to the values and skills of these peoples, and mixed-group camps fostered the bor-rowing of many cultural elements and foreign values from them. By 1800, when the Ojibwa were in close association with the Cree and Assiniboine and were ac-quiring horses from them, horses had assumed a position of importance among these peoples. This was the era of the flowering of plains equestrian cultures. For these people, horses were not only symbols of individual affluence and prestige, but, because of the burgeoning pemmican trade and the independence and power of mounted bison-hunting peoples, they were also both the means and the symbol of the affluence of these tribes. Given that the Ojibwa initially came west at least partly in search of material affluence and a high standard of living, and that they used certain trade goods as badges of personal social status, it is not surprising that some of them were attracted to the hallmarks of these traits among neighbouring peoples. Horses, and the finery and flamboyance associated with them by plains tribes, were such hallmarks. Reinforcing this admiration of the success of plains peoples was the fact that Cree was frequently used as a trade language by peoples throughout the West, including the Ojibwa.[113] The language of trade and negotiation commonly reveals power relationships. Where Ojibwa was the common tongue in the Great Lakes trade, Cree was in the West. This obvious shift of power may have reinforced the incentive for Ojibwa to emulate plains peoples.

What the Ojibwa took from their neighbours' example of independence and success, though, was only an external symbol. They adopted the horse, but not (at this date) the values of plains peoples surrounding the ownership, relationship with, and acquisition of horses. Charlo's relatives expressed their Ojibwa perspective on horses and horse raiding when they attributed his lingering death in 1801 to "bad medicine" being thrown on him by a Hudson's Bay Company trader, Mr. Goodwin, who was also a doctor (and therefore, in Native eyes, possessor of great spiritual power) when Charlo stole three horses from Goodwin's post. Such a negative assessment of the merits of horse stealing coupled with a strong affirmation of the importance of "medicines" in Ojibwa culture indicates a good deal of ideological continuity. Similarly, Tanner's repentance during the very act of his stealing a horse, and his abandonment of the animal because of his changed feelings, do not indicate an acceptance of the horse raiding and status complex among his group.[114] The attraction of the equestrian peoples' status and independence, the feeling of superiority when mounted, and the usefulness of horses as beasts of burden, were all factors in the adoption of horses by the early western Ojibwa. At the same time, horses were adopted on the Ojibwas' terms, to suit their own needs and agendas, and integrated into their own value system.

While possession of a few horses made little difference to hunting techniques, bison did become increasingly important to the Ojibwa in the Red River area at this time. The dwindling numbers of other large game species, the ready availability of bison in certain seasons, and the effects of Cree and Assiniboine cultural influences made bison hunting more attractive to the Ojibwa. By the late 1790s, many Ojibwa bands in the Red and Assiniboine River areas were relying on bison to support their more traditional activities. Increased use of bison provided food for the Ojibwa during the summer and in winter made it possible to continue trapping without long interruptions to find food. It is not surprising that at the same time they began relying on bison, many Ojibwa bands stopped commuting to their villages of origin or to eastern trade gatherings in the summer and began residing in the West year-round. The hunting of bison also allowed Native groups to escape the pressures of fur-trade competition to some extent if they so chose. As early as 1796 the Hudson's Bay Company trader at Fort Alexander complained about a "Red River gang," probably Ojibwa (though possibly Cree or Assiniboine), who "had done nothing but laid among the Buffalo the whole winter."[115] Typically, bison supplemented fish and game in summer and early fall, and were often hunted during winter when other game was scarce. Most bison hunting occurred in the parkland or at the edge of the prairie on both sides of Red River and south of the Assiniboine. Henry noted that some of the Ojibwa who traded with him preferred the east side of the Red "where the buffalo are as numerous as on the W., and much easier to approach in the willows and long grass." Some hunting was also done farther out on the prairie, most often in company with Cree hunting camps, as was John Tanner's experience south of the Assiniboine River one winter around the turn of the century.[116]

Not all the Ojibwa in the West adopted horses and bison during this period. Ojibwa in the regions north and west of Lake Winnipegosis, especially those living along the north Saskatchewan River, did not feel the need to integrate horses and bison into their lifestyle as the Red River groups did. Since they were less threatened by the Sioux, they did not need military assistance to lay claim to their hunting and trapping grounds. Nor do they seem to have been involved in either the Cree-Blackfoot conflicts or the Mandan trade. These factors meant that they spent less time with the Cree and Assiniboine and were less influenced by them. Finally, the more westerly Ojibwa were not faced with the shortage of large game that existed in the Red River area by 1804.[117] It was this condition in addition to the other incentives that compelled the Ojibwa in the Red River area to begin regular bison hunts.

CHANGING LIFESTYLES

As they spread out across the parkland and along western waterways, the Ojibwa encountered different ecological conditions, formed separate social networks, and participated differently in alliances with their Cree and Assiniboine neighbours. While all of the Ojibwa in the West shared some common background and experiences, they also developed several different adaptations to varying ecological, social, and trade conditions. By 1804, Ojibwa in the area west and north of the Interlake region had a way of life that was slightly different from that of the Ojibwa bands living in the Interlake area and along the Red and Assiniboine rivers.

Little information is available on the bands west of the Interlake, which included those trading at Lac la Biche, Edmonton House, Buckingham House and Nipawin, and several bands that spent much of the year in the wooded hills in the upper Assiniboine region. What is recorded about these people points to a number of small, tightly knit groups, often a mixture of Ojibwa and Ottawa, who frequently camped together and came in to the trading post together. The two largest recorded of these groups were a band that arrived in seven canoes (probably about forty people) around Edmonton in 1795-96 and another band with thirteen adult men, representing (at an average of three adult men per tent) some four to five lodges, possibly fifty persons in all. These families wintered around Lac la Biche in 1799-1800. Little contact between these people and neighbouring Cree, Blackfoot, or Assiniboine bands is recorded. Some must certainly have occurred (we may be hampered in our understanding of this region by the very limited documentation available), but one gets the impression that these people, unlike the Ojibwa who traded with Henry along the Red River, did not "feast and smoke" with non-Ojibwa neighbours or have significant kin ties with them. This isolation, the virtual absence of horses, and the smaller overall population distinguishes the most westerly Ojibwa adaptation.

It is unclear just how far and how often the Ojibwa in this area commuted for the summer in the mid-1790s. Many of them moved around a great deal, but some of the parties that arrived at the post in late summer to take debt may have been travelling from Red River or other places in the West rather than from the Boundary Waters or the Great Lakes. Some bands were certainly spending summers along the North Saskatchewan River, remaining in the West year-round.[118]

Except for the absence of wild rice, the lifestyle that they led did not differ significantly from that to which they were accustomed in the East. If they spent part of the summer travelling to and from the East, they were en route to their winter hunting area by late August. After obtaining supplies from the post, they hunted in the parkland and woods for moose, wildfowl, and other game. In winter they hunted for furs (mostly beaver, marten, and mink), and visited the post in mid-winter and spring. Most probably they fished under lake and river ice in winter and harvested small game for subsistence in addition to moose, deer, elk, and some bison that sought shelter in the more densely wooded areas that these bands frequented. What little data is available for this area after 1800 contains no references to Ojibwa hunting bison or using horses by 1805, and the exclusively woodland orientation of these Ojibwa was noted as being distinctive. In a letter to fellow trader William Tomison, James Bird wrote from the Hudson's Bay Company post at Setting River in 1798 that "saving the Bungees, all [the Indians] without exception are tenting in the plains, killing Buffaloe."[119]

In late winter, bands conducted intensive beaver hunts and came in to the post between the end of March and early May with their returns, which were as many as 400 MB. It is not known whether these people harvested sugar, although box elders (Manitoba maple) and birch would have been available for this purpose. In late spring, bands gathered at the post, fished, and hunted large game near rivers. Sturgeon were harvested from the Saskatchewan River, the Sturgeon River, and possibly other tributaries of the North Saskatchewan River in spring, which allowed the Ojibwa to remain in large groups for some time. This is the only evidence for spring gatherings that might have included religious ceremonies; otherwise, this adaptation seems more focused on individual extended family hunting and trapping groups. In early summer the people began to disperse, some travelling east and others moving to local hunting and fishing territories.[120]

Trade competition was intense in some of these more westerly areas, and the tensions certainly affected the Ojibwa. At Lac la Biche, they were forced to come "slyly at midnight" to trade with the Hudson's Bay Company during the winter of 1799-1800, and by January they were the centre of a deal struck between the two companies: "the Canadians promised to pay us 300 MB on conditions of our not sending to the Bungees & Ottaways Tents . . . [while the Indians] are to have free liberty to bring what furs they will in a Private but not public manner to our House to trade."[121] Such pressures quite likely affected other aspects of the adaptation of these bands to the West. Unfortunately, evidence for this area is slim for the 1790s and largely missing for the 1800-1805 period.

To the southeast, along the Red and Assiniboine rivers, other distinctive lifestyles were evolving. Ojibwa families began concentrating along the Assiniboine River, at the forks of the Red and the Assiniboine, at Pembina, along the shores of the Manitoba lakes and in the Interlake area, and immediately west of the Interlake at Swan River, Shell River, and Dauphin River.[122] In contrast to the way of life of the more westerly bands, these families were in close contact with each other, their bonds maintained through spring and autumn gatherings to harvest sugar and sturgeon and to celebrate group religious ceremonies.

The seasonal round that most of the Ojibwa in the Red and Assiniboine River area followed by 1800 did not change greatly for several decades. By the mid-1790s, most of these people were living year-round in the West. In late summer and early autumn, large numbers of Ojibwa arrived at the trading posts to socialize and take debt. By 1800, many were arriving with stores of both fresh and dried bison meat.[123] Ojibwa were also harvesting sturgeon in August in some locations; Henry noted such a fishery in operation on the lower Red River near Netley Creek in mid-August of 1800.[124] The autumn trapping period continued as before, sometimes preceded by a brief bison hunt to provision it. Generally, though, the Ojibwa hunted moose, deer, bear, and small furs in the parkland during the autumn. According to Tanner and the traders, a bison hunt during December or January became more common for these bands.[125] The Ojibwa do not seem to have adopted the Cree practice of living in large groups in winter and depending solely on bison. Of Tanner's band, only the men ventured onto the prairie and for only brief periods. Tanner indicated that at least some of the newcomers in the West still preferred to hunt moose and other more familiar game in winter, and that they felt less skilled or less certain of success hunting bison during this season. "Being . . . reduced to the apprehension of immediate starvation, I was compelled to go in pursuit of buffalo," he said, and in another instance, "The men having most of them come from a forest country, and having never hunted buffalo before, all failed to kill except myself."[126] This supports Lauren Ritterbush's conclusion that the early western Ojibwa in the Red River district displayed more continuity with the past than adaptation, and that they made use of patches of familiar wooded territory in the West, especially Turtle Mountain and the wooded river valleys and hills west of the Interlake region.[127]

The Ojibwa continued to make a mid-winter visit to the trading post before beginning to trap seriously in February and March. Women sometimes made this visit while the men hunted game. Trapping and sugaring sometimes overlapped, with the women producing sugar and the men trapping for beaver and other furs. This was probably also the case with a group of Ojibwa who spent most of February and March in the Netley Creek area, which offered good trapping and was close to sugaring sites.[128] Sugaring was a social occasion for those who used sugar groves along the Assiniboine and the Red rivers and their tributaries. Tanner described a camp of "ten fires," probably between sixty and 100 people, who co-operated in both sugaring and the spring beaver hunt.[129] Women and their families had rights to particular groves of trees for sugaring; families who were new to an area had to search for a decent grove that was unoccupied or ask to be allowed to harvest in a claimed area. Significantly, the process of laying claim to these family groves may well have created some of the Ojibwas' first permanent ties to the West.[130] These gatherings also reinforced kin ties among a larger group of people than the extended family that had wintered together, contributing to the formation of a group identity.

When the sap stopped running in late March or early April, some of the trapping and sugaring groups moved to their sturgeon weirs to await the spring spawning run, while others immediately gathered at the trading posts.[131] In some cases, weirs were located near posts, and the fishing sustained large social and trade gatherings. Unless they had earlier traded for or travelled to obtain caches of wild rice, dried sturgeon, sturgeon oil and fish pemmican may have been necessary alternatives to rice in order to complement lean game at this time of year. The spring run, usually three to four weeks long beginning in late April or early May, offered a prodigious food resource. Midewiwin and other religious ceremonies were held by the assembled families at these gatherings, which, like the sugar harvesting camps, also promoted "the renewal of friendships and social ties [and] the discussion of military and political affairs."[132] Fish, sugar, stored foods, and whatever game could be caught sustained the gatherings at the posts in April and May, when the posts were said to be "swarming with Indians of all descriptions" trading furs and sugar and enjoying their spring celebrations.[133] After trading, the large group at the post dispersed. Some returned east, while others went to take advantage of the end of the sturgeon run, the renewed abundance of wildfowl and their eggs in the marshes, or to hunt bison and other large game. In some years, Tanner's family, like many others, began making preparations for going to war soon after the spring trade gathering. This required laying in stores of food and leather for the warriors as well as for those who were left behind. Tanner's family "killed great numbers of buffaloes, and . . . dispersed [them]selves about to make dry meat" one year for this purpose; another year, they hunted elk and moose.[134]

An interesting picture of life for bands most deeply involved in the fur trade within the Interlake district at this time can be pieced together from journal references to one "Bad Governor," or *maji ogimaa* ("Matchi Huggemaw" in the journals, the Bad Chief). This man, whose leadership role may have extended beyond being a trading captain, led a fair-sized group of eight men and their families (probably fifty to ninety persons), most of whom were undoubtedly related. He appears first in the records at Bloodvein River, on the east side of Lake Winnipeg at its narrows, with a few furs and some venison in early September 1795. Several weeks later, he led ten canoes of his people to Jack Head River on the west side of the lake; the group seems to have traded at the Hudson's Bay Company outpost at Partridge Crop in the central Interlake region that winter. A few of their furs went to Canadian traders who also had an outpost there. The band came to the post at the beginning of April for their spring celebration but brought few furs. "About 100 Indians at ye houses and the whole did not bring a hundred beavers," complained Hudson's Bay Company trader John Best. Bad Governor's people left the post in early May, and met the traders in September on the western shore of Lake Winnipeg. They had a great deal of dried moose meat, many geese, and much wild rice. These stores give some indication of how the group spent its time during the summer. Bad Governor's bands took debt and left the post by the end of September. During the autumn the Indians traded part of their fall game hunt (moose meat and geese) and over 150 gallons of wild rice, mostly for liquor. In December and January they brought prime furs amounting to about 100 MB to the post, and in April and May they visited both the Lake Winnipeg and Fort Alexander posts with over 170 MB, indicating an intensive spring fur hunt. (The Fort Alexander trader remarked in 1799, "my Chief dependence is on them," and, as if to prove his statement, he then fetched 200 MB from their tents.) They also retrieved wild rice from their caches in early May, and traded at least twenty gallons of it for brandy. In late

May an invitation to go to war arrived for Bad Governor. He left, and he and his band returned to the post in September. The lacustrine orientation of Bad Governor's band, and their emphasis on wild rice – probably harvested in the waters east of Lake Winnipeg – suggest that this group may have been recent arrivals in the West from the Boundary Waters region.[135]

Post journals seldom mention Ojibwa women, as they do male trading captains such as Bad Governor. Given the general division of labour by sex in Ojibwa society, though, it is clear that women as well as men made crucial contributions to their families' comfort and economy. Wild rice and maple sugar, largely the products of female labour, were, as has been mentioned, important subsistence items and trade goods. Rolls of birchbark and bundles of wattap (spruce roots, used for sewing canoe seams and bark containers) provided sources of trade income. Women processed men's contributions, both for the support of their families and for trade. Pemmican, dried meat, fish pemmican, sturgeon oil, and dressed hides produced by women were staples of Native life, and surplus quantities were in constant demand by traders. Despite this, foods harvested by women were often assigned a lower social value than big game brought in by men. Native people frequently told fur traders that they were "starving" when they had no big game even when there were enough roots, rabbits, or other foods to sustain life. Thus, Henry noted in the spring of 1801 that "his people" (the Ojibwa who traded with him and probably some of his men) were "starving" but living on prairie turnips.[136] In practical terms, however, the Ojibwa commonly used a wide range of subsistence resources to compensate for the effects of environmental fluctuations on various harvests. In this practice, "women's foods" – rice, sugar, roots, and the small game that they snared – were an essential contribution to a balanced and productive seasonal round. The extent to which this translated into personal autonomy, self-esteem, and social status for women, however, is not reconstructible from the documents for this period.

In addition to processing goods for trade, women traded both the fruits of their own labours and those of their male relatives. Trading by women was most often done on behalf of their husbands or families, when Indian men were not in the camp at the time that fur-trade employees arrived to collect furs, or when for some other reason no men were available to fetch needed goods from the post.[137] Wives of Indian hunters hired to provide meat for European traders received gifts from the trader, just as "trading captains" or "chiefs" did. In September 1800, Henry noted that he had "equipped [his] hunter with clothing for himself and his wife." Gifts to other women in the band included awls, needles, net thread, vermilion, and tobacco.[138]

Women also had a good deal of power within the family. Significantly, as anthropologist Susan Rogers has indicated, the family was the central and most important part of many pre-industrial societies, and it was the place where many decisions about daily and long-term activities were made.[139] Given their involvement in resource harvesting, women must have had some input into the general seasonal round and specific movements of their families. Netnokwa, for instance, determined many of the movements of her own family, as when she rejected a poor sugaring site and immediately moved her family some distance to a better one. According to Tanner, "everything belonged to Netnokwa, and she had the direction in all affairs of any moment."[140] While Netnokwa was an exceptionally strong and charismatic woman who actually led a band, with a great deal of spiritual power backing her assertiveness and leadership, her influence was presumably neither unprecedented nor unparalleled.

Women's ability to make such decisions and influence their own and their families' lives depended to a large degree on their ages, as it did for men. Young adults had relatively little power or status, except that which was gained from their practical and decorative or artistic skills. Elders, on the other hand, were frequently consulted for advice and thus exerted a good deal of influence; this was one of the sources of Netnokwa's authority. Mothers of men and women of marriageable age frequently played important roles in choosing mates for them. Netnokwa and Tanner both made it quite clear that it was the duty of mothers to choose wives for their sons or husbands for their daughters, although in many cases it was men, in practice, who arranged marriages for their children. Netnokwa's disapproval of a son-in-law's laziness led her to throw him out of her tent – in effect, divorcing him from her daughter – another indication of the power older women were capable of exercising within their families.[141] (Netnokwa allowed the man back into her family when she heard he was without a wife and "destitute," another indicator of women's status and roles in Ottawa-Ojibwa society.) The gatherings of women during sugaring, ceremonies, and at trading posts gave them opportunities to find and observe potential mates for their children. This implies some control by older women over the composition of their families and camps.

Apart from these specific examples, the extent to which their economic contributions gave Ojibwa women the right to make decisions over their own and their families' lives during this era of adaptation is uncertain. In other cultures, women's contributions to household and family economy are not necessarily accompanied by social or political power or status.[142] Henry's comment that suicides were "not uncommon among the Saulteur women," and similar comments by other traders later in the nineteenth century, may indicate that despite their significant contributions to subsistence and trade, women did not enjoy an equally significant social status: women's suicides often signal acts of autonomy in a social and political context in which women are otherwise relatively powerless.[143]

In assessing the position of women in Ojibwa society at this time, one must ask to what extent and in what ways women's work benefitted women, how their work was regarded by their male kin, and what *power* (in the sense of authority) and *status* meant in Aboriginal societies. In the case of Ojibwa women's contributions to trade, for example, it is certain that Ojibwa affluence in the late-eighteenth and early-nineteenth-century fur trade was achieved only with a great deal of back-breaking female labour processing furs, hides, and other "country produce" for trade. Women's return on this labour came in the form of trade goods such as kettles and needles, and prestige goods such as jewellery and cloth, obtained by gifts from traders, by their own trading, and from their husbands trading furs and goods processed by them.

Other returns on women's labour were less material in form. Just as Ojibwa men parlayed skill in trapping furs into social prestige through their acquisition of trade goods, their ability to give things away to followers, and possibly through the institution of the trading captain, women also used their role and returns from the trade to achieve social prestige. Few women became trading captains themselves, and the position, with its (men's) military coat and top hat as trademarks, was male-oriented. Women's contributions to their families' well-being were crucial, but not publicly lauded or ritualized in the same way as were those of their male relatives. On the other hand, their skills and abilities were judged, and were in a sense public, just as men's skills in hunting and trapping different animals were known and judged. Women's decorative skills, in particular, were a public expression of private competence. As June Helm has noted, decorated garments worn by Native men "served as a kind of travelling art gallery" for their wives' work. Such displays of skill are frequently said to have made women desirable wives to men and sought-after teachers by other women. Did something comparable to the elaboration of men's social status through the institution of the trading captain and its material trappings happen to talented women through their display of competence in processing foods and hides and of skill in creating and decorating garments? What happened, for instance, when Ojibwa women began making leather coats for their husbands in the style of trading captains' coats? And again, to what degree did respect for a woman's many practical and artistic skills bring "power" and "status" for a woman? We need to continue to ask such questions of the separate but closely related worlds of Ojibwa men and women.[144]

One final point of uncertainty in determining women's status is the extent to which Ojibwa in the West included women as status symbols in their developing wealth complex.[145] Among plains tribes, the advent of the horse allowed the development of individual wealth: where once the hunt and the processing of the catch required a communal effort, horses made it possible for male hunters to make their own, marked kills. This led to the accumulation of individual, male-owned wealth. As the wealth complex grew, more wives were required to process the larger kills.

By the mid-nineteenth century, a man's status could be told by the numbers of his horses and wives. The Ojibwa did not immediately develop a horse-and-bison economy when they entered the West. However, their participation in the early western fur trade, with its abundance of beaver and ready access to trade goods, may have affected them as the horse affected plains tribes. The references, both by traders and by John Tanner, to these newcomers as "wealthy" people, and the descriptions of their clothing and lavish jewellery, indicates the presence of a similar individualized wealth complex. Women certainly shared in the material benefits of such a complex, as noted in David Thompson's description of Ojibwa "Women and Children, as well as the Men" being "rich" and wearing heavily decorated stroud clothing. But what did Ojibwa men imply about women's status when they informed Henry that "all great men should have a plurality of wives"?[146] Did they see women as partners in achieving status who shared in the prestige that came with the ability to obtain quantities of furs, trade goods, and food? Or did they, like plains tribes, see women as simply a means to and an indication of wealth? And, although recent studies have contradicted the many claims made by traders that Native women were "beasts of burden," stating instead that women took pride in their ability to harvest foods and process meat, hides, and furs, how does one explain Henry's comment about the frequency of Ojibwa women's suicides? For now, it may be all we can do to raise the questions about the effects of these historical forces and cultural adaptations on Ojibwa women's lives, and about whether Ojibwa women were affected differently by these changes from the way their male relatives were.

* * *

Many western Ojibwa bands made significant changes in their lifestyles between 1797 and 1804: living year-round in the Red River area, spending more time with the Cree and Assiniboine, increasing their reliance on bison, and beginning to hold their own Midewiwin ceremonies. These changes were not made simply because by that time they "possessed horses on such a scale as to permit success in hunting in a plains region," as Hickerson believed.[147] Some changes, such as the hunting of bison, were simply efficient accommodations to the different resources of the West or to pressures from fur-trade competition. Other changes signalled the roots that these Ojibwa were sinking into their new soil. The most important of these was the end of their seasonal "commuting" to and from their eastern villages and trade gatherings. This transition is marked in the historical records by evidence that Ojibwa were hunting bison and trading furs in the summer months, and, even more importantly, that they were celebrating the Midewiwin ceremony in the West rather than returning to the eastern villages to participate in it.

Midewiwin ceremonies are known to have been held in the spring at a number of locations, including Pembina, Reed River near its junction with the Red, and the Shell River (upper Assiniboine River) area, and were undoubtedly held at other locations, particularly major sturgeon fisheries. These gatherings, at once sacred and social, maintained and reinforced the identity and solidarity of Ojibwa families in the West.[148] The Midewiwin is a group-healing ceremony in which teachings central to Ojibwa world view and identity are re-told. According to William Warren, a multi-family group or a seasonal village was considered to be "actually separated from the common central body and Me-da-we lodge" and a "distinct branch of the same tree" when it "became of sufficient importance as to assume the privilege of performing the rites of the Me-da-we-win within its own precincts."[149] The gathering for and participation in such ceremonies defined social boundaries and networks. Many links, including periodic visits, between the older Great Lakes villages and the western Ojibwa continued after this time, and the western Ojibwa continued to feel bound to their eastern kin and communities by a sense of heritage and much shared culture. Vital social ties and feelings of shared identity were also created among those who gathered yearly in the West to share such an important ceremony, who shared similar experiences and patterns of living, and who had made similar adaptations to new lands.

While they had become "a distinct branch of the same tree" by 1804, the western Ojibwa still felt very much a part of that tree. Their adaptations to the different physical and human environments in the West, including their increased association with plains peoples, use of bison, and, for some bands, adoption of horses, did not immediately bring more profound cultural changes or changes in identity. Even though they had begun to uproot themselves from their eastern homes, the early western Ojibwa way of life "was characterized by the maintenance of many 'traditional' traits."[150] Many of the most basic details of daily life that reinforced Ojibwa everyday reality and identity continued as before. With the sole exception of wild rice, most subsistence pursuits, including fishing, the production of maple sugar, berrying, hunting and trapping, remained unchanged. Canoes continued to be used, and shelters of rush mats and bark continued to be made.[151] According to David Thompson about 1798, the Ojibwa, including those in the Red River valley, had "no Horses, and only Dogs for winter use and not many of these to haul their things in winter, they have very few tents of leather. They are mostly of rush mats neatly made, sometimes of Birch Rind, or Pine Branches."[152] This description would also fit Ojibwa communities in the Boundary Waters and the central Great Lakes. Other cultural elements such as mourning customs and religious ceremonies continued as before; as John Macdonell noted in the mid-1790s, "Amongst the Saulteux in the Assiniboil River the same customs & superstitions prevail as in their native places, Lake La pluie and Lac

Rouge."[153] Thus, when Alexander Henry purchased a white bison hide in 1804, he remarked, "The Saulteurs set no value on these skins." He would have got a very different response from the plains Cree and Assiniboine, to whom the bison meant life and was sacred, and who had legends about white bison.[154] By 1804 the Ojibwa were still, as Harold Hickerson wrote, "a woodland people with a few horses." Peter Grant reported similarly: "Many of the Sauteux families settle among [the Cree and Assiniboine], preferring those fruitful countries to their own, yet too tenacious to the customs of their own nation to conform to the manners of the others.[155]

Clearly, the adaptations that the western Ojibwa made to their new lands were balanced by a continuity of outlook and, as yet, of many practices. While they had become a "distinct branch" by 1804, they were yet part of the same tree and still rooted firmly in Great Lakes soil.

"More troublesome and daring," 1805 to 1821

3

The Ojibwa had barely begun to adapt to the Northwest when they faced a series of crises and changes. Foreshadowed by the beaver epidemic of 1800, the fur trade declined drastically after 1805, touching off the death throes of fur-trade competition between 1805 and 1821. Between the demise of the XY Company in 1805 and the merger of the North West Company with the Hudson's Bay Company in 1821, European traders literally fought for furs, a situation that produced escalating competition and, for Native trappers, continued access to relatively cheap goods. Even so, the effects of competition could not mask the decline of fine furs and large game that were the basis of the high standard of living the Ojibwa had initially enjoyed in the West. In addition to these changes, several years of unusual cold and drought, which affected the availability of important food resources, and an epidemic of measles and whooping cough made for a difficult period.

Developments in the human landscape of the West in these same years proved just as dramatic as changes in environment and economy. Within two decades, no fewer than three new peoples emerged to challenge the Ojibwa and other Native groups for the remaining furs and game in the western prairies and parklands. Freemen (European and mixed-blood men who left full-time employment in the fur trade but chose to remain in the West) and Métis (the children of country marriages between Native women and fur traders, who began to form a distinct society around Red River in these years) rapidly became full-scale communities and began to dominate certain sectors of the prairie fur-trade economy. Most startling of all, the first settlement of Europeans who were not fur traders was begun at Red River in 1812. With the settlers came the first treaty in the Canadian West and the first missionary and "civilizing" efforts aimed at Native people there.

Scholars have assumed, given the ecological and economic decline occurring in the West at this time, that these years witnessed the waning of Ojibwa fortunes:

that, having made the fur trade essential to their status and well-being, the Ojibwa became dependent on it when it failed and were trapped into a cycle of poverty that culminated in handouts of food to them from trading posts later in the century.[1] Such analyses reflect the fur traders' own commentaries on the state of the trade after 1805. "The country grows poorer every day, but does not diminish the Indians' wants," noted trader George Nelson in 1811, while in 1819 Peter Fidler commented, "The Indians I believe are becoming more lazy than formerly[;] they are also much more troublesome and daring."[2] If we probe such comments, though, we find that they reflect the traders' disappointments rather than the Natives' needs. Although they participated in the fur trade eagerly when it suited them to do so, and continued to participate to obtain basic goods even when conditions worsened, the fur trade was not the centre of the lives of the western Ojibwa. In difficult times, they balanced their needs and allocated their time to various activities – including trapping – accordingly, and found ways to cope with all but the most extreme conditions they encountered in these years. In fact, the western Ojibwa developed a number of strategies to provide themselves with alternate subsistence and trade resources to minimize the stresses of the period. This chapter will examine these coping strategies as they relate to the continuing development of Ojibwa culture in the West.

For Ojibwa who were still actively involved in the fur trade, the most important development in this period was the continuing decline of beaver and other high-status furs. Without beaver, even intense competition by trading companies could not sustain the affluence that the Ojibwa desired. Beaver populations continued to decrease after the beaver epidemic at the turn of the century in the parts of the Red and Assiniboine River valleys that were safe from the Sioux, and by 1805 the fur shortage was widespread. By 1815, beaver were scarce in the entire area from the Winnipeg River near its junction with Lake Winnipeg south to the middle Red River territory, north into the Interlake area, and west along the North Saskatchewan River, including the Cumberland House district, as far as Edmonton House: in short, throughout virtually all of the regions in the West where Ojibwa people resided.[3]

In response to the beaver shortage, Native people turned to muskrats, martens, otter, lynx, wolves, and other furs as alternatives.[4] Muskrat and marten populations hit a high point in their cycles between 1811 and 1817, but then began to drop in the Red River, Assiniboine River, Interlake, Swan River and Lake Dauphin areas. Red foxes and lynx increased after 1817, but none of the types of furs that were available in any quantity was of much value.[5] Table 1 shows the relative values of typical furs traded between 1795 and 1821. Thus, muskrats were worth only a tenth of the price of beaver, making the typical returns of 300 to 400 muskrat skins during the height of the muskrat population cycle barely equal to a decent

TABLE 1
Fur Values, 1795-1821, in Pounds Sterling and Made Beaver

Fur Type	Range of Value, Sterling	Range of Value, MB
Whole beaver	14s. 5d. to 36s. 1d.	1 [constant]
Lynx	3s. 7d. to 11s. 11d.	1 1/2 to 2
Red fox	3s. 8d. to 5s. 8d.	1 [constant]
Fisher	4s. to 6s. 4d.	1/2 to 1
Martens	4s. 10d. to 9s. 9d.	1/2 [constant]
Muskrats	6d. to 1s. 1d.	1/10 to 1/6
Otter, prime	13s. 10d. to 24s.	2 [constant]

Note: Fur values were often expressed by traders in shillings rather than pounds and shillings: hence figures such as "36s." (Sterling value is given as it appears in the account books and refers to London currency.)

Sources: HBCA B.105/a/4, Lac la Pluie Journal 1796-97; B.213/d/2, Swan River Account 1796-97; B.22/d/1, Brandon House Accounts 1810-11; B.213/d/3, Swan River Accounts 1810-11; B.160/d/1, Pembina Accounts 1811-12; B.213/d/4, Swan River Accounts 1811-12; B.213/d/5, Swan River Accounts 1812-13; B.22/d/4, Brandon House Accounts 1813-14; Hudson's Bay Company Standard of Trade, 1820.

beaver hunt of the period between 1790 and 1804 and "costing" many more times the work and energy.

Such "costs" were increased by poor weather throughout parts of the West between 1809 and 1819. Climatic problems were especially pronounced between 1816 and 1818, when unpredictable late and early frosts, and a three-year drought, seriously affected food resources.[6] Fluctuating water levels (generally high between 1812 and 1816, low after 1816) and killing frosts during late spring growth periods typically affect wild rice, aquatic mammals such as beaver and muskrat, waterfowl, other species such as moose that feed on aquatic plants, and cultivated crops. Although the climate was not uniformly bad over the entire West, harvests are known to have been affected in 1816 and 1817 along the Red and Assiniboine rivers, and unpredictable snowfalls affected hunting and fisheries in some areas in 1810-11 and 1813-14.[7] These conditions forced Ojibwa in these regions to diversify the resources they harvested and to work harder for their subsistence, a factor that may have prevented them from spending as much time trapping as before and may have further lowered fur returns. It is little wonder that during the final years of this period, Indians were frequently reported to be "starving," a term used in a peculiar sense by fur traders and Native people to mean hunting for food rather than furs.[8] Resource stress caused by climatic extremes may also have contributed to the mortality of the 1819-20 measles / whooping cough epidemic that ended the cycle of hardship, for the severity and mortality of measles is greatly worsened by malnutrition.[9]

As if they were not coping with enough, the Ojibwa faced competition for remaining furs and large game from the rapidly growing freeman and Métis populations.[10] These peoples had existed in the West before 1800, but their numbers were relatively small and scattered. This changed quickly with the union of the XY and North West companies in 1804, and the economy-oriented reorganization of the Hudson's Bay Company in 1810-11, when many lower-ranking employees were either dismissed or quit when their pay was lowered. A fair number of these "free men" chose to remain in the West with their Native or mixed-blood wives and made their living by hunting, trapping, and performing some labour at trading posts. As their numbers increased, freeman-Ojibwa groups developed in areas that the Ojibwa had formerly dominated: the Interlake, Swan River, Turtle Mountain and Pembina areas.

Even more aggressive than the freemen in claiming their share of the western fur-trade economy were the Métis. From the very beginning of the fur trade, marriages between European traders and Aboriginal women had created a population of mixed-blood children. In the Great Lakes region and other areas in the Northwest, the Métis formed their own society, separate from that of either of their parents though strongly tied to both. The need of the fur trade for huge amounts of provisions gave the Métis (as well as the plains Cree) a niche on the northern plains, and after the Red River settlement was established it became the focus of a developing Métis nation.

In the Cumberland House, Interlake, and Red River areas, Ojibwa also faced competition from Cree families who were moving into that area. These people may have been "Swampy" or northern Cree from the Hudson Bay Lowlands, or they may have been members of the northernmost bands of Ojibwa from the region northeast of Lake Winnipeg.[11] They were drawn south by the lure of furs and game, which existed in greater quantities there than in their homelands, and they may have hoped to use the ties between their Métis kin and the traders to make a better living than was possible farther north. They were generally favoured by traders as being more "industrious" than the Ojibwa and were thus viewed with some disfavour by the Ojibwa themselves. By 1810 they were trading with Nelson in the Interlake, and by 1820 they were jostling for casual labour and prestige with Peguis's band of Ojibwa at Red River.[12]

In their own ways, each of these new peoples offered stiff economic competition to Ojibwa in the fur trade. Because they had close ties to traders, freemen were commonly given higher prices for furs, meat, and labour at posts than were Indians. Peter Fidler stated in the Red River District Report for 1819 that, while Indians were paid less than one shilling per buffalo hide, freemen were paid between two and three shillings per hide. For much the same reason, freemen, Métis, and Cree also began to replace Ojibwa as labourers and hunters for traders after 1805.[13] And, well before 1821, the Métis dominated the bison hunt with their enormous, tightly organized seasonal parties, which set out from Red River. The large-scale bison hunts immediately caused difficulty for the Ojibwa, who lacked sufficient horses to follow the herds once the mounted hunts had driven them far away. By 1817, the Ojibwa were "Jealous of the freemen getting so much goods, and chasing the cattle [bison] with Horses."[14]

The problems faced by the Ojibwa between 1804 and 1821, then, were related to the decline of choice furs and the consequent loss of their economic advantages in the fur trade; bad weather and its effects on food resources; and new competition in the quest for diminishing fur-bearers and large game from the growing freeman, Métis, and mobile northern Cree populations. In response to these pressures, the Ojibwa developed several coping mechanisms. Some bands retained their basic seasonal round but began hunting and trapping in areas that had previously been only lightly harvested. A few began living with plains Cree, freeman, and Métis families, sharing the special skills and advantages of those groups, while others stayed in the areas to which they were accustomed but traded a wider variety of furs and began exploring alternate means of subsistence such as corn and potato cultivation, bison hunting, and fishing. Many families used several of these strategies at once or over the course of a year.

Hunting and trapping in still-productive areas was not easy to do, for by 1805 most of these regions were held by enemies. Beaver could still be found along the Souris River, for instance, but Ojibwa were often afraid to hunt there because of the danger from Sioux (and, in some years, from Blackfoot and Mandan) enemies.[15] The upper branches of the Red River were also productive but very dangerous. Despite this, according to John Tanner, there was around 1810 "a very general movement among the Ojibbeways of the Red River toward the Sioux country; but the design was not, at least avowedly, to fall upon or molest the Sioux, but to hunt."[16] With a large group for defense, Tanner and his family travelled south to the upper branches of the Red River to hunt beaver at the beginning of this "general movement." Most of the party lived in a fortified camp because of constant expectations of an attack by the Sioux. The upper Red River was far more productive than the secure parts of the Red River valley. Tanner claimed to have taken 100 beaver in one month, at a time when beaver were becoming hard to find. More typical hunts ranged from twenty to forty MB in mixed furs from other parts of the West. Similarly, two Ojibwa men arrived at Henry's post at Pembina in the spring of 1806 from Pelican River, where they had "seen Sioux repeatedly" but had stayed to obtain 300 beaver pelts and forty prime otters.[17]

A measure of the seriousness with which the Ojibwa regarded the beaver shortage is the manner in which they re-interpreted the nativistic teachings of The Shawnee Prophet, which swept the Great Lakes region and parts of the West in 1808. In discussing his decision to undertake dangerous hunts up the Red, Tanner said, "I know not whether it was that we were emboldened by the promise of the Prophet, that we should be invisible to the Sioux, but we went much nearer than we had formerly ventured to their country." In fact, the original teachings of The Prophet did not include such a message. Nor did Ojibwa in the Interlake district – which was more productive in beaver and game – interpret the teachings to mean this.[18] That the shortage of beaver should influence even the prophecies of the times indicates how deeply concerned the Ojibwa were about this problem.

Partly in an attempt to make trapping in these areas safer, Ojibwa from the Red and Assiniboine River region and their allies sent war parties against the Sioux in 1804, 1806, 1807, 1813, 1814, the winter of 1815-16, 1816, 1818, 1820, and 1821.[19] Sioux attacks occurred just as often, indicating that neither group had a real advantage over the other. Ojibwa war parties did not set out with the sole purpose of driving the Sioux from the upper Red River and gaining control of resources in that region. After nearly a century of enmity, Ojibwa-Sioux warfare was, by 1805, fuelled by the desire for avenging family members killed by Sioux, and by the opportunity for gaining prestige in battle. While Sioux and Ojibwa each may have been attempting to claim the upper Red River, neither was successful, nor were the naive peacemaking efforts of Lewis and Clark in 1805 or of other negotiators in succeeding years.[20] Gradually, the Ojibwa were forced to reconsider the feasibility of making routine trapping expeditions deep into Sioux territory. They did not entirely abandon the upper Red River area, though, nor did they abandon the Pembina region due to pressure from the Sioux, as Harold Hickerson believed they had. As Lauren Ritterbush has shown, Hudson's Bay Company documents to which Hickerson did not have access demonstrate that Pembina continued as a trading centre for Ojibwa for some time after 1809. The site's proximity to the still-abundant furs from Turtle Mountain and to the bison herds made it a favourable location, particularly so in view of competition between the Hudson's Bay Company and the North West Company, which attracted Ojibwa from Leech and Red lakes to the east and from the Assiniboine River and the Forks.[21]

Safer areas where game and furs could still be found during this period included the Interlake and the wooded hills and river valleys around it, from Cedar Lake in the north to the Red Deer, Dauphin, Carrot, and Swan rivers in the West. Arthur Ray has noted a pattern of seasonal movement among Ojibwa and Cree bands in this region, who left their summer fishing camps each autumn and moved into these valleys to hunt moose in winter.[22] The Turtle Mountain area became a refuge for several bands of Ojibwa on a year-round basis as well as for other bands on a seasonal basis; its wooded hills, good game populations, and distance from the Red River "war road" all proved attractive to these bands.[23] Ojibwa also abandoned some regions, possibly because of game and fur shortages there. There are few reports of Ojibwa inhabiting the North Saskatchewan River after 1805, although this may be a function of the lack of documentary evidence for that region and era. At least one band, however, was noted to be leaving Lac la Biche in 1810 for the Columbia River, "where they hoped to find beaver as numerous as blades of grass."[24]

In addition to focusing on still-productive areas, some Ojibwa sought to cope with the decline of resources by joining forces with freemen, who got better prices for furs, or with plains Cree and Métis relatives whose emphasis on the bison hunt and the important pemmican trade ensured their standard of living and some continued access to trade goods. The number of mixed-group camps rose with the increase of the freeman population in the West between 1805 and 1812. Ojibwa commonly wintered with Cree and Assiniboine in the Pembina Hills and at Turtle Mountain by about 1805, and Ojibwa-Cree bands were reported near Cumberland House in the winter of 1806-07 and around Setting River in the fall of 1808. One Setting River camp was described by Henry as containing "20 leather tents of Crees, a few Saulteurs, and two freemen," while another camp nearby was composed of "10 Crees, and a few Saulteurs and freemen, who had a number of horses."[25] This was typical of the composition of mixed-group camps, with most residents being Cree, and a minority of Ojibwa, freemen, and Métis.

Although the formation of mixed-group camps may seem paradoxical during a period in which ethnic groups in the West were beginning to compete for resources, such "increasing complementarity and interdependence" was in fact an efficient method of dealing with the problem.[26] The alternative was for one group to displace another, as the Ojibwa had attempted to do with the Sioux. Unlike Ojibwa-Sioux relations, the complex web of kinship ties between Ojibwa, Cree, freemen, and Métis conflict between groups and allowed groups to combine their strengths. As one trader remarked of inter-group marriages during this period, "These unions consolidate the interests of the tribes, and are foundations of much social harmony and good fellowship."[27] Conflict between these peoples was also reduced by the sharing of the advantages that freemen and Métis had in the fur trade with the Native kin with whom they lived. Some of these advantages were shared with Native people in the form of the trade goods they purchased or were paid. The Ojibwa, for their part, were relied upon for their skills in hunting moose, elk, and other woodland and parkland game, and possibly for their hunting magic, of which the Cree had less.[28]

An even-more-common response to declining fur and game – and one that was necessary to compensate for the effects of poor weather on several important resources – was to increase the number of significant food resources harvested in the annual round. Bison, garden crops (especially corn and potatoes), fish, wild rice, and other resources played important roles in maintaining the equilibrium of the seasonal round during this period.

Consistent references are made in trade journals to Ojibwa harvesting fish, particularly sturgeon. Some "775 sturgeon, weighing from 50 to 150 lb each, were brought into [Alexander Henry's] . . . trading post at the mouth of the Pembina River between 20 April and 20 May 1801; sturgeon may thus have equalled or exceeded bison in the stock of provisions at Henry's post that year."[29] A few years later, in June 1805, Henry reported that Indians and employees intended to live on fish for the summer at Red River near Netley Creek, close to the site of a major sturgeon fishery used by both Ojibwa and traders. Other fisheries were located on the Assiniboine River near Brandon House and at the mouths of rivers flowing into the Manitoba lakes.[30] Some fisheries were affected by fluctuating water levels associated with the climatic disturbances of these years. George Nelson reported in the autumn of 1810 that there was little snow and virtually no fish at the rapids of the Dauphin River, normally a productive whitefish fishery.[31] In general, though, fish remained a major staple of the Ojibwa diet.

Wild rice became somewhat more accessible to Ojibwa bands by 1820 despite a series of high and low water levels and the colder weather of 1816 through 1818, which must have damaged some harvests. Ojibwa deliberately extended the range of this crop by sowing rice in marshes and small lakes in the Red and Assiniboine River corridors. Rice was harvested at Netley Creek, in several marshes along the Red River, in small lakes east of Brandon House, and at the mouths of rivers flowing into the east side of Lake Winnipeg. Nelson's accounts of life in the Interlake between 1807 and 1811 mention Ojibwa families leaving the post for the annual rice harvest and retrieving caches of rice during winter, and Peter Fidler traded rice from Indians at Fort Douglas in 1814 and 1815.[32]

Far more important than the harvest of wild rice during this period was the adoption of corn and potato horticulture to augment wild plant foods and game. Long practised by the Ottawa, refugee Huron, Ojibwa, and other Great Lakes tribes, horticulture spread rapidly through the Boundary Waters and Red River valley regions around the turn of the nineteenth century.[33] Ojibwa-Ottawa gardens were first reported at Netley Creek in 1805. Other gardens were begun by mixed Métis, freeman, Ojibwa, and Cree families at the Forks by 1812 and at a site between Brandon House and Portage la Prairie in 1816.[34] Corn and potatoes provided a supplement to wild rice during years in which the rice harvest was poor or failed altogether, and later in the century Ojibwa deliberately planted larger gardens if water levels seemed unfavourable for rice crops in the spring.[35] This "short-term resource switching" was one of the successful strategies the Ojibwa used to maintain a productive seasonal round during more difficult times. Garden produce was in a sense a double addition to Ojibwa subsistence, for, as well as the food value of the crops, the gardens required little tending during summer and therefore freed the people to harvest other foods while the crops were ripening. The carbohydrates provided by corn and potatoes were also important in adding calories and energy to the diet, especially during winter when game was lean.[36]

Women, who did much of the gardening, would have played a crucial role in deciding how to balance these resources each year and how best to compensate for changing weather patterns and water levels. Interestingly, though, it was men who claimed the credit for introducing horticulture into the West. John Tanner stated that an Ottawa man, Shaw-gwaw-goo-sink, introduced maize cultivation among the Ojibwa at Netley Creek in the Red River area about 1805, though Alexander Henry claimed that he had supplied the first seed for Ottawa gardening efforts in the region.[37] In fact, both sources may have been at work. The Ottawa had long had productive gardens in their Great Lakes villages, so that Ottawa who migrated to the Red River region may have brought seed and knowledge with them. Ojibwa women married to Henry's men and other traders may also have learned to cultivate and obtained seed from their husbands. As Lauren Ritterbush has noted, Alexander Henry refers to Indian women – who may have been wives of traders – planting at Pembina in 1804.[38]

Most of these gardens were abandoned for all or part of the period between 1813 and 1818. The Ottawa abandoned the Netley Creek site about 1813, either because the poor weather made gardening less successful at that site or because of pressure from traders to produce more furs, and they moved their gardens to islands in the Lake of the Woods, which may have had more favourable microclimates.[39] Ojibwa gardened at Red River in 1815 and 1816; Peguis's band reestablished the Netley Creek gardens by 1819; and a map by Peter Fidler shows another garden on the southeastern shore of Lake Manitoba in that year as well. A group of six tents of Bungees (between fifty and seventy people) was reported near the freeman community at Birsay, just east of Portage la Prairie, in May 1819, camping near a fish weir and planting gardens.[40] Large Ojibwa gardens are noted in Hudson's Bay Company journals for 1819 in the Interlake district. The most important of these was the "Big Tent" site at the north end of Lake Manitoba, where they grew potatoes:

on an Island towards the north end of the Lake, they have erected what they call a Big Tent, where they all assemble in the spring, hold Councils and go thro' their Religious Ceremonies – The soil here is excellent and each family has a portion of it under Cultivation, which the women and old men remain, and take care of it during the summer – while the young men to hunting – In the fall of the year when they are going to abandon the place, they secure that part of the produce, under ground till spring, which they cannot carry along with them.[41]

As well as planting enough to supplement their diet, the Ottawa and Ojibwa began producing surplus crops after 1805 "to make corn a regular article of traffic" with the traders, so that by 1811 Lord Selkirk knew enough about their commercial operations to instruct his colony governor to attempt to purchase corn "from the Ottawa and Bungee Indians at Dead River."[42] For those who cultivated them, then, the gardens provided two partial solutions to the fur and game shortage: they supplemented the diet, thus bolstering game supplies and allowing more time to be spent obtaining furs, and they provided a new product to trade, partial compensation for the decrease in the number and quality of furs.

Bison was also used to provide stores of food for periods of intensive trapping. This began during the initial years of the game shortage just after 1800, and bison hunting remained a regular part of the western Ojibwa yearly cycle between 1805 and 1821. With the deterioration in the climate after 1809, bison may have become particularly important as compensation for lost or damaged harvests of plant foods and other fluctuations in game populations due to lowered water levels. Pemmican, with its high fat content, would have provided a high level of caloric energy to replace wild rice and cultivated crops in years and areas where these were not available.[43] The altered behaviour of the herds in 1817 and 1818, when due to severe weather they remained close to the Assiniboine River during seasons when they would normally have been far away from that region, made them an especially welcome alternative to other foods in those years, which were disastrous for garden crops and other resources.[44] Ojibwa hunted bison most frequently during the summer and the leanest mid-winter months. The camp of nine long tents that Henry observed at River aux Gratias in 1806 had been living on bison for a month, and he noted several other bands that had also had summer bison hunts. Some Ojibwa began arriving at the Swan River and Dauphin River posts in late summer from the plains after 1804, and bands from Dauphin Lake, White Mud River and the Hudson's Bay Company's Big Point House in the Interlake district all depended on bison for part of their subsistence, especially in summer and "to make a stock [of] Dry provisions to enable them to pursue the Trapping" in late winter. Bison were hunted in the parkland and prairie south and west of the Assiniboine River, and along the banks of the Red River south of Pembina.[45]

All of these strategies enabled the Ojibwa to survive the many difficulties they encountered after 1805, but they were often implemented at the expense of time spent trapping for furs. Between the decrease in the number of furs available and the need to work harder to obtain food, fur returns, especially those of beaver, fell dramatically. European traders therefore tended to interpret Ojibwa coping strategies as signs of "laziness." Peter Fidler was not the only trader to complain of this. The writer of the Manitoba district report for 1821 similarly complained that the Ojibwa who traded at Big Point House in the winter had "not exerted them selves in furs as last year, having followed the Buffalo." During Nelson's tenure in the Interlake, he lamented that more than one Ojibwa hunter "amuse[d] himself at hunting game only." The Cumberland House clerk also voiced this opinion in 1807, stating that the Bungees there "had done nothing this winter."[46] Some of this was simply traders' griping; the Cumberland House Ojibwa, after all, were able to pay their debts for several years after the Cree ceased to. However, even Nelson's fairly productive Ojibwa in the Interlake region spent enough time hunting and trading meat that Nelson frequently wished "that they should hunt wherewith to pay their debts [i.e., furs]."[47] Despite the traders' self-interested complaints, the Ojibwa were not becoming "lazy." The fur trade remained one part of their seasonal round, but it was a part that was increasingly diminished by changing ecological conditions.

In fact, the decision to spend more time hunting, fishing, and gathering, and less time trapping, was a coping strategy in itself. Rather than conduct an intense trapping period over a week or more, the Ojibwa began to combine trapping with hunting trips, and to make shorter trapping excursions over the course of the winter as game supplies permitted. One of the Ojibwa who traded with George Nelson arrived at the post with the meat of three beavers, the skins of four, and three otters, all "killed since three days past when he left his lodge to come this way."[48] This strategy did not require the laying-up of large food stores to sustain trappers and their families through periods of intensive trapping, but allowed them to fit a limited amount of trapping into their daily food quest. It did limit their access to trade goods, and while the Ojibwa were unconcerned about meeting the traders' expectations (i.e., paying their debts), they still had to obtain necessary goods. As Charles Bishop has recently observed, this strategy does not necessarily signal independence but may instead reveal a double bind in which Native trappers found themselves during the waning of the fur trade: it is possible that they could not spare the time to hunt for furs even though they may have required certain trade goods to hunt for food.[49] There is remarkably little evidence of this type of difficulty among all of the records pertaining to the Ojibwa in this era, though, something that may well have been due to the effects of continuing fur-trade competition.

Competition was an important factor in Ojibwa strategies between 1805 and 1821. Although Henry (and, undoubtedly, many other traders) gloated soon after the merger of the XY Company with the North West Company in 1804 – "our Indians in the beginning attempted their old tricks, coming into the house every two or three days to beg for free rum, . . . they were soon convinced there was no longer an X.Y. Co. to spoil and support them in idleness. They saw the need of hunting to procure their necessaries. . . . We obliged them to pay their debts, and not a drop of rum was given"[50] – he was more hopeful than accurate about the state of the trade. Far from being calmer after the removal of the XY Company, the years between 1805 and 1821 witnessed the most violent and deadly fur-trade rivalry in the West, including the harassment and routing of the Selkirk settlers, the "Athabasca War," and the battle of Seven Oaks. And, despite Henry's claim, the era of Ojibwa "idleness" (or economic leverage, depending on one's perspective) was not entirely over. The Ojibwa who traded with George Nelson were certainly not chastened by changes in the Europeans' fur trade. Their behaviour and attitudes were far from the desperate picture painted by Henry: they received respectable presents every spring, and were nonchalant enough about hunting for furs that Nelson had difficulty getting them to leave the post in the fall.[51] Many Ojibwa threatened to trade with the competition and used the still-competitive atmosphere in the trade to obtain credit and presents – often at least as much as given in previous decades. Competition also negated traders' efforts to cut costs and compensate for poor fur returns and mounting Native debts, for each time one trader attempted to limit or cut off credit to Native trappers, the rival company was likely to make that an opportunity to attract disgruntled Indians.[52]

Trappers who remained loyal to their traders continued to receive credit, usually between forty and seventy MB, in fall and spring. Within areas that experienced intense competition, loyal trappers were treated particularly well. Nelson gave between thirty and sixty MB credit in fall to principal hunters, and presents to encourage them to bring them their hunts.[53] Duncan Cameron of the North West Company distributed the following presents to Nelson's principal trappers in the Interlake in the spring of 1808: "[to] Ayagon he gave a Coat, hat & feather; to Old Muffle he gave an Illinoi capot; to old Cu fesse, he gave one Blkt 3 pts & one fathom HB's strouds . . . & after a long speech he gave them one keg mixed rum, six quarts of Powder Shot & Ball in proportion among them."[54] Similarly, the trader at Brandon House noted in October 1811 that a group of Ojibwa had arrived who were "old customers of ours"; among the items with which he outfitted them for the winter were ammunition, goods, and even two horses.[55] Remaining loyal to one trader was not simply a means of maximizing benefits, of course. Deep and lasting relationships ranging from friendship to adoptive parenthood to marriage developed between many Ojibwa and the traders and their employees. Thus, Ayagon was not merely manipulating George Nelson by angling for presents. Fur trade rhetoric aside, Nelson respected and admired the older Ojibwa, and there are indications that Ayagon held Nelson in similar regard. Even John Tanner, whose trading loyalties seem rather fickle in his narrative, said, "I had long traded with the people of the North West Company, and considered myself as in some measure belonging to them."[56]

Other Ojibwa continued to manipulate the competitive system as they had before 1804. Henry noted that despite the fact that the region was nearly trapped out by 1805, Ojibwa continued to trade at Pembina because they were able to get inexpensive goods due to the intensely competitive situation there.[57] The additional goods they obtained in this manner helped to maintain their access to luxury items as fur supplies diminished. Another manipulative strategy was displayed by an Ojibwa band that took debt from the Hudson's Bay Company at Brandon House in the fall of 1811 and then traded with the North West Company at Fort Dauphin during the winter. They re-appeared at Brandon House with only a few dressed skins and some fishers in the spring of 1812, provoking an irate journal entry there: "they are such a rascally set they do not deserve ever to be trusted with goods on debt from us."[58]

Other families, previously loyal to one company, switched allegiance during the period between 1805 and 1821 after what they felt to be poor treatment, hoping to receive better rewards and favours from their new traders. Despite his feeling of "belonging" to the North West Company, John Tanner traded for several seasons at the "Mouse River post" (an outpost of Brandon House at the Souris River?), apparently for the sake of convenience. He stopped trading there and went back to the North West Company after a horse that he had been promised was sold in his absence: "I told him, since the horse had gone to the north west [company], the beavers might go there also." Similarly, some of George Nelson's principal hunters in the Interlake area left his post one day stating, "They are determined not to have any more dealings with our people for they say themselves to be too pitiful with us." Peguis, who later became "Colony Chief" at Red River, also switched his allegiance to the Hudson's Bay Company around 1812 after a quarrel with the North West Company.[59] In some cases, then, relationships between Ojibwa and traders were broken by the feeling that the trader was not treating the Ojibwa as generously as he ought to.

At the same time as they took advantage of these continuing economic opportunities and created others for themselves, Ojibwa throughout the Northwest accumulated debts at trading posts between 1805 and 1821. Ayagon complained "much of not being able to pay his debt . . . owing to scarcity of beaver; and other peltries" as early as 1807.[60] This was part of the waning of the fur trade all across the West; the Ojibwa were certainly not the only people to accumulate post debts during this era. It was noticeable in the Ojibwa case because they had brought in such large numbers of beaver and other prime furs in previous decades. By 1819, one trader believed that Ojibwa debts with both companies in the Swan River district were of "such an amount that they can never be paid," and Peter Fidler commented in 1820, "Formerly, the Bungees were much more punctual in paying their Debts than now."[61] Like so much other information given by traders regarding Indians and the state of the fur trade, these statements were coloured by professional self-

TABLE 2
Debts, Interlake, Swan and Red Deer Rivers, 1815-1821

Post	Year Listed	# of Debts Debts	Range of amt., MB	Average	# Debts above av.	# Debts below av.
Red Deer	1815	10	3-23 MB	9.5	3	7
Swan R.	1815	16	1-42	18	6	10
Partridge Crop	1821	13	4-33	17.1	6	7
Big Point House	1821	36	1-63	13.5	9	27
Ft.Dauphin	1821	20	1-18	5.1	6	14

Sources: HBCA B.176/d/1, Red Deer's River Accounts, 1815; B.213/d/7, Swan River Accounts 1814-15; B.51/e/2, Manitoba District Report 1821, Indian Debts; B.51/d/2, Manitoba District Accounts 1820-21.

interest and were not strictly true. Information on Indian debts at Red Deer River and Swan River in 1815, and at Fort Dauphin, Big Point House, and Partridge Crop for 1820-21 indicate that just two hunters out of some ninety-five owed over sixty MB, while the majority had debts of less than twenty MB and several hunters paid off credits of twenty to seventy MB (see Table 2).

Despite the traders' accusations, the few excessively large debts that existed were created largely by themselves due to mismanagement and the competitive situation. By 1815, most Indian trappers were known to the traders, as were their abilities, and it was part of a careful trader's job to limit credit to amounts that could be repaid by average hunts. Unfortunately, careful trading was impossible in areas with intense rivalry, such as existed in much of the Interlake, including Big Point House, where the largest debts were recorded. Still, traders did sometimes refuse credit to Indians in bad years.[62] Competition also raised debts by tempting Ojibwa to refuse to pay outstanding debts at the end of a season, a practice that was of short-term benefit (by making the goods they had obtained less expensive or free), but which caused further tension between traders and Natives. Some Ojibwa were forced "to use every stratagem to keep out of [the Hudson's Bay Company's] way when they have Furs – In case we would take them in payment of their debts and prevent them from bartering them."[63] On the other hand, some bands responded to debts by taking less credit, such as the bands that Nelson described as being "not in the humour of taking so much [debt] as formerly."[64] Other debts were the result of the need to spend more time hunting for food rather than for the trade, and of the decrease in the quantity and significance of presents given to Indians, which deprived the Ojibwa of a significant part of their "income" of trading goods and required them to take more in debt. The state of the trade had changed considerably from the extreme competition that had caused the Cumberland House trader to lament in 1794 that the Ojibwa there would "not trade anything for their Furrs but cloth and guns. As for all other articles they look for to be given them."[65]

Large debts were also caused by changes in the kinds of goods wanted by the Ojibwa. Ojibwa tastes in trade goods became more expensive during these years, being more strictly limited to high-priced items such as "Cloth, Blankets, Guns, Kettles, [and] Capots [blanket coats]." The less-expensive silver ornaments that had been such a high priority for them in previous years waned in importance after 1805.[66] There are several potential reasons for this trend, any or all of which could have applied to different Ojibwa bands at different times. In general, the limitation of desired trade goods, particularly the focus on cloth, blankets, and capots, is a trend that has been interpreted by historical geographer A.J. Ray as a sign of growing dependence on the fur trade to support bands in a region becoming scarce in large game from which leather could be obtained.[67] This is entirely plausible for those bands that chose to remain in areas where large game was scarce, and it is borne out to a certain extent by the Ojibwas' increasing reliance on bison, which would have compensated for the lack of other large game by providing leather and robes as well as stores of meat. On the other hand, as will be seen, some Ojibwa families shifted from birchbark- or rush-mat-covered lodges to tipis made of moose, elk, or bison hide during this period. This would have been impossible to do if leather were truly scarce, for the average lodge required ten to twelve large hides.[68] Nor was this the first era in which cloth and blankets were desirable trade items. Cloth (particularly red cloth), had been much in demand in the 1790s, when leather was not in short supply. At that time it was a symbol of status and affluence, rather than a necessary alternative to leather. Some western Ojibwa – such as those around Red River by the 1810 to 1820 period – did face such a leather shortage that they turned to cloth clothing. Peter Rindisbacher's highly detailed images of Ojibwa at Red River in the 1820s show that much of their cloth clothing was made of red stroud.

Some bands, then, chose to use cloth and to re-focus their trading desires. Others were undoubtedly forced to; Ray's hypothesis is probably correct for some bands in over-trapped areas. But other western Ojibwa bands may have had still another reason for both their debts and the types of goods they demanded. For the more plains-oriented bands, this reason may well have been their growing desire for horses.

Ojibwa attitudes towards horses began to change noticeably after about 1815 in the Red River area. Before that time, they were interested in horses as useful beasts of burden, but few thought of them as items of prestige or wealth as did other western tribes. Henry stated in 1805 that "the Saulteurs . . . are not so thievishly disposed" about horses as the Cree and Assiniboine, and Fidler's 1815 survey showed that the number of horses owned by the Ojibwa had not increased appreciably since 1804, being still about one per lodge for families who possessed them. But by the summer of 1817, the Ojibwa around Red River were stealing horses, and the following year they were said to be "much addicted to Horse stealing in the summer Time." Numerous horses were stolen by Ojibwa in 1818 and 1819. At Swan River, the trader wryly commented that the Cree and Ojibwa were "fond of horses & frequently take the loan of stragglers for which they politely apologize but uniformly forget to return."[69] These comments strongly suggest not only that their interest in horses was increasing dramatically, but also that some Ojibwa were adopting the plains horse-raiding complex. War had long been an acceptable way to obtain horses – Tanner obtained a horse about the turn of the century that had come from a raid – but generally the Ojibwa traded for their horses. By 1820, horse stealing became a reason for war, a means to gain status as well as horses, and young men vied to outdo each others' feats. Where Tanner had once gone to purchase horses from the traders, the Ojibwa were now stealing them from the traders. While the Ojibwa around Red River still did not use horses to hunt bison, they may have been using them to transport the growing amount of bison meat they were eating.

As their desire for horses grew, some bands from the Red and Assiniboine River area obtained horses from the Mandan villages at the Missouri.[70] But Mandan horses were expensive, as the Cree had discovered some years earlier, and they were traded primarily in exchange for guns and other high-priced trade goods. In 1805, the Cree were giving guns to the Mandan "as fast as they take them in debt" – in return for which, the trader reported, "they get nothing in return but Indian corn and Buffaloe robes, this is a great means why often they slip their debts."[71] As well as corn and buffalo robes, though, the Cree were also receiving horses from the Mandan. Ojibwa who were obtaining horses from the Mandan would have found themselves in the same bind as the Cree: horses were expensive, costing guns, blankets, and other trade goods; they needed to obtain these items from the traders to obtain horses from the Mandan but became unable to repay their debts because of the growing shortage of fur-bearers and the difficult climate that made it imperative to spend less time trapping and more time hunting for food. Ojibwa who obtained horses from the Cree would also have faced the same problem, since the Cree paid high prices for their horses and needed guns to trade them from the Mandan. It is quite probable, then, that Ojibwa debts at some posts, and the more expensive goods they demanded, were in part the result of their growing trade with the Mandan, Cree, and Assiniboine for horses. If so, then these changes in Ojibwa trading patterns do not necessarily indicate a growing dependence on the fur trade but may instead signal a determination to participate less in the fur trade and more in its alternatives, including bison hunting for subsistence and trade, as such debts did for many Cree. To this extent, post debts were part of an attempt to maintain control over the quality of their lives and the nature of their participation in the trade.

If Ojibwa were obtaining horses from the Mandan, they must have been quite determined, given the complex political situation on the plains at the time. Several incidents recorded in the Brandon House journal indicate the Ojibwa position in this political tangle. By 1805, the Mandan relationship with the Cree, Assiniboine, and Ojibwa had been disintegrating for some time. Between then and 1820, relationships between Mandan, Cree, Assiniboine and Sioux constantly shifted, with open hostilities breaking out between the Mandan and the Cree several times, and peace (generally involving ritual horse trading) being made as often. Cree visited the Mandan to formally "renew Terms of Friendship between both Tribes" in the fall of 1817, and in April 1819, fifteen Ojibwa went from the vicinity of Portage la Prairie to the Mandan villages "as friends."[72] Ojibwa participated in most of the war parties that set out against either the Sioux or the Mandan-Hidatsa in these years, and many of these were concerned with obtaining horses as well as scalps. With high prices and hostilities limiting their access to the Mandan horse market, horse raiding may have become a more important priority for Ojibwa warriors as well as for Cree and Assiniboine men in these years.

Frustratingly little information is available on the daily lives of these early plains-oriented Ojibwa. A far better picture can be reconstructed for the different life led by Ojibwa bands in another region, the Interlake, from a combination of sources that date between 1807 and 1821. Hudson's Bay Company journals and district reports, and North West Company trader George Nelson's journals and reminiscences, provide unusual detail on the Interlake bands and particularly on the Ojibwa families who traded with Nelson.[73] Together, these sources give at least a partial picture of Ojibwa economic strategies, social relations, religion, and aspirations and allow us to see how the Ojibwa in the Interlake coped with the stresses of the period.

Nelson's writings on the band he traded with at the North West Company's Dauphin River House between 1807 and 1811 are particularly detailed, allowing a partial reconstruction of the composition of the band, which consisted of about thirteen related families and comprised at least fifty people. The area they lived in was a plentiful one, which Nelson referred to as a "Land of milk & honey" in his reminiscences.[74] For these people and others in the Interlake, the combination of fur and provisions trading, sugar and wild rice production, and hunting of large and small game, provided a reliable subsistence base that allowed for a comfortable life. While the families that traded with Nelson did not garden, others in the Interlake did. Those who had gardens cached surplus potatoes and corn in the ground in late summer and then went to one of the trading houses around the Interlake (which included, besides Nelson's, Fort Dauphin, Big Point, a number of small lakeside outposts, and Swan River) in September. A few families still made an intensive fur hunt in November or December, but most hunters brought in small numbers of mixed furs throughout the autumn. Large game, especially moose, was hunted during the fall. Game was still relatively plentiful, as evidenced by the success of the Ojibwa hunter hired to provide meat at Big Point House in the fall of 1819, who killed twenty moose by 10 December.[75] Hunting areas were "owned" on a usufructory basis, and newcomers apparently had to obtain permission to hunt in areas already in use.[76]

Bison were hunted in January, February, and sometimes March, when they could be found in the plains and parkland south and west of the Assiniboine River. Bison hunting and warfare must have brought the Interlake Ojibwa into sufficient contact with plains peoples to learn some of their ways, for one of the changes that occurred among the Interlake people during these decades was, surprisingly, the adoption of the plains-style skin tipi. As early as 1810, Ayagon invited the women of his Interlake camp to sew a twelve-skin lodge, and in 1820 Peter Fidler observed that, while the Ojibwa around Lake Manitoba used the traditional bark wigwams in summer, they had begun to use hide tipis in winter and were "now becoming more generally to follow the Cree construction of their wigwams."[77] Ayagon's invitation reminds us of one of the crucial roles played by Ojibwa women in the overall process of cultural change, which is the learning and incorporation of new forms, construction techniques, and design elements from neighbouring peoples.

Meat from the bison hunt sustained hunters and their families during a spring muskrat hunt that usually took place in March. After this, the people gathered in the sugar bush, where each family had its allotted grove of trees. About the use of these groves, it was emphasized, "The Indians generally keep the same spot they have before been at and no others interfere whilst the original owner as we may say remains in the spot or assigns his right to some other."[78] There is no evidence to suggest a division of spring activities by sex (men hunting for furs while women, children, and elders made sugar), as would seem to be the case for some earlier groups, though data from outside the Interlake shows continued female control of sugaring activities.[79] Some families had extensive sugaring operations, with "upwards of 1,000 roggans" or bark containers to collect sap in. Much of the sugar was eaten, though some was "put in Cache."[80] Some sugar was also traded: in

1819, fourteen tents of Ojibwa sugared around Portage la Prairie and traded 120 pounds of sugar.[81] In an effort to bolster their fur returns and maintain their standing with their traders, some Ojibwa groups began trading more maple sugar. By 1819-20, however, the Hudson's Bay Company frequently traded only liquor for country produce and seldom traded goods such as cloth or blankets for sugar, although this was what the Ojibwa wished.[82]

At their spring gathering at the post a few chiefs continued to be clothed, and there was the by-now-traditional social gathering. Religious ceremonies were held either during or just before this gathering. The nature of these ceremonies is frustratingly vague in the fur-trade records. Donald Sutherland noted that the Indians were gathering to *"cungor* or *manitocawsui"* – which could mean any number of ceremonies, including the Shaking Tent and Midewiwin rites – at White Mud River in May 1816.[83] At Big Tent Island the ceremony was almost certainly the Midewiwin. The "Big Tent" itself was a "church" referred to in the Fort Dauphin records as being arched, "30 yards by 5," covered with bark and bulrush mats, and a brief description of the proceedings in the post's daily journal notes that "all the Indians Dancing, the House contains near 160 Persons. They kept it up till sun set, eat 3 Dogs & drank 1 1/2 keg Rum due them."[84] At Jack Head in 1819, George Nelson witnessed the initiation of two men and a woman into the "Meetaywee": certainly the Midewiwin.[85] Following this gathering, the Indians enjoyed "a holiday Time till winter commences," as trader William Brown phrased it.[86] Frequent visits were made to the post until early summer, when the traders usually left for the season. For several years the Ojibwa received *paroles,* or invitations to war, in the spring, and groups of men left the Interlake before Nelson. Families gradually left the gathering to hunt, to harvest wildfowl and their eggs in the marshes, to go to war, and to plant their gardens for the summer.[87]

Ojibwa in the Interlake apparently did not begin gardening until after the worst of the climatic disruptions, but by 1819 they had large gardens on an island at the north end of Lake Manitoba. The island may have provided a microclimate more favourable to horticulture in the previous few years of killing frosts. Given the size of the garden reported in 1819, and the degree to which horticulture seemed by that time to have been incorporated into the seasonal round in surrounding areas, it is possible that earlier, unreported efforts at growing crops had been made. Nelson had gardens at Dauphin River in 1810, and, though he claimed that they were "the first attempt towards gardening that was ever made" there, a freeman and his Native family were quick to raid the potato patch when Nelson was away for a short while, and the Ojibwa with whom Nelson traded had a word for potatoes and enjoyed eating them when given some by traders.[88] Not all of the Interlake Ojibwa gardened, though, including the Ojibwa families who traded with Nelson.

When traders returned in late summer, the Ojibwa were busily harvesting wild rice at sites located mostly on the east side of Lake Winnipeg. Those who had gardens also took up their produce and cached part of it in the ground. Large stocks of whitefish were taken during the fall run at fishing sites which, unlike hunting and sugaring sites, were apparently owned for just one season. Though not as large as sturgeon, whitefish were as numerous. Of the fishery at the Dauphin River near his post, Nelson recalled that the fish were "so numerous as to exceed all credibility."[89] After the fishery, bands generally camped around the post for several weeks while they obtained their fall outfits. Finally, small groups began leaving the main camp near the post for their winter quarters, where they first hunted for moose and deer. They hunted game and furs during the winter, and visited the post (or visited with the runners sent to collect their furs) several times during the season. As was the custom, game caught was shared throughout the camp. Such reciprocity was an effective means of "storing" food, as author Bruce White has recently observed, for the recipients were obliged to return an approximately equal share of meat or another product to the giver at a later date. The practice worked rather less to the advantage of European traders who desired to buy meat, as Nelson ruefully observed: "I am now so well acquainted with Indian oeconomy [I know] – that although Cu-leve killed two moose only these few days past that but a very short time longer would be sufficient for them to give too good an account of the remainder."[90] Finally, there was a more intensive fur hunt by small groups of related men in late winter, and then the families returned to the camp near the post.

The families who traded with Nelson communicated a clear sense of well-being and independence in their well-balanced annual round, their relationship with and expectations of Nelson, and their appearance. Ayagon gave Nelson companionship and the benefit of his influence as a patriarch, but Ayagon's expectations of Nelson are clearly expressed in Nelson's references to the older man as "My Lord." Another older hunter actually kept a tally of the amount of liquor given out by Nelson and the amount that would be left for the spring celebration, so as not to be cheated of any he felt was due him.[91] Their confidence and well-being was also expressed in material ways, as Nelson's visual memory of them indicates: "We, here found all our Indians collected and waiting our arrival. They were dressed in their best; that is, painted faces, . . . The hair carefully & neatly braided in one, two three or four plaits . . . covered with Silver brooches, as thick as they could be set . . . & the remainder also carefully gathered up into a knot of 4 or 5 in. long covered with thin hoops of Silver & filled with the handsomest feathers. Ring of one to 2 ins. broad in the ears . . . with quills or Silver hoops in their nose."[92] The similarity of this picture to Thompson's description of the Ojibwa in 1798 is unmistakable, and it is a clear statement that these Ojibwa had done well despite the difficulties of the time. And judging by the amount of time they spent together, and the difficulty with which Nelson persuaded them to leave the post and hunt furs, it is also clear that these people were hardly slaves to the fur trade. They certainly enjoyed the convenience of trade goods, and their drams and filled pipes in spring and fall, and they bemoaned their fate when the fur hunt was poor. But aside from food shortages caused by unusually harsh winters, they lived well and coped quite successfully with the challenges that faced them.

The information we have on these Interlake bands also allows us a glimpse of Ojibwa family life at that time. Fifteen named hunters and their families, totalling at least fifty persons, traded with Nelson at Dauphin River between 1807 and 1810; of these, nine hunters (and their families, about thirty persons in all) belonged to two extended families. Nelson's comments about the relationships between these individuals emphasize the adult men and show Nelson's EuroCanadian perspective. However, his many references to sons-in-law may be a clue that these households, like the ones in which John Tanner lived, were probably composed of several related older adults and one or more daughters and their spouses and children.[93] Several of the adult men trading with Nelson had more than one wife, and a few years later Peter Fidler noted that Ojibwa women usually married shortly after puberty (at about fourteen years), that polygamy was common, and that the sororate was practised.[94] Typically, the women in these families were responsible for such tasks as harvesting sugar and rice, processing and storing foods, preparing hides and furs, gathering bark and spruce roots, sewing clothing and lodges, and raising small children. They also traded when the men were away hunting, and planted and tended the gardens where these existed.

Though both Nelson and Fidler had Native wives, they viewed Ojibwa women and women's roles through European eyes. According to Fidler, the women performed "all the drudgery work such as, fetching meat, Cooking – Dressing skins – cutting the necessary fuel & then generally have the largest & most weighty sled to drag." Several comments by Nelson suggest his European views on Native women; in one incident, when he had been annoyed by the behaviour of one of his employee's wives, he called the woman "a vixen & hussy" in his journal, and stated that he "began to think that women were women not only in civilized countries but everywhere also."[95] On the other hand, the traders were evidently ready to accept many of the roles of Ojibwa women when it suited them. When Nelson's Ojibwa wife and the Indian wife of one of his men saved all of them from starvation in the winter of 1815, he expressed only pride, muted perhaps by his embarrassment at being reduced to that situation: "My woman brings home 8 hares & 14 Partridges making in all 58 hares and 34 Partridges. Good." Nelson's self-conscious term for his wife during this incident (*she-hunter*), and his consistent use of the term *woman* to refer to her, rather than *wife*, underscore the cultural gap between them – though this does not seem to have seriously limited her activities or behaviour during these years.[96]

These perspectives are obviously shaped – or misshapen – by cultural and occupational biases. We have no comparable remarks by the Ojibwa themselves to indicate how they thought of women. On the one hand, these were obviously functional families in which men and women both knew and performed their "proper" roles and in which family members showed affection and tenderness for one another. Nelson recorded a naming ceremony for an infant Ojibwa girl, who was encouraged by her father to "Be a wise & sensible woman & thou shall be loved & respected," and another incident in which an Ojibwa man led a divination ceremony "not only because he was the only one able to do it, but on account of his wives & children's sicknesses to know what was their sickness; & what medicine would be most proper for his giving them."[97] Ayagon also invited, rather than ordered, the women in his camp to sew a skin lodge for his family's use.[98] Still, there were certainly boundaries within Ojibwa culture beyond which women were forbidden to go. In May 1810, Ayagon "nearly killed one of his women on account of his war pipestem that was lost. This he tells me is occasioned by the woman's getting into his (leather) lodge contrary to their laws." In another incident, Ayagon purchased "a small keg of rum to pay Old C-fesse for medicine that he got from him to put on his sore leg, occasioned by a woman inadvertently passing over it."[99] And Ojibwa women – but not men – were punished for adultery by having their noses mutilated, even occasionally by death.[100]

These few references suggest that Ojibwa men perceived women as having potentially dangerous and polluting sexual power, and that they constructed and enforced rules to contain and control that power: from physically punishing women who had sexual intercourse with non-sanctioned partners, to ritual cures or purification of illnesses and damage caused by improper forms of contact with women. But women's "dangerous" and "polluting" powers were only so to men; whether women thought of themselves in these terms is unknown. Nor is it certain to what extent such attitudes were aboriginal or the result of post-contact absorption of European and Christian attitudes towards women, which emphasized the negative powers of women and justified their highly controlled and subordinate position in society. Women themselves may have interpreted their power simply as based on their relationship with life-giving (rather than negative or polluting) forces, and as being strong enough to overwhelm the power of men and their ritual objects (rather than being evil or polluting). Whether they did so, or whether they already identified with the negative self-image portrayed a century later in anthropologist Ruth Landes's study, *The Ojibwa Woman,* is unknown.[101]

Nor can we be certain, due to the limited nature of the data available in these fur-trade sources, how concepts of women's power affected or were affected by women's economic, social, and political roles in Ojibwa society. Given the apparent dichotomy in male attitudes towards women, though – sometimes tender and respectful, sometimes vicious and fearful – it may be useful to consider a model proposed by Jennifer S.H. Brown, who, in reflecting on data garnered by anthropologist A. Irving Hallowell in the 1930s from Ojibwa at Berens River, on the east side of Lake Winnipeg, suggests that Ojibwa men and women might well be regarded as two intersecting but distinct subcultures.[102] This model has many intriguing possibilities, not the least of which is its allowance for differing male and female perspectives on women's roles and power, and its reminder that the changes involved in the emergence and development of the Ojibwa may have been more challenging and less rewarding for Ojibwa women than for Ojibwa men.

For both men and women, some of these changes were easier to cope with than others. While the Ojibwa adapted their harvesting and trading strategies readily to environmental and economic pressures, their social lives exhibited the effects of continually mounting tensions in the fur trade. Like Henry's journals, Nelson's reminiscences include mentions of injuries and deaths caused by alcohol, including a pattern of spousal abuse during drinking bouts. Both of the incidents involving Ayagon and women cited above involved alcohol: in the first, Ayagon was drunk when he "nearly killed his woman," and in the second he paid for medicine with rum. While there are instances in the documents of both men and women becoming aggressive and injuring their spouses and others, women were more frequently the victims of alcohol-related violence.[103] The Ojibwa were also jealous of the "Mashkiegons," Northern Cree who entered the region during Nelson's tenure and who were favoured by Nelson because of their greater "industry" in hunting for furs. Though no actual violence is recorded between them, threats of violence and magical feuds between them were frequent and ongoing.[104] Other strains were evident in the Ojibwas' adoption of the teachings of The Shawnee Prophet after 1807, the nativistic tenets of which caused alarm among traders and appealed widely to Ojibwa and Ottawa across the Northwest.

The commandments of The Shawnee Prophet, Tenskwatawa, were the result of long years of instability for Native people in the Great Lakes region. For decades before 1800, the Shawnee and many neighbouring tribes in the lower Great Lakes had been harassed and murdered by American settlers, had been driven from their homelands, had suffered great hunger and poverty because of the effect of settlement on game supplies, and had vainly struggled to turn back the tide of invading "Long Knives." With no justice or coherent aid forthcoming from the Whites, the Shawnee succumbed to social chaos, alcoholism, and despair. It was in this context that in early 1805 The Prophet received a series of visions in which he saw Heaven and conversed with the Master of Life.[105] His subsequent teachings were sparks cast on dry tinder: the prophecies "spread like wild-fire" throughout the Great Lakes region and were "felt by the remotest Ojibbeways," including John Tanner's family and the Ojibwa who traded with Nelson. The movement is not mentioned in post journals farther west than the Interlake, however.[106] The Prophet advocated a return to traditional values, roles, lifeways, and material culture and urged his followers to treat each other with respect and kindness and to relinquish European technology and material culture. The Prophet ordered his followers to destroy their medicine bundles and amulets, saying that the power these things contained had "lost its efficacy" and that those who obeyed him on this matter would see their dead relatives and friends restored to life someday. Furthermore, by praying earnestly to the Master of Life, as The Prophet showed them, followers could restore game animals to their former plentiful numbers.

Tenskwatawa created prayer boards incised with power figures to remind his followers to pray, and inducted "disciples" to spread his teachings.[107] Tenskwatawa's teachings were brought to the West by both Ottawa and Ojibwa who remained in contact with relatives and trading centres in the western Great Lakes, where many villages had been proseletyzed in 1807-08 by the disciples of The Prophet. Tanner's account of the spread of the prophecies into the West mentions a special ceremony conducted to give the teachings to his family. He also notes The Prophet's injunctions against letting the fire in the lodge go out, against drinking, lying, and hitting, and against some European goods, including dogs, which Tenskwatawa and later prophets assumed to be European introductions. As well, according to what Nelson heard of the movement, the men were "not [to] go about at nights after [the young] women as they are accustomed to do." The teachings were adopted with all seriousness by many Ojibwa in the Interlake and Red River valley.[108] It took close questioning, even harassment, for Nelson and his colleagues to coax information on the developments from the Ojibwa they knew, for followers had been forbidden to speak of the new ways to Whites. When one man finally did explain, he also confessed a plot to pillage the traders' canoe brigades and outposts.[109] Nelson suspected the Indians were in league with Whites or Métis regarding this plot, which amounted to nothing but a few days of alarm on the part of the traders, though it was a logical extension of The Prophet's nativistic doctrine. The effects of The Prophet's teachings were "very sensibly and painfully felt," according to Tanner. "For two or three years drunkenness was much less frequent than formerly, war was less thought of, and the entire aspect of affairs among them was somewhat changed by the influence of one man."[110]

Why should such beliefs, which arose hundreds of miles away in response to pressures that were not directly felt in the northern interior, be so compelling to the western Ojibwa? Like the circumstances behind Tabashaw's dream in 1801, the Ojibwa were feeling pressures stemming from unrelenting fur-trade competition, the decline of beaver, and the effects of alcohol. Thus, John Tanner's family felt emboldened to venture farther south along the Red River in search of beaver because of "the promise of the prophet that we should be invisible to the Sioux."[111]

Similarly, the ready acceptance of the injunction not to use items believed to be of European manufacture or import was a means of asserting some feeling of control over an increasingly chaotic fur trade in which they had less power (due to the lack of beaver, and perhaps to the aggressive and often hostile tactics of competing traders) and in which "their pleasure [was] not much consulted nowadays."[112] Others were surely attracted by the promise of success and happiness that was supposed to be the lot of believers. According to the information given Nelson, The Prophet's disciples advocated that "any person who conforms himself to these [teachings] is sure to be for ever happy both in this world & in the next."[113] The nativistic elements of The Prophet's teachings, and the hints of danger to the traders that so alarmed Nelson's colleagues, echoed conversations that Nelson later recalled as having with the Ojibwa he dealt with, in which the Indians expressed great dissatisfaction with their lives and the state of the fur trade. The "General tenour of the Speeches of the indians on our advent among them," he said, was that before traders arrived in the Northwest,

we always had plenty to eat & be warm; but you have taken these things from us, & given us your flimsy cloth. Your looking glasses, beads &c. &c. dazzled our young people your knives, axes &c. &c. deceived us. And when you found that we began to see through these things, you distributed your fire liquor (rum) which, indeed, when we first tast of it exhilarates, makes us loose site of our misfortunes; but then this joy gradually gives way to madness, & how many, both of yourselves & us, have to lament & mourn over the calamities bro't on us all by that bad water – that poison. – You know our foible & you avail yourselves of it to destroy us: – Begone! go away in peace.[114]

Such comments, combined with the fervour with which the Ojibwa adopted (if only temporarily) The Shawnee Prophet's teachings, indicate that the Ojibwa were feeling pressures related to the fur trade and wished either to disentangle themselves from the trade or at least to gain a greater measure of control and power over their lives within the trade. In that sense, the nativistic elements of The Shawnee Prophet's teachings that appealed to the Ojibwa were adaptive responses to fur-trade pressures, for they promoted a renewed commitment to Native values and lifeways. Their fervour stemmed from their hope that, by following the teachings, "their golden age was at the moment of returning, when their lands would once more enjoy all the happiness & comforts they did before the advent of the white."[115]

When adherence to The Prophet's strict rules failed to produce any change in their lives, their appeal faded, and within a few years they were abandoned. As Tanner noted, "gradually the impression [made by the Prophet's teachings] was obliterated, medicine bags, flints, and steels were resumed, dogs were raised, women and children were beaten as before, and the Shawnee prophet was despised."[116] The pressures that had made them appealing were still present, however, and in this context the establishment of the Red River settlement in 1812 created a new set of conditions for Native people to adapt to and take advantage of.

The settlement was a hopeful sign to Ojibwa in the Red River and Interlake areas, who were aware of the decline of the fur trade in the Red River valley and welcomed what they saw as a permanent, year-round market in the colony. As one trader expressed it, "They imagine that for the future they will want nothing." Their motives may have been more complex in this regard, with overtones of The Shawnee Prophet's teachings, for The Black Man, an Ojibwa leader, was recorded as saying that "all the Indians are much pleased with the People coming to settle upon their lands, to teach them how to manufacture European articles."[117] Whether this was a widespread sentiment, or whether The Black Man, like Tabashaw before him, believed there was a "secret" to producing trade goods, is uncertain. It is known that the Ojibwa also looked to the colonists in hope that these new arrivals would become "a powerful support to them against their enemies the Sieux." They were, unfortunately, to be sadly disappointed in this in the coming years.[118]

The colonists' need for hides, furs, and all manner of provisions provided an important new economic opportunity for local Native bands. Indeed, the Red River Ojibwa and their Cree, freeman, and Métis relatives are generally credited with keeping the settlers alive through the first desperate years of the settlement's existence. Even after the settlers began to establish themselves, meat, leather, maple sugar, and other types of country produce commanded high prices in the colony. Maple sugar, for example, brought prices as high as four shillings (forty-eight pence) per pound, considerably higher than the price of nine pence per pound (less than the value of a single muskrat) listed in the Hudson's Bay Company's "Standard Price of Country Produce, 1820." Better still, sugar, wild rice, and other country produce sold to colonists was paid for in cloth, blankets, and other goods, while only liquor was given for sugar traded at Hudson's Bay Company posts in the Manitoba district.[119] Almost immediately upon the arrival of the settlers, some Ojibwa drastically reduced the amount of time they spent trapping to take advantage of this new market. Some Natives and Métis were hired specifically to hunt for the Hudson's Bay Company and colony. Others simply made the settlement another stop on their annual round, and counted on trading country produce there. Hudson's Bay Company trader George Sutherland met a group of Ojibwa near White Mud River in 1815 who "seemed to be very sausey, and told me that they wear to be as well paid for provisions by the Coloney as they would be for their skins from us."[120]

Traders were predictably critical of the effects of the colony market on the Ojibwa: it made them "avaricious with anything they have to trade," complained one, while another noted that, because of the high prices given in the colony "for sugar & Drest Moose skins, they have not now that spur to exert themselves in the fur hunt as before." In a similar vein, Peter Fidler noted in 1819 that "since the colonists arrived . . . [the Bungees] receive many presents which enables them to live without that exertion they had become accustomed to."[121] Again, such comments must be inverted to be properly interpreted. If the Ojibwa were "avaricious," they were also sharp traders who were doing quite well from the Colony trade, and if they had no "spur to exert themselves in the fur hunt as before," then neither were they dependent on the fur trade.

The colony also provided opportunities for prestige and preferential treatment from Europeans, which the Ojibwa still very much desired but which they now seldom received because of the decline of furs. Providing aid to the inexperienced and ill-equipped colonists helped to compensate for this, especially for the band of Ojibwa led by Peguis. Peguis and his family had arrived at the established Ojibwa-Ottawa settlement at Netley Creek, near the mouth of the Red River, some time between 1800 and 1810. Netley Creek was an especially resource-rich area that had the advantage of being near a marsh plentiful in muskrats and wildfowl, a fishery in the Red River, and elk and bison on the plains to the south.[122] By 1812 Peguis led "the best hunters of furs in this part of the country." Peguis began trading with the Hudson's Bay Company around 1810 after a dispute with the Northwest Company, and he was thus poised to take on a very special role with the establishment of the Selkirk Settlement within his territory.[123]

Because of their location, Peguis and his band had frequent contact with the colonists. In the autumn of 1812 they helped one of the first parties of travel-weary Selkirk settlers to finish their journey from the mouth of the Red River to a temporary camp at Pembina for the winter, and provided them with some food. In return for his band's assistance to the traders, Peguis came to occupy, as "Colony Chief," a favoured position, which the Ojibwa regarded quite seriously. As well as being treated with respect by colony officials and settlers, Peguis was taken by Hudson's Bay Company officials in 1814 to see the ships and forts at Hudson Bay. Macdonell reported that Peguis was "highly pleased with the attention he has met with – he slept two nights on board H.M.S. Rosamond."[124] While this was meant to impress Peguis with the strength and importance of the Hudson's Bay Company, the special treatment he was given actually reinforced the chief's sense of his own status. It is not surprising that at least one Ojibwa leader in the Interlake district had "the ambition of being a Colony chief" like Peguis.[125]

Peguis's behaviour did not spring entirely from charity. Just as Macdonell had orders from Lord Selkirk to establish friendly relations with the Ojibwa to accomplish certain ends (peaceable coexistence and aid for the settlers), so did the Ojibwa have certain expectations of the Europeans at Red River.[126] They did not accept the presence of the settlers merely because they hoped the colony would be a source of goods and of military aid; they expected these things. Peguis was conforming to traditional Native ideas about alliances, which were based on the metaphor of kinship and involved reciprocal aid, including military aid. Thus, the Ojibwa readily offered assistance to the settlers in the full expectation that they would themselves receive aid from the Europeans some day. On the other hand, the settlers appeared sufficiently like traders (in fact, Macdonell was instructed to attempt to disguise them as traders for the first few months) that the Ojibwa felt entitled to ask for payment for some of their services. Alexander Ross later recalled that the Natives (both Indians and Métis) "generously brought in large quantities of buffalo meat, wild berries, and 'prairie turnips'" for the settlers, but that the settlers had to barter for much of this, sometimes dearly.[127] Despite the settlers' affront at such demands, something like an alliance was indeed created between Ojibwa and settler. Ross recalled, quite romantically, that the settlers' experience of passing the winter "according to Indian fashion," and receiving aid from the Indians "tended to foster kind and generous feelings between the two races, who parted with regret" in the spring of 1813. It was perhaps not unexpected, then, that, in keeping with the Native concept of how allies should behave, the Ojibwa expected that the settlers would provide military aid in their struggles against the Sioux; and, for their part, colony officials speculated that, should the Americans attack the colony during the war of 1812, the Ojibwa would aid them in "bid[ding] defiance to the Yankies."[128] The apparent good will between settler and Ojibwa for the first few years of the colony's existence seemed to confirm the validity of these mutual expectations.

This new relationship was tested repeatedly during the colony's troubled early years. The location of Selkirk's Hudson's Bay Company–affiliated colony at the junction of the Red and Assiniboine rivers, a crucial node in fur-trade shipping routes, threatened the North West Company and its largely Métis staff, who feared that the partisan community could blockade the transportation of their furs and goods. Matters were inflamed still further in the winter of 1814 when Macdonell further threatened the North West Company supply system by issuing a proclamation (intended merely to keep colonists supplied with food) which forbade the export of pemmican from the area around the settlement, and shortly thereafter forbade the hunting of the bison by mounted chase: the favoured technique of the Métis. Furious, the Canadians vowed to destroy the tiny settlement. Many of the Ojibwa around Red River were confused by "these quarrels between relatives," as John Tanner expressed the situation, but most refused the bribes offered by the North West Company to attack the colony. These bribes were offered to Cree and Assiniboine people from the Assiniboine River area and to Ojibwa from Kaministiquia to Fort Alexander. One group of Indians whom the North West Company were attempting to persuade to travel to Red River to destroy the colony took the liquor offered them as bribes, and then drank to the health of the colony and refused to go.[129]

Métis and North West Company harassment of the settlers and Hudson's Bay Company personnel at the Forks began in earnest in the spring of 1815, and, in June, Hudson's Bay Company and colony officials appealed to Peguis and his young men "to see what they can do for us in making Peace & remaining here."[130] When they arrived at the Forks, the Ojibwa were bribed by the North West Company with liquor, but after they had drunk the bribes they crossed to the Hudson's Bay Company's Fort Douglas and conferred with trader Peter Fidler and colony officials.[131] There, Peguis was reminded that his pipe stems had been sent "to our Great Father, that he may be charitable to you and your friends" – a reminder of the reciprocal relationship between them – and was told that the Ojibwa would be "prized for having been the Friend" to the Great Father's British children.[132] Fidler and the colony officials pleaded, "We know these Lands are yours, if you tell us to leave them we [will], . . . but if you tell us to remain here we will not leave these lands, but you must make peace for us with these people." Peguis's reply indicates firm commitment: "We will offer these people the pipe of peace," he said, "and if they will not smoak with you, we will not restrain our young men more, but shall join them in the cry of war."[133] He then crossed the river and attempted to negotiate with the North West Company, without success. Returning to Fort Douglas, he told the officials, "My Children my heart is grieved – I return with shame. Those people have no ears to listen to the words of peace; . . . go you to Jack River and collect a force & we will send word to the Chief of the Red Lake and elsewhere. . . . When you embark myself and my young Men will sit down in your Boats, for I fear these peoples hearts are bad & perhaps they would pillage you."[134] They did accompany the settlers to Netley Creek, where they were given a generous present to reward their loyalty.

From the Ojibwa perspective, their relationship with these Europeans was perfectly functional; they were allies. The Black Man's reaction to the subsequent burning of the colony by the Canadians is thus readily understandable: "The day after the last buildings were burnt The Black man an Indian chief from Turtle River arrived with a few others, he went to the foundation of the Captains room now in ashes and wept bitterly over it, vowing vengeance against the Canadians."[135] The settlers were persuaded to return but faced more harassment in the following years. The Ojibwa offered their assistance again in 1816, both before and after the incident at Seven Oaks in which twenty-one settlers and the colony Governor were killed by Métis forces. Two Ojibwa men attempted to warn Governor Semple of the impending attack several weeks before the incident, and they offered their support, but Semple dismissed both. One account of the incident states that Peguis restrained his men from joining the Métis in the battle, but this is not substantiated. According to some sources, Peguis and his men gathered up and buried some of the bodies after the battle, and then once again assisted in the peaceful removal of the settlers.[136] Again, the behaviour of the Ojibwa conformed to their expectations of inter-group relations. Even the colony officials praised the Ojibwa, calling them "Our true friends and late protectors."[137]

Once the furor in the colony died down in 1817, though, the relationship between colonists and the Hudson's Bay Company on the one side and the Ojibwa on the other began to sour. After 1817, the Ojibwa were consistently disappointed that, although they behaved as they felt they should towards an ally, their "allies" failed to do so, and, indeed, intentionally scorned them. Despite the crucial support that they had consistently offered the colony, no reciprocity was forthcoming. Instead, the Europeans did everything they could to deny the existence of anything but a token relationship.

Since the years 1816 through 1818 were poor for crops, the Ojibwa could at least take advantage of the colony's continuing economic opportunities. While their goods were wanted in the settlement, though, they themselves were not. As hostilities between the two trading companies waned and the colony began to stabilize, the Ojibwa were not needed for the defense of the colony, and they did not have to be wooed on that account. As early as March 1817, Hudson's Bay Company and colony officials were voicing a very different opinion of the Ojibwa and their relationship with them from what they had just a few years earlier. "Many of the Indians offer us their assistance," wrote Bird to Macdonell, "but I hesitate to employ as allies savages whom it would be impossible to restrain within the bounds prescribed by humanity."[138]

The chasm that was opening between the two groups was widened by the signing of the Selkirk Treaty in July 1817. By this treaty, the Ojibwa, Cree, and Assiniboine in the region "sold the land to Lord Selkirk extending two miles on each side the two rivers from Lake Winnipeg to Muskrat River above Portage des Prairies and up the Red River to the mouth of the river going to Red Lake."[139] In return for the land, the Native people received an annuity of 100 pounds of tobacco per tribe, which was calculated by Lord Selkirk to be preferable to outright sale for the purpose of forming "a permanent hold over [the Indians'] behaviour, as they must be made to understand that if any individual of the tribe violate the treaty, the payment will be withheld."[140] It is doubtful whether any of the Native signators understood Selkirk's motive. Rather, the similarity of the annuity to their annual presents from the traders would have implied, from their perspective, a similar ceremonial honouring of a valued business associate or relative rather than the imposition of a hierarchical relationship such as Selkirk had in mind.

To Lord Selkirk, the 1817 treaty was necessary to refute the North West Company's claim that the violence in the settlement was the result of Native dissatisfaction with colonists for not properly compensating them for their land. For the Ojibwa, and particularly for Peguis, the treaty was a formal acknowledgement of the relationship between themselves and colony officials and offered some protection for their remaining lands and the resources they relied upon. The Selkirk Treaty worked two ways, though. While it acknowledged Ojibwa rights to unceded lands, it also meant that after the signing of the treaty the Ojibwa literally had no place in the settlement. This reinforced the process of alienation from the colony that the Ojibwa experienced after 1816, a process hastened by the fact that freemen and Métis were becoming an ever more important part of the Red River community.

The Selkirk Treaty also proved to be a divisive force between the Red River Ojibwa and local Cree bands. Until this time the Cree had made no protest against Ojibwa occupation of what had once been Cree territory. On the contrary, one account has it that they invited the Ojibwa to live in the Red River area after the smallpox epidemic of the 1780s. During and after the treaty negotiations, however, the Cree disputed the right of the Ojibwa to sign the treaty. The Cree threatened "to expel their rivals from RR altogether, and the Whites along with them, unless the names of the Ojibwa chiefs are expunged from the compact, and the annual payment be made to the Crees only."[141] It is uncertain whether the Cree objected to the Ojibwa signing the treaty because they wished to maintain formal rights to the land even though they seldom used it, or whether they found the terms of the treaty – which included annual gifts of tobacco and an official relationship with the Colony – appealing. The situation was finally resolved after some negotiation amongst themselves and some persuasion by Peguis. The Cree gave the Ojibwa "Liberty . . . to grant the lands" to a certain point, which has been given variously as Muskrat Creek and the Riviere aux Champignon.[142] The leaders of bands that frequented particular areas were responsible for signing for the transfer of their own lands. Thus Peguis transferred the land from Lake Winnipeg to the Forks; the Premier signed for the area between the Forks and Pembina; Black Coat (also called Blue Robe) sold from the Forks to Musk Rat Root River, beyond Portage la Prairie.[143]

The narrow width of the land included in the treaty reflected the settlement's layout, with its farms on river lots strung for miles along the Red River and for a short distance up the Assiniboine. It was also an attempt by some Ojibwa to ensure continued access to the bison, for some of the signers feared that if they "granted more, the white people would come and frighten away the buffalo."[144] With the shortage of large game in the Red River valley growing ever more acute, maintaining access to the bison herds had become a real concern for Ojibwa. Soon after the signing of the treaty, The Premier's son expressed this concern, stating that "tho' they had sold the lands in the neighborhood of Red River they did not the lands more out on the plains, and that they would not allow people to be rearing the cattle." Not only did they continue to claim the lands outside the treaty limits, but The Premier's son also complained that the freemen and Métis were "chasing the cattle [bison] with Horses."[145] This focus on bison is heightened by the fact that only after the treaty was signed did the Ojibwa realize they had not left themselves a legal access to the Red River, an error that may well have been the result of their unfamiliarity with the purpose of land treaties; certainly, the river and its resources remained central to their lives. The problem was solved when the Native signators negotiated the right of occupancy along the river at certain crucial points. Peguis claimed the shoreline "from Sugar Point to Lake Winnipeg; Les Grands Oreilles wished to have the point below Upper Fort Garry, where many of his relatives were buried; and Blue Robe selected Portage la Prairie."[146]

More serious complications in the relationship between the Ojibwa and both Hudson's Bay Company and Red River colony developed just after 1817 over the issue of the Company's trade with the Sioux. Agents for the Hudson's Bay Company and the settlement justified the trade by arguing that as both warring tribes "border[ed]" on Selkirk's grant of land, it was "absolutely necessary for the safety of the Colony to endeavor to make peace, between these ferocious people."[147] Whether the Company actually believed that the centuries-old feud could be ended by trade or whether they simply wanted to gain another market in a period of economic decline, Hudson's Bay Company agent Robert Dickson persuaded some Sioux to attempt it. In 1817, 1819, 1820, and 1821, groups of Yanktonai and Sisseton Dakota visited Fort Douglas to trade and to attempt to negotiate agreements with the Ojibwa so that they could continue to come and trade unmolested.[148] Predictably, they were harassed by the Ojibwa, who even went so far as to steal the horses of the 1819 delegation. The Ojibwa protested bitterly at what they perceived as the Company's disloyal treatment of them. One said "that it was very hard, we [the Hudson's Bay Company] were giving goods and ammunition to the other nation to the South of them to kill [the Ojibwa]," and after an 1817 clash in which three Ojibwa were killed by Sioux the Ojibwa were said to be "enraged," claiming it was the traders' fault for "sending goods up the Red River to their old and inveterate Enemies."[149] The Company's attempts to initiate trade with the Sioux disillusioned many Ojibwa who had previously thought of the Company as their ally.

The Red River colony had one additional surprise for the Ojibwa to deal with before 1821, one that would profoundly affect Native-White relations in decades to come. In 1818, the first Christian missionaries arrived in the Northwest in response to the needs of the large, nominally Catholic mixed-blood population. The Fathers had instructions "to reclaim from barbarism and the disorders that result from it the Indian nations" of the region.[150] The missions they established at Pembina and the Forks had relatively little to do with the Ojibwa, being largely concerned with the Métis. Still, Catholic teachings, prayers, concepts of saints and the Holy Family, and sacred objects such as rosaries, would have entered Ojibwa consciousness through discussions with their Métis kin. The influence of the priests was not always so benign, however. During their first years in the West, the very presence of the priests gave impetus to rising racist and assimilationist sentiments in the region. The wording and intent of their instructions, along with Bird's 1817 remark that the Ojibwa were "savages whom it would be impossible to restrain within the bounds prescribed by humanity," and similar attitudes held by other colony officials about the need to demonstrate "the collateral advantages which they will obtain from a progress in the arts of civilized life," all composed the first glimpse of a tide that would work sea changes in Rupert's Land within a few generations.[151]

The Ojibwa were able to ignore these omens for a few years more. They could not ignore the epidemic of whooping cough and measles, which spread through the Red River colony and the western tribes between the summer of 1819 and the spring of 1820. The Ojibwa were not as badly affected by the epidemic as the Cree and Assiniboine, among whom twenty-five to forty percent of the adult men died, but they did not completely escape the disease. Tanner recalled that "Seven died out of the circle of my near relatives with whom I then lived, and an alarming mortality prevailed throughout that part of the state." George Nelson's journal at Tête-au-Brochet for the 1818-19 season does not mention any deaths from illness in that area, but he was aware of deaths at the Forks. Mortality was high for Ojibwa in the area just east of Lake Winnipeg, and on the west side of the Interlake the Indians (who were mostly Ojibwa) were noted to be doing little because of illness in the early months of 1819. Fur returns dropped in the Cumberland House and Swan Lake regions as a result of the epidemic.[152] Combined with the other problems they faced, the epidemic reinforced the trend among the Ojibwa of limiting their participation in the fur trade and spending more time pursuing a diverse pattern of subsistence activities. Thus, in the spring of 1820 at the Dauphin River House, the trader reported that Ojibwa were keeping their dry provisions for sugar making, rather than for hunting furs.[153]

The epidemic was the last of many extraordinary challenges that Native people experienced in the Northwest between 1811 and 1820. It was also an event that joined the cycles of Aboriginal and non-Aboriginal history, for it corresponded with the end of an era in fur-trade history as well. After the merger of the Hudson's Bay Company and the North West Company in 1821, much would be different for all peoples involved in the western fur trade.

* * *

The challenges faced by the western Ojibwa between 1805 and 1821 resulted in continuing cultural adaptations. The Ojibwa used a number of different strategies to cope with declining fur and game populations and with environmental fluctuations, and to maintain their economic autonomy. For a minority of the western

Ojibwa, life was marked by greater change in these years. Declining game populations and disenchantment with the state of the fur trade led to the beginning of their adoption of an alternate system of values and new symbols of status and prestige. These were Ojibwa men, characterized by Fidler as "becoming more lazy . . . troublesome and daring" who, after close contacts with plains Cree and Métis people, signalled the beginning of their adoption of the horse wealth and raiding complex by stealing horses in the Red and Assiniboine river region.[154] The genesis of multi-ethnic bands containing Ojibwa, Cree, and Métis, and an increase in the use of bison, are other developments during these years that indirectly support the idea that the Ojibwa were adopting ideas from the peoples around them. So does their adoption of the skin tipi, which women in some otherwise traditional bands in the Lake Manitoba area began making between 1810 and 1820.[155] The adoption of hide tipis underscores the fact that life in the West opened up opportunities among women for learning new skills and designs, and that, quite logically, material culture changed along with other aspects of Ojibwa culture.

These were as yet tentative steps, taken by only a few bands, and even among these people many basic elements of everyday life remained unaltered. Despite their plains leanings, there is no evidence that the spirituality of these bands began to change at this time. The Sun Dance would not be adopted by any Ojibwa bands for several more decades, and there is far more evidence for cultural continuity among the western Ojibwa at this time than there is for cultural change.

Rather than looking to the plains, many western Ojibwa bands simply made adjustments to their seasonal round to compensate for declining fur and game populations, diversifying their subsistence activities and altering the nature of their participation in the trade. When they began limiting the length and intensity of their trapping periods, traders labelled them "lazy," although they generally continued to satisfy their material wants during this period. William Brown's 1819 description of the Big Tent Island people, cited earlier, is certainly not one of poverty or dependence. Nor is Peter Fidler's 1820 description of "the young Bungee men," which demonstrates that the Ojibwa he encountered were still able to satisfy their desire for material affluence. They were, he said, "very flashy & decorated with a variety of silver ornaments. . . . Such as necklaces made of whampum about 2 inches broad – Arm & wrist bands with gorgets Broaches &c – Scarlet Leggins garnished with Ribbands and Beads and a number of small Brooches which is very tastefully arranged."[156] The similarity of this description to those by David Thompson and George Nelson is remarkable, and illustrates the continuity of values that remained at the core of western Ojibwa culture even during the process of cultural adaptation.

Even the other peoples with whom the Ojibwa began to reside in these years recognized that the bases and boundaries of Ojibwa culture and identity remained unchanged. "The Mashquegons," noted Henry in 1808, "are afraid of the Saulteurs." Traders noted these boundaries as well. The continuing preoccupation of the Ojibwa with the supernatural, with medicines, and with "magic," which reinforced their identity in the eyes of others, is also seen in an 1818 incident in the Interlake. When Nelson moved to the Jack Head / Tête-au-Brochet post in 1818, most of the Ojibwa from Dauphin River followed him, not only because of their established relationship with him, but also because Nelson had a supply of medicines at his post that the Ojibwa perceived as having both curative and spiritual powers. In accordance with Ojibwa concern with "medicines," both herbal and spiritual, Nelson also noted, "It is surprising to see what a stress these people lay upon their medecines – they sell nothing to each other whatever, but their medecine they sell amasingly dear."[157]

Trader Peter Fidler's 1815 census of Red River Indians also demonstrates that the Ojibwa remained closely tied to their cultural heritage. The census shows that Ojibwa still had more guns and fewer horses than their plains neighbours, a pattern that reveals the continuing economic and social differences between the groups. An analysis of Fidler's census shows approximately the same numbers of people in each lodge among the Assiniboine, Cree, and Ojibwa (11, 10.9, and 11.4, respectively); 1.7 horses per tent among the Assiniboine, 2.9 among the Cree, and only .9 among the Ojibwa; and .33 guns per tent among the Assiniboine, 1.71 among the Cree, and 2.72 among the Ojibwa. Nor, despite their horse raiding and the changing values this implied, did the Red River Ojibwa "pound" bison or hunt them with horses.[158] If anything, Fidler's survey suggests that the Red River Ojibwa were still strongly attached to the fur trade, and that their adoption of horse stealing after 1815 was an addition to, rather than simply a replacement of, the value they placed on success in the trade.

Despite cultural adaptations made during these decades, then, the western Ojibwa maintained an identity and a way of life that was based on their eastern heritage. In the decades after 1821, this trend would continue. Regional conditions would foster the development of distinct adaptations of Ojibwa in different parts of the West, forcing the western Ojibwa to build on their heritage and to exhibit the flexibility and tenacity that has marked their history.

"To take advantage of the times," 1821 to 1837

4

After years of increasingly fierce competition, the Hudson's Bay Company and the North West Company merged in 1821. The transition to a monopolistic trading system has been interpreted by historians as having had profound effects on western Native peoples. A.J. Ray, for example, has referred to the post-1821 period as one of "declining opportunities," and H.A. Innis wrote that, after the merger, "The Indians were assured of the supremacy of the Hudson's Bay Company and brought under the control of monopoly."[1] While Ray's statement is true in the sense that game and fur-bearing species continued to wane after 1821, the Ojibwa took advantage of and created new economic opportunities for themselves in these decades just as they had in years past. The significant business activity carried on by private traders, American traders, and the colony market challenged the Company's monopoly control throughout much of the West, and, for western Ojibwa who chose to participate less in the fur trade, an increasing plains orientation can be seen after 1821: it is during these years that the term *plains Saulteaux* was first used by traders. Thus, while the union of the two companies did have drastic effects on Native people in the Northwest, they were not necessarily the exact effects that were intended by Hudson's Bay Company officials. As one Hudson's Bay Company trader noted in chagrin, "These people know well how to take advantage of the times."[2]

Historians trying to gauge the effect of the merger on Native peoples have been greatly influenced by the attitudes and policies of George Simpson, who was appointed Governor of the Company's Northern Department (which included the lands west and north of Red River) in 1821. Preoccupied with the problems of creating an economical, efficient department, Simpson had clear ideas about the place of Indians in the reorganized fur trade: "but of course the scenes of extravagance are at an end. . . . I am convinced they must be ruled with a rod of Iron to bring and keep them in a proper state of sub-ordination, and the most certain way to effect this is by letting them feel their dependence upon us."[3] Among the reforms that Simpson hoped to make to the trade were the closing of certain posts, the elimination of presents and the reduction of credit to Indians, the reduction of the trade in liquor, and the introduction of conservation practices to maintain fur yields in over-hunted areas.[4] Like Henry's earlier, equally over-confident statement about the effects of the merger of the XY Company with the North West Company, though, Simpson's plans never came to pass on the plains or in the parkland. He was able to introduce all of his intended reforms in varying degrees in different areas, but their effectiveness was seriously hampered by a number of factors that gave the Ojibwa some freedom to make decisions and adapt within the confines of Simpson's rigid policies.

For instance, the Company did reduce the amount of credit given to individual Indians, limiting each hunter to an amount that might reasonably be expected to be repaid, given local conditions and seasonal fluctuations. However, most examples of credits as noted in the post journals do not show a great deal of difference from the pre-1821 era, except that the largest excesses were trimmed. Credit of between twenty and forty MB for most known hunters, with larger sums for trading captains, seems to have been the norm for western Ojibwa bands even after 1821. This was largely because Simpson was hesitant to introduce radical changes in the trade in the plains and parkland, for he recognized that most of the Native population in that region was "independent of" the Company, and he feared that they would simply stop trading altogether if they were angered.[5]

Aboriginal people did react angrily to the changes that accompanied the merger. One group marched in a body on the Red River post with their faces painted black in mourning to protest the withdrawal of their posts, while others chose to leave the trade altogether or to a large extent following the merger, and either traded provisions or adopted a bison-hunting lifestyle.[6] While there are no accounts of Ojibwa protests specifically against the limitations on credit, John Tanner's response to an earlier implementation of a monopoly system at Pembina, when the remaining trader announced he would no longer trade on credit, is illuminating. On hearing from other members of his band of the new terms of trade, Tanner

reproached the Indians for their pusillanimity in submitting to such terms. They had been accustomed for many years to receive credits in the fall. They were not entirely destitute not of clothing merely, but of ammunition, and many of them of guns and traps. How were they, without the accustomed aid from the traders, to subsist themselves and their families during the ensuing winter? . . . I went immediately to my hunting ground, killed a number of moose, and set my wife to make the skins into such garments as were best adapted to the winter season, and which I now saw we should be compelled to substitute for the blankets and woolen clothes we had been accustomed to receive from the traders.[7]

Even though Tanner's statement does not apply specifically to the post-1821 situation, it is important, for it shows the capacity of the Ojibwa and their neighbours to cope with the loss of credit. His lament that he and his fellow Indians were rendered "destitute" and in danger of death without trade goods was echoed by bands across Rupert's Land in 1821 and 1822. While undoubtedly true for some families, this claim seems related to the use of the term *starving* by Indians to traders: not necessarily literal, but connoting a less-than-ideal state of being (poor in goods, and poor, deserving of pity). Since credit was only reduced after 1821, rather than ended, few Ojibwa would have found themselves as "entirely destitute" as Tanner's family.

As well as limiting credit, Simpson reduced the amounts and values of presents given to Indians, particularly to trading captains of whom far fewer were clothed after 1821. This was a trend that had begun some time earlier in an attempt to reduce the costs of fur-trade competition, but, again, Simpson was unable to discontinue the practice entirely. Trading ceremonies continued at posts that faced competition from Americans and free traders, although the remaining captains received less ammunition than they would have a decade earlier, and gifts of status such as flags, knives, and clothing were often replaced by alcohol and tobacco.[8] Combined with the loss of their ability to play off opposing traders to increase the amount of their credit, the reduction in presents resulted in a further limitation of the goods readily available to the Ojibwa. This may have been eased by the lowering of the price of goods (a change that was also implemented by Simpson), but subsequent drops in the value and availability of furs largely cancelled out the beneficial effects of the lower prices.[9]

Both as part of his scheme to bring new order to the fur trade and to adhere to new British Parliamentary regulations on the trade, Simpson was also determined to reduce the amount of alcohol traded and given to Indians. After 1822, alcohol was no longer traded for furs, and the amount given as gifts was reduced by half. Simpson admitted the former importance of liquor to the trade, noting that it was "the grand Stimulus to call forth the exertions of the Indians," and warned the London Committee that if it were immediately and completely withheld it would "discourage" the Indians to such an extent that they would not trade.[10] A transitional period was followed by an almost complete ban in the northern part of the Northern Department. Simpson's concern about the effects of this change was confirmed by James Leith, Chief Factor at Cumberland House, who complained that there was a noticeable reduction in the number of furs taken there in 1824-25, and ascribed this to the new policy of not fetching furs from Indians' tents and of trading less liquor.[11]

Of all Simpson's proposed policies, this one might have been truly beneficial for the western tribes. Unfortunately, like the rest of his reforms, Simpson was unable to fully implement it in the parkland and plains, where, as he noted, liquor was the only trade good with which sufficient provisions could be purchased from the Natives to meet the Company's needs. As he stated, the plains tribes were "so independent of European commodities that they would not take the trouble of hunting in order to provide themselves with any other articles." To minimize the effects of competition with Americans, liquor continued to be given to trading chiefs in the parkland and plains.[12] Since they traded at posts that also served the plains Cree and Assiniboine, the Ojibwa continued to receive liquor.

One change Simpson did make that directly affected the Ojibwa was the temporary closure of certain posts for reasons of economy and, in some areas, to allow the fur-bearing populations around them to recover. Within a few years after the merger, the Brandon House, Fort Hibernia, Fort Dauphin, Swan River, and Red Deer River posts, as well as Big Point House and others in the Interlake, were closed. In addition to these, all of the former North West Company posts opposing them were shut down.[13] Native people actively protested these closures, and the group that marched to Red River in 1825 stated that the closure of their posts had brought them to "the extemity of distress."[14]

Like Tanner's claim that his people were made "destitute" by the withdrawal of credit, the claim made by these people that they were in "the extremity of distress" as the result of the post closures is more the language of anger and manipulation than a genuine cry of distress. This is not to say that the post closures did not cause hardship. Many families were forced either to relocate altogether and find new hunting, trapping, and harvesting grounds closer to the remaining posts, or to make longer and less frequent trading trips from their existing territories to posts and outposts that were maintained or later re-opened. These included Red River, Cumberland House, Fort Pelly, Fort Ellice, Fort Carlton, Qu'Appelle, and Swan River, and outposts at Shoal River and Lake Manitoba. One result of this was an increase in the Ojibwa population in the upper Assiniboine and Qu'Appelle River valleys during the 1820s. The Carrot River, Shell River, Red Deer River, Beaver Hills, Duck Mountain, and the area between Brandon House and the Qu'Appelle River remained popular hunting areas for Ojibwa who traded at Fort Pelly (built in 1824) and Cumberland House. Families circulated within this area, perhaps moving from The Pas to Red Deer River to Swan River in the course of a year.

Another western Ojibwa response to Simpson's reforms was to trade with the American rivals of the Hudson's Bay Company. As one Hudson's Bay Company trader noted in 1826, the Indians were "exasperated at their posts being abandoned," and complained "that they had been cast away by their old traders, but that they have now found others in their place."[15] Combined with the limitation of credit and of the other fur-trade courtesies, the post closures were a hardship and an insult. It was little wonder that Ojibwa loyalty to traders and trading companies largely dissolved after 1821 and that many Ojibwa began travelling to American posts along the Missouri River, sites near Turtle Mountain, Pembina, and Grand Forks. American firms also sent small groups of traders like pedlars through the prairies and parkland fringe, and some freemen acted as middlemen doing the same thing and taking the furs across the border.[16] In the spring of 1827, a frustrated trader at Red River wrote that Ojibwa there were trading little, having chosen instead to "hoard up their furs for them [the Americans], in expectation of receiving high prices."[17] The Fort Pelly journal records one instance in which two Indians "would not send in their Furs, & make threats of paying a visit to the American Traders established at the Moose Deer Hills, only Five days march from this Post maintaining that we have not the means of supplying them in their wants nor on equal terms." Such threats were common across the West.[18]

The very real competition posed by American traders made it difficult for the Hudson's Bay Company to effect other reforms such as the discontinuation of steel traps as trade goods, and injunctions against taking beaver during summer. Indeed, the Council of the Northern Department recommended that in districts faced by competition, the Natives should be encouraged to trap the beaver to the point of extinction and thus create some protection against American opposition.[19] Across the parkland and plains, the Company's boast of monopoly rule rang hollowly. By virtue of their position and mobility, the Ojibwa had a ready alternative to the Company's policies when these displeased them.

Another healthy alternative to the Hudson's Bay Company's rigid policies and diminution of credit was the established trade with the Red River settlers. Smug statements such as that in the Fort Douglas journal in 1826 indicating that "debts they never get here and increased industry on their parts is the consequence," were countered by the frustration experienced by the Company in trying to stem the Indians' trade with the settlers: "Some of these rascals have come all the way from Fort Dauphin, and others from Swan River for the purpose of trading with the settlers at Red River, and until some measures are adopted for punishing those Colonists who carry on this illicit traffic it cannot be supposed that Indians will bring their skins to the Company's Store, whilst they meet with such . . . ready purchasers, who allow them better prices, than what the Company is in the habit of paying."[20]

Efforts by Company officials to end the illicit trade were never successful. As they had from the beginning of the colony, settlers paid high prices and desirable goods for leather, furs, and provisions. Especially attractive to the Ojibwa were goods such as rum and clothing, which the settlers were able to offer even during years when these things were otherwise difficult for the Ojibwa to obtain.[21] Aided by Simpson's schemes to defeat the Americans, settlers were also able to buy goods cheaply at the Fort Garry shop, using these to buy furs from the Indians, which they traded at the shop. This put some check on the flow of furs to the Americans, although it did cause some difficulty for the Brandon House trade, for the journal writer there complained in 1828-29 that the area was "overrun" by colonists who got most of the furs and robes from the Natives.[22]

Perhaps equally important to the Ojibwa as these changes in the climate of the fur trade after 1821 was the rapid growth of the Métis population. With the post-merger reorganization of the Hudson's Bay Company, approximately two-thirds of the fur-trade labour force, most of whom were Métis, became redundant and was dismissed. In 1821, there were at least 500 Métis in a settlement at Pembina as well as those established in the Red River colony. The Pembina group moved to Red River in 1823, and by 1831 there were 1,300 Métis in and around the colony.[23] These people retained strong ties to their Native kin, and like them they relied on a mixed subsistence base of hunting, fishing, growing small garden plots, and harvesting berries and maple sugar.

During the 1820s, the Métis began organizing large-scale bison hunts that set out from Red River each summer and autumn. If the Ojibwa had been jealous of the Métis' mounted hunts before 1821, they were simply overwhelmed by the size of them after that date. According to Alexander Ross, a retired trader living in the settlement, the 1820 bison hunt involved 540 Red River carts, a number that grew to 680 in 1825 and 820 by 1830.[24] The huge scale of the Métis hunt meant that the Métis dominated the colony and Company market for provisions. This competition caused some tension at times, particularly as the Métis and freemen were paid more for their hides and meat than were the Indians. What the Ojibwa lost in trade to Métis competition, though, they gained in access to the herds. Few of the Red River Ojibwa hunted bison by horseback themselves, but they accompanied their Métis relatives on foot and received shares of the meat.[25] The Ojibwa benefitted from the large size of the main camp of the Métis hunt in another way, for it made them less vulnerable to Sioux attacks and therefore enabled them to venture farther into Sioux territory after both bison and scalps.[26] More than one hunt was disrupted, or ended in payments to cover the dead, by Ojibwa camp followers picking a fight with a party of Sioux encountered by chance.

The effects of all these changes, and Ojibwa strategies for coping with them, can be seen in the choices and movements of the Lesser Slave Lake trading chiefs Tolibee and Baptiste Desjarlais during the 1820s. Their reactions demonstrate the adaptive flexibility of the Ojibwa during the period after the merger, and are linked to Ojibwa responses across the Northwest. Tolibee, an Ojibwa, was a trading captain appointed by the Hudson's Bay Company at Lesser Slave Lake in 1819-20, as was his Métis half-brother Baptiste Desjarlais, or Nishicabo.[27] These two men were related to a sizeable group of freemen, Métis, Ottawa, Ojibwa, Iroquois, and other eastern tribespeople who had gathered in the Lesser Slave Lake area by 1810.

Such mixed groups were common by the early 1820s; they offered the chance to combine the preferential rates given freemen for their furs with the rights and skills of their Native kin in hunting and gathering. Since their kinsmen included nearly all the best hunters around Lesser Slave Lake, Tolibee and Baptiste Desjarlais wielded considerable power and received sizeable presents to prevent them from defecting to the North West Company. Of Tolibee, it was reported that "In spring & fall he receives a full suit of the finest clothing brought up (and a keg of Indian rum)." The half-brothers' skillful use of threats to defect prompted Hudson's Bay Company trader Robert Kennedy to write bitterly, "These people know well how to take advantage of the times but it is to be hoped that a time will very soon come when these fellows will be more kept under by the power of a single Trader without opposition."[28]

Kennedy had his revenge in the fall of 1821. When Tolibee, Baptiste, and their relatives arrived at the Lesser Slave Lake post with their usual ceremony, they found that the salutes they fired from their canoes were not returned from the post. As happened to Native trappers across Rupert's Land, the group was disappointed and offended to discover that, as part of the Company's new policy, all presents save a foot of tobacco and a dram of liquor had been abolished and their credit was to be strictly limited. Neither Tolibee nor Baptiste Desjarlais was reconfirmed as a trading chief; several Cree were clothed instead. As Tolibee and his relatives realized the extent of the changes, "their disappointment at not finding their expectations realized [was] . . . scarcely to be described."[29]

To Tolibee, Baptiste, and their relatives, these changes were devastating. The Ojibwa and their Métis kin took great pride in their ability to obtain trade goods easily, in the prestige and power that their desirability as procurers of fine furs gave them, and in the trade goods and other tokens that denoted their status in both Native and European fur-trade worlds. Tolibee himself "[spoke] french like a Canadian and [dressed] the same as the white people."[30] To lose the positions and gratuities that were the source of so much of their status was a disaster. The miserly tone adopted by the new company was also an insult: this was poor payment of gratitude to hunters who had for decades supplied posts with furs and food, and who had long-established relationships with trading companies. When Baptiste Desjarlais was made a trading chief in 1819, he received his clothing and then presented a gift of twenty-five beaver in return. As Bruce White has written, this custom not only sealed the bargain, but also evoked Native adoption ceremonies and the expectation that each party would treat the other as loyally and generously as relatives would. Similarly, Tolibee was reported in the spring of 1821 to have "conducted himself with his usual fidelity" over the winter.[31] After the changes of the following year, and the stripping away of familial overtones and customs from the trade, both men must have felt betrayed.

The band took decisive action in response to the changes. The entire group left the Lesser Slave Lake area and their former traders there, and moved to Lac la Biche where they lived for several years, spending more time fishing and hunting instead of trapping for furs. The group disappeared from the region in the spring of 1823, at which time Tolibee joined a Cree war party and headed for the Saskatchewan River – something he had once promised the trader he would never do while he was a trading chief.[32]

These actions demonstrate an intensified determination by the former chiefs to participate in the fur trade on their own terms. Still, while they sought alternatives to the fur trade when the Hudson's Bay Company's new terms were unveiled, they did not leave the trade altogether. They continued trading for necessary items but undoubtedly missed the prestige, the gifts, and the preferred rates the freemen had been given before 1821, for four years later, in the summer of 1827, the band was trading again – but this time far to the east, at Cumberland House, and trapping along the Carrot River. This area still had good game and fur populations in the late 1820s, and here they may have hoped to make a fresh start and regain their former status. But again, they were treated with less respect than they felt they deserved. Tolibee's step-son was unable to obtain credits for the band at Cumberland House as he had hoped to do, since they came from another post district, and Tolibee himself "begged hard" for meagre advances for his group later in the season.[33] The group hunted and trapped in the fertile territory between Nipawin and Swan River for the next year, and then seems to have broken up. Tolibee and several followers remained in the Cumberland area, later spending several years near Carlton House, while the Métis in the group attached themselves to Fort Pelly, where Baptiste Desjarlais satisfied his ambition of becoming a trading chief again. Both groups found niches within the changed fur trade, and, after attempting to regain their former status, both became less involved in the trade and found other sources of prestige and personal satisfaction.

Tolibee's decision to leave Lesser Slave Lake altogether and seek his fortunes elsewhere shows that, while the Ojibwa found themselves under significant new pressures after 1821, they were not overwhelmed by these changes. To counteract the new terms of trade, the loss of fur-trade posts, the rise of the Métis, and the continuing decline of the fur trade and large game populations, they relied on a whole set of economic alternatives and supplements to maintain control of their lives after 1821. For most Ojibwa, credit restrictions and other changes in fur-trade policy did not result in "greater industry" and higher fur returns, although these changes did limit Ojibwa access to trade goods and thus, both directly and indirectly, to personal prestige through the trade. The trade no longer brought wealth or status but became merely a source of everyday goods. The importance of the trade therefore changed somewhat within the Ojibwa seasonal round, continuing a trend that had begun some years before 1821. Like variations in the water level or in populations of game and fur-bearing animals, changes in the trade were merely additional factors to be added to the complex web of data that informed Ojibwa decision making and planning: adaptive strategies, based on human and environmental conditions and needs.

The nature and success of the strategies used by the Ojibwa after 1821 varied from region to region, and the changes themselves worked to produce distinct regional adaptations and social networks. Different conditions and decisions in each area shaped several variations on the larger Ojibwa theme: a parkland/forest orientation, which for many families involved increasing amounts of time spent hunting bison; mixed-group camps, which followed what was essentially a plains Cree way of life, producing the first "plains Ojibwa" bands; and the families of Peguis's band near Red River, who were faced with assimilative pressures from the colony.

THE TRANSITIONAL OJIBWA

The way of life that Tolibee chose in the area around Fort Pelly was typical of the pattern that developed there after 1821. Many Ojibwa chose to maintain their familiar seasonal round in the transitional area encompassing the forest and parkland belts that included the Interlake and the western shores of Lakes Winnipegosis and Manitoba, the Assiniboine River valley and the wooded hills surrounding it, and· the lower Saskatchewan River. Between 1,000 and 2,000 Ojibwa occupied this region in the 1820s and '30s, trading at Swan River, Forts Pelly, Ellice, Carlton House, and Edmonton.

This region had always been popular because of its rich resources. More Ojibwa families either entered the area or shifted their territories westward within it after the measles–whooping cough epidemic of 1819-20 and the closure of posts in and around the Interlake after 1821. Deaths from this epidemic thinned the combined population of Ojibwa, Cree, and Assiniboine in the area, possibly making the Ojibwa more welcome than they might otherwise have been. As well, the temporary closure of posts in the Interlake induced a number of families to shift their hunting grounds to the western edge of the Interlake, closer to remaining posts such as Fort Pelly on the upper Assiniboine.[34] The re-opening of posts around the Interlake in the late 1820s did not completely reverse this westward trend, for, during the time they were closed, many families who shifted their hunting grounds developed new social ties around the alternate posts. Other bands moved south rather than west after 1821. In 1829, Francis Heron of Brandon House recommended that posts be established at Portage la Prairie and Turtle Mountain for the

Lake Manitoba Ojibwa, which gives some indication of their pattern of dispersal.[35]

Heron's recommendations for the locations of new posts also reflected the growing Ojibwa trade with American firms at Pembina, Turtle Mountain, and the Missouri (and their outposts and free traders much closer to the Assiniboine and Qu'Appelle rivers) in response to the changes in Hudson's Bay Company policy. Because of the rapid increase in illicit trade, Fort Dauphin was re-opened in 1827 and Brandon House in 1828, Fort Ellice was opened in 1831, and outposts were opened or re-opened in a number of locations (Manitoba House, Shoal River, Duck Bay, and, after 1850, Touchwood Hills, Guard Post, Fort Qu'Appelle, Egg Lake, Shell River, and Last Mountain House) to minimize temptation to Native trappers.[36]

Trade with Red River settlers provided yet another economic opportunity. Hudson's Bay Company traders complained that in spring the Ojibwa traded much of their maple sugar at the colony "for Cloth, Blankets to the settlers at a very high price, in several instances more than 4 shillings per lb."[37] Trade with the settlers was particularly appealing during 1826, after the great flood that virtually destroyed the colony, and during the harsh winter that followed it, when the bison stayed far away from the colony. This opportunity, as well as the muskrat trade, which grew rapidly in the late 1820s and early 1830s, may have offset westward migration of Ojibwa out of the Interlake region somewhat.[38]

After the initial changes in trade that had so angered Native trappers, the readiness with which the Ojibwa made use of these trading options, and particularly the threat of American competition, led to a warmer welcome for them at the posts by the mid-1820s. At some posts, particularly those with close American competition, chiefs continued to be clothed, and Ojibwa bands were welcomed to the fort with the old ceremonies. At Fort Pelly, the trader "fired a volley of small arms and Hoisted the Flag for them, Presented them with Four Kegs reduced Rum."[39] No fewer than seven Ojibwa men were given chief's outfits in 1825 at Fort Pelly, a post that faced keen American competition.[40] These chiefs and their bands emphasized diversity in their fur hunts and relied most heavily on whatever species were currently plentiful: "Our Fort Hunters *Seauteaux* giving themselves airs and little or no exertions in Hunting large animals, Rats being abundant and easier killed to pay their advances and requisite supplies."[41]

Muskrats were indeed abundant in the late 1820s. In the spring of 1829, four Ojibwa brought 8,000 skins to Fort Pelly.[42] Returns such as these led to their being characterized as the "most industrious" Indians at Swan River in 1825, and allowed the Ojibwa to maintain their access to necessary trade goods, even after the muskrat population plummeted in the winter of 1829-30.[43] When the muskrat population was low, they were often able to obtain "the usual Debts" by emphasizing their former hunts and reputation and by promising to "make good hunts in other furs," usually marten and lynx.[44]

In general, though, trapping was far less important to the Ojibwa after 1821. Even formerly active trappers such as Tolibee, to whom fur returns and the favours of non-Native fur trade society had once meant a great deal, gradually drifted out to the very periphery of the trade. Tolibee was noted in the Carlton records in the late 1820s as bringing in small hunts of beaver and spending time close to the post, probably doing odd jobs and hunting for the traders, an indication that he was trying yet again to regain some status through the trade.[45] The shortage of beaver and the changes in the trade made this an impossible goal, and he joined the ranks of other Ojibwa in the region whose fur production was exceeded by that of the Piegan and certain Cree and Assiniboine bands.[46]

Having finally abandoned his dreams of glory in the fur trade, Tolibee and his family adopted the more independent, subsistence-oriented way of life typical of Ojibwa in the transitional zone. By the fall of 1829, Tolibee's step-son had a summer cache of leather and provisions at Bloody Berry Lake (a spot that was popular with more established Ojibwa for berrying and hunting wildfowl), suggesting a growing emphasis on subsistence hunting over fur trapping.[47] In doing so, Tolibee's family joined dozens of Ojibwa bands who used the still-rich resources of the western forests and parkland to the fullest throughout the 1820s. These resources allowed the Ojibwa to maintain the diverse and productive seasonal round they had developed before 1821. Sugaring, fishing, berrying, hunting (large parkland game when it was available; small game and bison when it was not), and trapping continued as before.[48] The gardens at Garden, or Big Tent, Island continued to be cultivated. The Reverend John West mentioned Indian gardens of pumpkins and potatoes on an island in Lake Manitoba in 1821, and large numbers of Indians – such as generally convened on garden or fishing sites – were met at Duck Bay and "the Grand Lodge" in the spring of 1830. Gardens were also "transplanted" from established sites to the Fort Pelly region and continued to supplement other food resources.[49]

This was a satisfying way of life, but it did not last; Tolibee's family was almost too late to enjoy it. By 1830, large game other than bison was becoming seriously depleted in the region, and the muskrat population cycle plummeted as well. Still-abundant fisheries and other resources might have compensated for these serious setbacks, had it not been for a series of hard winters in the early 1830s. Hunger became a more frequent complaint throughout the region as the decade wore on.[50] Several of the Ojibwa who traded at Fort Pelly starved to death (or died of causes related to hunger) during the following winters, when the bison stayed far away from their usual winter grounds and lack of snow made hunting even more difficult.[51] Others frequently claimed they were "starving," although the term was most often used in its by-then-ordinary sense of action taken to prevent hunger, rather than hunger in the present tense.[52] The actions they took to prevent hunger were extensions of older coping strategies. Some bands added gardens to their seasonal round: at Fort Pelly, "the whole of the Indians who winter in the vicinity of this Post" applied for garden seed in the spring of 1834 because of the scarcity of large game.[53] Most began spending virtually the entire mid- to late-winter season hunting bison, reinforcing their choice to participate less in the fur trade. Some bands chose to seek their fortunes on the plains as bison hunters, leaving the region altogether for much of the year; the emergence of these plains-oriented people is detailed in the next section.

During the worst winters, the parkland Ojibwa relied on the Hudson's Bay Company for provisions and meat for bait. This was not simply an indication of dependence on the fur trade but should rather be seen as an adaptive coping strategy used only during extreme conditions. Even after the radical changes in the nature of the trade and Native-trader relationships that had been implemented after 1821, the Ojibwa still considered it good manners for the traders to offer food when they arrived at the posts and believed in their right to be fed. Asking for food still had the connotation of reciprocity, the sharing required of those who have more, as among Native societies, rather than of begging, as among European societies. Not only did the Ojibwa consider this their right, their part of the bargain, but they were also ready to remind the trader of it periodically – perhaps to test this aspect of the relationship against some time when it would be needed.[54] During the bad winters of the early 1830s, then, they had no qualms about asking for food from the traders.

As the experience of The Jackfish's band shows, they also knew just how to ask for support. In mid-January 1832, women from The Jackfish's band arrived at Fort Pelly and asked for provisions and meat for bait, arguing that if they were supplied with food they would be able to continue trapping; otherwise, they would have to go to the plains to hunt bison, where they had been headed a few days earlier. They obtained what they asked for and returned with the same request a month later.[55] The trader acceded to their requests largely because he was concerned about the growing number of Ojibwa who chose to hunt bison rather than furs during the winter. The comments of the Fort Pelly trader on these incidents shed light on the differing Ojibwa and European perspectives on grants of food from the post. They also suggest strong continuity in at least this aspect of Ojibwa attitudes and expectations towards the trade despite all the changes in previous decades. The trader stated, "This party by hunting in the strong woods, considers that they have some claim on us for support, in the event of being hard pressed. It appears there is no want of fur bearing animals . . . but the country is completely exhausted in Moose and Deer, So that if they had not a . . . supply from the House, they must follow the Buffaloe, they therefore prefer submitting to a few privations to pay their debts."[56] He also noted that other Ojibwa families "[consider] it a right to be supplied with ammunition or otherwise [be fed] at the House" when they had been trapping in an area where game was scarce.[57] One senses from the timing of the requests that The Jackfish and his band may have decided that getting pemmican from Fort Pelly was easier than getting it in the plains. The trader's wording twists the Ojibwa perspective into the European one, implying ("they therefore prefer submitting to a few privations to pay their debts") their dependence and lack of options from which to choose. From the Ojibwa perspective, though, the food provided by the Company was already theirs, by right and for the asking. Far from being an indication of dependence, obtaining supplies from the post was yet another resource-use choice to be added to the seasonal round. It was a choice made only in more difficult times, whether as a reminder or in necessity, and when game and fur populations increased later in the 1830s, the Ojibwa stopped asking for food and bait at the posts.

The Pelly trader's statement – "there is no want of fur bearing animals . . . but the country is completely exhausted in Moose and Deer, So that if they had not a . . . supply from the House, they must follow the Buffaloe" – indicates both the dilemma in which many Ojibwa found themselves during these years and their other solution to it. Many Ojibwa claimed that "real starvation" in mid-winter drove them "out to the Plains after the Buffalos."[58] This was an intensification of a pattern that had been developing for decades. This seeming solution to the lack of other large game sometimes backfired, for the Ojibwa had come to rely on bison during lean seasons, and failure to find the herds presented serious problems ranging from literal starvation to bare survival during cold months of misery. A family of Ojibwa that arrived at Carlton House in late April 1833 had "killed no Furs during the Winter and have had much difficulty in making themselves live; . . . they saw no Buffalo on their way down the River."[59] For the most part, though, bison did provide an adequate supplement to other resources available in the transitional zone, allowing the Ojibwa to maintain their way of life there.

The actions of one band in the Fort Pelly region illustrate many of the coping strategies on which Ojibwa relied after 1821. In the spring of 1832, two members of a band led by Wisiniw arrived at Pelly, saying they were starving and would be unable to pay their debts. The band was not literally starving; they had escaped starvation by hunting solely for food, which was why they were unable to pay their debts. They used the term *starving* in its manipulative sense, holding up the image of privation to encourage the trader's "pity," or generosity. Eight months later, in December 1833, Wisiniw sent in no less than 125 MB of furs from his camp at Shell River; this was when the trader called him "the most valuable [Indian] belonging to this post." The remainder of the winter was apparently difficult, for in the spring he came in to the post and pleaded for garden seed on the grounds that he was unable to support his family. At the same time, he brought in the rest of his winter's hunt, which amounted in total to 202 MB: a very large return from a single hunter for the 1830s. We do not know whether he actually planted his garden, but the band did spend the summer of 1834 in the plains hunting bison. He arrived at Pelly again in October to trade, and two and a half months later he sent in 2,000 muskrats.[60] Times were certainly difficult, but Wisiniw was clearly managing to cope with them.

Like Wisiniw's band, most Ojibwa in the transitional zone retained their diverse seasonal round, trapping when they could and augmenting their diet with food from gardens, food from the post, and bison. Midewiwin and other traditional ceremonies also continued to be held in this region, often at Fort Pelly.[61] For some bands, however, the gradually increasing reliance on bison, changes in the fur trade, and the shortage of large game and furs in the transitional zone, led to the development of a more plains- or bison-oriented economic and cultural adaptation. The actions of the second half of the Tolibee–Baptiste Desjarlais band illustrate the development of this plains orientation quite clearly.

THE PLAINS OJIBWA

While Tolibee remained in the parkland, hunting bison close to his trapping territories in winter and early summer, Baptiste Desjarlais and other members of the original Lesser Slave Lake band took a path that led them towards the plains. This band was of mixed ethnicity, containing Métis, Ojibwa, and probably plains Cree, and several more Ojibwa from around Fort Pelly joined Desjarlais's band about this time as well. Their path to the plains was not as common as the lifestyle that Tolibee chose but was another pattern of response to the challenges they all faced. Moving onto the plains with their Métis and Cree relatives, these were among the first "Plains Ojibwa."

In the fall of 1830, after trading there for only a year, and again in 1832, Baptiste Desjarlais was clothed as a trading chief at Fort Pelly.[62] During this period he and his band continued to bring in substantial hunts and receive good credits. But the group also began trading more meat and fat, and fewer furs, and followed the regional trend of "pitching farther out in the plains in quest of the Buffaloe" during the leanest winter months.[63] Their reasons for doing so were the same as those that prompted the Ojibwa of the transitional zone to hunt bison: a scarcity of other large game, and the decreasing rewards of fur trapping. The collapse of the muskrat population after 1829 acted as a watershed and catalyst for the plains-oriented bands. If muskrat pelts were worth very little, there had at least been plenty of them, and their availability served as an anchor in the parkland for some bands.[64] Without them, the Ojibwa were placed in a double bind: they were forced to spend more time hunting fur-bearing species that were much harder to find, but they needed to spend longer periods hunting for food as well. Often, they were forced to choose between eating well and trapping. Nor did the Ojibwa feel as compelled to trap or to pay their debts after the changes and insults of 1821.

Several factors combined to encourage the emergent plains Ojibwa orientation. All of the western Ojibwa faced a shortage of large game and fur-bearing animals in the parkland. Some families, such as Tolibee's, chose to deal with these challenges by remaining in their familiar cycle of harvests and campsites, using their established sugaring groves and fishing weirs, trapping the remaining furs, and hunting small game and bison to maintain their way of life and pay some of their debts at the posts. Other Ojibwa families, who had stronger kin ties to plains Cree and Métis, chose a very different alternative. It was for this group of western Ojibwa that a new way of life began to open up after 1821, especially after peace negotiations between the Cree and the enemy Blackfoot in the late 1820s. As one trader described it, "seeing that they cannot pay their debts [the plains Ojibwa] have joined the Crees in the plains.[65] In essence, the plains-oriented bands chose to switch from fur trapping to the provision and wolf-pelt trade, from a forest/parkland to a parkland/grassland cycle. It was seldom a permanent move; the hallmark of the western Ojibwa was their flexibility and resourcefulness. Nor did they abandon their old cycle when they moved onto the plains but rather overlaid a plains adaptation (both economic and social) on top of their existing way of life and culture. Some families wore this new cultural cloak lightly, able to remove it at will. For others, though they moved back into the forests and closer to the posts at need, it was seeking shelter in an empty house: the transitional zone and the ways of life within it no longer felt like home.

At first, this pattern was virtually the same as that followed by the other parkland Ojibwa. It differed only in that a few bands pitched a little farther away on the plains, stayed a little longer, and traded fewer furs. Even after the plains orientation became firmly established, these bands continued to harvest berries, roots, fish, and other foods as they had before, often in the same areas. The plains orientation differed in that these bands did not merely "resort to the Plains" when necessary but rather preferred the plains and bison hunting above all other locations and subsistence activities. By the late 1820s and early 1830s, some mixed Ojibwa-Métis-Cree bands were living primarily on bison both in summer and in winter, and they spent little time hunting for furs or other game. The returns of these bands were sometimes indistinguishable from those of bands composed wholly of plains Cree and Assiniboine: "A Small Band of Crees & Sotteux arrived and brought 1,500 lbs dry meat and 1,000 lbs Grease."[66] For these bands, bison hunts and the Thirst, or Sun, Dance became social and economic mainstays of their annual round, instead of being one point on the wheel. The large gatherings for these events largely replaced the social functions of the late winter periods of group-intensive trapping and fishing, which had been so important for the early Ojibwa. The term *plain(s) Saulteaux* was used for the first time in the spring of 1833 at Pelly, and in the fall of 1837 one Tian, "a principal Sauteaux chief who passed the summer in the plains," arrived, "heavily loaded with provisions his horses unable to get further."[67] It is little wonder that traders were concerned about this trend and refused to establish a post at a place called "the Squirrel" because they feared it would "draw some of our fur hunters from the Strong woods to the plains."[68]

Ojibwa kin ties with Métis and plains Cree had much to do with this process. During the 1820s, the growth of the Métis population, the custom of Ojibwa participation in large Métis bison hunts, and more frequent contact with Cree through bison hunting, resulted in ever-denser kin ties among the three peoples, so that nearly all reports of plains Ojibwa link them, as in the case of Baptiste Desjarlais's band and the histories of the Turtle Mountain people, with Cree and Métis kin. Most plains Ojibwa were a minority in these mixed camps. The multi-ethnic nature of these bands lent itself not only to the development of a plains Ojibwa orientation, but also to the absorption of much of plains Cree, Métis, and Assiniboine culture by the plains Ojibwa. An early mention of one such camp noted that it consisted "of Forty Tents Crees, Seauteaux & Stonies; . . . they have no pound."[69]

Along with this more bison-oriented way of life, the plains-oriented Ojibwa adopted the desire for autonomy displayed by other plains tribes, spending most of their time far away from the trading posts and closer to the bison herds. Living comfortably on fish and bison, Baptiste Desjarlais's band wintered at the Fishing Lakes along the Qu'Appelle River, a few days' travel west of Pelly, in 1833-34, and although they brought in moderate fur returns they were much less interested in trapping or the prestige associated with it than they had once been. Another family that wintered with them spent even more time in the plains and did "little or nothing" in the way of fur hunting. Of other bands from the southern end of Lake Manitoba, it was said that they "have not exerted them selves in furs as last year, having followed the Buffalo."[70]

Their close ties with Cree and Métis and the time they spent hunting bison linked these plains-oriented Ojibwa bands with regional inter-tribal feuds. In the southeastern part of the region, the Ojibwa supported the Cree in their conflict with the Mandan, which continued throughout the 1820s. Battles in 1828 and 1831 caused temporary unrest (after the 1828 incident, most of the "Crees Bungees & Stone Indians belonging the Southward" moved into the Carlton region for several months). More importantly for a developing plains population, hostilities with the Missouri tribes meant that the supply of horses from that source was intermittent at best.[71] The Cree-Mandan disputes complicated the more serious situation to the west, where escalating hostilities between the Cree and the Blackfoot made the northwestern plains unsafe for much of the 1820s. The desire for peace and, for the Cree, for Blackfoot horses (to augment the Mandan supply) led to peace negotiations in the late 1820s, which made the region somewhat safer for a few years. After the harsh winters of the early 1830s, when the Cree and some Métis were forced to travel well into Blackfoot territory to find bison, some fighting resumed, but this was limited by the effects of the smallpox epidemic of 1837.[72]

After the Cree made peace with the Blackfoot in 1829, the safer state of the region encouraged the Cree and their Ojibwa relatives to venture farther and oftener into the prairies in search of bison, thus fostering the development of a true plains Ojibwa subculture. Such was the case with a band of Cree and Ojibwa led by an Ojibwa named Black Powder (Mukatai). These people moved into the Jackfish Lake area on the north side of the Saskatchewan River between Forts Carlton and Pitt during the 1820s, in response to the same forces that prompted many other Ojibwa bands to move westward following the union of 1821. According to Hugh Dempsey, who has recorded some of the oral history of Black Powder's band, they "normally camped near Jackfish Lake, ranging onto the edge of the plains for buffalo in the summer and into the woods to trap and hunt in winter" during the 1820s. The wooded areas of Turtle Mountain and the upper Assiniboine and Qu'Appelle River valleys were also frequented by bands such as Black Powder's.[73] By the mid-1830s, Black Powder's band, like other mixed Ojibwa-Cree-Métis bands that became more plains-oriented in that decade, spent less time in the woods and had become far more bison oriented. During this period, Black Powder ranged "south of the Saskatchewan River to the Red Deer Forks." He was probably one of the first Ojibwa to "pound" bison, and may have participated in some of the eight "Cree" bison pounds that were recorded as being on the north side of the Saskatchewan between Forts Pitt and Carlton in the winter of 1830-31.[74] Some plains Ojibwa may also have had enough trained horses to have been employing the mounted chase at this time.

Bison-hunting techniques were by no means the only plains traits that Black Powder and his people absorbed from their Cree and Métis kin. A note in the Fort Pelly journal in 1831 hints at the nature and depth of these changes. According to the journal writer, the plains-oriented Ojibwa bands "were formerly excellent fur hunters But having got a taste of the Buffaloe by bordering on the meadows since the rats failed they are from their dress and habits little better now than the meadow bucks."[75] This statement implies changes in dress as well as economic orientation, social organization, and possibly personal identity, the "habits" to which the journal writer referred.

Apart from the Pelly trader's statement, it is difficult to identify changes in Ojibwa dress from the existing body of Ojibwa material culture from this period. Several specimens of clothing labeled "plains Ojibwa" survive in museum collections, and several other items are portrayed by artists such as Catlin and Rindisbacher. Of these items, however, most are problematic in some way, eluding certain identification and thus frustrating attempts to draw conclusions about this aspect of culture change among plains-oriented Ojibwa bands.

Working with artifacts from museum collections is especially problematic, for most early pieces were collected as curios or gifts, and seldom have any provenance (that is, information about the maker's tribal affiliation, date of creation, or purpose or meaning of the artifact). Most artifacts are tentatively identified long after they have been acquired, by curators working on the basis of stylistic similarity to somewhat better documented pieces. Given these limitations, most artifacts can be assigned only a regional identification (for example, "Great Lakes," "eastern plains"), and very few can be assigned tribal or specific community identification. This system does not lend itself to taking into consideration the complexity of artifact identification created by multi-ethnic camps or inter-tribal trade. Ojibwa, Cree, and Métis women in mixed camps would have compared and imitated each other's decorative styles, a process that now frustrates researchers attempting to identify the specific tribal origins of the artifacts they produced and makes it especially difficult to use material culture as a source of data such as documents or oral history. Given that such artifacts are a crucial expression of aspects of culture that are not generally recorded in the documents, though, it is important to analyse these pieces for what scraps of information and nuance they can give us.

To give a detailed analysis of one such garment, and the problems of using material culture in reconstructing ethnohistory, a plains war-shirt drawn by artist George Catlin provides an excellent example. James Howard, writing in the 1950s, made much of Catlin's portrait of an Ojibwa man, The Six ("Sha-co-pay"), drawn in 1832.[76] Catlin claimed that this man was "The chief of that part of the Ojibbeway tribe who inhabit these northern regions," and portrayed him in a northern plains-style "war" shirt decorated with hairlocks, quilled rosettes and quilled shoulder strips. Catlin claimed that the shirt belonged to The Six and represented his war record, and that "this, and also each and every article of his varied dress, had been manufactured by his wives, of which he had several."[77] He also sketched one of The Six's wives, whom he shows wearing a painted and quilled or beaded bison robe with feathered circle designs[78] (see Illustration 1). Howard, in turn, made this sketch the primary basis for his conclusion that by the 1830s the Ojibwa had been completely transformed from a woodland to a plains culture.[79]

Unfortunately, inconsistencies about this sketch raise questions about Howard's use of it as documentary evidence for the adoption of plains identity and cultural traits by the Ojibwa. The robe worn by The Six's wife, in particular, is problematic, for it is of a style that has been documented as Teton Dakota and as being a man's, not a woman's, garment. (Interestingly, Catlin stopped to paint the

1. George Catlin, 1832, "The Six, Chief of the Plains Ojibwa" (courtesy National Museum of American Art, Smithsonian Institution, gift of Mrs. Joseph Harrison, Jr., accession no. 1985.66.182).
George Catlin, 1832, "Wife of the Six" (courtesy National Museum of American Art, Smithsonian Institution, gift of Mrs. Joseph Harrison, Jr., accession no. 1985.66.195).

Teton Dakota on his way to Fort Union the same year; did he collect the robe? Or did it belong to The Six, and Catlin ask her to put it on?) The Six's shirt, too, seems Siouan, with its double quilled rosettes, though its painted pictographic-style figures suggest a style similar among both the eastern Dakota and western Ojibwa. These and other questions about the authenticity of Catlin's costuming have been raised by a number of scholars, suggesting that The Six's clothing may not have been what Catlin claimed it to be.[80] If these items were indeed made by The Six's wife, one wonders if she herself was Sioux (or, perhaps, Assiniboine?), whether Catlin was mistaken, or whether the items had been acquired in trade or gift instead of being made by The Six's wife.

Nor does there seem to be any corroborating evidence for Catlin's statement that The Six was "the chief of that part of the Ojibbeway tribe who inhabit these northern regions." In fact, there is good evidence to suggest that The Six was not Ojibwa, but Dakota. Catlin's rendering of The Six's Indian name, Sha-co-pay, is similar to the name of a famous Mdewakanton Dakota chief, Shakopee (Dakota *sakpe,* "Six"), whose village on the upper Mississippi River near the mouth of the St. Croix River and Fort Snelling was well-known.[81] James Howard went as far as to admit that "'The Six' (Sha-co-pay) is apparently a name borrowed from the Dakota tribe," but he did not admit that, given these coincidences (why would an

Ojibwa have a Dakota name?) and the fact that The Six's garments appear to be Siouian, The Six might actually be the Dakota Chief Shakopee.[82] Catlin encountered The Six far from Shakopee's village, and did identify The Six as a plains Ojibwa, but these many problems certainly call into question the validity of Catlin's documentation – and, by implication, of Howard's use of the sketch.

In the end, the questions surrounding the garments sketched by Catlin make it virtually impossible to use them as evidence of the type of change in material culture to which the Fort Pelly trader was referring. Similar problems come with the few other early-nineteenth-century objects identified as being western Ojibwa in origin. There are simply no garments clearly identified as being made by Ojibwa people in these years that are northern plains rather than western Great Lakes in style. One early collection of plains-style clothing identified as being "plains Ojibwa" in origin serves only to further underline the difficulties of using material culture as documents of cultural change. This collection was made by trader Joseph Klinger of Gorz, or an agent of his, and attributed on the original accession documents to the "Chippeways Indians." Gorz presented the material in 1825 to Emperor Franz I. Some of the objects have been identified by James Howard, on the basis of their style and their original documentation, as being "plains Ojibwa" in origin. The collection includes Great Lakes–style ball-headed war clubs, a spreading eagle-feather headdress, several pairs of quilled moccasins, and a plains-style leather shirt and leggings. The association of the Great Lakes clubs with the plains clothing suggests that the collection may, indeed, have come from a plains-oriented Ojibwa band. However, the total dissimilarity between the two decorative styles makes it seem likely that the clothing, at least, may well have been acquired in trade rather than being produced by Ojibwa women. (One set of moccasins from this collection has been identified by another researcher, on the basis of style, as being Crow.) Further research on the collector is needed to support the identification of this collection as plains Ojibwa in origin.[83]

The lack of documented plains-style western Ojibwa clothing for this era is more likely the fault of the many problems in the documentation of museum collections than of the Fort Pelly trader's faulty vision in identifying the Ojibwa who had begun to dress like "meadow bucks." The prevalence of mixed-group bands among these plains-oriented Ojibwa supports the trader's statement, even if we do not have any artifacts that readily do. However, it is necessary to remember that change was not total among the western Ojibwa, and that plains-style artifacts would have supplemented rather than replaced older, Great Lakes–style clothing and personal possessions. Even if the early plains Ojibwa did adopt plains-style war shirts, they may have been carrying Great Lakes–style gunstock clubs such as those in the Gorz collection, or another collected in Saskatchewan, "with incised figures reminiscent of Ojibwa Midewiwin scrolls," when they went off with a war party[84] (see Illustration 2).

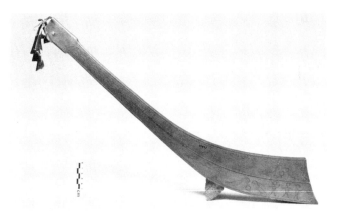

2. Western Ojibwa–style war club; found in Saskatchewan (courtesy Royal Ontario Museum, Toronto, Canada, accession no. 37592).

If changes in dress and material culture were external, readily observed by the Fort Pelly trader who commented on them, so too were many changes in Ojibwa "habits" as they left their old lifestyle behind. But behind these lay a host of deeper, subtler changes, including ones affecting group organization, personal goals and identity, and familiar language. Many of these can be seen in the history of Black Powder's son, born in 1825. With an Ojibwa father and a mother who was either Cree or Ojibwa, Black Powder's son acquired a Cree name with Ojibwa religious connotations: *mistahai maskwa*, or Big Bear. This was the same Big Bear who would decades later emerge as a prominent "Cree" leader in the Rebellion of 1885. The child and his upbringing reflect the process of cultural change at the individual level, which was intimately involved in the emergence of the plains Ojibwa. Though his father was Ojibwa, and he was perceived as Ojibwa by the Cree in his camp (both in childhood and adulthood), Big Bear's first language was Cree. As Hugh Dempsey has written, the young Big Bear was taught both "the secrets of hunting moose and deer in the woods and stalking the buffalo in the open prairies."[85] His upbringing was most affected by strong plains Cree cultural influences, including emphasis on the bison hunt, on the extended social network within the large-scale encampments formed for the bison hunt and the Sun Dance, and on the use of horse raiding to gain personal prestige.[86]

Big Bear's childhood raises the intriguing question of the process by which personal ethnic identity develops in a multi-ethnic family. If Dempsey's reconstruction of his life is correct in these details, why did Big Bear speak first Cree and then his father's language, conform to plains-style peer pressure in his teens, and ultimately emerge as a "Cree" leader? The fact that he learned to speak Cree first, and that plains Cree cultural elements dominated within his family and band, implies a status differential between Cree and Ojibwa languages and cultures within multi-ethnic camps. This possibility is reinforced by later comments about plains Cree-Ojibwa interaction. As Peter Erasmus, a Métis participant in the treaty negotiations of the 1870s, commented, "The Prairie Crees looked down on the Swampy and Saulteaux as an inferior race. They would be intolerant at being addressed in Swampy or Saulteaux words." This would also have been reinforced by the fact that there were generally far fewer Ojibwa than Cree in these mixed camps.[87] If Cree was indeed perceived to be a higher-status culture and language than Ojibwa, then Big Bear's experience suggests that children growing up in such mixed camps were affected both by cultural exchange and by the maintenance of cultural boundaries reinforced by the difference in status. On the one hand, Big Bear and other children would have learned behaviours and beliefs from non-Ojibwa in their families and camps; on the other, they would have been consistently identified as Ojibwa and their Ojibwa heritage maintained because of the ethnocentrism of the status differential, much as Dempsey implies when he observes that "Having an Ojibwa father [made Big Bear] . . . different from the Cree boys in camp."[88]

The complexity of such interaction, and the mixed signals for children that it generated, have implications for existing theories about cultural change among the plains Ojibwa. In particular, it allows a refinement of ideas such as James Howard's, who concluded that the plains Ojibwa had completely abandoned their old, woodland-based culture and identity and replaced these with plains-based ones. Looking at the process from the perspective of an individual such as Big Bear, it is apparent that while many plains elements were added, a core of eastern Ojibwa identity and culture remained. Not everything was so neatly replaced as Howard believed. Nor was the ethnicity of a child growing up in a multi-ethnic band simply a homogenous fusion of its parents', as Susan Sharrock has suggested. Ethnic fusion did occur, but it involved the more complex process of maintaining a core of older Ojibwa values and creating and donning a plains Cree outer cultural "garment."[89]

Part of the reason for this cultural continuity was undoubtedly the fact that it was the plains Cree who were the most crucial role models for the western Ojibwa in the process of their adaptation to the West. While I am emphasizing the adoption of so-called plains traits by the western Ojibwa from the Cree and other peoples in this process (plains-style clothing, the horse complex, tipis, warrior societies, and an emphasis on the bison hunt), it is important to note that these were relatively new facets of plains Cree culture. As Dale Russell has concluded, the Cree from the mid-1700s through the nineteenth century were primarily a parkland people. Russell's findings indicate that we need to begin thinking of "plains" peoples such as the Cree in a broader way. There was, for instance, a great deal of overlap between the subsistence practices of the "plains" Cree and the western

Ojibwa, for both peoples as well as the mixed bands they created relied on fish, vegetable foods, small game, elk and deer, and some fur trapping, as well as bison.[90] This fact challenges the traditional definition of "plains" cultures as having, among other traits, "an absence of fishing," and an almost complete economic reliance on the bison: a definition that overemphasizes the "plains" element (both the time spent in that ecological zone and reliance on bison), at the expense of understanding other aspects of their culture, which made use of the resources of the parkland and forest zones of the West.[91] Recent studies of plains Ojibwa and plains Cree resource-use present a more balanced picture of "plains" societies, which differed from the parkland/forest adaptation of the transitional Ojibwa only by degree.[92] This revised picture of plains Cree culture means that many aspects of Cree life would have been familiar to their Ojibwa kin, creating a core of continuity on which to base change in other aspects of their lives, and contributing to the maintenance of an Ojibwa heritage in this most distinctive of western Ojibwa adaptations.

There are no accounts comparable to that of Big Bear's experience to tell us what effects this new way of life had on Ojibwa women, or how plains Ojibwa female children were socialized. As seen in the example of Big Bear's childhood, the process by which cultural identity is passed from generation to generation in mixed-group camps is complex, dependent on teachings from male and female kin of several generations, all of whom may be of different ethnic backgrounds.[93] For the first few years of a child's life, the mother and other women of the household provide the most important socialization. They may also, as Harriet Gorham has suggested, provide the foundation of the child's ethnic identity: "Often, women may provide the most consistent element in a family unit, and thus may be the most available cultural role models. . . . Could ethnic orientation or identification be linked with acquired gender roles and social roles as learned through the socialization process?[94] After the first few years, though, young children of any Aboriginal society are socialized within the subculture of their gender: girls are taught by older women, boys by men. In a multi-ethnic camp it is thus possible for children to be exposed to teachers of a variety of ethnicities and cultural backgrounds. Does Big Bear's adoption of a largely plains Cree identity stem from his exposure to male teachers other than his father? Does this also apply to the socialization of his children, who assumed Cree identities even though their mother was Ojibwa? One wonders if Big Bear's three daughters saw themselves as Cree or Ojibwa.

One further complication in understanding the relationship among gender, ethnicity, and the process of cultural change lies in the fact that plains cultures may not have offered as many attractions to Ojibwa women as they did to Ojibwa men. Nor can we be certain that the changes involved in the emergence of the plains

Ojibwa were as positive or as meaningful for women as they were for men. Plains cultures were in many respects male-oriented ones. As bison hunting and horse raiding became new sources of wealth and status for men, plains Ojibwa women, like women in other plains societies, stood to lose control of the sources of wealth and prestige. Where before they themselves could trap and snare, and they could trade the products of their varied labour for trade goods, in the plains context they were increasingly limited to processing the fruit of men's labour, and since they did not participate in horse raids themselves they were forced to rely on the wealth of their male relatives. Furthermore, in bands that hunted bison from horseback (male hunters on male-owned horses) rather than by the communal pound method, women were excluded from the process of hunting. Though women were said to own the products of the hunt, the obligation on the part of the hunter to share with poorer members of the band and the right of soldier societies to destroy the tipis of men who committed offenses suggests that by not participating in the hunt, women "owned" the products of the hunt less fully even when these products were supposedly given to them. In bands that participated in the bison-robe trade, Ojibwa women may have become part of the plains wealth complex: not only did plains women process items that could be converted into wealth, but they themselves became objects of wealth, status symbols for their husbands. Certainly, women did not achieve the same prestige or social rewards as men did in plains Ojibwa society, nor were the same means to do so open to them. One of the most glorified institutions of plains cultures, the warrior society, described at length for the plains Ojibwa by Skinner and Howard, was not shared in any general way by plains Ojibwa women.[95]

Frustratingly, there is virtually no evidence at all on the changes that plains life brought to Ojibwa women's activities, roles, and powers. Following the lines of analysis developed for the Sioux, Blackfoot, Assiniboine, and plains Cree, however, we may speculate that the adoption of plains values, ceremonies, and other cultural components proceeded more quickly among Ojibwa men, and that this process may have had more profound, and negative, implications for some aspects of the lives of Ojibwa women. Since Ojibwa women's labour in processing furs and country produce had been crucial to the success of their people in the fur trade, the shift to an altered economy based on the bison hunt may not have involved important changes in social structure or economic roles. Plains Ojibwa women may have prepared more pemmican and bison hides than other western Ojibwa women, but the tasks of food and hide preparation and other duties were essentially the same. We do not know whether the incidence of polygamy and the average number of wives per household rose when the Ojibwa entered the fur trade or again when the plains Ojibwa began participating in the robe trade. Indeed, the degree to which the plains Ojibwa participated in the robe trade is uncertain. Still, the general trend among plains women during the nineteenth century was the loss of control over their own lives, increasing exclusion from sources and symbols of group prestige, and a much poorer return for their labour than when they were involved in a more broadly based subsistence-oriented economy. Where men obtained more efficient means of hunting bison (through the uses of the horse in hunting), women did not obtain or develop a correspondingly more efficient method of processing meat or hides.[96] Apart from the advantages that horses offered women in moving camp, the plains lifestyle had far less to offer women than it did men. All in all, Ojibwa women may have been less enthusiastic to adopt this new way of life than their male relatives.

In seeking to understand how the plains Ojibwa adapted to their newly chosen lifestyle, and what the ramifications of these changes were for men, women, and their accustomed roles and behaviour, it is clear that the entire process was far more complex than implied by Howard's statement, "by the 1830s the westernmost Ojibwa were fully adjusted to life on the Plains."[97] The process embodies the most extreme meaning of Fredrik Barth's statement about cultural variation within ethnic groups: "One ethnic group, spread over a territory with varying ecologic circumstances, will exhibit regional diversities of overt institutionalized behavior which do not reflect differences in cultural orientation."[98] While the plains Ojibwa were certainly still Ojibwa, by virtue of the continuity of cultural boundaries, ascription by other peoples, and self-ascription through cultural continuity, they had also begun to shift the very basis of their cultural orientation and identity. The next few decades, which contained events of moment for all plains tribes, would play a major role in the next steps of this fascinating dynamic between continuity and change.

PEGUIS AND THE RED RIVER OJIBWA

The Ojibwa of Red River faced a somewhat different set of challenges after 1821 than did bands farther from Selkirk's colony. As well as having to cope with the changes in the trade and with ecological fluctuations, the Red River Ojibwa were subjected to intense assimilationist pressures from Christian missionaries and colony officials based in Red River. These pressures were balanced by the attraction of the trade with the settlers, the opportunities offered by the missionaries for status and reciprocity, and the opportunity to participate in the bison hunts of their Métis kin.

In 1822, there were at least 180 adult male Ojibwa (representing a population of about 500 in all) trading at Fort Garry and the Netley Creek and Pembina outposts. These families were based in a wide arc ranging from the Turtle Mountain and Pembina Mountains to Peguis's encampment at Netley Creek and Black Robe's spring camp along the shore of Lake Manitoba.[99] In addition to these established groups, delegations of Ojibwa from Red Lake (Minnesota), Lake of the Woods, and Rainy Lake visited the settlement periodically to renew ties with their Native kin and with the colony administrators. Red River was also host to the annual payment of the quit rent to Ojibwa leaders who had signed the Selkirk Treaty.[100] Throughout the year, Ojibwa from the north and west also passed through the colony to trade their furs and country produce with the settlers. Red River was thus a centre for communication among Ojibwa in the entire Northwest and Boundary Waters region, and events there were a barometer of what was to come for more remote bands.

A first ugly storm arose there in August 1821, when a delegation of Sioux arrived at Fort Douglas to trade with the Hudson's Bay Company. The Sioux had been invited and encouraged to trade at the Forks by the Company, but Peguis's men, who had learned of the impending visit, felt rather differently about it. On their arrival at Fort Douglas, the Sioux were confronted by a force of more than fifty Ojibwa warriors. Dismayed colony officials found the two sides "drawn up in hostile array," and barely prevented a battle. The incident caused consternation among both the settlers and the Ojibwa. John Pritchard wrote that if any of the Highlanders had "found a conveyance out I believe very few would now be re-maining in the [Red] River." It was more ominous for the Ojibwa, however, who found that their loyalty and military assistance during the crises of 1813 to 1816 was being poorly repaid. Instead of offering military support in return to the Ojibwa as their allies, the colonists attempted to persuade officials to call out the resident Des Meurons troops to drive the Ojibwa away from Fort Douglas during the inci-dent.[101] This was certainly not the reciprocity that Peguis and his men would have expected. Ironically, it was largely because of this incident that Hudson's Bay Company trade with the Sioux was discontinued, a decision that was communi-cated by what must be two of the greatest understatements in fur-trade documen-tary literature. In early September 1821, barely a week after the confrontation at the Forks, Simpson advised: "I conceive it important that the Connexion with the Sieux should be broken off as early as possible . . . [as] they will be exceedingly troublesome and expensive." The London Committee replied the following year that they were also "disposed to think that it will not be found to be expedient to continue the trade into the Sioux country."[102]

The 1821 confrontation was part of a pattern of disturbing events in relations between Ojibwa, settlers, and Hudson's Bay Company at Red River. Although the Company backed down on its initial decision to trade with the Dakota, its decision to open trade with them at all was a signal to the Ojibwa of Red River that the Hudson's Bay Company was not the ally they had hoped for and expected. The non-Natives they dealt with were probably never fully aware of Ojibwa perceptions and expectations of their relationship. The illusion of an alliance was sustained by European behaviour only as long as it benefitted the Europeans to cooperate with the Ojibwa. After the colony was placed on a solid footing, the officials, settlers, and Company employees pursued their own interests, to the detriment of the Ojibwa. Rather than being an about-face, European behaviour at Red River towards the Ojibwa after 1817 merely acknowledged the realities of their relationship.

Political and economic ties between the Ojibwa and European groups were further strained after 1821 by changes in the nature of social relations between races. At the same time as these other links were deteriorating, the kinship metaphor ceased to function as an effective bond between Native and non-Native people in Red River. At about the same time as the incident with the Dakota, Peguis expressed the hope that his daughter would marry the son of James Bird, Chief Trader at Fort Douglas.[103] This was an attempt to use the longstanding and honoured custom of marriage to create social links between Natives and non-Natives in the fur trade. Unfortunately for the Red River Ojibwa, the fur-trade society in which this custom had functioned was virtually gone. The appointment of men like Simpson, who neither knew of nor cared about the values and customs of fur-trade society and Native-trader relations, coincided with the merger and the new company's focus on economy and efficiency and with the introduction of Victorian ideas about race and social class to Red River. Missionaries reinforced these prejudices as they strove to "civilize" Natives and Métis by persuading them to adopt Christianity, sedentary agriculture, and other hallmarks of Victorian society.[104] It was the advent of a world in which the Ojibwa and other Native peoples were unimportant, unappreciated, and essentially unwanted. On his son's behalf, Trader Bird refused Peguis's offer of his daughter's hand. All ties between them, it seemed, were being broken.

Having won the battle over trade with the Dakota, Ojibwa around Red River began to fight another over the post-merger credit terms implemented at Fort Garry. While credits had been reduced across the Northern Department, the Fort Garry traders adopted an especially miserly policy and, in their journals, claimed to be strict about debts.[105] This was greatly annoying to the Ojibwa but was made worse by the fact that because the settlers were given first chance at the goods when they arrived in the fall, the shop was often sold out of desirable items (such as clothing and blankets) before the Indians could trade what they needed. For Ojibwa living around Red River, where large game – and therefore leather for clothing – was in short supply, the new policies posed a significant problem. The Ojibwa made their opinions of the situation perfectly clear: "They say matters are come to a strange pass, indeed, when with furs in hand and clear of debts, they cannot obtain their necessaries. The consequence of this . . . is that many packs of rats have already gone the way of the Americans."[106]

Ojibwa and Cree from the lower Red River and Assiniboine River area travelled regularly to American posts at Pembina and the Missouri River, a continuation of their earlier trips to this area to trade for horses. Besides this "Roguery in trading their debts" to the Americans, the Ojibwa also maintained a busy trade with the Red River settlers.[107] Simpson's policy of selling goods to the settlers cheaply, encouraging trade between settlers and Native people to discourage Indian trade with the Americans, was quite successful.[108] Indians were given the first chance at the new goods at the Fort Garry shop beginning in the autumn of 1828,[109] but by then the years of poor treatment at the colony fort and the stresses caused by the difficult years between 1825 and 1827 had caused significant changes in the relationship between the Company and colony, and the Ojibwa. Peguis maintained an official relationship with officials in the colony, but he and his band were made less and less welcome in Red River as the decade progressed, and they consequently spent little time there.

The cool welcome they generally received in the colony became even frostier when in 1822 Peguis led a group of Ojibwa to Fort Douglas to complain that they had not received sufficient compensation for the lands ceded in the Selkirk Treaty. In his written report of the interview, Andrew Bulger, Governor of Assiniboia, confirmed the change in the relationship between the colony and the Ojibwa in his comment, "Their mouths may . . . be stopped by the presence of a Company of Soldiers."[110] It was not the last time Peguis would express dissatisfaction with the compensation his people received for the use of the lands in Red River. Throughout the 1830s, Peguis repeatedly raised this issue, more often and more bitterly as Red River grew, and increased demands were made on surrounding lands. In 1832, Peguis was offered a keg of rum and three blankets for Sugar Point, the riverside land he had requested after the signing of the Selkirk Treaty, and that had subsequently become a source of valuable timber for the settlement. Despite further pressure to sell the point in the early 1830s, he managed to retain it.[111] Still, Peguis justifiably complained in 1830 about "the many infringements the whites had made upon his privileges, as a native of the soil; The infamous manner they had failed in nearly all their promises made to him; and their ingratitude and inattention to all the favors and protection granted them when they were too feeble to help themselves."[112]

These changes in the fur trade and Native-White relations did not alter the Red River Ojibwas' way of life. Nor did they become more "industrious" or produce more furs because of the changes, although this was the intended effect. When the new trading goods arrived at Fort Douglas in the fall, members of Peguis's band would trade a few furs for supplies, receive their annual treaty present of

3. Peter Rindisbacher, "Winter fishing on the ice of the Assynoibain and Red River. Drawn from nature in December 1821, Manitoba" (courtesy National Archives of Canada / C-001932). Note the winter clothing, bows and arrows, and interaction between settlers and Native people.

tobacco, and then go to fish and hunt muskrats near Netley Creek where they spent much of the winter.[113] Essential supplies of fish, waterfowl, sugar, plant foods, muskrats and other small game remained steady around Netley Creek after 1821, though hunters were forced to go far afield, sometimes unsuccessfully, in search of moose, deer, and bison. Winter was often a lean and sometimes a precarious season, depending on weather conditions, but the continued presence of bison in the Red River valley in winter provided economic support. The Ojibwa hunted bison on the margin of the plains in early winter, but many Ojibwa left the hunt and returned to the settlement "to share in the good things of this life, during the Holidays." On New Year's Day, Peguis and others were ceremonially welcomed at the fort, and were each given some tobacco and a dram.[114] Peter Rindisbacher's painting, "Winter Fishing on the ice of the Assynoibain and Red River," drawn in December 1821, shows Indians, Métis, and settlers alike fishing with nets and spears through the ice at the Forks during this mid-winter gathering (see Illustration 3).

The band returned to the plains and hunted bison after Christmas until mid-March or early April. Rindisbacher sketched one Ojibwa man in mid-winter, holding his bow and arrows, wearing a tailored shirt or coat, probably of leather, with

4. Peter Rindisbacher, "A savage of the Sautaux Indians on the Red River. Drawn to a twelfth part of his natural size. P.R., Manitoba, ca. 1822" (courtesy National Archives of Canada / C-001935).

blue wool leggings decorated and gartered with red, a trade blanket, moccasins, a peaked cloth hood, and trade silver brooches; he appears very well dressed (see Illustration 4).

When the snow began to melt, the Ojibwa visited the fort and received "a small present of Tobacco, ammunition, and provisions" as well as some liquor. They then set off to make maple sugar and held a spring muskrat hunt around Netley Creek. Since the lower Red River district was "exhausted . . . in animals of the fur kind," muskrats and country produce were the staple items of trade for Peguis's band. Spring ceremonies were held after these activities, and trading continued until late May, when some men left on war parties against the Sioux.[115] Although war parties left Red River virtually every summer during the 1820s (including 1823, 1824, 1825-26, 1828, 1829), some turned back from their goal, and most war parties seem to have been for the purpose of retaliating against attacks made on Ojibwa on the upper Red River, rather than as a defense against a local threat or as an attempt to gain access to resources. Other conflicts involved freemen and Métis, often in the region south of the Forks to Pembina, suggesting that the summer bison hunts were encroaching on Sioux territory.[116]

5. Peter Rindisbacher, "A family from the tribe of the wild Sautaux Indians on the Red River, Manitoba, ca. 1821" (courtesy National Archives of Canada / C-001929). Note the variety of jewellery worn by this family; the strap dress with separate sleeves worn by the woman at right; the bows and arrows; and the different housing styles.

Those who remained at home during the summer planted fields of maize and fished about the mouth of the Red River. They also lived well for several weeks on large numbers of wildfowl and their eggs, which were to be found in the marshes. Many of the early missionaries found that their arguments about the virtues of farming fell on deaf ears during the summer, "when the Indians are roaming from lake to lake, and meeting with provisions every where."[117] Rindisbacher's painting of a Red River Ojibwa family in summer shows an adult man, his face painted, wearing a bear-claw collar and pendant, and an extended family of two women, another adult man, younger than the first, three toddlers, and four older children. They are cooking a fish and a bird over their fire, and wear stroud clothing and some beaded and silver ornaments (see Illustration 5) .

These families visited the post occasionally "to beg a pipe of tobacco," but brought nothing to trade until late August.[118] As well as visiting the post, they socialized with eastern kin and with other Ojibwa who came to Red River to trade with settlers or negotiate with officials. Summer ended with the harvesting and caching of crops and the arrival of the boats from York Factory with fresh trading goods.

This satisfying round of activities produced a life of confidence and plenty for the Red River Ojibwa. In 1822, the Lower Red River District Report commented on "the want of Industry in the Natives, who, during the Winter instead of employing themselves collecting the few Furs which are to be procured, resort to the Plains, to live on Buffaloes, or linger away their time about the Settlers' Houses or in the neighborhood of the Fort." The passage concludes by saying that these Indians lived on "the precarious charity of those who throw them the refuse of the fish they catch," a claim that is inconsistent with the picture of leisure and resource choices implied earlier in the same passage.[119] Other remarks about the productivity of the fisheries in Red River, the abundance of muskrats, and the Ojibwas' generally amused responses to the missionaries' suggestions that they adopt sedentary agriculture, all sharpen the image of plenty for the Red River Ojibwa in the early 1820s.

This situation quickly changed from relative feast to absolute famine in the mid-1820s. Between 1824 and 1827, settler, trader, and Ojibwa alike were buffeted by a series of ecological disasters that made life extremely difficult for everyone in the Red River area. The bison remained far out on the plains to the west of the river during the winter of 1824-25, causing food shortages; the summer of 1825 was very poor for crops, and the plains west and south of Red River burnt to a great extent, which kept the bison far away the following winter. Many of Peguis's band were forced to beg in the settlement during the winter of 1825-26 but were largely unsuccessful since the settlers were no better off than the Indians. When spring came, the Red River flooded to record levels, forcing Natives and settlers to abandon their homes and property and take refuge along the Assiniboine River; this delayed planting, and crops were further damaged by frost later in the season.[120] Things began to improve by the spring of 1827, but then whooping cough broke out in the settlement. It was not a major epidemic, and mortality among the Ojibwa was limited in comparison to that among the Cree and Assiniboine, but the deaths that occurred must have been keenly felt after the problems of the previous two years.[121] Throughout these difficulties, the Ojibwa also had to deal with assimilationist pressures from Anglican missionaries, who wished them to convert to Christianity and adopt a way of life based on sedentary agriculture.

The Ojibwa survived these crises by maintaining their economic diversity and by making use of every ecological, spiritual, and human resource available to them. Under these pressures, some Red River Ojibwa looked hopefully at the newly arrived Anglican missionaries as a potential source of aid, just as they had hopefully greeted the arrival of the settlers a decade before. The missionaries' Christian charity quickly became a slender but important new resource for the Ojibwa to harvest, and the missionaries' status in the settlement prompted Peguis to maintain close relations with them. The Ojibwa – especially Peguis – may have hoped that the missionaries would replace the Hudson's Bay Company as allies during these troubled times. Unfortunately for the Ojibwas' hopes, the missionaries had their own agenda. Far from agreeing to participate in Ojibwa reciprocity, the Anglicans wanted the Ojibwa to abandon their culture and adopt British Protestant religion and culture.[122] The Ojibwa quickly learned that, while they might ask for certain things from the missionaries, they themselves would be asked to give a good deal more in return. As an intermediary between the Ojibwa and the missionaries, Peguis had good need of his talents as a shrewd leader.

After the Catholics, who at first had relatively little contact with the Ojibwa, the first Protestant missionary to come to Red River was Reverend John West of the Church Missionary Society, who arrived in the settlement in 1821. He and his successors David Jones and William Cockran (sometimes spelled Cochrane[123]) attempted to persuade Peguis's band to adopt Christianity and the lifestyle and values that accompanied it. Chief among the "civilizing" changes they hoped to accomplish was the elimination of polygamy and Native ceremonies and the adoption of sedentary agriculture. In the missionaries' words, "if we cannot make them industrious, they will never be pious."[124] Peguis, in turn, saw in the missionaries an opportunity to regain the recognition and support that his people had lost with the Hudson's Bay Company. Given the difficulties with which they had to cope in the 1820s, the Red River Ojibwa were eager to take advantage of all the missionaries had to offer.

In most cases, what the missionaries offered consisted of small amounts of food they were able to give from their own scanty provisions and the basic supplies they gave the school children. In one instance, Peguis's sister asked Reverend West to accept her son into the missionary's school for Indian children. Pleased at the opportunity to instruct the child, West took the boy but was upset the following week when the child's mother came to take the child back, saying "that they had parted from him in consequence of their not being able to obtain any provisions."[125] The family was affronted when West insisted that the child return the clothes he had been given and even threatened West with "bad medicine for those who displeased them": apparently, the family was hoping for a winter outfit for the boy. The Ojibwa also used the missionaries' houses as relief stations when they were ill or hungry.[126]

Peguis himself was a crucial figure in the course of Ojibwa-missionary interaction at Red River. Ever mindful of his own status, he kept the missionaries at arm's length partly out of concern that they might diminish or usurp his influence over his band. At one point he decided to have his house built near that of Reverend Cockran's servant so that Cockran's servant could take care of it when Peguis was away hunting. Cockran felt that one of the main reasons he had difficulty convincing the chief of the merits of the Church's settlement scheme was that the missionary's "arguments did not weigh so heavy in [Peguis'] mind as his own objectives."[127] This was made quite clear in an 1828 exchange: "I asked him [Peguis] when he intended to begin to cultivate the ground? He answered, not till he had visited England, as he was going in company with the Great Governor next Spring, and when he returned, he might perhaps begin. . . . At present he had come to pay me a visit of ceremony, and he hoped that I would treat him in a generous manner."[128] This conversation is particularly meaningful in light of an 1818 comment by a colony official to Selkirk to the effect that Peguis was already, in that year, "determined to establish his garden and village; . . . [he] finds it beautiful and has applied for the seeds of Bread and Potatoes for next spring, which of course I promised him."[129] That he was "determined" in 1818 "to establish his garden and village," but was equally determined not to for Cockran a decade later, suggests that in each conversation he was pursuing his own and his band's interests, and that he was presenting a different and deliberately chosen image of himself in each case.

What was particularly galling to the missionaries about not just Peguis, but also all of the Ojibwa with whom they interacted, was that the Native people dealt with them as equals, one nation to another. The missionaries, on the other hand, thought of the "savages" as inferior beings. Jones, Cockran, and Smithurst were therefore nonplussed to find that their patterns of interaction with the Ojibwa did not proceed according to their expectations, and that the Ojibwa were essentially uninterested in the missionaries' teachings and exhortations. "The Savage . . . sits down at your feet," summarized Cockran, "but it is not that he may hear your instructions, but that you may hear him."[130]

These patterns of interaction reveal a relationship between the Ojibwa and the clergy that involved far more than simple manipulation. Communication within this relationship was always obscured by cross-cultural "static." Each side, quite understandably, interpreted the other from within its own cultural framework, and there was an astounding lack of "fit" between the two cultural systems. The Ojibwa, for instance, likened the missionaries to their own religous specialists – shamans – and expected them to perform the same functions, including curing and the use of spiritual power to lend physical protection to vulnerable humans. They were thus disillusioned by the deaths of children sent to an early missionary school in Red River. The missionary was told that the Natives "think it is of no use to send you their children as you can no more keep them from dying than they can themselves."[131] They also expected the same sharing and reciprocity of these newcomers as they did of fur traders and other potential allies, and were not reticent about asking for food and other necessities.

The missionaries, for their part, interpreted these requests from their own cultural perspective: as begging, with all the negative connotations this implied. Similarly, they failed to understand the functional qualities of reciprocity or, indeed, of the Ojibwas' widely based annual round of hunting, gathering, and fishing, or of the values of a society based on the extended family. Believing that "the advantages of civilization are so great and self-evident," it is hardly surprising to find William Cockran also expressing the sentiment that "it was more honorable for a man to supply his own wants, than to live by begging."[132]

Given such a wide gulf between Ojibwa and missionary, relations between them were predictable. The missionaries persevered, using every opportunity to teach, lecture, and challenge; the Ojibwa refused to change. And if Peguis's band did not want to give up its familiar way of life, the missionaries, on their part, were hard pressed to demonstrate the advantages of Christianity and sedentary agriculture to the Indians. The settlement was a poor advertisement for Christianity. Its members ranged in their religious beliefs from rigid Scots Presbyterian to Métis who were nominally Catholic but who frequently held syncretic Native-Christian beliefs and participated in Native ceremonies. On one occasion when John West tried to convince Peguis to give up polygamy, Peguis retorted that "there was no more harm in Indians having two wives than one of the settlers," who also did.[133]

As to the values of Christian civilization and settled farming, the colonists' crops of wheat and barley failed with predictable regularity due to frost, drought, and grasshoppers, leaving the Europeans largely dependent on the Indians and Métis for food, while the Ojibwa were able to harvest their potato patches and corn fields and maintain a productive fishery during most of the difficult years.[134] Given the backbreaking labour required to break sod, plant, and hoe with hand tools and the poor results usually obtained from the settlers' gardens, it is little wonder that the Ojibwa found their guns lighter than hoes. Nor did agriculture have the same enjoyable associations for Ojibwa men as hunting and fishing, as Peguis made clear when he came upon Cockran spreading manure in a field in 1828. Cockran told him that it was by doing this that the Europeans had their wealth. In reply, Peguis "looked at [Cockran] with a satirical smile, and pointed to the plains and river," to indicate his own, less odoriferous, source of wealth.[135]

Ojibwa aversion to adopting sedentary agriculture was probably also fostered in part by their reaction to the success of a number of northern, or Swampy, Cree who moved into the area of the colony from the northern Interlake during the 1820s.[136] The "Swampies, as they were known, were attracted by the economic opportunities offered by the colony. Eager to make better lives for themselves, these individuals adopted Christianity, took advantage of the missionaries' offers of material assistance, and commenced farming just north of the Red River settlement, where Cockran had hoped to settle the Ojibwa. Peguis and his people became jealous of the Swampies' success in farming, of the esteem in which they

were held by Whites as a result of their "exemplary" conduct, and by the assistance given the Swampies by their Métis relatives. When urged to imitate the
Swampies' success, the Ojibwa told Cockran that it was only the Swampies who
were able to benefit from the adoption of sedentary agriculture and Christianity:
"It would be contrary with us were we to adapt [sic] the same customs," Peguis
said in the fall of 1830.[137]

In keeping with the tradition of the Ojibwa as being people very much concerned with magic, members of Peguis's band responded to the stresses in their
relationship with the Swampies by attributing Cree success to supernatural power.
This may explain Cockran's comment that "the Crees are considered the greatest
conjurors: the Seaultaux or Chippewas imagine that the Crees can conjure a man
to death at a very great distance, consequently they are unwilling to come into
close contact with them." Stricken by a run of personal bad luck, one Ojibwa
concluded that the Swampies were conjuring him. Acting on his behalf, Peguis
decided to shoot the Swampies. He was dissuaded, with difficulty, by Cockran.
Reverend David Jones, on the other hand, wrote that the Swampies were "too
much afraid of the Saulteaux to amalgamate" with them.[138] The magical rivalries
between the two groups were an indication both of the stress that they were under
to maintain their economic and social niches in their relationship with Europeans
at Red River and of the continuation of traditional means of dealing with such
stress.

Despite such pressures, and despite the severe weather and subsistence strains
that might have induced them to agree to the missionaries' proposals, the Red
River Ojibwa maintained their way of life during the 1820s. During the harsh
winter of 1825-26, when some Indians were forced to beg for food in the settlement, Reverend David Jones remarked that the people of Peguis's band were "very
proud and haughty, but I see with pleasure that they are become much more friendly
of late."[139] Even in the most difficult years, though, the Ojibwas' friendliness –
whether genuine or born of hunger – did not lead to missionary successes. Their
resistance became even more defined after 1829, when Reverend Cockran received
permission from George Simpson to begin an experimental farm for the purpose
of settling, civilizing, and converting the Indians around the colony.

Ironically, as noted earlier, Peguis's band had raised substantial quantities of
corn and potatoes since 1805 as conditions permitted. It was not simply the growing of crops that the missionaries wished so fervently to teach the Ojibwa. What
they also wanted the Native people to learn was the growing of European crops
(especially wheat), planting in the straight furrows used by European farmers,
being "industrious," obeying the Biblical injunction to live by the sweat of one's
brow, and the whole complex of work ethic, nuclear family, and European gender
roles (men, not women, were to be the farmers) that was embodied in the concept

of the experimental farm. Not only did the missionaries feel that "civilization," in the form of sedentary agriculture, was necessary for true conversion, but by the late 1820s they also hoped it might be the means to effect any conversion at all. In the annual reports sent to the Church Missionary Society in London in 1828 and 1829, Jones and Cockran both admitted: "We have not yet made a single step towards the civilization and evangelization of the pure adult Indians. There seems to be an insurmountable barrier between us and them."[140] In the mounting fervour of the missionaries' efforts to break down this barrier, and the resultant frustration when they did not, Cockran and his colleagues succeeded only in provoking more widespread and more serious resistance from the Ojibwa.

For some years, when he was pressured by the clergymen to adopt European habits and Christianity, Peguis often stalled for time by saying that he was unable to find his councillors to discuss a matter with them, or that he was too much in debt to the Hudson's Bay Company to stop trapping and begin sedentary cultivation.[141] After plans for the settlement became a reality, Ojibwa reasons for refusing the missionaries escalated. Having told him for years that they would not convert, in the fall of 1830 the Ojibwa told Cockran that they could not abandon their traditions. "If they were to accommodate themselves to the customs of the Whites; embrace their religion, and lay aside their medicines, dreams & Conjurors," Cockran reported them as saying "they would soon all die." In a similar exchange between Peguis and Cockran, Peguis stated that "it was not likely that any thing he sowed would prosper, for all his ancestors had lived by hunting, and when he ceased from following them he could not expect to prosper."[142] Indeed, during the unfavourable weather of 1831, the Ojibwa became convinced that the climatic (and their own) problems were caused by the "Troublers of the ground" being near their camp.[143]

As his frustration at the Ojibwas' resistance mounted, Cockran's persuasions became as intense as the Indians' own rationales. Fostered largely by the missionaries' claims that the Christian God was more powerful than their own supernatural beings, and by pressures to abandon their traditional religion, a kind of shamanic rivalry developed between Cockran and members of Peguis's band in the early 1830s. Cockran argued that the Master of Life had deliberately taken the animals from the Ojibwa to get the Ojibwa to assimilate and convert, and taunted a "conjuror" (actually a medicine man or Midewiwin leader) who had asked him for food, saying: "Call upon your gods for assistance, . . . call upon them to fill your kettle with fishes. . . . We cultivate the ground in the proper season, according to the Master of Life. . . . We are growing rich and fat in the land which your gods cannot preserve you in life."[144]

In fact, the Ojibwa had already called on their gods. In the spring of 1831, the traditional religious leaders of Peguis's band held a ceremony and feast "for the purpose of ascertaining whether the change to agriculture . . . would be beneficial or otherwise."[145] The answer they received is not known, but the Ojibwas' continued reluctance to agree to Cockran's plans may echo the advice the spirits gave them during the ceremony. The resistance was not limited to threatened Midewiwin practitioners and shamans who stood to lose their status to Christian missionaries; it was widespread, including the young men as well as the social and religious leaders. About the time of the feast in 1831, the young men of the band refused to fetch seed intended for themselves from the settlement when asked by Cockran and Peguis.[146] The following spring, similar unrest combined with the effects of Catholic-Protestant rivalry led to an eight-day "conjuring" session in which the Ojibwa again sought guidance from the supernaturals. Again, group feeling was anti-missionary. Cockran wrote, "During this period they threw the hoes out of their tents, and threatened to throw us in the river."[147]

Within a few years the feud progressed from the theological to the personal level. Cockran informed one of the "conjurors" in December 1835 that "the man's spiritual Master . . . is afraid lest you should hear any of the word of God, he knows that it is more powerful than any of the chains by which he has you."[148] By boasting that his source of spiritual power was stronger than the shaman's, and by denigrating the shaman's power, Cockran was essentially (though perhaps unknowingly) challenging him to a shamanic duel. This man clearly saw Cockran as a professional rival and did his best to limit the missionary's influence among his people. The shaman informed the young men of the band in the spring of 1833 that unless they went to war the Master of Life would punish them for deserting the old ways. Peguis obviously felt caught in the middle of this rivalry: if he did not support the shaman he risked losing the support of his band; if he supported the shaman, he risked losing the status he had acquired in the eyes of the missionaries. His diplomatic reply to the young men was to ask if going to war would keep them warm in the winter, and to say that the only war he was going to wage was with his potatoes and wheat.[149] Needless to say, such rivalries greatly complicated relations among Ojibwa factions and between the Ojibwa and the missionaries.

Though they would have liked to ignore Cockran for spiritual reasons, the Red River Ojibwa may finally have been forced to pay some heed to him for temporal reasons. Large game was scarce around Red River, and subsistence could be precarious in winter if the bison hunt failed or if the winter were severe, as in the mid-1820s and the winters of 1830-31 and 1831-32. For these reasons, Peguis exhorted his people in the spring of 1832 to accept the missionaries' proposals to settle the Ojibwa. "The animals of the chase have failed," he said. "We must look to the produce of the ground for a subsistence, the same as the Colonists. By it we have lived the last two winters, if we had not received a little from one and from another, we would have starved."[150] Even these pressures were insufficient to convince the Ojibwa. In 1833, three Native families settled on the site chosen by Cockran for the Indian settlement, but there is no record that they were Ojibwa; they may have been Swampies, settling down near their kin. Peguis himself began breaking ground and sowing crops in 1833 but did not live in the Indian settlement year-round for some time. Missionaries continued to lament that, just at seeding time, warm weather and the ready availability of fish made the Ojibwa forget their promises of settling that they made during the lean winter months.

What Peguis had done was to make a minor concession – a public commitment to agricultural settlement for himself, and public exhortations to the rest of his band to follow his example – in order to further his own goal of forming a personal alliance with the missionaries and thus creating a source of European material aid for his people. These actions were interpreted by the missionaries as important steps in the accomplishment of their own goals, the conversion and civilization of the Ojibwa. In his gratitude for Peguis's efforts, Cockran praised Peguis in terms that sounded very much like those that might have been used by the Ojibwa themselves to describe an ally. In 1832, Cockran said of Peguis, "The old Chief has been exceedingly faithful to his promise, stuck close to us, supported us in all difficulties, labored hard with us, is gradually throwing off the distant reserve, and treating us as confidents."[151] Peguis's efforts, it would seem, had been successful, but since it quickly became evident that more significant actions were not forthcoming on the part of the Ojibwa, the missionaries themselves soon began to question the validity of this new alliance.

In 1834, only two years after praising Peguis's labours and support, Cockran wrote in frustration to the Canadian Missionary Society, "The Saulteaux have been so inimical to the Gospel, that they have no claim upon our assistance. . . . This spring when they ought to have been sowing their farms, they were conjuring, and . . . unanimously agreed that they would never forsake the custom of their ancestors."[152] Apart from Peguis's personal relationship with them, the would-be alliance with the missionaries was crumbling almost before it was completed. By the late 1830s, the Ojibwa had acquired a reputation for "obstinacy" and "prejudice against Christianity" because of their decision to continue their own way of life as much as possible. This decision was especially clear in their lack of participation in missionary schools. By the early 1840s, the Ojibwa school at Netley Creek had only fifteen to seventeen students, while the Cook's Creek school, started for the Swampy Cree about the same time as the Ojibwa school, had as many as ninety pupils. As they realized that the Ojibwas' "prejudice against Xtianity [was] greater than the Crees," the missionaries began concentrating their efforts on the Cree.[153] Peguis's band continued to hold traditional ceremonies long after Peguis promised to accept the missionaries' plans. As late as the 1860s, annual feasts and ceremonies were held at Lower Fort Garry by the members of Peguis's and surrounding bands. These traditional Ojibwa maintained not only a reputation for "heathenism" but also a strong group identity and cohesion.[154]

In a development about the same time that must have greatly frustrated the Protestant missionaries, Father George Belcourt established a Catholic Ojibwa settlement at Baie St. Paul on the Assiniboine in 1833-34. Father Belcourt's efforts at Baie St. Paul (also known as Baie des Sauteux), seem to have initially been somewhat more successful than Cockran's at Red River. Ojibwa there were apparently persuaded to cultivate crops and build cabins, although they continued to hunt bison. Because the Ojibwa felt that the location of the mission was too exposed to the Sioux, the village was moved after just a year and re-established some eighteen miles west of St. Francois Xavier. There the physical development of the mission continued; the Ojibwa built ten new log cabins in 1835-36, and thirty families planted crops in the spring of 1835. As at the Protestant mission, though, religious progress was much slower. Although Belcourt claimed in 1835 to have 150 catechumens and to have baptized seventy-two children and adults and married eight couples, he also noted that the Ojibwa resisted becoming catechumens because they feared that they would no longer be able to pray "to their *manitou* or author of life for help for the sick." Other problems arose when Belcourt persuaded them to give up all but one wife before baptism: rather than keeping the first (and, in Christian eyes, legitimate) wife, some men wished to keep the youngest. The mission school was likewise as sparsely attended as the Protestant one, but, because a Métis woman, Angelique Nolin, who may have been bilingual, was the teacher, it is likely that some of the religious and literacy lessons were fully assimilated by the Ojibwa students. Although it was a promising beginning, Belcourt's efforts were not satisfactory to his supervisors, and the village was abandoned in 1847 when Belcourt left the area.[155]

The adaptations made by Peguis, Tolibee, and the "plains Ojibwa" were all variations of a common cultural heritage. These adaptations enabled them, as Robert Kennedy wrote in exasperation, "to take advantage of the times": to exploit the opportunities offered by the particular ecological, social and political situations in which they found themselves and to maintain as much autonomy vis-à-vis the fur trade and European newcomers as they possibly could. This ability to exploit and to adapt made the Ojibwa a match for even the determined and ruthlessly efficient George Simpson. After nearly a decade of monopoly control, even Simpson proved unable to make these people truly "feel their dependence upon" the Hudson's Bay Company.[156]

The changes faced by the Ojibwa between 1821 and 1837 were the result of human as well as natural forces: changes in fur-trade company structures and policies; the decline of fur- and game-animal populations; the rise of competition for remaining resources; the effects of missionary pressure and racism. The Ojibwa, of course, may not have attributed these causes to the challenges they faced, but may have posited spiritual reasons instead of or as well as these others. Certainly their spirituality was a central and crucial part of their response to these changes. So was the influence of particular individuals. Tolibee, Baptiste Desjarlais, Wisiniw, Black Powder, and Peguis were respected, capable leaders whose personalities and social status, and acceptance or rejection of new ideas and behaviours, certainly influenced the process of change in their larger kin groups.

Given the nature of leadership in Native societies, of course, the process also worked the other way: since most members of a band had some input into decisions affecting the group, the actions of leaders often expressed the thoughts of their "followers." Women, though they emerge less often in the non-Native records as leaders, also played an important role in accepting, rejecting, and initiating new ideas and behaviour. Their decisions about how to switch between resources to cope with short-term changes, their relations with non-Ojibwa marriage partners, their role in socializing children within mixed-group camps, their acceptance or rejection of new decorative techniques and means of clothing construction all affected Ojibwa responses to change. And it was the interplay among all of these factors – Native and non-Native, natural and supernatural, human and nonhuman, the influences of leaders and the desires of followers, the similar and different needs of men and women – that formed the very basis of the development of Ojibwa strategies for coping with change.

"Saucy & Independent," 1837 to 1857

5

For the Ojibwa, the two decades between 1837 and 1857 were bounded by a major smallpox epidemic at one end and the Hind and Palliser expeditions – the beginnings of organized exploration that would lead to large-scale White settlement of the West – at the other. Between these momentous events were relatively quiet years, a period marked by the resurgence of fur- and game-animal populations in some areas. There were disquieting elements to this era, notably the effects of missionization as it spread into the Interlake and the parkland to the west of it, the shrinking of the great bison herds, and the beginning of the buffalo wars as the plains tribes fought for access to the remaining animals. But, in general, for the Ojibwa as for all the Native peoples of the West, the 1840s and 1850s were the oppressive calm before the storm of White settlement, the demise of the bison, and the beginning of the reserve era.

These peaceful decades began with calamity. In early autumn of 1837, disturbing reports of an unidentified sickness at the American trading posts on the Missouri River began to filter north. The gates of Fort Union had been shut, it was said, and no Indian was allowed to enter them. Fearing the worst, trader William Todd of Fort Pelly immediately began to vaccinate Indians with cowpox vaccine and explained the mechanics and danger of contagion. His diagnosis of smallpox was not confirmed until mid-winter, but as early as November the plains tribes had fled north and scattered in a desperate attempt to avoid the epidemic. Indians in the areas of Shoal River, Swan Lake, Carlton, Île-à-la-Crosse, and some at Edmonton were vaccinated through Todd's effort; he even sent vaccine into the plains with several bands.

When the epidemic abated the following spring, as many as two-thirds of the Assiniboine and Blackfoot, who stayed too far south to receive the vaccine, as well as many Cree and Ojibwa who either did not receive the vaccine or were given faulty vaccine, were dead. Thanks to William Todd's vaccination campaign, "many of the Plains Cree and nearly all of the Parkland and Woodland Indians living in south central Manitoba, Saskatchewan, and Alberta were saved."[1] Most of the Ojibwa were among the survivors. Tian, one of the "principal Souteaux" of Fort Pelly, spent the summer of 1837 in the plains without hearing anything of the epidemic; he brought some 2,000 pounds of dried meat with him to the post that autumn, was vaccinated, and left again. Black Powder's band was less fortunate than Tian's. His people were hit by smallpox, and his son Big Bear bore the scars for the rest of his life.[2]

In just a few short months, smallpox had once again changed the human face of the West and altered the established inter-tribal relationships on the plains. The epidemic was the end of an era that had begun with the epidemic of 1781-82, just as those years had been the end of an earlier cycle of history. The Cree emerged from the epidemic a larger and more powerful people than the Assiniboine or the Blackfoot, among whom mortality was much higher.[3]

For the western Ojibwa, the epidemic had two effects. Firstly, it encouraged the ongoing process of the formation of multi-ethnic bands among the Cree, Assiniboine, and Ojibwa.[4] In this way, decimated bands could maintain the numbers needed for labour (especially tasks such as bison hunting, which required a large group) and for defense, while providing grieving survivors with a new kinship and support network. Secondly, since mortality among the Blackfoot had been higher than among the Cree, the Cree felt safe to venture farther out onto the plains in pursuit of bison without fear of Blackfoot attacks. The same was true for the multi-ethnic bands. This re-opened the path to the plains that had earlier been created by the truce between most of the Cree and Blackfoot in the late 1820s but blocked soon after by renewed hostilities arising from harsh winters in the early 1830s, which had forced the Cree deep into Blackfoot territory after bison.[5] For the plains Ojibwa and the mixed groups in which they generally lived, the path to the plains was once again clear.

The renewed safety of the plains led to a westward shift for the Cree and plains Ojibwa. By the late 1850s, one explorer noted, "The Ojibways of Lake Winnipeg may now be discovered, summer and winter, near the Grand Forks of the Saskatchewan, . . . where they have permanently established themselves."[6]

As territorial boundaries shifted after the epidemic, Forts Pelly and Ellice, which once catered largely to the Cree, gained numbers of Ojibwa and mixed-group bands, while Fort Pitt changed from a Blackfoot to a Cree and plains Ojibwa post.[7] The Touchwood Hills, the Fishing Lakes and other sheltered spots in the Qu'Appelle River valley, and Turtle Mountain were also popular as protected bases close to the bison herds for bison-oriented Ojibwa bands.[8]

The annual cycle of these bands incorporated activities and camp sites famil-

6. Isobel Finlayson, 1840-1843, "Souteaux family in the plains" (courtesy Hudson's Bay Company Archives, Provincial Archives of Manitoba, no. E.12/5/ fo. 73).

iar to the plains Cree as well as to the Ojibwa and transitional Cree members. After the ice broke in the rivers, the people fished and harvested maple sugar during the spring runs and then left their winter camps and began hunting for bison. As the weather warmed, they continued to hunt bison and moved onto the plains, toward the site of the Sun Dance encampment. Their movements at this time might have taken them into the plains west of the Assiniboine and Souris rivers, and along the South Saskatchewan River; the Fort Pelly journal records "a camp of two hundred tents Crees [and] Saulteaux in the middle of the bison" four days from the Touchwood Hills in July 1856. Isobel Finlayson's sketch, "A Souteaux Family in the plains," drawn between 1840 and 1843, shows one such family with a tipi and bison robes (Illustration 6).[9]

After the great gathering for the Sun Dance, some men went on raiding parties, while a few might have gone to trading posts. Depending on how far south they already were, they might well have travelled to the Missouri River to trade with the Americans.

Most of the people began concerted bison hunts in late summer, and the women harvested quantities of roots and berries to dry and store for winter. Hunting peaked in early fall, when many bison, elk, and deer were killed for winter use. Once this supply of food was secure, the people moved north to make their fall visit to the trading post, exchanging pemmican and robes for their goods.[10] After trading, some bands made a last intensive bison hunt on the prairies or at the edge of the parkland and then moved into sheltered areas to winter as the snow began to fall. To the southeast, at Turtle Mountain, the plains Ojibwa and their Métis kin followed a parallel sequence of movements and harvests. Their activities varied only in their location and in the fact that they frequently accompanied the Métis on their large summer bison hunts to the south and west of Turtle Mountain.

Winter sometimes brought an economic division within mixed-group camps. Some families moved into more densely wooded areas where they could trap, while others, who were less involved in the fur trade, simply lived on stored foods until the winter bison hunt, visiting nearby winter camps and socializing. By December, when the bison herds had moved closer to the parkland to seek shelter from winter storms, the plains-oriented people moved out to the edge of the plains again to hunt bison. There are numerous reports of large winter camps of Ojibwa and Cree that spent considerable periods "in the middle of the Buffalo" between December and February in the mid-1850s. For some Ojibwa, hunger and the influences of these plains-oriented people led them to repeat the winter pattern developed during the harsh years of the 1830s. The Cree and Ojibwa who traded at the Guard Post, located at Egg Lake, trapped for only a few weeks in December after the last fall bison hunt and before the winter pounds, and for several years they refused to pay their debts. They were described by traders as "a most unruly set," "very saucy and independent." Clearly, the bison-hunting lifestyle continued to have two attractions: the food resources it offered, and the autonomy it allowed in relationships with fur traders.[11]

According to their own oral traditions, mixed bands such as Black Powder's contained people of differing cultural orientations. Most members participated in plains Cree cultural activities, such as the Sun Dance and bison pounding. Some people also chose to maintain aspects of their former orientation and spent considerable time in winter trapping, some travelling long distances to productive trapping areas. In Dempsey's words, these families "never completely abandoned their woodland ways and were content to live off fish and small game during the cold weather. Others in the camp were pure plainsmen who would disdain to eat moose or deer and considered buffalo to be the only proper food for an Indian." Big Bear himself, Dempsey feels, "tended to think like his father, and though he may have been more oriented to the plains, he still sought the protection of the woodlands as long as the buffalo were within reasonable distance of the Little Hills."[12] Among these bands, the distinctions between people of "plains" and "woodland" orientation were often blurred by the activities they pursued, by their perceptions of themselves, and by outsiders' perceptions and categorizations of them.

All of these factors give us a picture of the plains Ojibwa that is considerably more complex than the straightforward transition to a culture "neatly adjusted to life on the plains," as Howard expressed it: "In place of the birchbark or cattail-mat covered wigwam of the forests, they learned to use the bison-hide tipi of the Plains. Instead of the canoe they employed the horse and travois. . . . The deer, moose, and beaver . . . gave way to the buffalo and pronghorn antelope."[13] The nature of this complexity, and of the recombination of different cultural elements, deserves further consideration here. Howard was correct in that, on the surface at least, the plains Ojibwa exhibited strong plains Cree cultural elements. Black Powder's was one such band, and according to Dempsey this was a crucial element in Big Bear's youth. These influences were so evident that, when artist Paul Kane encountered Black Powder in 1847, he assumed (on the basis of the leader's appearance, language, association with Cree friends, and, presumably, ascription by others) that Black Powder was plains Cree. Kane noted that Black Powder was a second chief, or "aide-de-camp" (Dempsey says "close friend"), to the well-known Cree chief "Man that Gives the War Whoop" (Kee-a-kee-ka-sa-coo-way), and described the Ojibwa leader as "a great warrior and horse thief, the two most important qualifications for a chief."[14]

Big Bear was raised in this plains-oriented (and male-oriented) value system, in which horses were associated with a cluster of idealized male behaviours and values, including "spiritual potency, bravery, military prowess, wealth, largesse, and prestige." Mandelbaum notes of this value system among the plains Cree, "The legitimate way of procuring horses, in terms of that social system, was to steal them from an enemy tribe."[15] One of Big Bear's first measures of adult success was gaining prestige by stealing a number of horses and then giving them away. Elsewhere, a missionary's buffalo runner was the favourite target of young Ojibwa men.[16] Big Bear also participated in a number of raids, both for horses and revenge, on Blackfoot camps, in the context of largely plains Cree participants, and was both a "Worthy Young Man" and member of the warrior society.[17] Alanson Skinner and James Howard have described warrior, or soldier, societies among the Ojibwa in detail, characterizing them as one of the distinguishing features of plains Ojibwa society, reaching levels of complexity similar to this institution among the plains Cree, Sioux, and Blackfoot.[18] Like their Cree counterparts, plains Ojibwa *okitcita* used horned backrest decorations, a significant fact in light of the other plains-oriented values they acquired: the associations of leadership, bison, and especially with horns, a sign of power among the Ojibwa, suggests the powerful attraction that such plains-oriented institutions had for Ojibwa men.

Big Bear, like other members of these mixed bands, also participated in Cree rituals during these years. He was present at a Cree Thirst, or Sun, Dance at the time of Man that Gives the War Whoop's revenge party, and later sponsored Thirst

7. Paul Kane, "Muck-e-too [Mukatai],"
Black Powder, sketch (courtesy Royal
Ontario Museum, Toronto, Canada,
accession no. 946.15.54).

dances himself.[19] Other mixed bands also celebrated the Midewiwin and developed a shared repertoire of Cree and Ojibwa ritual, myth, and medicines. That some members of these mixed bands celebrated both of these major ceremonies, participating in different spiritual and ritual traditions as well as proclaiming their membership in overlapping but different social networks, says much about the complexity of personal and group identity among the "plains" Ojibwa.

Though we have no early portraits of Big Bear, Kane's 1848 portrait of Black Powder shows the leader wearing a bison robe, a simple but convincing statement of the effects of this new lifestyle on such bands[20] (see Illustration 7).

In addition to Kane's portrait, and Finlayson's sketch of a plains Ojibwa family in similar robes, artist Rudolf Kurz sketched a group of some 100 Ojibwa who visited Fort Berthold in mid-summer of 1851. Kurz's tiny, preliminary sketch of the arrival of the Ojibwa party shows, as he described in his journal, several mounted men flanking a line of men on foot, and the chiefs going before, five abreast. Though the figures are small and only roughed out, he shows the chiefs as wearing plains-style shirts, one of which has a triangular neck flap. Several wear

8. Ojibwa backrest banner (courtesy Collection of Glenbow, Calgary, Alberta, artifact no. AP 1525).

either feathers or headdresses, and they carry their long pipe stems as they advance towards the Mandan.[21] In his journal entry describing the trading session that followed between the Ojibwa and the Mandan, Kurz also notes that the Ojibwa were given clothing, "magnificently ornamented," by the Mandan.[22]

There is another item of material culture that suggests that some plains influences were penetrating deeply into western Ojibwa culture by this time. This artifact is a backrest banner dating from the mid-nineteenth century or earlier, collected over a century later among the Ojibwa of Nut Lake, northwest of Fort Pelly[23] (see Illustration 8).

Backrests were standard furniture in plains tipis, and they were hung on tripods so that a person could recline against the panel and be supported by the tripod. Backrests could be decorated for special persons by hanging ornamental panels from the top of the tripod. The Nut Lake banner is such a panel. Of wool trade cloth and the skin of a bison head, with beaded decorations representing the pound and the spiritual power necessary to call the bison into the pound, the banner was a mark of power and status, displayed on the man's backrest within the tipi. This banner is typical of a small group of such pieces, all but this one attributed to the plains Cree. It is, as curator Ted Brasser states, "one of the frequent reminders of the extensive intermarriage and cultural interaction of Cree and Ojibwa in this part of the country." The style of this banner replaced an earlier version that consisted of the skin of a bison head, which was draped over the backrest in such a way that a man leaning against the backrest would appear to be horned. Such horned banners were described by Alanson Skinner as being used by plains Ojibwa members of the *okitcita*, or soldier's society, an institution adopted from the plains Cree and Assiniboine. Other decorated cloth panels are mentioned by James Howard as having been used in the ritual of calling bison into a pound.[24] The Nut Lake banner embodies the personal, social, and supernatural aspects of the kinds of change that stemmed from multi-ethnic camps such as Black Powder's.

These images and artifacts confirm the Fort Pelly trader's 1831 observation that some of the Sauteaux he saw resembled "the meadow bucks" in their dress.[25] If evidence for such change is slender before 1837, it is certainly present – at least for Ojibwa men – in these images from mid-century. Where once stroud clothing and trade silver had been the marks of prestige and accomplishment, the bison-hunting life had ushered in a new set of symbols of achievement, and, indeed, new goals for Ojibwa men. The plains Ojibwa rejected the symbols of their ties to the fur trade and instead donned decorated bison robes, northern-plains leather shirts, garments of bison and elk hide, horse hair, and quillwork, and beaded objects of power with bison heads: symbols of the economic and social independence of their new lifestyle from the fur trade. During these decades, which coincided with the powerful burgeoning of the "classic" plains cultures, new styles of clothing may have helped the plains Ojibwa to clarify their changing identity.

Balancing these plains innovations was a rich and persistent heritage rooted in the woodlands. Big Bear's first wife, Sayos, was Ojibwa, and his first son was named Twin Wolverine, which according to biographer Dempsey is a name associated with Big Bear's woodland heritage.[26] Ojibwa social structures did not necessarily give way to Cree ones in these bands. Hind's party met several "Cree half-breeds" who had clans, and who recognized relationship with Ojibwa clan members even though they had never met. Since the Cree themselves did not have clans, this incident suggests the intimate adaptations that evolved in mixed-group bands.[27] And for all the Sun, or Thirst, dances in which Ojibwa in these mixed bands participated, the Midewiwin and other Ojibwa ceremonies continued to flourish.[28] Two artifacts found near Fort Carlton in the 1850s by Henri Bourgeault, botanist for the Palliser expedition, show no adaptations to plains Cree spirituality at all. The artifacts – a water drum of the type used in the Midewiwin, and a board with pairs of incised animal figures, which may have been used in the Wabano ceremony – could, by their appearance, have been found in any western Great Lakes or Boundary Waters Ojibwa community; and, indeed, they may originally have come from one such village. The water drum bears symbols typical of Great Lakes Midewiwin equipment – including two incised *missepeshu* or Underwater Panther figures – unaltered by at least sixty years of Ojibwa experience in the West. The wooden board is inscribed with four pairs of animals, and the figures depicted on it are animals of the woodland and parkland rather than of the plains: moose, bear, otters, and beaver, providing an especially revealing comment on the continuity of western Ojibwa world view.[29]

The continuity of Ojibwa world view and identity is further emphasized by the fact that, according to Dempsey, Big Bear's major source of power, a bear spirit, was perceived as "Ojibwa" in nature by the Cree elders to whom Big Bear described his dream. Though the bear was also a potent figure among the Cree, Dempsey implies (presumably on the basis of family testimony) that it took on a more ominous power when in relationship with the Ojibwa: "the Cree . . . were aware that the bear figure among the Ojibwa also had vicious powers; if offended, it could wreak havoc upon those who insulted it." This accords with information given to Mandelbaum by the plains Cree, who stated that the Ojibwa were regarded as having especially potent supernatural powers. According to Mandelbaum, even many "Cree" medicines were obtained originally from the Ojibwa, and "Whenever it was possible, Saulteaux practitioners were called in to treat the sick."[30] Furthermore, "the Plains Cree regarded the Saulteaux and the Wood Cree as 'bad medicine' men who fought by magical means rather than by strength of arms."[31] This fear of Ojibwa supernatural powers was also shown by the Cree around Fort Pitt, who were said to be "in terror" of Ojibwa rituals in the early 1840s (although their fear may have been exaggerated by the Methodist Reverend Rundle who recorded it, and whose aversion to "heathen ceremonies" was plain). Interestingly, after Reverend Rundle reproached these Ojibwa for practising such "idolatries," as he termed their rituals, they angrily left and went hunting bison.[32] Despite the claims of anthropologists such as Howard that the Ojibwa had been completely transformed by the western plains environment, it is clear that much of the ritual and cosmology which were the touchstones of Ojibwa culture and personal identity were maintained within these and other Ojibwa bands.

Plains Ojibwa dress was not entirely "plains," either. In contrast to the descriptions of men's clothes given above – bison robes and northern plains-style shirts – Kurz's sketch of one of the women in the group at Fort Berthold shows her

9. Rudolph Friedrich Kurz, Fort Berthold, 27 July 1851, "Sauteuse," western Ojibwa woman, probably from Red River, sketch (courtesy Bernisches Historisches Museum).

in a traditional Great Lakes strap dress such as those depicted by Rindisbacher in the 1820s and Finlayson in the 1840s[33] (see Illustration 9).

Cree women also wore strap dresses, or a variant, the side-fold dress, but by mid-century these had begun to give way to the two-skin dress with a deer-tail yoke accented by wavy rows of beads. George Catlin painted one Ojibwa woman in a plains-style dress in 1832, but this is the only piece of evidence for an early adoption of this style by the western Ojibwa.[34] That the Ojibwa woman sketched by Kurz was wearing the older-style strap dress, still common in the Great Lakes region, rather than the more fashionable northern plains two-skin dress, may mean either that she was from a more easterly community, or that – at least in some regions – Ojibwa women's dress remained more conservative than men's and was slower to reflect plains influences.[35]

Older, and more easterly, design influences are also seen in the decoration of her dress, which has rows of ribbon appliqué or beadwork across the chest in designs reminiscent of those on western Great Lakes artifacts. As well, the straps of the dress bear several stylized anthropomorphic figures similar to those on Midewiwin scrolls, and typical of Great Lakes pictographic style.[36]

The influence of Great Lakes design on this dress is echoed by a woman's legging collected by Paul Kane during his tour of the West in the 1840s, and attributed to the Ojibwa by museum curators on the basis of decorative style.[37] The legging is of red wool cloth, with blue ribbon binding and hawk bells at its outside edge. Horizontal lines of straight and scalloped beadwork on the lower third of the legging are reminiscent of curvilinear, floral, Great Lakes border designs, which by the time of Kane's visit had become integral to the sinuous floral style employed by the Red River Métis.

Kurz provided no information as to the home district of the Ojibwa he sketched, although they arrived at Fort Berthold just after a group of Métis from Red River and may have accompanied them. His sketches, like many other ambiguously documented "western Ojibwa" artifacts, leave tantalizing gaps in our understanding of changes in Ojibwa material culture. If the group sketched by Kurz was Ojibwa, from the Turtle Mountain or Red River region, perhaps, then the stylistic difference in men's and women's clothing would support the idea that plains Ojibwa adaptation was to some extent gender based. Given the greater social and material rewards offered to men by the plains lifestyle and value system, it is not surprising that plains Ojibwa men may have been more eager to acquire plains-style clothing than plains Ojibwa women were. True, women helped to make plains-styled items for their men (the backrest banner discussed above was probably beaded by a woman), but – with the exception of Catlin's portrait of Kay-a-gis-gis – they do not appear to have made such items for themselves. This process would echo the gender differences in the eighteenth-century adoption of European-influenced dress. Then, as on the plains, it was men who desired to adopt the latest fashions, and whose clothing reflected social status. In both of these eras, the referents for male social status and prestige changed, and with them the visual symbols of status changed as well. Women, whose status was not linked to such public displays, were slower to adopt new fashions for themselves. In the eighteenth century they cut new materials (woollen cloth) in old patterns, and in the nineteenth century they may have been similarly reluctant to alter this badge of their identity without reason.[38]

Taken together, the maintenance and adoption of these various traits constitutes not merely a balance between, but a blurring of, plains and woodland cultural orientations. This recombination of cultural behaviours and knowledge produced a plains Ojibwa ethnicity and culture that was more complex than earlier models have posited. Plains Ojibwa culture was not simply a wholesale adoption of plains

Cree and Métis life, as Howard claimed. Alanson Skinner was more correct when he suggested that plains Ojibwa culture was "half and half" of woodlands and plains traits. In a similar vein, Sharrock's model of ethnic fusion is also useful, but both of these require refining. I would argue that the plains Ojibwa exhibit a very special kind of ethnic fusion, which I call "layering": the maintenance of a core of older, woodland-adapted heritage and the adoption of a set of plains-adapted cultural elements over top of this core. Or, to state it another way, these Ojibwa were not divided between plains and woodland cultural adaptations and identity, as Skinner proposed, but were comprised of both elements in a wholly different adaptation that creatively combined them on different levels. And to the extent that this process conformed to standard interpretations of ethnic fusion or hybridization, western Ojibwa culture was not simply a homogeneous mixture of equal parts from both "parent" groups.[39] The identities and affiliations of the composite bands had different-sized borrowings from their different components. While Big Bear's was virtually plains Cree in nature – indeed, some of its members identified themselves as plains Cree – others were clearly identified as Ojibwa, but their behaviour, and personal and group identity, ranged along a continuum of orientations. Kinship and a sense of heritage and identity probably played a crucial role in creating and sustaining these different adaptations and the links between them, and they were likely of more import to the Ojibwa themselves than concerns of personal or group distinctions between themselves and the bands around them.

The complexity of plains Ojibwa culture has implications for standard ethnographic distinctions between woodland, parkland, and plains-adapted societies. In particular, the reality of "plains" Ojibwa culture suggests that such standard categories may be accurate only as points on a continuum, and that the use of these terms to designate wholly separate peoples may require considerable reworking. This becomes clearer when we examine activities and interactions within one of the most complex areas in the West: the Touchwood Hills and Qu'Appelle valley. These wooded, sheltered areas within the prairie functioned as ecological "borders" or transitional areas between the plains and the parkland. Within these areas, bands had ready access to bison, parkland game such as elk and deer, furs, berries and roots, fish, and waterfowl.[40] These resources drew both plains and transitional Ojibwa and Cree to the region, often at the same time. In winter, eastern Cree bands as well as mixed Cree-Ojibwa and Ojibwa bands camped in wooded areas in and around the Qu'Appelle valley.[41] A number of these bands spent part of the winter at the Qu'Appelle Lakes, taking advantage of the autumn fish run and living on fish and bison for the winter, a pattern that had begun in the 1830s. Other Ojibwa and mixed bands moved into the area in winter to have readier access to bison as parkland game became scarcer in their trapping areas to the north. Bison were also accessible from the Touchwood Hills in summer.[42] One mixed Ojibwa-

Cree band was even noted as gardening in the Little Touchwood Hills in the late 1850s.[43] Other bands harvested fish during the spring runs in the lakes and the Qu'Appelle River. The productive fishery in the "Fishing Lakes" in the upper Qu'Appelle valley had been used for several thousand years, and it continued to provide abundant food: missionary Charles Pratt caught as many as 1,000 per night in a basket weir in October 1852.[44]

With these many attractions, it is hardly surprising that this region was one of human and cultural diversity, or that this diversity led to much sharing of ideas and cultural practices. As Henry Youle Hind concluded after passing through the region in the late 1850s, "Many of the wood Indians now keep horses, and enjoy the advantage of making the prairie and the forest tributary to their wants."[45] But if the Ojibwa, with their "woodland" origins, readily crossed the line into the prairie and back again in this region, they were joined by bands with varying degrees of commitment to the "plains" lifeway who took advantage of forest and parkland resources here.[46] Ojibwa returning from the Touchwood Hills to Fort Pelly to sugar may well have been joined by some Cree, who, according to Mandelbaum, also made sugar and stored it in birchbark rogans similar to those of the Ojibwa.[47] Other Ojibwa, far less committed to the fur trade, used this region as a resource-rich shelter from which to hunt bison far to the west and south.[48] In all, the region lent itself to such connections between ecological zones and cultural orientations.

The most extraordinary sharing that occurred in this region was not of natural resources and subsistence practices, however, but of religious beliefs and ceremonies. Not only did some Ojibwa adopt the Sun, or Thirst, Dance, but the Midewiwin continued to be celebrated in this area and even spread to the Cree. The Midewiwin was celebrated at the Qu'Appelle Lakes in the mid- and late nineteenth century, and collections of Ojibwa material culture from this region that are now in museums include both Sun Dance and Midewiwin equipment.[49] Cree oral tradition recorded by Mandelbaum included a story about the adoption of the Midewiwin by the Cree. A Cree man is said to have gone to the Ojibwa to obtain medicines. The Cree "took with him two horses loaded with fine clothes. The Saulteaux were especially glad to get the horses, for they had very few. They took him into their *mite.wiwin* lodge where they taught him the use of many plants for medicinal purposes."[50] That the Ojibwa were still trading horses for medicines decades after Henry recorded them doing so with the Assiniboine suggests the continuing, shared needs and relationships amongst these peoples. Many of these ties between Cree and Ojibwa, and between different Ojibwa adaptations, were most tangibly felt in this Touchwood Hills–Qu'Appelle valley region.

Clearly, neither ecological zones nor ethnological constructs such as "culture areas" were rigidly bounded in this region. Both were permeable, and the proximity and kinship amongst people in different camps in the area led to the sharing of ideas and customs. The sharing of ceremonial activities is particularly interesting in this context, for it leads us away from the concept that cultural change among the western Ojibwa was simply a response to different environmental zones, and it upholds the role of human choice, identity, and heritage in determining the course of cultural adaptation and change. Concomitantly, while the adoption of a more bison-oriented lifestyle was an important marker of change in the emergence of the plains Ojibwa, it was more so for the fact that it brought them into contact with plains Cree cultural institutions and values than because of the importance of bison as a resource. The true hallmarks of the plains Ojibwa were not simply the use or importance of bison or the amount of time spent on the open plains, but rather the shift in the importance and esteem they assigned to bison within the total spectrum of resources used, the changes in values, especially the shift from the fur trade to horse raiding as a major source of prestige and wealth, and to other changes in language and identity caused by association with other plains-oriented peoples.

Finally, some of the aspects in which the western Ojibwa resisted cultural change in this atmosphere of example and choice are significant, for they point to important continuities in identity. These people (plains-oriented, as well as those in other bands) retained the continued use of canoes, Great Lakes–style artifacts and decorative styles, the clan system, and ritual and belief brought with them from the western Great Lakes, to give just the more obvious examples. When maintained in a different environmental setting in the face of alternate behaviours and adaptations, these formed core elements of personal and group identity. In the end, resources and geography do play a crucial role in orienting or "framing" a culture – and its evolution – but they do not determine all of its aspects.

By mid-century, just as some Ojibwa were beginning to truly absorb aspects of northern plains culture, the very foundation of this way of life – the bison – began to disappear. The range of the herds gradually contracted westward and southward, so that after the late 1850s they could generally be found only west of the Touchwood Hills and the Souris River or to the west and south of Turtle Mountain.[51] The northern range of the herds similarly withdrew to the south and east; by the 1830s they were gone from the upper Assiniboine River, and by the late 1850s they were seldom seen along the lower Saskatchewan River north of the Touchwood Hills.[52] As the range of the herds contracted, relations between tribal groups on the northern plains tautened in one of two ways: they became either more cooperative, working together to gain access to the herds in enemy territory, or more hostile, seeking to prevent other groups from hunting in their territory. Given their widespread distribution and affiliations, different Ojibwa bands experienced both of these changes.

West of the Assiniboine River, the bison drifted away from the heart of plains Cree and Ojibwa territory, into the more dangerous areas held by the Blackfoot and Sioux. By the mid-1850s, bison hunts more frequently resulted in warfare.[53] In response, Cree and Ojibwa entered the area together in large numbers for security. The camp of "two hundred tents Crees [and] Saulteaux in the middle of the bison" four days from the Touchwood Hills, recorded in the Fort Pelly journal in July 1856, was typical of the large multi-ethnic camps that became more common after 1850.[54]

The difficulties and dangers posed by the need to hunt in enemy territory made the plains Cree and their Ojibwa kin increasingly hostile towards the Métis, whose large hunts took such a toll on the herds and who had usurped the role of the plains tribes as provisioners to the Hudson's Bay Company. Tensions rose still higher when some Métis began travelling west from the White Horse Plains on the Assiniboine River, well into Cree territory (west of the Souris River and between the North and South branches of the Saskatchewan) to hunt.[55] Such a direct challenge to Cree use of the region met an equally direct response. Beginning in the 1850s, Cree leaders considered the situation serious enough that they tried to limit access to the herds to Indians only. The Cree limited their enforcement of this decisions to "threats and lectures" delivered to traders and travellers such as the Hind party, but it was obviously a matter of concern to them.[56]

Ojibwa who were related to both the plains Cree and the Métis must have felt caught in the middle of this rising tension. The situation was even more volatile closer to Red River and Turtle Mountain, where the herds had taken the brunt of the Métis hunts. By the mid-1850s, bison could rarely be found north or east of Turtle Mountain or the Pembina region.[57] This happened virtually at the same moment as Ojibwa in the Pembina and Turtle Mountain region were completing their adaptation to a bison-oriented way of life: these were the same bands from which the elderly plains Ojibwa with whom James Howard and Alanson Skinner worked in this area in the twentieth century came.

The contraction of the herds meant that these Ojibwa were forced to venture deep into Sioux territory to find bison – when the herds had not been frightened completely away by the enormous hunting parties of the Red River Métis. In 1831 there were some 1,300 Métis in and around Red River, as well as the settlement at St. Joseph near Pembina, and approximately 820 carts accompanied the 1830 hunt. By 1843 there were 2,600 Métis, and 1,210 carts accompanied the 1840 hunt; by 1856, the Métis population had risen to 3,250 and the hunts had continued to grow.[58] Ojibwa from the Red River, southern Interlake, Assiniboine River, Turtle Mountain, and Pembina areas almost always participated in these hunts, both to gain the benefit of large-scale communal hunting and to allow them to approach the herds in enemy territory.[59] When hunting near the border without Métis protection, Ojibwa travelled in large parties, such as the 100 or so bison hunters who arrived at Fort Berthold on the Missouri in July 1851.[60]

Though the Ojibwa used the Métis hunts for their own purposes, their relations with the Métis were by no means free of tension. Some were angered by what they saw as the Métis slaughter of the bison. Green Setting Feather, leader of one of the plains-oriented Ojibwa bands at Turtle Mountain, rebuked the Métis in 1852: "The manner of his hunt is such not only to kill, but also to drive away the few he leaves, and to waste even those he kills." Green Setting Feather stated that the Métis had been allotted a hunting territory by the Turtle Mountain Ojibwa but were also encroaching on Ojibwa hunting grounds near Turtle Mountain. He echoed the Cree decision to limit hunting to Native bands only, saying that the Turtle Mountain Ojibwa wished to keep their hunting lands "and let not your half-breeds take them."[61]

Nor were the Ojibwa the only people to protest the Métis toll on the dwindling herds. The Sioux also resented it, and, as the herds contracted and the Métis themselves were forced to strike deeper into Sioux country, hostilities broke out over access to the bison.[62] This was greatly compounded by the presence of Ojibwa on the Métis hunts, which made the hunting parties natural targets for any Dakota they encountered. Furthermore, the Ojibwa did not accompany the Métis merely to hunt. Ojibwa war parties often used the cover and safety of the huge Métis hunting camps to penetrate deep into enemy territory before striking at the Dakota.[63] The Ojibwa even tried sometimes to persuade the Métis to lend their numbers and firepower to their attacks. In one incident, a group of Ojibwa men accompanying the hunt became angry when they could not persuade the Métis to attack some Sioux they encountered, and they expressed their anger by breaking the rules of the hunt and frightening the bison away.[64]

* * *

For peoples who were not so dependent on the bison and the plains horse culture, these decades held other threats; and, like the waning of the bison herds, the unease felt by other Ojibwa bands during these years was but a warning. For Ojibwa at Red River, in the Interlake, and in the more densely wooded areas west of the Interlake, the most disturbing element of these years was the growing influence of European settlers and missionaries. Some of these bands coped more successfully with their diminishing influence and autonomy than others, and most retained their spirituality and way of life in the face of determined efforts by Europeans to dispossess, convert, and assimilate them. This continuity was not easy, and though the Ojibwa managed, it was, as they would discover, but a minute fraction of the pressures they faced after 1870.

RED RIVER

The Ojibwa became an ever less important segment of Red River society as the nineteenth century proceeded. By the late 1830s they were physically separated from the community at the Forks through the Selkirk Treaty, the establishment of the Indian settlement some distance from the rest of the colony, and the building of Lower Fort Garry twenty miles downstream from the Forks in the 1830s. The position of the new fort, closer to the Indian settlement and Netley Creek, eliminated the journey through much of the Red River colony to the Forks to trade. This, as well as the rapid growth of the Métis and mixed-blood population and the continuing influx of Swampy Cree, meant that the Ojibwa were less visible in the settlement than before, and although their economic role as suppliers of country produce continued, their contributions were less than the huge amounts of meat supplied by the Métis. They were also separated by religious beliefs, because many "stubbornly" retained their own spirituality and scorned the work of the Church Missionary Society. Socially, racially, and politically, the Ojibwa were placed outside the pale of the Victorian society that began to emerge in Red River as legal and political institutions evolved and as Victorian concepts of racism gripped the colony. The ties that the Ojibwa retained with the colonists were insufficient to bridge these divisions, and by mid-century the Red River Ojibwa were essentially isolated from the Red River settlement.

While it is clear that the White settlers and elite of Red River perceived the Ojibwa by mid-century as being on the lowest rung of Red River society (with themselves at the top of that society), it is not clear whether the Ojibwa themselves understood the changes occurring in Red River or whether their isolation mattered to them. The intellectual and religious currents that surged through the colony in these decades, particularly those to do with racism and social class, largely affected only those persons who wished to be part of Red River society. In many ways the hardening and elaboration of this society did not matter to or affect the Ojibwa, who led their own lives and continued their accustomed seasonal round.

In other ways, though, the Ojibwa certainly were affected by some of the developments in Red River. An incident that occurred in 1845 at the very heart of Red River illustrates the shift in the balance of power in the settlement that accompanied the gradual isolation of the Ojibwa. The year before this incident, during the bison hunt, a battle had occurred between the Red River Métis and some Sioux. The hostilities were ended by gift giving and a peace treaty, and in late August of 1845 some of the Sioux involved set out to visit their new allies at the Forks. The delegation met some Ojibwa at Upper Fort Garry, who were gathered there "as is usual on the arrival of strangers," according to Alexander Ross. One of these Ojibwa was in mourning for a brother who had been killed in a Sioux raid, and according to tribal custom he avenged his brother's death by shooting one of the Sioux.[65] The incident radically departed from tribal custom at this point, however. Settlers were greatly alarmed by the shooting, fearing that Red River would become the scene of a prolonged and escalating conflict between the two tribes. The "murderer" was imprisoned in the jail at the Forks, was tried by jury (which did not contain any Native representatives), and less than a week later was publicly hanged.[66]

The hanging was intended to send a message to the Ojibwa that, although life in and around Red River continued in some ways as it had for the previous fifty years, the balance of power had shifted. True, the Europeans genuinely feared an Indian war in their midst; in that sense, the Ojibwa were still a force to be contended with. The hanging was, however, an emphatic attempt to assert European standards of justice over tribal standards. To his own people, the Ojibwa had done no wrong in killing the Sioux; on the contrary, he would have been regarded as having set a serious matter to rights. Alexander Ross expressed the European perception of the incident in his statement that "few acts more daring in its nature, or more insulting to the whites, had ever been committed in this quarter, and the universal voice cried aloud for justice."[67] But the "universal voice" did not speak in Ojibwa, nor was it Ojibwa justice that was dealt out. Red River was changing, and in its new social and political reality and structures the Ojibwa were seen as pitiable and primitive: a people to be distrusted, and certainly not to be regarded as the allies they had once been. Ross's description of the Ojibwa as both dangerous and slothful ("Many of them abide in the colony from one end of the year to the other, not as hunters, nor as labourers, but as vagrants and evil-doers; they beg, roam about, and annoy the settlers") provides the clearest expression of this shift in Ojibwa standing in the colony.[68] The hanging was a symbol of the developing European society in Red River and the desire of this society to control those whom it marginalized. In reality, it would be decades before the Ojibwa were subject to any real legal control; the Red River court records in the years after 1845 are not full of prosecutions of Ojibwa people. Still, the hanging was a powerful symbol, reinforced by the arrival of a regular British regiment in Red River in 1846 to uphold the Hudson's Bay Company's monopoly against free traders and to serve as a reminder that Red River was subject to British law. These two events marked a great change not only in Red River society, but also in relations between Ojibwa and Whites at Red River.

The physical and demographic structure of Red River provides another indication of the changing position of the Ojibwa in the colony. By mid-century, the Red River settlement stretched nearly fifty miles along the Red River and extended along the Assiniboine for some distance as well. Of the thirteen Métis, Scots, and half-breed communities that made up Red River, the Ojibwa occupied just the most remote one, St. Peter's, at the extreme northern edge of the settlement, and the Catholic settlement, Baie St. Paul, on the western edge.[69] Their minority position was confirmed by the 1849 census, according to which there were just 460 "Swampies" and seventy-seven Ojibwa of a total population in Red River of 5,391.[70] If this figure represents adult male heads of families, rather than total persons, it is comparable to an earlier, 1838, census of "Saulteaux Attached to New Fort Garry," which listed all the male heads of families of Peguis's band (and their names) and the number and gender of their dependents: 58 male heads of family with 63 wives, 88 sons, 55 daughters; 17 female followers (who would have been widows or other relatives), 12 boy followers, 13 girl followers; total, 308 persons.[71]

Despite being greatly outnumbered, the Ojibwa did maintain a presence in Red River. They continued to supply vital country produce, including meat, corn, wild rice, salt, fish and fish oil, bark and pitch, and canoes, to the settlers and mixed-bloods.[72] As well, the Ojibwa maintained a social presence in Red River, though interaction with European members of the settlement was limited. According to Ross, there were generally a number of Ojibwa gathered at the fort at the Forks, watching for strangers, and Warre's 1845 sketch of the fort confirms this.[73] They were also familiar with the settlers nearest the Indian settlement and maintained a civil or political presence in the colony and particularly with these settlers.

Individual settlers made appeals to Peguis for permission to use lands outside the two-mile treaty boundary, some of which were granted. One settler in St. Andrews obtained Peguis's permission to use Ojibwa lands outside the boundary, only to be accosted by a number of Swampy Cree who came to collect rent on the land. In response, Peguis called a council at the Indian settlement (St. Peter's), "took off his ordinary dress of a settler and in full Indian fashion, moccasins, fringed leggings, and breech cloth with a scalping knife in his belt, held a pipe ceremony declaring that [the settler] was his son and threatened to rip open anyone who molested him."[74] This story reminds us that the longstanding tension between the Ojibwa and the Swampy Cree persisted and may have been intensified by stress relating to land rights: the Cree who came to collect the rent were challenging Peguis's right to make such land grants, though Peguis later publicly re-asserted this right. The fact that the Cree were all men the settler "knew well" also underlines the different patterns of social interaction between European settlers and the Ojibwa and Cree at Red River; the Cree had much more to do with the settlers than did the Ojibwa. Finally, Peguis's symbolic changing of his clothes before speaking to the council is a reminder of his leadership skills. European clothing worn by Native people often functioned as a symbol of willingness to adopt civilization, so Peguis's "ordinary dress of a settler" represented his strong ties to Europeans. The Native clothing he changed into to speak to his band, on the other hand, signified his Ojibwa identity in that context and his solidarity with his band as well as "cultural integrity and resistance to the domination of whites."[75] Such skills enabled Peguis to exert a high degree of control over land use around Red River until his death in 1864, despite the fact that his people were a tiny minority of the settlement's population and had become marginalized in other ways as well.

The changes looming on the horizon of Rupert's Land during these years did little to alter the seasonal round of the Red River Ojibwa. Members of Peguis's band continued to leave the Indian settlement in spring to fish and to harvest sugar, eggs, and ducks. Spring sturgeon runs remained extremely important to the Red River Ojibwa, as can be seen from the isinglass returns for the lower Red River district. An average of 259 pounds of isinglass – a product made from the inner membrane of the sturgeon bladder, and used, among other things, for making glues – was traded annually between 1841 and 1857.[76] Given that one pound of isinglass represented some 283 dressed pounds of sturgeon, the average amount of sturgeon harvested annually in the lower Red River district during these years was thus a staggering 73,409 pounds. Nor were all sturgeon harvested processed for their isinglass. The production of this substance was extremely labour intensive, and we may assume that a good part of the annual harvest was not so processed.[77] Much of the sturgeon was dried, and the oil rendered and stored in fish-skin jars. About the time of the sturgeon run, gardens were also planted.

Later in the summer the Ojibwa went to the bison plains, often in company with the great Métis hunt. After harvesting the garden crops, they conducted a fall fishery and game hunt around the shores of the lake, and a fur hunt in December and January. The band probably sold furs to the private, or free, traders who operated in the region as well as to the Company. Some families, though not all, conducted a bison hunt in winter as they formerly did. They had a late winter ice fishery at the lake, which continued to be very productive: "In this way one Indian will frequently take in a day from 50 to 100 fish weighing 8 to 12 pounds ea." In all, the Red River Ojibwa still had access to considerable food resources by mid-century.[78]

Their subsistence round was not the only thing that the Red River Ojibwa maintained virtually unchanged during these years. Ojibwa attitudes towards Christianity also remained essentially the same, and the agents of the Church Missionary Society were just as frustrated as they had been during the 1820s and '30s. Peguis himself did convert to Christianity in 1840, after putting aside three of his four wives so that he could be baptized, and other members of his family followed during that decade. It is unclear whether Peguis had experienced spiritual doubts about his own traditions and felt strongly attracted to Christianity, or whether he became baptized to pursue his own political ends and to reinforce his relationship with the missionaries. That he and some of his family converted, but few others of his band did, suggests that they may have been at least partly motivated by political reasons.[79]

Despite Peguis's example, conversions on a broader scale were not forthcoming, nor did his band heed his advice in 1840 "to give up their children to be taught in the school, and to come to Church themselves." After this direct appeal, Smithurst, Cockran's successor, concluded, "Such alas is the . . . prejudice of the Saulteaux tribe against Xtianity, that though the assembly consisted nearly of the whole tribe not one expressed a desire for instruction."[80]

Even for the few who decided to become baptized, the acceptance of Christianity did not necessarily mean an acceptance of "civilization." As Smithurst lamented in one annual report, "of the 17 children in the Saulteaux school, . . . 6 are gone with their parents to the plains."[81] In the face of such limited progress, Smithurst's correspondence assumed a note of rather determined optimism in these decades, such as his comment when several families broke ground for the first time in 1842: "I have some encouraging hopes respecting this hitherto obstinate tribe."[82] This situation changed very little throughout the 1840s and '50s. Apart from Peguis's conversion and other minor gains, Smithurst's one "victory" was to break the Ojibwas' habit "of wearing their best clothes on all occasions." Given the relationship between fine clothing, well-being, and spiritual power, Smithurst's success may signal a change in Ojibwa values and spirituality. Like the missionaries' other victories, though, it was not a universal change; Smithurst also encountered a "heathen Saulteaux" at Red River wearing rabbit-skin clothing in the winter of 1844, and, given the messages of cultural allegiance signalled by clothing, this in turn may indicate the rejection of "civilization" on the part of some of the Ojibwa from Red River.[83]

A related settlement at Portage la Prairie was little more rewarding for the missionaries than were their efforts with Ojibwa at St. Peter's. In fact, the Ojibwa at Portage la Prairie may have been partly comprised of a group of Christian Ojibwa that split away from the St. Peter's group; at least one man on the 1838 Lower Fort Garry census of Peguis's band, Muchekeewis, is listed as a member of the Portage la Prairie settlement in 1850s. Other members of the settlement were on the site when Cockran arrived there in the early 1850s, implying that they may have been remnants of earlier Ojibwa communities in the south Lake Manitoba – Portage la Prairie area. Some residents may have remained from Belcourt's Baie St. Paul settlement. Before Belcourt was forced to abandon his mission to the Ojibwa in 1847-48 (after he came under fire from George Simpson for championing the cause of Métis rights to free trade[84]), he had made a good deal of progress. In 1838 he claimed to have 150 catechumens amongst his Ojibwa and Métis parishioners, and the 1840 Red River census listed ninety-eight persons resident at Baie St. Paul.[85] More Métis moved into the community in the 1840s, apparently changing the nature of the village. By the time Belcourt left, it was said that the Ojibwa there did not farm, and relied on the hunt for their subsistence.[86] There were about twenty-eight Ojibwa families at Portage la Prairie, and while Cockran found them "not so easily persuaded" as the Cree he had worked with at St. Peter's, he did encourage some of them to build cabins and to garden.[87]

One progressive Ojibwa at the Portage la Prairie settlement, Pachetoo (a man who was described elsewhere as Métis and who may have been a son of John Tanner), a free trader in furs and horses, had the second-finest house in the settlement, with shingles, bright red doors and window frames, and the latest American mechanical toys for his children. (Given the ostentatious overtones of Pachetoo's house and possessions, one cannot help but wonder if these were simply the latest manifestations of Ojibwa symbols of prestige and well-being: from trade silver and red cloth leggings for competence in trapping, to factory-made toys and red window frames for competence in trading?)[88] Even such progressive men did not live entirely upon the produce of their farms or trading, though; like all other residents of Red River, they depended on hunting and fishing for their staple diet. The Hind party noted Ojibwa fishing for sturgeon with spears and a weir at Portage la Prairie in June 1858 and were later approached by these Ojibwa, who wanted to barter fish for tobacco and tea.[89]

Other than a few isolated cases such as that of Pachetoo, the missionaries met with continued resistance from the Ojibwa after 1837. Most of them continued to believe that "the Master of Life intended them to live by hunting and fishing, but the white man were to live by the plough being a more degrading occupation."[90] By 1841 there were only three Ojibwa communicants in the Indian congregation, out of an adult Ojibwa population of over 130; by contrast, there were fifty-six Cree communicants.[91] The number of confirmed Ojibwa remained low throughout these decades, and, while the original wooden church at St. Peter's, built in 1836, became too small and had to be replaced by a larger stone one in 1853, its congregation was mostly Swampy with but a sprinkling of Ojibwa.

If anything, observations by missionaries and others for the late 1840s and 1850s reveal strong continuity in Ojibwa ceremonial life and world view. During Paul Kane's visit to an Ojibwa camp near the mouth of the Red River in early July 1846, he saw a woman in mourning, wearing old clothes, as was traditional; and a medicine man offered to bring wind for Kane's party's boats in exchange for a gift of tobacco. Kane may have interrupted a ceremony, for he was offered part of "a large roasted dog," another traditional Ojibwa ceremonial food.[92] The persistence of traditional ways of thought is also evident in the Ojibwas' syncretic perceptions of baptism, which they believed to be an effective protection against the sending of malevolent forces by evil shamans. In fact, some of the Ojibwa regarded Smithurst as "an English Conjuror" and were willing to "try the effect of [his] putting water upon [the sick] in the performeance of what they regard as one of our conjuring operations."[93]

If the Red River Ojibwa felt anxious enough about their security in the 1840s to have occasional recourse to "English Conjuror[s]" – and the other-than-human powers to whom Smithurst was connected – they still did not forsake their own "conjurors" or guardians in these years. Their kin in the Interlake, more deeply affected by changes in the fur trade and game populations, felt a greater need to call on the Christian God, though even these Ojibwa did so in patterns that conformed to their own traditions. And in the decades after 1857, when Netley Creek and St. Peter's were threatened by the flood of would-be settlers and developers from the East, Peguis and his kin would have cause to call on every source of supernatural aid available to them. At mid-century, though, they were secure enough in their own way of life to give the Reverend William Stagg the unpleasant surprise of seeing, as he entered the Red River from Lake Winnipeg in the summer of 1854, "so large a number of Saulteaux Indians still heathen. A great many were tenting on the banks of the river."[94] They would be there for some time yet.

THE INTERLAKE: PRESSURES AND PROPHECIES

While the Red River Ojibwa maintained a firm but quiet resistance to missionization and assimilation, the Ojibwa of the Interlake region felt these pressures more keenly, and they responded in a variety of ways. Some of these responses were political: direct challenges to the missionaries' authority and goals by Ojibwa religious leaders. Other responses were syncretic experiments, attempts to explain and use Christian "power," holy objects, and sacred persons in traditional Ojibwa ways, including individual re-interpretations of Christian belief and a series of nativistic prophecies that incorporated Christian symbols. These syncretic responses were also attempts to forge a cohesive and comforting belief system from two very different and very divided religious traditions.

By the late 1830s, the Interlake was no longer the "Land of milk & honey" it had been before 1821. It was by no means barren of either food or fur-bearing animals, but the availability of prime species for food and trade was limited, and the fur trade had not improved since George Nelson's day. For instance, while returns from Manitoba Post in 1820-21 and 1856-57 actually rose over the years, one of the species that made up the bulk of this increase (muskrat) has wide cyclical variations in population, so that the 1856-57 figures may simply indicate a high point in their cycle that was preceded and followed by years in which very few were to be found. The other species that increased greatly was mink, which was relatively valuable. At prices ranging from 2s. 3d. to 5s. per mink pelt in the

TABLE 3
Fur Returns, Manitoba Post, 1820-21 and 1856-57

Fur Type	#Traded, 1820-21	# Traded, 1856-57	
Bear	35	38	
Beaver	19	6	
Cats	840	155	
Fishers	31	67	
Red fox	25	285	
Mink	19	1,261	
Muskrats	1,021	2,500	
Otter	39	31	
Total furs reported	2,029	4,343	

Sources: HBCA B.51/d/4, Manitoba District accounts 1820-21 [may include outposts around Manitoba House]; HBCA B.160/d/6, Manitoba Post accounts 1856-57.

Note: Only major fur categories are compared here, and only comparable categories are included in chart: e.g., black bears are compared only with black bears, red fox with red fox.

1850s, the 1,261 mink traded at Manitoba Post in 1856-57 were worth from £142 to £315. Muskrats were worth from 1d. to 6d., making the 2,500 muskrats traded worth only £6 to £10.[95] While the mink figures look impressive, there were probably over fifty hunters bringing them in, making individual hunts quite small and of little value. Despite the increase in the number of furs traded, then, Ojibwa hunters were not necessarily doing well in the trade.

Nor were the advantages offered to the Interlake people by fur-trade competition or by the Red River market very significant. Free traders were present in the region throughout the 1850s, but there is no evidence that they drove fur prices up, and the trade in country produce that continued with the Red River settlers was taken over to a certain extent by the Métis and seems to have made no real contribution to Ojibwa economy in the area.[96] The Interlake bands traded at Manitoba House; a short-lived post at the Partridge Crop; Berens River; Fort Alexander; and sites to the west and south of the Interlake (Fort Garry, Brandon House), as well as with free traders closer to home. All in all, they found that trade goods became much harder to obtain than they had been before 1821, given the decrease in the more valuable furs and the Hudson's Bay Company's limitations on credit, presents, and liquor.

A similar situation existed in regard to food resources. Sugar making, gardening, fishing, gathering plant foods and eggs, and hunting wildfowl and game, remained the cardinal points on the seasonal round. Mid-winter moose hunts were held each year, though they were not always successful, and the paramount importance placed on the fisheries by these bands may indicate that large game was unreliable. At the Lake Manitoba post in 1838, Indians (presumably Ojibwa) expressed dissatisfaction because the trader was unable to supply them with the bison robes he had promised them – another indication of the lack of large game.[97] Fortunately, the fisheries were extremely productive, and the fall fishery and duck hunt supplied crucial sources of food for winter. Fish pemmican made with pounded fish mixed with fish oil was the staple winter food, and enough was produced that some was traded to the missionaries at Fairford for clothing and other trade goods.[98]

It is difficult to evaluate how well these resources served the Ojibwa. Most of the documents from this period were produced by missionaries, who were eager to prove the inadequacy of Native subsistence strategies to convince the Indians of the superiority of their own, and even the missionaries contradicted each other. Belcourt, the Catholic priest who travelled through the Interlake, exclaimed at the "prodigious" numbers of ducks, geese, and fish around Manitoba House in 1840, and to the northwest of the Interlake, Reverend Budd stated in 1841 that one could obtain moose and deer meat in exchange for tobacco and ammunition around Cumberland House. Reverend Smithurst, on the other hand, claimed in 1843 that the Cree around Cumberland were "very poor, the fur animals as well as deer being nearly exterminated." Non-missionary sources do not resolve these contradictions. The members of the Hind party who travelled through the Interlake in the late 1850s had difficulty finding game, though they noted productive fisheries, the use of fish pemmican and the storage of fish oil, and Indian potato gardens on "Sugar Island," probably the same location as Garden, or Tent, Island. Some of these difficulties were caused by typical fluctuations in weather, water levels, and animal population cycles: in the summer of 1857, for instance, high waters led to a poor rice harvest and fishery in some areas, a situation that coincided with a low point in the rabbit population cycle.[99]

While resources were certainly not at their peak in the Interlake in these years, they were far more abundant than they were in what is now northern Ontario, the area directly east of Lake Winnipeg and north of the Boundary Waters at this time. According to ethnohistorian Charles Bishop, the Ojibwa of northern Ontario were by the 1820s well into a subsistence pattern that relied upon fish and hare, which they found precarious and unsatisfactory. Comparing these conditions to those during the heyday of the fur trade in the Little North, Bishop concludes that the Northern Ojibwa experienced considerable stress due to "a long period of deprivation involving reduced resource availability."[100] Fish and hare did not provide an adequate diet for the Northern Ojibwa, due to the cyclical variations in the hare population, the high amount of energy necessary to snare the numbers of hare required, and the fact that the fish and hare diet was dangerously low in fat, a critical component of the diet in a region with such cold winters.[101] The situation was different in the Interlake, however, where intensive spring and autumn runs provided an efficient means of harvesting tens of thousands of pounds of fish, and where fish species such as sturgeon had large amounts of oil and fat, which could be rendered and stored. Certainly, the fish runs were able to support large gatherings for short periods of time throughout the Interlake, or the Midewiwin could not have continued to be such a force there. Ojibwa in the Interlake also had access to seasonal harvests of sugar, garden produce, and small game and wildfowl.

This is not to say that supplies of food were always adequate, especially in winter, and large game, especially moose, does seem to have been scarce. So were prime furs and the trade goods they bought. Economic and material scarcity has often been used to explain religious change and movements of religious revitalization, including phenomena such as the religious unrest and experimentation in the Interlake during these years.[102] In this regard, it seems likely that resource deprivation alone did not cause the religious prophecies and syncretic experiments in the Interlake, for the Ojibwa were neither literally starving nor economically destitute in the trade. Still, they were relatively deprived, especially of the most prestigious meat and fur species. Decreased availability of furs combined with Hudson's Bay Company reductions in credit also produced a relative poverty in trade goods. In short, there was more than enough to sustain life, but not life as the Ojibwa wished it.

Other causes of discontent are not directly reconstructible from the documents, but they can be inferred from other known aspects of Ojibwa life. Though admittedly a more speculative reconstruction than one that depends on direct observations of physical conditions, I think we can point to a number of social and spiritual ramifications of relative material poverty for the Ojibwa. Even relative poverty must have had social connotations, for without game, furs, or trade goods there was little to give away and thus few opportunities to gain social prestige. For an Ojibwa, it was embarrassing not to be able to reciprocate or redistribute, and poverty would have made them feel stingy and mean: truly "poor." And since material wealth was a mark of a relationship with an other-than-human spirit protector or guardian and the powers bestowed by such beings, poverty connoted spiritual impoverishment and powerlessness as well. The Ojibwa also experienced powerlessness in their relationship with the traders, for without a steady supply of prime furs and intense competition they were unable to exert the control over the trade that they once had. Adjusting "to a subservient status in a trade they had once dominated" was frustrating, humiliating, and stressful.[103] They experienced similar frustrations as missionaries attacked the authority of established Ojibwa religious leaders and the validity of the Ojibwa belief system. All of these developments threatened what, according to Mary Black-Rogers, is a central goal for

Ojibwa individuals: "to be in control [of one's] . . . destiny and self-determination. Stated another way, the ideal is not to be controlled by one's environment – 'environment' including other people as well as other beings or forces that could affect one's outcomes and render one helpless."[104] Given their changed fortunes, many Ojibwa in the Interlake felt – as they would reveal in their prophecies – that they were not in control of their environment, and they intensely disliked being controlled.

These conditions set the background for tensions that developed between Anglican (Church Missionary Society) and Catholic missionaries and the Ojibwa they sought to convert in the Interlake, and for the syncretic and nativistic beliefs of Ojibwa in the region. This was a fascinating era in the history of these bands, as they sought to use new conditions and beliefs to their own advantage. Their creative recombinations of Ojibwa and Christian beliefs were efforts to bridge the growing gap between the remembered conditions of the past and the less satisfactory reality of the present, and to use Christian powers to improve their situation. Their new beliefs were also attempts to bridge the gap that emerged between Ojibwa and Christian ideologies, and between Protestant and Catholic faiths.

Beginning in 1842, from a base at Fairford Mission in the central Interlake, Reverend Abraham Cowley and his successor, Reverend William Stagg, conducted a determined and aggressive campaign to convert the Ojibwa and Swampy Cree of the area. They followed in the footsteps of the Methodist James Evans, who had been located at Norway House at the northeast corner of Lake Winnipeg since 1840; other Church Missionary Society representatives, including West, Jones, and Cockran, had been at Red River since the 1820s; and Peter Jacobs, of the Wesleyan Missionary Society to the southeast, had been at Fort Frances and Fort William since the late 1830s. By the late 1850s, Stagg could boast that he and his colleagues had spread the Gospel to "nearly all of the Saulteaux north of Red River," including many bands in the Interlake as well as a large territory to the west of Lake Manitoba.[105] These people also heard the sermons of Catholic priests who worked in these same areas. Catholics had missions at Partridge Crop near Fairford for several years during the 1840s, and at Duck Bay, and conducted periodic tours through the area to convert and to serve the needs of Catholic converts. With each denomination striving to overcome what it felt were the pernicious influences of the other, as well as to assert the greater truth of Christianity over Native religion, missionization proved confusing and threatening for many Ojibwa. As it had in Red River, missionization in the Interlake touched off a bitter struggle for power between missionaries and the traditional Ojibwa religious and civil leaders, and a larger struggle amongst the Ojibwa population as a whole to reconcile these new teachings with their own world view.

The missionaries found their efforts hampered by the strong presence of the

Midewiwin society in the Interlake. Midewiwin and other ceremonies were held at "Potatoe Island" (the same site formerly known as Garden Island and Big Tent Island), Manitoba Post, Jack Head, Dog Head, Berens River, Black Island, Fort Alexander, and other native camps around the time of the spring and fall fisheries. Father Belcourt described a Midewiwin gathering of about 200 Ojibwa near Manitoba Post in late September 1840; he actually interrupted the ceremony to preach against what he called "their ridiculous practices." Despite such pressures, the missionaries were never successful in eradicating the Midewiwin and other Ojibwa ceremonies. Although many Ojibwa did convert to Christianity, Midewiwin ceremonies continued to be held at virtually all of these locations until the last decades of the nineteenth century.[106]

The preservation of the Midewiwin was not an easy struggle. Missionary attacks on it produced an atmosphere of tension, causing many Ojibwa to feel confusion over the implications of the new Christian doctrines and fear for the future. Just as had happened among the Ojibwa of Rainy River in the 1840s, Midewiwin leaders were the most vocal opponents of conversion, and they took the brunt of missionary attacks on "heathenism." One technique used by Stagg and Settee was to isolate Ojibwa Midewiwin leaders from their followers, either attempting to convert the leaders (and thus lead their followers to Christianity as well) or to discredit the authority and power of the leader (and thus gain influence with his followers). Midewiwin leaders were forced to campaign to retain members: at Fairford, feasts were held for individuals who showed signs of converting to Christianity, and the persons were warned about how much they would lose by neglecting the Midewiwin.[107] Such overt competition led to tremendous tensions between Native and European religious specialists. Stagg claimed that these feelings stemmed wholly from the Ojibwa leaders' jealousy of missionary authority and of their frustration in being unable to collect gifts (useful goods and marks of status) from followers.[108] This was true to some extent, although the real issue was the erosion of the Midewiwin, an important part of Ojibwa spirituality and society. The Midewiwin leaders themselves challenged Stagg on larger issues, including the very justness of missionization. As had the Ojibwa of Red River, they argued that "God gave the Metewin and a drum to the Indian; and a Church and a Book to the White man." The Black Duck, a Midewiwin leader, argued against Stagg's proselytization in similar terms: "What would you do," he asked Stagg, "if the Metawin had been the religion of your country, and the Book the religion of mine, and I were to offer you my religion?"[109]

Native leaders were not the only ones affected by Stagg's attack on the Midewiwin. The missionaries' tactics divided whole communities into Christian and traditional factions and caused personal confusion and bitterness. When a number of Christians refused to attend a Midewiwin ceremony, one Ojibwa elder "was so disappointed that he openly declared he would be no religion at all." Another old man lamented the waning of the Midewiwin, commenting sadly in 1857 near Manitoba Post, "There is scarcely any held about here now."[110] Although the Midewiwin was ultimately maintained, this was an era of often painful change and challenge. Missionary attacks on Ojibwa culture went far beyond the Midewiwin, of course, affecting Ojibwa on many levels. One rabbit-fur-clad Ojibwa man took his children away from Fairford Mission because the missionary's European style of physical discipline appalled him, and he stated, in defiance of the missionary's conviction that fur clothing was a mark of poverty or lack of civilization, that "rabbit-skin robes were as warm clothing as cloth." In this sense, rabbitskin clothing was a symbol of Native autonomy and a rejection of symbols of "civilization" – and Christianity – such as wool clothing.[111]

Such personal and emotional responses were caused in part by uncertainty over the benefits of Christianity as opposed to traditional Ojibwa beliefs. On the one hand, the Ojibwa feared losing the healing and protective properties to be gained from the Midewiwin ceremony. The individuals around Fairford who were feasted and warned about how much they would lose by neglecting the Midewiwin were undoubtedly reminded of this. Their concern was summed up by Stagg, who repeated comments made by Ojibwa to him like "many around us think that when an Indian becomes a Christian and gives medicines in a Christian manner it will do no good."[112] Given the relative deprivation and powerlessness they felt, these people had more need of "medicines," both herbal and spiritual, of healing and protection, than ever before; their need sharpened the tensions arising from being urged to choose between traditional and Christian means of obtaining these life-giving powers. And despite the continuation of the Midewiwin, the fact that Midewiwin members and leaders were being converted suggests that the events of the previous decades had shaken some Ojibwas' faith in the efficacy of their ceremonies, and in their entire traditional system of relations with the supernatural, and that they were looking to Christianity for other sources of protection and aid in these changing times.

Although they were urged to choose between Christianity and their older beliefs, many Ojibwa responded to missionary pressures by combining the two religions. The syncretic bridges they created were also responses to the other pressures they felt resulting from their relative deprivation and powerlessness. The Ojibwa were eager for new sources of assistance, and they saw in Christianity new guardian figures and sacred objects, which they added to their own belief system. Such multi-faceted reactions are present in virtually every missionization effort involving North American Native peoples; they represent a universal pattern of making sense of new phenomena by explaining them in familiar categories. In a subtle way, such recombinations are nativistic, for they reinforce the validity of traditional beliefs by fitting new ideas into old. By combining new sources of power with older ideas about power, the Ojibwa addressed their very real needs in a spirit of creativity and hope, and by absorbing Christian ideas into their existing framework they re-asserted many aspects of their culture in this difficult era.

The very nature of missionization promoted the rise of syncretic beliefs. Non-Christian families often attended Stagg's sermons, in addition to receiving his lectures on the evils of "idolatry" outside church. The Interlake Ojibwa would also have discussed Christian beliefs and their ramifications for Native culture with kin from Red River, Baie St. Paul, and Rainy River, where Protestant and Catholic missionaries had been at work for some time. Belcourt found an Ojibwa woman from the Baie St. Paul mission at Manitoba Post during his tour of the Interlake in 1840, illustrating the ease with which Christian ideas were communicated to a wide circle of bands around mission stations.[113] They also went back and forth between Catholic and Anglican missions, in the Interlake and elsewhere, to the frustration of the missionaries, absorbing ideas from both sources.

The resultant attempts of the Interlake Ojibwa to integrate new and old cosmologies are seen in events such as one reported by Stagg in 1854, when "some heathen Indians at one of the fishing places were very much frightened. . . . It appears a moose went very near to their tents, and they imagined it was something bad sent by the Swampies." At first, this incident and the analysis of its causes by the Ojibwa conformed to existing patterns: suspicion of the Swampies, and their magical "feud" with them. When the incident occurred a second time, though, the "heathens" had some Christian Ojibwa read the Bible as protection, drawing on the power of God through the use of a sacred object in the same manner as they would have drawn on their guardian spirits and medicine objects.[114] Similarly, by 1843, at least one old man at the Partridge Crop Catholic mission was so afraid of the power of the Catholic Ladder (a visual portrayal of Christian history and Catholic doctrine) that he would not look at it.[115]

Rivalry between Catholic and Protestant missionaries at the Partridge Crop and around the Interlake also encouraged nativistic responses by the Ojibwa. One leader told Father Tissot that "the English, French, and Sauteux nations each had their own prayers, suitable to them, and not transferable to others." Ojibwa at Partridge Crop – where for several years there were both Catholic and Protestant missions – likewise told Father Edouard Darveau that, "when you both agree, and travel the same road, we will travel with you; till then, however, we will adhere to our own religion."[116]

All of the pressures with which the Ojibwa were faced in these years – mild resource deprivation, the decline of their fortunes in the fur trade, and pressures from competing missionaries – combined to produce stronger and more dramatic responses in some Ojibwa families. These responses included millenarian and nativistic prophecies, recorded at and around Fairford Mission in the 1850s by Church Missionary Society agents Abraham Cowley, William Stagg and James Settee. The prophecies were spread by a number of Ojibwa (just how many is never certain from the records) who claimed that God had spoken to them in their visions. One person also claimed to have received a book from heaven. Collectively, the prophets' message was that "God will rain down from heaven Cloth, Cotton, Lead & Iron, yea, Gold & Silver & make the Indian richer than the white man. That the white man will beg his bread from the Indian. That any Chief Indian that wishes to possess those riches when they come let him, give the prophet without reserve as much goods as he can get to secure himself a portion of the riches which is to be send down to the Indian from heaven." The prophets also foretold that a great ship would descend from the heavens and that Noah himself would return in it, bringing back all the wild animals to the Indians.[117] Significantly, this last prediction was made by the religious leaders who campaigned to retain Midewiwin initiates, and it was part of their reassurances during the feasts they held for individuals who wavered toward Christianity.

The Interlake prophecies were not an isolated occurrence. They were related to a series of similar prophecies that spread throughout the Northwest between 1842 and 1864, and they were also related to conditions that sparked a brief revival movement at Oxford House, northeast of Lake Winnipeg, in the late 1820s, and to the earlier, Shawnee Prophet movement and similar, but individualistic, dreams and revelations such as those of Tabashaw. The mid-nineteenth-century prophecies erupted first along the coast of Hudson Bay at Fort Churchill, Moose Factory, and Albany, and later inland at Norway House in 1842 under the influence of a Cree man named Abishabis. Much of this movement was based on Cree appropriation of the power of writing, using James Evans's new system of syllabics for the transcription of Native languages, and on the prophet's claim of being able to produce maps of the "track to Heaven" (similar to the Catholic Ladder?) – an element echoed by the Interlake prophet's claim to have received a book from Heaven. Abishabis collected many gifts from his followers, just as the Interlake prophets expected to. Abishabis himself fell into disfavour and was ultimately killed as a *windigo* in late August 1843. The movement was temporarily suppressed after his death but recurred at points around the Bay and at Norway House for several years before re-emerging in a different form at Berens River and Fairford in the 1850s. Other, similar, prophecies and bouts of unrest occurred across the Northwest at Île-à-la-Crosse, Portage la Loche, Lake Athabasca, and Great Slave Lake in the 1850s and 1860s.[118]

As much as the Interlake prophecies were related to these other movements and spiritual currents and hint at cargo cults and full-blown movements of revitalization, they were themselves not a "movement" of any kind. Even allowing for the fact that the missionaries might have downplayed or underreported the spread of such beliefs to protect themselves, there is no evidence that large numbers of Ojibwa believed or followed the prophets. Rather, the prophecies were the extreme end of a spectrum of syncretic and nativistic responses to the pressures felt by Ojibwa in the Interlake during these years. Many other – probably most – Ojibwa in the region at this time pursued traditional means of interacting with traditionally conceived other-than-human beings, such as fasting for guardians and ceremonies such as the Midewiwin and the Shaking Tent. Despite the fact that they may have had a limited acceptance, though, the prophecies are worth examining in depth, for, as the most extreme response, they are also the clearest message both of the pressures that the Ojibwa felt themselves to be under and the creative solutions that the Ojibwa sought to their problems.

The prophecies have several obvious themes: a desire for easier access to trade goods; a desire to escape the growing authority of Europeans over them and to return the balance of power to Native people; a desire to re-assert the authority of Ojibwa religious leaders vis-à-vis the missionaries; a perceived need for larger game populations; and a desire to return to what they saw as a better and more rewarding life in the past. And beneath these more obvious meanings lie a number of others, subtler, but just as important. The prophecies incorporate Christian teachings but twist these into Ojibwa forms, asserting the validity of the Ojibwa world view. Thus, the prophets identified themselves with Jesus, the Christian shaman – although the elements of their dreams work in a traditional Ojibwa manner. Their authority was derived from both traditional sources (dreams as contexts for revelation and receiving power from supernatural helpers) and Christian ones (Jesus, God, Noah, and a book from Heaven).[119] The prophets' appropriation of symbols of Christian authority – revelations from God, the figure of Noah, the gift of a holy and powerful Book – reveals their willingness to augment their traditional world view. It is also an attempt to make use of what the missionaries claimed was the greater power of Christian spiritual beings over Ojibwa ones.

Other cultural re-assertions implied by the prophecies include the implication, in the promise that the Europeans' god would send trade goods to the Indians, that Native concepts of sharing and reciprocity would be reinstated in the fur trade world. Likewise, the prophets' suggestion that followers give them goods parallels the practice of gift giving when one wishes to learn medicinal or spiritual secrets, or to Midewiwin leaders and shamans when asking them to perform a ceremony. The prophecies are also a strong re-assertion of the validity of Ojibwa culture in their forceful answer to cruel statements by missionaries, such as Reverend Cockran's comment to Peguis in the fall of 1830 that the Master of Life had deliberately taken the animals away from the Ojibwa in order to get the Ojibwa to assimilate and convert.[120] Not only do the prophecies deny this reasoning, but they also make Christianity literally the vehicle by which the animals – and the Ojibwas' former way of life – would be returned to the Ojibwa.

The prophecies give voice to what must have been felt by many Ojibwa in the region. Certainly the Ojibwas' feelings at having to "beg [their] bread" are reflected in the predictions of a time when "the Indian [would be] richer than the white man; . . . the white man will beg his bread from the Indian." The inability of trapping and hunting conditions in the Interlake to support traditional means of attaining social prestige was further reduced by the missionaries' undermining of Native leadership and by their generally divisive methods, heightening the Ojibwas' feelings of powerlessness and subjugation. It is thus little wonder that the Ojibwa longed for a reversal of the prevailing balance of power and the return to a mythological "golden age."

Again, the prophecies were not heeded by most of the Ojibwa in the Interlake; nor did they persist for long. The rain of trade goods never happened, and Noah did not return the game to the Ojibwa in the Interlake. One ceremonial leader died, and others were baptised shortly after the height of the prophecy movement. The report of the Hind expedition of 1858 describes Fairford Mission but does not mention either the prophecies or their aftermath.[121] As the most extreme example of nativism and syncretism in the Interlake at this time, the prophecies reveal the attempts by the Ojibwa to re-affirm their way of viewing the universe, to use new powers to improve their situation, and to cope with the changing world.[122] Despite their short lifespan, the prophecies were, I would argue, a means of empowerment, of claiming aspects of a new era and reality for the Ojibwa by means of prophecy and syncretism. Ultimately, the prophecies and other syncretic responses to missionization made it possible for the Interlake Ojibwa to feel that they were active participants in, rather than merely victims of, the new reality.[123]

BETWEEN THE INTERLAKE AND THE PLAINS: THE TRANSITIONAL ZONE

In the forest and parkland zones west of the Interlake, life continued for Ojibwa much as it had in the past five decades, and missionization had much less effect than in the Interlake district. If anything, trade and ecological conditions were better for the Ojibwa in this region between 1837 and 1857 than they were in the decades before or after. The posts and outposts of this region included Forts Ellice, Pelly, the Guard Post, Shoal River, Red Deer River; Fort-à-la-Corne, Carlton House, and Pitt; and the Touchwood Hills and Qu'Appelle Lakes. In such a wide area, the Ojibwa population was mixed. Towards the northern and western edges of the region, along the North Saskatchewan and Qu'Appelle River valleys, it contained a highly complex combination of plains- and parkland-oriented bands, while references in the Fort Pelly journal to "our Northern Sauteaux" designate bands that spent a good deal of time hunting and trapping in the wooded areas between Pelly and Fort Pitt.[124] The heart of the region, along the upper Assiniboine, also contained bands that were tied in varying degrees to the fur trade. Some, such as Gabriel Coté's mixed Métis and Ojibwa group near Fort Pelly, qualified almost as a "Home Guard," while others spent far less time around the post or trapping.

Despite this diversity, the Ojibwa of this region emerge from the records as generally being well off and able to cope. They certainly do not appear to have been, or to have perceived themselves to be, impoverished, as did their kin in the Interlake. This may in part be due to the difference in the nature of the records, though: where the Interlake records are virtually all missionary sources, which tend to emphasize difficulties or upheaval in Native life as a foil for the virtues of "civilization," the records for this transitional region are dominated by fur-trade journals and accounts, and the Ojibwa were still doing well in the trade in this area.

The confidence of the Ojibwa west of the Interlake resulted in an even more assertive response to missionization. Church Missionary Society agents established a mission station at Fort Ellice in 1843 in response to Native requests, and James Settee, Charles Pratt, and Charles Hillyer laboured at Shoal River, Carrot River, Fort Pelly, Fort Ellice, Duck Bay, the Touchwood Hills, and the Qu'Appelle Lakes between 1843 and 1857. Missionaries of other denominations, including Catholics and Methodists, also laboured in this region and in the Edmonton area. In general they were met with similar responses from the Ojibwa. Although Belcourt claimed to have some success with Ojibwa at Duck Bay, those at Swan River threatened to shoot him if he spoke to them of prayer.[125] Nor was the Church Missionary Society particularly successful in this region. Within two years after responding to the call from the Fort Ellice Indians, Church Missionary Society agents recognized that the request had in fact been made "to induce us to make them presents" rather than for any desire for salvation. Ten years later, James Settee wrote from Shoal River that "the prejudices of the Saulteaux to the Xtian religion is a great hindrance"; and his colleague, Native catechist Charles Pratt, wrote in 1859, "I find the Soties indians very obstinate to the word of truth."[126] In the years between, Ojibwa responses to missionary teachings were much the same. Over a decade after the Swan River Ojibwa threatened to shoot Belcourt, Indians in the Pelly area circulated tobacco amongst themselves, "to join, . . . to keep off the Missionaries from their lands," and broke up a fish weir that Settee used; and failed bison hunts were blamed on the missionaries. Charles Pratt, despite being Native himself, was told bluntly to "go back," and his horses were regularly stolen by the Ojibwa members of his would-be congregation.[127]

As at Rainy River, Netley Creek, and to some extent in the Interlake, the Ojibwas' hostile response to missionization stemmed in part from the vitality of the Midewiwin society and traditional spirituality, cornerstones of Ojibwa identity. From Fort Pelly to Edmonton House, there is much evidence during these years of strong continuity of identity and of group strength in reports of vigorous ceremonial life. The Midewiwin continued to be held at Fort Pelly, the Qu'Appelle Lakes, Fort Ellice, and around Fort Carlton (as well, undoubtedly, as at many other locations), and other aspects of traditional religious practice, including healing and divination ceremonies, are also recorded in the post journals.[128]

The cold welcome that the Church Missionary Society agents received in the transitional zone also had much to do with the more abundant large game and fur resources of the region and the more intense competition for furs. The Shoal River Ojibwa, for instance, had a number of free traders as well as the Hudson's Bay Company post to trade their furs at, a situation that was similar to conditions before 1805, with the result that they were said to be "getting Lazy and spoilt saucy & independent of the Company." As the missionaries themselves observed, the Indians in this region were uninterested in Christian teachings "in the day of their prosperity"; furthermore, they admitted, the Indians of the upper Assiniboine region were "much more independent" than those of Red River or the Interlake.[129]

In general, these bands tended to travel between the more densely wooded areas of the region, including Swan River, Duck Mountain, the "Sandy Knolls" near Fort Pelly, the Thunder Hills, the Touchwood Hills, and river valleys.[130] Here they hunted moose and harvested other plentiful resources. Fish continued to be an important seasonal food. Sturgeon and other species were especially plentiful around Fort-à-la-Corne and in the North Saskatchewan and upper Assiniboine rivers, and in small lakes in the region. Sugar was harvested, and the Ojibwa continued to make birchbark rogans to store it. Small game, wildfowl, prairie turnips and other wild plant foods, and some garden produce also continued to be important parts of the Ojibwa diet.[131]

Despite the paucity of records for this region in the 1840s, it is clear that the moose population in the region increased greatly between the starvation winters of the 1830s and the relative plenty of the 1850s, a brief reprieve in the general course of the nineteenth century. Many Ojibwa in the region relied on moose, a trend that may have been encouraged by the increasing travel needed to reach the contracting range of the bison herds. Rather than pitching off to the plains as had been the custom in the 1830s, some of the Ojibwa trading at Pelly "pitched off to hunt moose for the summer" in May 1854. Between April 1853 and April 1854, meat and skins representing at least 104 moose kills were traded at Pelly, and some 700 moose skins were traded at Fort Pelly in 1844, a staggering figure. The presence of moose, which Peter Grant once called the "staff of life" for the Ojibwa, was a major factor in their continuing independence during these years.[132] According to the Swan River district returns, elk, deer, and bison were also important large game species.[133] Even parkland-oriented bands continued to hunt bison at times; one of Charles Pratt's horses, which was repeatedly stolen by the Ojibwa near Fort Pelly, was a bison-runner. Ojibwa bands hunted bison south of the Touchwood Hills and in the Squirrel Hills and the region south and east of the south branch of the Saskatchewan.[134]

As noted by A.J. Ray in *Indians in the Fur Trade,* some of the best moose hunters in the region continued to apply for handouts of food at the post during winter even when moose and small game were readily available. These families sometimes arrived at the trading post in mid-winter with moose meat and dressed skins to trade, indicating that their hunt had been successful until then, but claiming that they were starving, and would have to go to the plains after bison.[135] Gabriel Coté, for instance, a Métis leader of a largely Ojibwa band, sent one of his wives to the post to beg food in March 1853, saying that they were starving; nineteen days later, Coté brought in his spring hunt, which included thirteen moose skins, a sign that his band certainly had not "starved" all winter. (One is reminded of ethnohistorian John S. Long's definition of "starving" as meaning that a band had "just enough food, with none to spare.")[136] Other families seemed to prefer the food they received at the post as an alternative to – or perhaps simply to complement – rabbits and other small game when moose were harder to find. When moose were scarce during the winter of 1855-56, the Pelly trader noted, "it is surprising when all the Indians complain of starving when the Rabbits is so thick they surlie donte strive to hunt them."[137]

Neither of these complaints involved literal starvation. Rather, both were related to manipulative uses of the term. As Ray suggests, the incidents are expressions of food preferences: an Ojibwa accustomed to feasting on moose may indeed feel he is "starving" or impoverished when moose are unavailable, even if the alternate food – in this case rabbit – is abundant. As well, these were the same bands, or their relatives, who felt that they had "some claim upon [the Hudson's Bay Company], in the event of being hard pressed," if they had become hungry because they had been trapping.[138] There is no reason to believe that this expectation had changed. Asking for and receiving food at the posts had multiple meanings and functions. In some cases it relieved literal want and was a supply of food when there was otherwise none. In other cases it relieved metaphorical want, supplying pemmican where there had been rabbits. At the same time, the traders' provision of food reassured the Ojibwa that the Company would indeed fulfill what they saw as its obligation toward them and maintain them when they truly needed it: a form of reciprocity for their skill at procuring furs. Rather than simply being a sign of dependence on the posts, as some scholars have suggested – a transition from "self employment" to post employees receiving food for furs – Ojibwa demands for food had more complex meanings and were part of an adaptive strategy, the goal of which was to ensure a supply of food during lean times and adequate reciprocity for their work and loyalty.[139]

Whatever difficulties the Ojibwa experienced obtaining food in these years, they seldom had trouble paying their debts. Fur populations recovered a good deal by the 1850s, and once again these bands brought in excellent returns. Indians from Red Deer River were able to pay "considerably more than" their fall debts by early January 1848, and a band that arrived at Pelly in May 1848 brought over 1,000 MB in good furs. The trader remarked that several of these "had paid their debts before, they will of course leave empty stores." Debts of 129 to 250 MB were paid by Ojibwa hunters at Fort Pelly in the early 1850s, and except during the harsh winter of 1855-56 most Ojibwa men routinely paid their debts and had furs to spare; several even took and paid two or more separate debts of over 100 MB each. These returns were particularly remarkable given that the length of the trapping season was increasingly limited by the availability of large game.[140]

The ready availability of furs meant not only renewed affluence and prestige for these bands, but also the heightened fur-trade competition that developed in the region once again shifted the balance of power from trader to trapper. Not since before the coalition of 1821 had the Ojibwa done as well out of European rivalry. The competition was linked to the rise of free traders, men who traded privately with Indians for their furs in defiance of the Hudson's Bay Company's monopoly. Throughout the 1840s, the numbers of free traders grew as mixed-blood children of Hudson's Bay Company officers found their career possibilities increasingly restricted. As racist attitudes penetrated the Hudson's Bay Company hierarchy, even the mixed-blood children of senior officers, who were well-educated and brought up in an atmosphere of some gentility, found themselves limited essentially to labouring positions, while officers were appointed from outside the Northwest.

Given these restrictions, it was only a matter of time before the bolder mixed-blood men in Red River began trading and shipping on their own. The resulting tensions culminated in the 1849 Sayer trial in Red River, during which a Métis man, Guillame Sayer, was tried for illegally trading liquor for furs. Although Sayer was found guilty, he was not punished – partly because officials were concerned that the colony's regular defense force, the retired Des Meuron soldiers, would be attacked by the incensed Métis community. The Métis interpreted the outcome of the trial to mean that the Company was unable to stop them from trading privately.[141]

In response to the proliferation of free traders after the Sayer trial, and the inroads they made on the Company's fur return, fur prices were raised in areas of intense competition and the number of sub-posts increased.[142] In many ways, it was a return to the days of intense competition before 1821: runners were sent to collect furs from Indian tents, goods were slightly easier to obtain, and once again loyalty was rewarded by the traders.

This competition was keenly felt in the region west of the Interlake. In the 1850s, free traders were common around Duck Bay, Egg Lake, Devil's Lake, the Red Deer River, Jackfish Lake, the Thickwood Hills, and along both branches of the Saskatchewan.[143] This prompted the re-opening of Hudson's Bay Company outposts in several of these areas as well as the establishment of several new outposts along the Qu'appelle River to provide a barrier against the free traders. Fur prices and the quantity of presents given, especially alcohol, increased. By the early 1850s, competition was having a serious effect on the trade. The Fort Pelly trader admitted in late 1853 that he was "anxious to do all this winter to prevent any Indians from trading with the freemen," and he was surely not alone in this sentiment. Having had a few lean years since the trade was so good, the Ojibwa were quite ready to turn the competition to their own advantage. Not only did many bands trade with the first trader who happened along or simply refuse to pay their old debts, but some even refused to trade at the Hudson's Bay Company's tariff and instead set prices themselves.[144] By 1855 the situation was such that James Settee complained that the Indians (mostly Ojibwa) at Shoal River were "independent, the free traders is making them great cheats"; the following year, the Fort Pelly trader similarly complained that the Shoal River bands had become "Lazy and spoilt saucy & independent of the Company."[145] In retaliation, some traders began refusing all credit to Indians, but the presence of so many free traders in the region likely negated any hardship this might have caused the Ojibwa.

The material advantages that came with furs and fur-trade competition were accompanied by stresses. The pressures of renewed competition once again made alcohol an important factor in the trade, and more incidents of alcohol abuse and alcohol-related violence are recorded in the Fort Pelly journals during the 1850s than in the 1840s. Gabriel Coté's "customary gratuity of Rum" was eighteen quarts, which was shared amongst his band during a single drinking party. Another senior hunter, Saucy Fellow, traded 114 pounds of moose meat all for rum in one trading session, typical of what Ojibwa received for country produce during these years.[146] Alcohol also brought out tensions in the relationship between traders and Ojibwa. Coté and his Ojibwa followers became rowdy after being given their annual present of liquor, and they threatened the traders with physical violence if they did not receive more.[147] Free traders and American traders were generous with alcohol, and the deaths and injuries associated with this only compounded the fear and stress caused by the continuing dwindling of the bison herds, the overall decline of the fur trade, and the changing political control of the Northwest in the following decades.

To these stresses were added the disquieting implications of the 1851 Turtle Mountain Treaty. A well-established refuge for Ojibwa bands, affording access to the bison herds as well as parkland resources, and with strong ties to Métis kin there and at St. Joseph (Father Belcourt's relocated Catholic community just east of Turtle Mountain), this area had done well out of the American border trade. But as the fur trade waned on the border after its heyday in the 1840s, and tensions rose between the Ojibwa and Métis of the area over the dwindling bison hunt, the Ojibwa complained to government officials about the state of things around Turtle Mountain.[148] As the great American westward migration began in earnest, the American government began to negotiate treaties with the western tribes in the early 1850s to facilitate settlement. The Turtle Mountain Treaty of 1851 was one such negotiation. It was initiated by Native protests, the arrival of American settlers in the region, and by the Governor of what was then Minnesota Territory, Alexander Ramsey. During the negotiations, one Ojibwa elder, Clear Weather, interrupted the Governor's speech, "asking that Ramsey cease his "sugared words or honeyed phrases" and tell the assembled natives exactly what they stood to gain from the treaty. The government agent was either unable or unwilling to tell them the truth and did not answer Clear Weather. And, although they finally came to an agreement about land cessions and compensations, the treaty was never ratified.[149] Consequently, as the American land rush began in the area just south of the border, the Turtle Mountain people were horrified to find themselves dispossessed, landless, and caught in a decades-long, frustrating struggle to have their land claims recognized and a settlement made. They were granted a small reservation, but much of the land they claimed was opened to White settlement in the 1880s.[150] This bitter lesson was not lost on the more northerly Ojibwa. The fate of the Turtle Mountain people would inform rumour, fuel anxiety, and serve as the symbol of what was to come for the entire Northwest.

By mid-century, the western Ojibwa had made a complex adjustment to the prairies and parklands, to rephrase James Howard's statement. While some Ojibwa bands looked, behaved, and felt like the classic "plains" peoples whose heyday this was, others remained in the parkland and forested areas and retained the way of life that they had developed virtually on their entry to the West. All the western Ojibwa, however much they absorbed from the plains-oriented peoples around them, retained a crucial core of older culture, identity, and sense of heritage, and, in all the western Ojibwa adaptations, change was balanced by continuity. During the turbulence of the decades to come, these dual qualities of adaptability and stability would stand the western Ojibwa in good stead.

"Mischiefmakers . . . [and] shrewd men," 1858 to 1870

6

In the late 1850s, the storm that had been building over the old Northwest finally broke. Within a scant three decades it swept away so much of the old way of life that those who lived through it looked back with astonishment at the speed and totality of the change. These decades saw, in rapid succession, the organized exploration and survey of the West by Whites; the transition from Hudson's Bay Company "rule" to the rule of a country that had not existed at the beginning of the period; the intensification of contacts with the outside world through steamboat and rail; the negotiation of the first treaties and the move onto reserves; and, unthinkably, the virtual extinction of the bison. These winds of change caused other, more immediate, damage. Dakota bands fled into the lands of their Ojibwa enemies in 1863 as the result of conflict with White settlers in their homelands. And, for the plains Ojibwa, the final, frenzied, *danse macabre* of the buffalo-robe trade was also the height of the whiskey trade, resulting in many deaths by violence; they were also caught up in inter-tribal warfare given deadly impetus by disputes over the right to occupy the ever-contracting lands roamed by the bison. To violent death and despair was added the mortality of a vicious smallpox epidemic in 1870, immediately before the treaty negotiations began.

The Hind and Palliser expeditions across the Northwest mark the beginning of this period. These expeditions (the Palliser expedition sent by the British government, the Hind/Dawson/Hime expedition sent by the Canadian), traversed the West between 1857 and 1860 to assess the region's potential for agricultural settlement. They recorded an amazing amount of information about the natural conditions and human populations they encountered along their separate routes, and H.L. Hime of the Hind party took the first photographs of the Northwest. These images, together with the records of both parties, provide a "snapshot" of Ojibwa life across the West in the late 1850s and 1860s.

10. H.L. Hime, 1858, "Birch Bark Tents, west bank of Red River, middle settlement," photograph (courtesy Provincial Archives of Manitoba, Hime Collection 17, negative no. N12554).

The Hind expedition stopped for a fortnight at Red River in early June of 1857 and again on its return journey in 1858. On his second visit to the settlement, Hime photographed views of Ojibwa and Cree camps, portraits of several Natives, and views of the settlement. The Hime photographs confirm the strong suggestions of cultural continuity given in earlier archival evidence (see Illustrations 10 and 11).

Hime's work included several photographs of Ojibwa lodges, which he took on the banks of the Red River in the Middle Settlement. These structures were conical in shape, though one is oval-based with a central ridge pole running the length of the lodge. Several are covered with rush mats as well as birch-bark, and around the base of one are arranged neatly bundled bunches of what appear to be rushes, ready to be made into mats.[1] These are scenes unchanged from Peter Rindisbacher's paintings of Red River Ojibwa in the 1820s.

The combination of traditional and Christian religious practices by Red River Ojibwa is attested by a variety of sources. Several of Hime's images show tradi-

11. H.L. Hime, 1858, "Ojibway Woman and Child," photograph (courtesy Provincial Archives of Manitoba, Hime Collection 31, negative no. N12579).

tional Native graves roofed with boards and bark, which may either have been in the Indian Settlement or at the graveyard at Point Douglas near the Forks itself.[2] Other evidence that the St. Peter's Ojibwa were maintaining their ceremonial life comes from Hind's note that dog feasts were held on two Sundays during his stay in Red River. These feasts may have been part of Midewiwin ceremonies, which were reported as being held near Lower Fort Garry and elsewhere around the settlement throughout the 1860s.[3] Another ceremony, the Trade Dance, was still being held by the Ojibwa and Cree in the region at this time, for a set of equipment used in the dance – tiny bows, arrows, guns, knives, and hatchets with offerings of tobacco tied to them – was collected in the Winnipeg area in the 1870s. The Trade Dance was dedicated to Pakuk, a supernatural figure associated with winter and starvation, to bring snow so that game might be easily tracked and fur-bearers easily trapped during the winter.[4]

Other sources confirm that Ojibwa participation in Christianity was still tentative around Red River and that syncretism remained an important element of the "new" faith of those converted. At Fort Garry in 1867, one Ojibwa claimed (perhaps hopefully) that the last flood in the colony had washed away all the Indians' debts on the Hudson's Bay Company books, just as baptism had washed away their sins. And there were some who steadfastly refused to convert. Even at Portage la Prairie, where Cockran's agricultural settlement for Ojibwa was reported to be doing well, Hime and his colleagues encountered "an Ojibwa encampment in which were some of the refractory personages who had hitherto resisted the humane and unceasing efforts of the Archdeacon Cochrane to christianize them."[5] The Ojibwas' position towards Christianity seems not to have changed greatly since the 1820s. Peguis, the missionaries' ally and the stoutest proponent of Christianity, died in 1864.

Hime's other photographs at Red River suggest the persistence of Ojibwa subsistence practices. His image of bark and dug-out canoes drawn up on a bank in the Middle Settlement is a reminder of the continuing importance of country products (including canoes) sold by the Ojibwa to residents of the settlement. On a visit to Red River in late winter of 1869, Walter Traill also confirmed the settlement's reliance on country foods, some of which were sold by Ojibwa. The settlement was "in a desperate way" at the time of his visit, he said, with "no crops, no buffalo, no fish, and no rabbits."[6]

The importance of the fishery to the settlement was demonstrated in an 1865 resolution of the Council of Assiniboia, which determined that "it shall be unlawful to erect any Weirs or Barriers in any part of the Red River or Assiniboine" because by these "the majority of the people were prevented from catching a fair share of the fish on which, even in ordinary seasons, and much more in a season like this, so many were dependent for their means of living."[7] There is no evidence that this was enforced against the Ojibwa fishery, but the very passing of the resolution underscores the desire of Europeans in the settlement to exercise control over resources and over the Ojibwa, whom the Council did not consider to be part of "the majority of the people" or to be deserving of "a fair share of the fish" on which they had relied for so long. Like the 1845 hanging, the resolution demonstrates the development of European power structures at Red River. If the Ojibwa were not affected by these structures through the 1865 weir resolution, they would be after the signing of Treaty Number 1 in 1870 and afterwards, as Euro-Canadian administrative and legal structures enmeshed them.

The Ojibwa continued to cultivate small plots at their cabins in the Indian settlement, but even after the treaties they supplemented their crops with game, wild rice, fish (and fish oil and fish pemmican), berries and roots, sugar, and wildfowl from around the lake. Much of this was the product of women's labour, though as hunting became poorer around the settlement it is likely that Ojibwa men altered their subsistence activities and contributed to some of this work as well as seeking short-term wage labour in the settlement. They also trapped small quantities of furs and traded at Upper and Lower Fort Garry for ammunition, kettles, cloth, and clothing.[8] Both the Ojibwa photographed by Hime (a woman with a child and an "Ojibway half breed") wore cloth, European-style clothing.

Their economic participation in Red River sustained a nominal social presence in the settlement for the Ojibwa as well. The annual spring gathering described by Walter Traill was only partly for trade: "The Common between the village of Winnipeg and Fort Garry is the camping ground in summer for both Traders and Indians, being occupied by hundreds of tents and bands of horses. Here is where our local tribes, the Crees and Saulteaux, collect after the spring hunting and trapping season is over."[9] Hime's photographs of Ojibwa tents in the Middle Settlement also imply that Ojibwa were frequent visitors in Red River.

Those of Hind's party who travelled through the Interlake found Ojibwa life there similar to that near Red River. Spring brought the muskrat hunt, the duck and goose hunt, and the sugar camp; summer, more hunting and fishing; autumn, the Midewiwin ceremonies, the crucial fall fishery, another muskrat hunt, and the fall goose hunt; winter, some ice-fishing and sporadic trapping.[10] Life had not changed much for these people in several decades.

Though the urgency of the prophecies had died down by the late 1850s, many of the Interlake Ojibwa maintained their resistance to missionization. At Scanterbury, near the mouth of the Brokenhead River, the people were so against having a mission that the chief threatened Cree missionary James Settee with a gun, while at Fairford the Midewiwin leader reproached William Stagg for always telling people about Heaven "as though you want to get rid of them."[11] Other evidence that these Ojibwa still lived within their traditional world view came in a conversation between Settee and an old man who explained that a violent thunderstorm that occurred at Scanterbury was in fact Thunderbird fighting a great sturgeon or serpent (*missepeshu*?), and in Stagg's complaint that Ojibwa parents at Fairford refused to discipline their children in European fashion but allowed them, as was customary for Native parents, "to run about as they please."[12] For the Interlake people, the period between the prophecies and the treaties was also characterized by continuity. That they were slightly removed from the path of the main "invasion" from eastern Canada and America buffered them somewhat from the changes that swept the Northwest in these decades.

After the party left Red River, Hind and Hime travelled to Portage la Prairie, then to the confluence of the Souris and the Assiniboine rivers and up the Little Souris River, north to Fort Ellice, and along the Qu'Appelle valley to the Fishing Lakes. The party then divided. Hime's group travelled to Last Mountain Lake and then returned to rendezvous with the other group at Fort Pelly. Later, they explored the Riding Mountain area before going to Red River to winter. Their route thus took them through the heart of the region occupied by both plains- and parkland-oriented Ojibwa, and gave them a glimpse of the changing situation in both areas at this time.

In the late 1850s and 1860s, many of the bison-oriented Ojibwa continued to camp in and around the Touchwood Hills and the upper Qu'Appelle River valley. This pattern was not affected by the dwindling of the herds until the bison retreated southwest beyond the limits of Cree territory. By 1867, it was said that the Touchwood Hills were no longer a good place to wait for bison. Small herds occasionally approached Forts Qu'Appelle and Ellice, but only sporadically. Rather than being camping areas where bands could await the arrival of the herds, this region became a series of rendezvous points at which bands would collect and then, in large groups, make extended trips in search of the herds.[13]

Competition for the remaining bison provoked varying tensions among the peoples of the northern plains. The most serious of these was the renewed violence between the Blackfoot and their Cree and Ojibwa enemies, provoked by hunting parties forcing yearly deeper into Blackfoot territory to locate the remainder of the herds. Palliser said that the region between the Souris and the Saskatchewan rivers "may be called a buffalo preserve, being the battle-ground between the Crees and the Blackfeet, where none go to hunt without fear of meeting enemies."[14] Decades later, Alanson Skinner recorded memories of Ojibwa participation in this warfare, a series of retaliatory murders in which a marked tomahawk, left in the body of a victim, appeared the next year in a body of an enemy killed in revenge. In the 1860s and 1870s, as the whiskey traffic grew and the Blackfoot obtained repeating rifles from Americans, warfare would claim even more lives. Hime's photograph of the open prairie, with a human skull in the foreground, was a more apt metaphor than he knew for the situation on the plains.[15]

Nor were the Blackfoot the only serious threat to the plains peoples. The Métis hunts continued to deplete the dwindling bison herds, and, under such conditions, decades-old resentment against them escalated into real hostility. Hind had a council with a Cree band at the Sandy Hills in 1858 at which the Cree "objected strongly to the half-breeds hunting buffalo during the winter in the Plain Cree country," and the Cree also objected to the establishment of a mission at Qu'Appelle because they were afraid it would attract Métis who would then drive away the bison. Within mixed-group bison-hunting camps, the Métis "were required to pitch their tents individually at wide intervals and surrounded by many an Indian lodge."[16] A Métis post employee, Terry McKay, incurred the anger of the Natives in a camp in the late 1860s: "He had been hunting and had loaded some of his carts which displeased the Indians."[17]

In response to the changed pattern of the herds' movements and the competition to gain access to them, the Cree led an "armed migration" into the Cypress Hills region in the late 1860s. There, large multi-ethnic camps containing Cree, Assiniboine, Ojibwa, and Métis began forming in the summer months to provide protection against the Blackfoot as well as to ensure that straggling bands did not frighten away the herd. The reason that Terry McKay's loaded carts "displeased the Indians" was that by hunting on his own he had run the risk of stampeding the herd, something the camp was specifically trying not to do. Isaac Cowie found one such camp consisting of some 350 lodges of Cree, Assiniboine, Ojibwa, and Métis just northeast of the Cypress Hills in 1868; and Walter Traill, another Hudson's Bay Company employee, visited either this one or a similar one in the same area in the late 1860s.[18]

The Ojibwas' presence in these camps does not seem to have been resented as that of the Métis was. Plains Ojibwa continued to use and indeed emphasized their kinship with the plains Cree to gain access to the bison. As Hind noted in the official report of the expedition, the Ojibwa and Cree "are often found hunting the buffalo in company, and not unfrequently form family connections." Historian John Milloy has also theorized that, with the dwindling of the herds, the Cree may also have become more interested in Ojibwa hunting magic than previously, a factor that would have made the Ojibwa welcome in Cree camps when the Métis were not.[19]

The large multi-ethnic camps observed by Traill and Cowie demonstrate the social effects of the tensions that were building on the plains in these decades. The camp observed by Cowie had come together for mutual needs but broke up as soon as its goals were accomplished. And, though they had begun the gathering with a mutually celebrated Sun Dance, which affirmed the social cohesion of the assembled bands, the various peoples remained to some degree ethnically separate, for they each pitched their tents in a different area of the camp circle. As Traill noted of one such camp, "there was no small amount of jealousy amongst themselves as is always the case when many Indian tribes meet."[20] This "jealousy," which existed even between some Ojibwa and Cree, illustrates the hardening of the ethnic boundaries and status differential that had always existed between them. Reflecting on the treaty negotiations during the 1870s, Peter Erasmus, a Métis, commented that "the Prairie Crees looked down on the Swampy and Ojibwa as an inferior race." The Hind expedition made a similar observation and noted also that "notwithstanding this intercourse and blending of different nations, most of the superstitions and customs peculiar to each are still maintained and practised."[21]

For the Ojibwa, some of this continued separation was based on their reputation as having great spiritual power. A comment made by the Reverend George McDougall during treaty negotiations in the 1870s is instructive: "Big Bear and his party were a very small minority in camp. The Crees said they would have driven them out of camp long ago, but were afraid of their medicines as they are noted conjurors."[22] While the Ojibwa had always had this reputation, and had maintained a separate identity from the Cree with whom they lived and intermarried, the strident tenor of comments such as this and those by Erasmus and Hind in the 1858-1875 period suggests that stresses caused by the many changes in these years may have hardened these differences. If this were so, the strengthening of these boundaries between Ojibwa and Cree would have contributed to the preservation of a distinctly plains Ojibwa identity, somewhat different from that of the Cree.

Such distinctions between Cree and Ojibwa would not have been immediately apparent to observers such as Hind, Palliser, Traill, and Cowie. By mid-century, plains Ojibwa people were using bison pounds, complete with bison callers who had the spiritual power to call the bison to the pound, as well as the mounted chase; had adopted the warrior society, or *okitcitak*; lived in tipis arranged in camp circles; and celebrated the Sun, or Thirst, Dance. These camps may, as well, have had a more formally structured organization (with their *okitcita*, council, chief, and careful discipline during the bison hunt) than did the more parkland-oriented, transitional Ojibwa bands living just to the north and east. As described by elders who came to young adulthood during the third quarter of the nineteenth century and who later worked with anthropologists Alanson Skinner and James Howard, much of plains Ojibwa culture was virtually indistinguishable from that of the plains Cree (or, in some respects, from that of the Métis), particularly with respect to men's activities and values.[23]

Ojibwa men continued to adopt and internalize the roles and expectations of "plains" men more quickly than Ojibwa women adopted corresponding "plains" behaviours. This differential was partly due to the greater advantages that "plains" cultures offered men than women, although our understanding of such dynamics has been hampered by male-oriented anthropologists working primarily with Ojibwa men, who failed to collect data on women's perspectives and priorities. The gender differential did exist, though. Consider the gender orientation of some of the continuing adaptations in plains Ojibwa culture during this third quarter of the nineteenth century. The ceremonies that the Ojibwa adopted and purchased from the Cree were virtually all male-oriented. Women participated in some, including the Sun Dance, but they played lesser roles in the ceremonies and stood to gain fewer social or spiritual benefits from performing them.[24] All in all, plains Ojibwa men stood to gain far more prestige, self-esteem, and material and social benefits from participating in the bison hunt, the robe and pemmican trade, and the *okitcita* and other societies than did their female relatives.

An example of the special appeal of plains cultures to western Ojibwa men is warfare. Escalating warfare on the plains during the nineteenth century was related not only to competition over access to the bison herds but also to the deep internalization of the plains system of counting coup and stealing horses as a means for men to obtain prestige and social status. A breechcloth design illustrated by Skinner showing a symbolic camp circle, enemy tents, and the hoof prints of stolen horses is a singularly plains symbol of male prowess (see Illustration 12).

Like Big Bear, the men with whom Skinner worked noted that on his return from a war party a leader would give away all the horses and trophies he had captured, "thus acquiring great reknown" – and fulfilling the expectations held of a plains Ojibwa man, a value system acquired from the plains Cree.[25] Objects such as the full-length trailing eagle feather headdress and bonnet collected by Alexander Morris from a Manitoba Ojibwa also underscore the attraction of plains-oriented symbols and behaviours to men.[26]

Even for plains Ojibwa men in these decades, though, plains traits remained a veneer over a deeper heritage of cultural continuity. For every overtly "plains" custom and behaviour, there was other evidence of the retention of a much older cultural system. The water drum and the board with incised animal figures found by Eugene Bourgeau of the Palliser expedition at Fort Carlton, described in chapter 5 of this volume, both express this heritage. Perhaps even more telling than these artifacts is Skinner's observation that, among the plains Ojibwa, "The *okitcita* tent alone was furnished with the triangular willow stick backrests found more generally in use among other Plains tribes."[27] Even the men among the plains Ojibwa, it would seem, adopted only the most obvious symbols and elements of plains male culture; items found in the *okitcita* tent were not incorporated into all households, as would have been the case among the plains Cree or Assiniboine.

Since the household was the domain of women, this may be yet another piece of evidence for a gender differential in the adoption of plains culture: did women resist such changes? Certainly the Ojibwa women seen by the Earl of Southesk at Fort Qu'Appelle in 1859, waiting with their families for others to join them before going to the plains for the bison hunt, were wearing dresses that sound from the Earl's description like the old-style Ojibwa strap dress sketched by Kurz in 1851, rather than the deer-tail or wave-yoke dresses then favoured by Cree women.[28] In

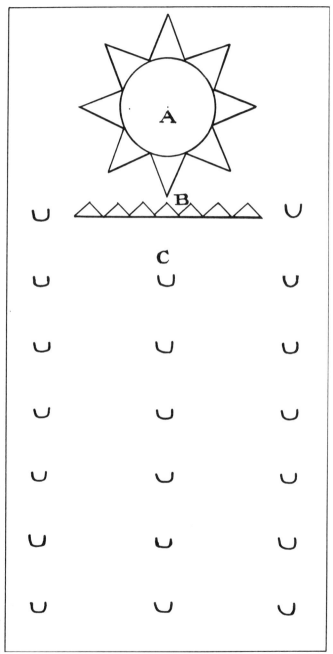

12. Western Ojibwa breechcloth design, originally illustrated in Alanson Skinner's 1914 paper, "Political and Ceremonial Organizations of the Plains-Ojibwa," p. 484, photograph by J. Beckett (courtesy Department of Anthropology Archives and Department of Library Services, American Museum of Natural History, negative no. 338391).

contrast to the style of their dresses, however, the camp in which the Earl saw these women looked to him like a typical plains camp, with skin tipis arranged in a camp circle, and Southesk himself was seated in the typically Cree guest spot in one of these, opposite the door.[29] Again, though these people adopted many customs from their Cree relatives, and looked – to nineteenth-century observers and twentieth-century ethnologists – like "plains" people, the reality of plains Ojibwa culture was a good deal more complex below the surface.

Several items of Ojibwa and Ojibwa-Cree material culture from this period visually demonstrate this complex recombination of elements. A man's shirt in the collection of the Haffenreffer Museum provides a vivid illustration of the cultural dualism that even the plains-oriented Ojibwa bands retained (see Illustration 13).

Collection records on the shirt identify it as part of an outfit belonging to "a Plains Cree chief" about 1860 to 1890; it may well have come from one of the mixed bands in the region at the time. While its sleeve and shoulder strips, beaded in a diamond pattern, and the rosettes on its chest and sleeves, conform to essential elements of classic nineteenth-century northern plains style, as do the fringes and painted rib-like striping, other aspects of the shirt's decoration reflect a Great Lakes heritage. Its neck and cuffs are beaded "in early Ojibwa style, with the linear, openwork designs commonly used in the eighteenth and early nineteenth centuries," including bands of small diamond and straight-line designs, similar to the Ojibwa otter-tail pattern. These designs are worked in white on the cuffs, reminiscent of the lace and braid trim on European military coats and, perhaps, on the coats given to trading chiefs. As Barbara Hail concludes, "The shirt provides a most interesting example of the movement of design styles from East to West with the movement of peoples, and of strong cultural continuity in the carry-over of certain favored design motifs, coexistent with a ready acceptance of new design ideas."[30]

Other shirts with similar black, white, and red concentric bull's-eye chest rosettes are attributed to the Ojibwa. One is illustrated in Howard's work on the Turtle Mountain people, and another, now in the collection of the Royal Ontario Museum, was collected by Alexander Morris from a Manitoba Ojibwa during or after the treaty negotiations.[31] The Morris collection shirt is also an interesting mixture of styles: a square neck flap of red stroud, with the beaded "bull's-eye" chest rosette, and striped, beaded cuffs, joined by loom-woven beadwork on sleeve and shoulder strips. This shirt also has a series of horizontal black lines (cruder versions of the "ribs" on the Haffenreffer shirt, or possibly a record of war honours or "coups") below the chest medallion. The woven strips are of a complex pattern, similar to strips from Minnesota and Wisconsin Ojibwa, just as the beaded cuffs on the Haffenreffer shirt are reminiscent of Great Lakes design. The composite nature of these shirts reflects the similarly composite makeup of western Ojibwa

13. "Plains Cree" shirt (courtesy of the Haffenreffer Museum of Anthropology, Brown University HMA 77-171).

culture and identity: though they have a plains cast overall, bits of Great Lakes and fur-trade heritage ornament these garments. Kinship was the metaphorical stitching that held the regionally disparate pieces of this cultural garment together; to the wearers of these shirts, the people who made them and the events, dreams, powers, and marks of status the shirts connoted were of far more import than the ethnic or regional identity they denoted.

Though anthropologists emphasized the "plains" aspects of plains Ojibwa life, these were in fact but one level of Ojibwa culture. And while Ojibwa bands who had assumed different adaptations generally lived apart, they did not always. The close interrelationships between plains- and parkland-oriented Ojibwa in the Touchwood Hills and Qu'Appelle valley continued during these years, with the continuum between forest and plains being occupied by both Ojibwa and Cree. Not only had the Ojibwa emulated their Cree relatives, but, as James Settee observed in 1861, "There is a good deal of Saulteaux customs among [the Cree]."[32] Again, it was kinship that tied all of these disparate elements together, often in the same individual. One man, named Paskwaw, who traded at Forts Ellice and Pelly, emerges in Walter Traill's account as a "Wood Cree," closely tied to the fur trade: "one of our best customers and hunters."[33] Yet this Paskwaw was said to be the son of a plains Cree leader, was leader of an Ojibwa band at the time of treaty, and once stole a herd of Gros Ventre horses to pay his debt at Traill's post (Fort Ellice) in the late 1860s. And not only was he one of the principal trappers in the region, but he was also given power by a bison spirit to have many bison, and painted his tipi with figures representing this power.[34] Pasqua's identity, like the Haffenreffer "Cree" shirt, linked him to several heritages and ecological zones, and, unlike later anthropologists, he saw no barriers between these.

As the members of the Hind expedition journeyed back from Fort Pelly, through Riding Mountain, they travelled through Pasqua's territory. The wooded areas north and east of the Qu'Appelle valley were home to many Ojibwa, a number of whom were well known to local traders such as Cowie and Traill. These more parkland-oriented bands were the most common Ojibwa adaptation, despite the anthropologists' later fixation on the plains-oriented bands. For the parkland-oriented Ojibwa west of the Interlake, life after mid-century could be summed up by Walter Traill's comment that places such as Riding Mountain were excellent for furs but had to be abandoned in mid-winter because of shortage of provisions. If provisions could be had, returns were very good indeed. "The Indians were rich in furs," Traill stated of a camp in the Touchwood Hills, and the fur returns at Pelly and the outposts around it actually climbed from year to year during this period.[35]

The continued presence of free traders in the region kept fur prices up and maintained the Natives' bargaining power. One trader in the Carlton House area offered $4 per fisher pelt in the late 1860s, comparable to the Hudson's Bay Company's price of about 18 shillings, or, using nineteenth-century exchange rates, between $4 and $4.77.[36] The maintenance, even proliferation, of posts and outposts west of the Interlake testifies to the continuing vigour of the trade in these years. There were Hudson's Bay Company posts and outposts at Pelly, the Guard Post, Ellice, Qu'Appelle, Egg Lake, Pitt, Carlton, Little Touchwood Hills, Riding Mountain, Water-Hen River, Fort-à-la-Corne, and Last Mountain, and free traders around Prince Albert, Egg Lake, Ellice, Touchwood Hills, Pelly, Shoal River, and Duck Portage.[37] The availability and demand for furs fostered an especially defiant attitude among some of these Ojibwa, who were cursed by traders in their account books and journals as "d——d Rascals."[38]

Much of the friction between Ojibwa and trader in this region stemmed from the difficult subsistence, especially in winter, that prevented the Indians from spending their time trapping and often resulted in their being unable to pay their debts. The moose population in the Fort Pelly area dropped in the early 1860s and remained low through the 1870s. Ojibwa complained that they were unable to kill moose in the early winter of 1863 and had a very difficult season as a result. Nor could they readily hunt bison as an alternative, for by the 1860s the herds seldom came nearer than a week's journey from most of the wooded areas that were the Ojibwas' winter grounds.[39] This problem was intensified by overcrowding at Duck Mountain and other wooded locations to which Ojibwa bands had moved in previous decades to exploit formerly plentiful game populations.[40]

With these drastic reductions in the resources available to the Ojibwa, seasonal variations in availability had greater impact and often sent them to the trading posts for food. Every winter, traders recorded Ojibwa "starving" and begging or trading for pemmican at Fort Ellice and Riding Mountain almost as a matter of course. The Fort Pelly journal entry for 20 November 1863 is typical of the more difficult winters: "the poor wretches [at Duck Mountain] are starving from the scarcity of Rabbits in the Mountain & they are unable to Kill Moose; it is rather early to complain of starvation on the part of our Indians, I wonder what the story will be later in the season." While there were no reports of death from starvation, there were mentions of camps being moved frequently in mid-winter in a desperate search for food, of children too weak to walk, of Ojibwas' dogs being "starved and useless," of a trading captain exchanging part of his spring gratuity of rum for pemmican, and one mention of an Ojibwa hunter trading his gun for provisions, a puzzling exchange that may indicate that his situation was desperate. These people were quite obviously hard-pressed to sustain themselves during winter, and suffered great hardship because of food scarcity.[41] In this context, Traill's statement that 3,000 to 4,000 pounds of pemmican was traded to the Riding Mountain Indians over a single winter has been interpreted by several scholars as a measure of the impoverishment and dependency of these Ojibwa and Cree: "Henceforth, the

Ojibwas were dependent on the trading company for food. . . . By a sleight-of-hand, it must have seemed, these Ojibwas had exchanged the autonomy of a hunting-gathering band for employee status and food."[42]

This image of entrapment is only one part – or, rather, one season – of the whole truth. The Ojibwa did not request food during late spring, summer, or autumn. Some continued to garden, and wildfowl, fish, and sugar remained available. Traill reported finding a lake on Riding Mountain that was "teeming with jackfish" and noted the abundance of wildfowl in the area.[43] Even during winter, the Ojibwa did have a staple food source: rabbits. They often traded rabbits for pemmican and tea at the posts to supplement their diet – the fat in pemmican would have been an important requirement for their diet in winter – but they are often noted in the journals as managing to survive on rabbit and other small game. After his concern for the Ojibwa in the fall of 1863, the Fort Pelly trader wrote later in the season that, while moose were still scarce, "all our Indians are so far instead subsisting on rabbits which are luckily numerous this year."[44] Furthermore, the fur returns at Pelly and the outposts around it climbed from year to year during this period, contrary to the normal pattern during periods of resource scarcity.[45]

The increases in fur returns provide a strong clue as to how the pemmican rations should be interpreted. The close relationship between many of these Ojibwa and the traders suggests that there may well have been a good deal of continuity in the Ojibwas' expectations of receiving food at the post when in want (in both senses of that word), and that they felt the same way as the band described in 1832 at Fort Pelly: "this party by hunting in the strong woods, considers that they have some claim on us for support, in the event of being hard pressed."[46] Most of the Ojibwa who obtained food at the posts were, like this band, potentially good trappers. In part, they were playing on their relationship with the traders, obtaining "domesticated" pemmican from the post rather than abandoning their trapping areas altogether. The comment of the Fort Pelly trader on the arrival of several Ojibwa seeking food in January 1864 sums up this relationship quite aptly: "they have been starving they say & could not hunt: & have come for what they can catch in the shape of food."[47] In effect, the post became another gathering site, like a sugar bush or a fish weir: one got fish at the weir in spring and fall, and pemmican at the post in winter.

To a certain extent, the parkland Ojibwa were tied to the posts by the debts they incurred in "gathering" this food, and by their requirements for trade goods. For people who had "exchanged their autonomy," though, they were remarkably assertive. The Riding Mountain bands had in fact burned down the fur post the year before Traill arrived, partly because the post ran out of provisions for them and partly because that lack compelled them to take their furs all the way to Fort Ellice, an onerous trip that they resented. They also made Traill agree to their own conditions (that their post would remain open until the end of the spring trading season) before they allowed him to build another outpost.[48] At Qu'Appelle, the "Plain Crees, the Stonies . . . and the Wood Saulteaux" demanded an increase in the prices paid to them for meat, and the Company was forced to comply. At Riding Mountain, too, the Ojibwa demanded an increase in prices paid for their furs and a decrease in the prices of goods, which Walter Traill avoided only by his wit and a feast.[49] A warning inside the front cover of the Fort-à-la-Corne post journal conveys both the conflicts involved in the fur trade during these years and Native attitudes towards the trade, which do not sound subservient: "There should be no rum brought here for these Indians as there is never any thinge got for it but the losse of the Company's property – and they should never get one skin in debt unless a few skins in ammunition for to enable them for to commence their winter's hunt – there is not one honest Indian among the whole squad one and all are d——d Rascals." These responses were a reflection of the difficulties of the times. As Traill commented, the Natives were "very difficult to deal with when they have too hard a struggle for what is necessary to support life."[50]

Food from the posts did become an important part of the Ojibwa subsistence round, and it certainly prevented deaths from literal starvation during winter. Still, these people had by no means reached the bottom line of dependency. They were still able to choose from a number of options regarding resource use, and they did not simply become a welfare or even a Home Guard population, completely dependent on the posts. The enduring strength of these people and of their resource base became evident again during treaty negotiations in 1870s, when the Ojibwa were still economically secure enough to adopt a hard bargaining strategy for treaty benefits, while the plains-oriented tribes, who faced immediate starvation because of the disappearance of the bison, were forced to comply more readily with the government's terms in order to gain an ally to see them through the immediate crisis.[51]

Nor did the difficulty of subsisting make these Ojibwa any more eager to accept the missionaries' claims of the economic and spiritual virtues of sedentary agriculture or Christianity than in previous years. A number of them cultivated small plots of potatoes and other crops in the traditional way, abandoning them in summer and returning in autumn to harvest. They thus made use of the availability of seed from the missionary without forming the permanent, Christian villages he had in mind. They further discouraged James Settee, the Cree convert and Anglican clergyman who had a mission station at Fort Pelly, by making it clear that they tolerated him in large part for his contributions to their subsistence. At a camp of some fifty Ojibwa near the Beaver Hills in the winter of 1861-62, one old man commented on Settee's visit: "Our minister is come to see us, . . . we are all ready & willing to hear him. But not unless he gives us a good meal."[52] Such rebuffs indicate persistent faith in the efficacy of their own spiritual helpers, powers, and ceremonies. Their nicknames for James Settee clearly indicate their opinion of missionization in general: they called him "The Pest" and "Talking too Much."[53] Ojibwa decisions not to convert to Christianity because they "saw too little of worldly goods in the hands of the preachers" echo traditional beliefs that supernatural powers were supposed to assist them in this world as well as the next.[54] Their traditional ceremonies must, in their own eyes, have continued to fulfill their expectations, for they were held throughout this period of rapid change. Spring and autumn Midewiwin ceremonies are reported at Fort Ellice, White Mud River near Fort Pelly, and they were probably held in other locations as well.[55]

Some leading men and spiritual leaders did convert, but it is difficult to determine whether their conversions were genuine or whether these leaders were attempting to ally themselves with representatives of the outside world in these changing decades. Those who did convert displayed considerable syncretism. Of Thomas Manitou Keesik of Fort Pelly, Cowie noted, "Each Monday after receiving communion on a Sunday . . . Thomas resorted to the forest bearing a strip of red and another of blue cloth . . . and offered these up in aboriginal fashion to his ancestral deity or deities."[56]

The majority of Ojibwa, even their leaders, outwardly rejected Christian doctrines and missionary pressures. After Settee left the tent of one old man at Fort Pelly, the man took up his drum and drummed nearly all night, as if to re-assert his own world view and means of relating to the supernatural.[57] Despite the old man's drumming, however, neither his, nor all of the Ojibwas' spiritual power would be able to avert the events of the coming decade.

THE WANING OF THE OLD NORTHWEST

The Hind and Palliser expeditions were part of the first trickle in what eventually became a flood of arrivals from the east in the next two decades. With them were other curiosity-seekers: artists such as Kane, who passed through Red River in the late 1840s, and his colleagues Kurz, Catlin and Bodmer, who crossed the plains in the 1830-1850 period; and gentlemen adventurers, such as the Earl of Carnegie, who travelled across the West on private safaris between 1850 and 1870. Unlike the curiosity-seekers who came to view the land and its people, though, Hind and Palliser represented the end of the Native way of life in the West, for their reports laid the foundation for the beginning of agricultural settlement from eastern Canada and abroad. Rupert's Land had never been completely isolated from the rest of the world and had changed somewhat with it, but it had always been set apart by virtue of its relative isolation and the unique societies that developed within it. By 1850 the geographical and social barriers that isolated it were weakening, and by 1860 they were virtually gone. Two symbols of the intrusion of the outside world into the Northwest – the first steam-boat from the United States, ushering Red River into the Industrial era, and the settlement's first newspaper, run by Upper Canadian immigrants – arrived at Red River in 1859. Between 1860 and 1880, the very nature of the Northwest was altered.

Peguis was probably the first Native leader in the Canadian Northwest to grasp the implications of these changes. Throughout the 1850s, and until his death in 1864, he actively pressed the point of the Ojibwas' right to lands and resources at Red River. His granting of permission to individual settlers to cut hay outside the two-mile treaty limit was a continual reminder of the validity of the Selkirk Treaty and the rights to lands outside it that the Ojibwa had always claimed. So, too, were the notices posted around the settlement on Peguis's orders in 1858 and 1861, warning settlers not to cut hay outside the two-mile boundary without permission or payment of a fee.[58] In his efforts to entrench rights to land and resources during this era of uncertainty, Peguis also looked to authorities outside Red River. In 1857 and 1859, he dictated two letters regarding the land situation, one to the Aborigines' Protection Society and the second published in the British *Aborigines' Friend and Colonial Intelligencer.*[59] In both of these he stated that the Ojibwa and other chiefs who had signed the Selkirk Treaty in 1817 had believed it to be preliminary, and that they had understood the annuity would be followed the second year by actual payment for their lands. Given that this had not happened, Peguis felt that he and his fellow chiefs had not sold the lands, and that the lands should be formally ceded and compensation made before the change in government of the Northwest occurred.

Unfortunately, the fears of dispossession that drove Peguis's efforts were felt by all groups at Red River, and caused vicious in-fighting in the settlement as Native, Métis, and European settlers alike scrambled to lay claim to their own rights. The conflicting claims that these stresses produced emerged in a series of letters in the *Nor'Wester* responding to Peguis's petition to the Aborigines' Protection Society. Seeking a way to present their own case for land rights in Red River, many of the Métis publicly agreed with Peguis that the Natives – both Ojibwa and Métis – should be compensated for their lands, and that they should not be ignored by the Hudson's Bay Company as it "sold" their land to the Government of Canada. Other settlers were furious at what they perceived as an attempt by Peguis to "sell" the land a second time. Andrew McDermott expressed the common European reaction to Peguis's stance by attempting to discredit Ojibwa claims to the region altogether, noting that neither Peguis nor many of the members of his band had been born in the region.[60]

The debate raged on into 1861 and continued as an undercurrent of concern and discontent in the settlement for the remainder of the decade. It was not an issue that could be resolved in Red River. Ultimately, it would require the 1869-70 Métis resistance and the 1871 treaty negotiations to bring federal attention to the matter – and even then, the land question would not be resolved to the Ojibwas' satisfaction.

These fears of change and the future were given a brief respite in the early 1860s by an interruption caused by a remarkably familiar scene at the Forks: a conflict between Ojibwa and Sioux. But this confrontation was considerably different from earlier ones, for this time the Sioux sought neither revenge nor trade. Instead, they sought a place where they could live in peace after the Dakota War of 1862. For the Dakota of the Minnesota River Valley, the old war-road to the Forks had become a trail – they hoped – to shelter.[61]

The fate of the Dakota in Minnesota was yet another warning to the Ojibwa about what they stood to lose in the coming decades. Pressured to abandon hunting and take up farming, with treaty annuities given only to those who promised to farm, with their hunting grounds settled by Whites who offered them only abuse, and then forced to give up much of the agricultural land they had begun successfully farming, relations broke down between the Dakota and the government and settlers, and even between Dakota farmers and warriors.[62]

Their frustration finally erupted in the killing of nearly 500 White settlers in August 1862. The Dakota paid a terrible price for their actions. Thirty-eight were hanged; dozens of others died in prison camps; and most of the survivors were permanently exiled onto tiny, inadequate reserves. Several bands fled, moving west and north, meeting at Devil's Lake (North Dakota), and made ready to fulfill plans made early in the war itself to move north across the boundary line.[63] After a series of trial visits to the Forks by Dakota leaders in late 1862 and early 1863, and attacks by United States troops on the refugees which left many Dakota dead and wounded, 445 Dakota arrived at Fort Garry in December 1863.[64]

Pathetic as they were when they arrived, wounded, starving, and impoverished in the bitter cold of a Manitoba winter, the Dakota caused panic among Europeans at Red River. Emergency meetings of the Council of Assiniboia were held, frantic requests for troops were sent to Britain, and a civilian cavalry was formed. Settlers feared more armed attacks or, just as bad, an inter-tribal war between Dakota and Ojibwa in their midst. In fact, the Europeans judged the Dakota too quickly and too harshly. These were not the same bands with whom the Ojibwa had generally fought.[65] They were related, true, and the Ojibwa were certainly not friendly to them because of that. But when they arrived at the Forks, the Dakota knew they were making their last bid for freedom. Provoking conflicts with the Ojibwa would have ended their slim chances of being allowed to stay on British soil.

The strength of the Dakotas' determination is evident in the remarkably peaceful history of their relations with the Ojibwa after their arrival in Red River. This is not to say that it was an uneventful relationship. One Canadian Dakota recalled that, when the refugees first arrived, "There was a lot of trouble between the Sioux and the Saulteaux near Portage [la Prairie] in those days." Some of that trouble was described by Ogimauwinini, an Ojibwa elder who worked with anthropologist Alanson Skinner in the early 1900s, who told of visiting the Dakota camp at Portage la Prairie when he was a young man. Ogimauwinini was lectured by the Dakota chief, for he rode a fine pony that the chief feared might prove too tempting for the young Dakota men. The Dakota did attempt to steal the horse that night, but Ogimauwinini wounded the leader of the raiding party and took tobacco to the Dakota chief the next day, recounting the incident. The chief rebuked the young men in the camp, but the wounded man and his family had fled.[66]

There were only two documented attacks on the Dakota by Ojibwa. One occurred during a Dakota visit to Red River in 1866. The attacker was from Red Lake, though, rather than Red River, and there was no Dakota retribution. Ojibwa also attacked a Dakota camp near Portage la Prairie during the same year, killing two; again, there was no retribution.[67] Other than these few events, relations between Dakota refugees and the Ojibwa were tense but peaceful, and the Dakota generally took care to keep them that way. When the refugees dispersed from Red River, they went to other locations that had Ojibwa populations: Turtle Mountain, the Interlake, and Portage la Prairie. In these places they made formal requests to the Ojibwa for permission to occupy land, and they sealed the bargains with gifts of sacred pipes and horses. The Dakota man quoted above described the ceremony that was held at Portage la Prairie. According to his account, twenty Dakota men dressed for war marched, singing, into the Ojibwa camp, one carrying a pipe. The Dakota requested a formal council and "wanted to smoke," that is, to hold a pipe ceremony to create an alliance between the groups. Despite some opposition from the Ojibwa, the offer was accepted, and the combined group danced to celebrate. Later, the Ojibwa came to the Dakota camp and the entire ceremony was repeated.[68]

In other areas, where they were not so deliberate, the arrival of the Dakota aroused hostility. Several bands that moved to Forts Ellice and Qu'Appelle stole horses and usurped Ojibwa positions as labourers around the posts. Of Fort Ellice, Cowie noted that there were "seventy Sioux women cutting wood and dressing leather at that place to gain a livelihood. They are far more industrious than any other tribe of Indians that we have seen." With traders taking this attitude, it is little wonder that Cowie reported years later that the Ojibwa around Forts Ellice and Qu'Appelle "had long viewed with resentment" the presence of the refugees.[69]

All things considered, the presence of the Dakota aroused not so much open hostility as uneasiness, a sense that the proper order of things had been violated. As Walter Traill expressed it in 1864, "I never go out without my gun for one knows not what he may see before he gets back. There is also fear of being scalped and Tomahawked by the totaly uncultivated Sioux."[70] This uneasiness, the uncertainty that "one knows not what he may see," was not only due to the unpredictability of "uncultivated" Sioux who did not possess longstanding allegiances to either the Hudson's Bay Company or the Native people north of the boundary line. Rather, the Dakota were a symbol of change and of the potentially devastating effects of change on the Northwest, so that the uneasiness they caused was shared by all the peoples bracing for change in the 1860s. Given the uncertainty of the times, one did not, indeed, know what one might see next. At least in Red River, such concerns may have tempered the Ojibwa response to the Dakotas' arrival. After the hanging in 1845, they knew what the European response to inter-tribal violence in the settlement would be, and they knew from kin to the east and south, as well as from the Dakotas' plight, that, with the transfer of the region to Canada and the flood of settlers already flowing along the Red and Assiniboine, there would probably be a treaty.[71] They may not have wanted to initiate a battle with the Dakota that would set the course of their larger campaign against them.

The sense that the rightful order of things had been violated became stronger as the 1860s progressed: the haven to which the Dakota had fled was vanishing even as they arrived. In the 1860s and 1870s, the bison herds became scarcer, the whiskey trade thrived, and inter-tribal warfare intensified and became more deadly. Isaac Cowie claimed to have heard of some 700 violent deaths in the 1860s and '70s.[72] Adding to the deaths from warfare, the smallpox epidemic of 1870 raced like some last, dreadful prairie fire across the Northwest. More than anything else, these were decades marked by loss.

All of these changes were experienced by the western Ojibwa. The plains Ojibwa were part of the "armed migration" of Cree into the Cypress Hills, which ended in the battle of Oldman River, during which the Blackfoot re-asserted control over their territory by dealing a terrible military blow to the Cree and their allies; and in 1873 they were part of a raiding party that stole horses from some American wolf hunters, an incident that sparked the tragic Cypress Hills massacre of a camp of Assiniboines.[73] Though they were less affected by warfare, parkland-oriented Ojibwa experienced problems related to food shortages in winter and the over-use of alcohol in the fur trade. Gabriel Coté's spree in the fall of 1860, during which he and his family consumed some fifty-six quarts of diluted rum in two weeks, and the drinking bout at the Assiniboine camp slaughtered in the Cypress Hills massacre, are all-too-typical events of this period.[74]

The anxieties created by the dreadful reality across the West were only worsened by fears arising from the unsettled state of the region and the rumours that swept the Native populations about the future of the country. The fact, if not the exact purpose or ramifications, of the 1857 review of the Select Committee of the British House of Commons of the affairs of the Hudson's Bay Company, and the failure of the Hudson's Bay Company to obtain the renewal of its licence for exclusive trade in 1859, was known to many traders, Métis, and freemen in the Northwest, and an uneasiness over the future of the trade and the well-being of Natives who dealt with the Company swept the region. In 1860, William Stagg wrote to the Church Missionary Society that the Ojibwa and Cree around Fairford Mission were "very unsettled as changes are expected in the Government of the country."[75] Natives were angry, as well, at what they perceived as this final abandonment, the breaking of their longstanding (if often unsatisfactory) relationship with the Hudson's Bay Company, and were confused by the change. As late as 1863, some Ojibwa came to Swan River "to hear about the new Company they dont like to hear that the Company sold out the Country they do not understand the subject."[76]

In Red River and the Interlake the fears of change set off another, short-lived wave of prophecy and nativism. According to Reverend William Stagg, an Ojibwa from Red River arrived at the Fairford mission station in March 1860:

He pretended to be sent by Pigwys . . . to prepare the Indians here for the reception of some Americans who were soon to take their country, and drive the English from it; and to request their attendance at the Settlement next spring, to arrange with other Indians about the country. . . . He . . . told the Indians to cast off prayer and to cling fast to their old superstitions; if not, they would be obliged to fight with the English against the Americans who, he said, had no religion and that when the great masters would come the heads of all the praying Indians would be cut off, and boiled in large kettles. [77]

While this particular agitation seems to have quickly subsided, anxieties continued in the Interlake throughout the 1860s. By the late 1860s, tensions between missionary James Settee and the Ojibwa and Cree at Scanterbury had focused on land and resource rights. The chief there called a general assembly at which, after proclaiming that he had "full authority from the late Chief Pewygis," he told Settee that the missionary could not cut more hay than one cow could eat. Settee's son was later attacked returning to the mission building with fish from the weir, his potatoes were stolen from the field, and in another assembly the people were told "to stand their ground" against his work.[78] This assertiveness was echoed by Ojibwa beyond the Interlake: at the mission station near Fort Pelly, the Ojibwa demanded payment for the land occupied by the mission buildings, while at Egg Lake an Ojibwa argued that he had a right to take fish from the Company's nets because "the fish belong to Indians, who had a right to take what was their own from the whites, who were mere intruders in the country."[79]

At Red River, the fears of the Métis and their Native kin also became more specifically oriented towards the control of land and resources as the flood of outsiders arriving in Red River swelled. The Ojibwa had special reason to worry, for they were by then a tiny minority of the population of Red River. According to the 1871 census, there were 1,600 Europeans, 5,720 Métis, 4,080 Protestant half-breeds, and just 560 Indians (both Swampy Cree and Ojibwa) in the settlement. Socially and numerically, the Ojibwa were so alienated from the larger community that they stood to be ignored and dispossessed without some skillful political manoeuvring on their part. Nor were Peguis's skills and experience available to them at this critical time; he died in 1864.

Rising tensions caused by fears of change finally erupted in the winter of 1869-70, when the Métis stopped a land survey party from surveying the Métis river lots, prevented the new lieutenant-governor of the North West Territories from entering the region, and seized control of essential stores at Upper Fort Garry. As the Métis movement evolved, setting up a provisional government and outlining terms on which it would be prepared to negotiate with the Canadian government for entrance to Confederation, and, finally, when troops from Ontario arrived in Red River to assert Canadian rights in the Territories, the Ojibwa were pressed by Métis kin to join forces with them.[80]

In a move that was as calculated as the Ojibwa response decades earlier to the "Pemmican War" of 1814-16, Peguis's son and heir, Henry Prince, refused to support the actions of the Métis. Indeed, Prince made an obvious show of support instead to the Hudson's Bay Company and colony officials. After Upper Fort Garry was taken by the Métis, Prince led nearly 100 warriors to Lower Fort Garry and offered their assistance to officials. Their offer was gratefully declined, but a dozen remained as guards. Prince also met with Riel and other Métis leaders but failed to sway them, as his father had failed with the North West Company in 1814. Prince did prevent his men from participating in the uproar, though, and the following summer, when the long-awaited treaty was finally being negotiated, he reminded the negotiators: "all last winter I worked for the Queen. . . . My people had nothing to do with [the uprising]."[81]

Though both the Ojibwa and the new government officials in Red River were eager to negotiate a treaty, it was obvious during the negotiations that having "worked for the Queen" was no guarantee that Ojibwa interests would be looked after in the treaty. In fact, Treaty Number 1, the Stone Fort Treaty, was initiated only after it became clear to the Ojibwa that their interests would not otherwise be protected during the settlement of the West. As historian John Tobias has stated, "the treaty process only started after Yellow Quill's band of Ojibwa turned back settlers who tried to go west of Portage la Prairie, and after other Ojibwa leaders insisted on enforcement of the Selkirk Treaty, or more often, upon making another treaty."[82] Such emphatic and cohesive responses by Ojibwa leaders, in the absence of seasoned statesmen such as Peguis, suggests the continuing vitality of Ojibwa society and the effectiveness of the communications network among Ojibwa and other Native peoples. Yellow Quill, Henry Prince, and the other Ojibwa and Cree leaders who demanded a treaty in 1870 and attempted to obtain specific concessions during the negotiations for Treaty Number 1 showed their familiarity with the nature of terms of treaties, something that must have been fostered not only by memories of the Selkirk Treaty but also by reports of treaty negotiations from Turtle Mountain and Minnesota.

Not only did the Ojibwa understand the basic nature of treaties – which they saw as protective – in 1871, but they also had clear goals during the negotiations. According to historian Jean Friesen, the Red River Ojibwa saw the treaty as a form of economic planning, a means of ensuring continued access to natural and economic resources during the era of White settlement, and they demanded what they saw as a fair exchange for the transfer of their land rights.[83] That they had a fairly clear estimate of the value of what they were ceding is indicated in the treaty negotiator's response to their "excessive" demands. As the official report of the treaty proceedings notes, "much difficulty was experienced in getting [the Ojibwa] to understand the views of the Government – they wishing to have two-thirds of the Province as a reserve."[84] The Ojibwas' "excessive" demands were based on their estimates of what they would need to support themselves and their descendants in the coming years; at least one Native leader told the government officials during the Treaty Number 1 negotiations that he "calculated on being maintained by you" in exchange for the rights to the lands occupied by his people. Part of these calculations involved the assumption, confirmed by government officials at the treaty negotiations, that the Ojibwa would maintain rights to use resources, and to hunting and fishing, on the land that they transferred, just as in the earlier Selkirk Treaty.[85]

As a result of these verbal assurances and their own expectations and understanding of the protective nature of the treaty, the Ojibwa had reason to believe that, even though their "excessive" demands for land were refused, they had still fulfilled their goals: that they had retained hunting and fishing rights to the lands ceded, that they had been granted adequate reserve lands and annuities, and that they had a binding agreement and a working relationship with the new provincial government and with the Crown. Their satisfaction with the treaty was short-lived. Just two years after Treaty Number 1, a petition was filed by the Ojibwa and Cree stating that their annuity and their reserve were both too small and that game was too scarce for adequate subsistence, and requested an increase in their annuity. They also discovered that, not only did both the provincial and federal governments have different interpretations of what had been promised during the negotiations, but also the Ojibwa were essentially powerless in the new order of things, and that their determined and well-reasoned protests and petitions seldom brought results. Within fifteen years of the signing of the treaty, both federal and provincial governments began restricting Ojibwa rights to hunting and fishing, and, in 1909, as the result of bribery and corrupt practices by civil and government officials, the band was forced to surrender their reserve in Selkirk (for which they received insufficient compensation for lands) and move to a new reserve some 100 miles north, at the mouth of the Fisher River in the Interlake.[86]

To the north and west of Red River, other treaties followed in quick succession. By 1877, the entire area between Lake of the Woods and the Rockies from well north of the North Saskatchewan to the border had been ceded and opened to White settlement. In the aftermath of the 1870 smallpox epidemic, inter-tribal warfare, the effects of alcohol, and the disappearance of the bison, the other Ojibwa bands and their Cree kin attempted to deal with the final threat to their very being: loss of land and of autonomy. Ojibwa signed Treaties Number 2 and Number 4 in 1871 and 1874, with other bands signing adhesions to these treaties for several years afterwards. As John Foster has noted, many of these bands retained a sufficiently rich resource base that they were secure enough to negotiate quite aggressively, and in several instances they disrupted or held up treaty negotiations as part of their bargaining strategy.[87]

Reverend George McDougall's comment sums up the negotiators' experience of the Ojibwa during this process: "These Soto are the mischiefmakers through all this Western country and some of them are shrewd men."[88] Once they were on their reserves, however, as the Red River Ojibwa quickly discovered, they would need every ounce of both of these qualities to survive.

The Ojibwa and their Cree and Métis relatives had a few more years of relative freedom in the 1870s. Even after the signing of the treaties, life continued as usual in some areas. Treaty negotiator Alexander Morris met several bands of Cree and Ojibwa returning from bison hunts during his work in the 1870s, as well as a mixed band from Jackfish Lake, Big Bear's home territory, who stated that the bison hunt was very important to them.[89] Elsewhere on the plains, the Ojibwa were not so nonchalant. In 1876, the Ojibwa and Cree still in the Cypress Hills sent a message to Morris, saying, "We are now all gathered together in these Cypress Hills . . . and we see with our own eyes that the buffalo are gradually dying," and requesting an increase in their ammunition supplies.[90] In the forested areas and parkland, Ojibwa maintained much of their seasonal round for decades.

Still, while many Ojibwa coped admirably with their changed situation, as they had coped with change and crises in the past, they found their way of life gradually eroded by the constraints of reserve boundaries, permanent villages, government restrictions and incompetence in administering the treaties, the loss of territory to settlers, and the effect of non-Native, commercial resource-harvesting operations such as fisheries and logging companies. Sarah Carter has demonstrated that the bungling of the Department of Indian Affairs agents in administering the treaties, particularly their failure to provide the equipment and education that would allow the western tribes to farm, virtually dictated the retention of as many traditional subsistence practices as were still available to the reserve communities.[91] With these older ways becoming impractical because of the loss of territory, and with bureaucratic and cultural barriers preventing them from wholeheartedly adopting agriculture, the last decades of the nineteenth century were particularly frustrating and disheartening for the Ojibwa and their Cree kin.

* * *

The Ojibwa coped admirably for nearly a century with decreasing game and fur populations, environmental fluctuations, the arrival of European settlers, shifting inter-tribal alliances and deadly warfare, epidemics, and the waning of their power in the fur trade. Over the course of the years between 1780 and 1870, they showed themselves to be remarkably resilient in the face of change and deprivation. They were just as tenacious and capable during and after the treaty negotiations, driving the hardest bargains they could with the government agents and seeking to fulfill their goal of obtaining sufficient resources and government assistance to create a decent life for themselves and their children. Even as their old way of life was gradually eroded by the development of the West, they sought to participate in the new economy, bolstering traditional sources of food and goods with wage labour when they could obtain it and with agriculture when it was practical.

What the western Ojibwa found more difficult to cope with was the loss of so much of their land base combined with the loss of control over resources and over autonomy that accompanied their designation as wards of the government. The Stone Fort Treaty marked the beginning of a new era in the West for all Native peoples, the era of government control. The passage of the Indian Act consolidated the government's control over Native peoples. After the Treaty and the Act, no matter what strategies they used, the Ojibwa were ultimately subject to laws not of their making and to government policies arising from racist and ethnocentric attitudes. The cycle of history begun by the Stone Fort Treaty, one that is still being played out in the provincial and federal courts, has been marked by continuous efforts on the part of the Ojibwa to regain control of their rights, resources, and destinies.

Conclusion

During the pivotal century from 1780 to 1870, the Ojibwa maintained a constantly shifting balance between cultural continuity and adaptive change. This balance was not identical among all Ojibwa bands in the West; rather, diverse environmental, economic, and human factors across the West fostered different coping strategies, different adaptations, and different elements of continuity. The western Ojibwa were by no means a uniform people, despite the shared heritage that continued to form the basis of their identity in the West. They were a varied and complex people, as was their history.

There are, of course, many ways of viewing western Ojibwa history. I have presented only certain aspects of their histories in this work; I have told one of many stories, in my own style, if you will. There are other stories and other perspectives, all of which are useful in helping us to understand different parts of the historical experiences of the western Ojibwa. Twentieth-century scholars have tended to study human responses to change from a broad, rather distant perspective – the "bird's-eye view," examining change at the level of the group as a whole, as I have generally done within this study. Writing history in this manner demands that we integrate the stories of individuals and individual families and bands into the larger categories of regions and tribes. Writers and readers alike would do well to remember that such abstracted stories begin with decisions made "on the ground," with the actions of individuals such as John Tanner, Peguis, Black Powder, Big Bear, Machi Huggemaw, Wisiniw, Pasqua, and their wives and families. The stories of these individuals and their smaller-scale worlds complement and enrich larger-scale works such as this, for they examine with a jeweller's eye and report in experienced detail the conditions faced and decisions made, and the longer-term ramifications of these. There are as yet only a few of these kinds of stories that have been made available for study: John Tanner's narrative, a collection of brief life histories made for the Canadian Ethnology Service in the late 1960s, and a number of stories passed down in the family of Pinayzitt (Partridge Foot) and recently published by Pinayzitt's great-grandson Alexander Wolfe.[1] These are all invaluable for understanding another side of the story presented here, and I hope that other such stories will be made available in the future.

One might also take a different perspective on the manner in which the Ojibwa made their decisions, both as individuals and as groups. My own perspective follows Fredrik Barth's idea that humans "tend to choose the personal action that they feel will gain them the greatest benefit (or avoid the greatest loss) with the smallest expenditure of resources."[2] In part, my adoption of this interpretation was based on the kinds of information most readily available in the historic records, although it is also a legitimate perspective on certain aspects of Ojibwa history. Based on this reading of the documents, I feel that the Ojibwas' decisions were intended, in part, to bring economic benefits, to allow them to obtain the most food and trade goods possible with the least risk. Their choices were made after weighing a myriad of interrelated data about weather conditions, water levels, the state of the fur trade, and many other variables. Their strategies did not always work, of course, but they were generally successful at coping with the vicissitudes of nature and the fur trade. It was individual responses such as these that combined to make what I have called a balance between change and continuity among the western Ojibwa as a whole.

Other perspectives on western Ojibwa histories might well be less economically oriented than mine. For the Ojibwa, as for other tribes, not all the benefits that they constructed their coping strategies to obtain were economic or material in nature, and not all the data they juggled to arrive at their decisions were so easily measured as water levels or the amount of credit they received at the post. The Ojibwa were strongly influenced by social and spiritual factors. The material benefits of the fur trade were less important to some of them than the social prestige to be gained from redistributing trade goods. And while what they achieved in practical terms can be interpreted as optimal foraging theory or logical strategies for coping with changing environmental and trade conditions, these actions were as likely to be seen by them in spiritual terms.

The spiritual side of the Ojibwa story cannot be entirely reconstructible from the fur trade documents, though I have tried to emphasize such things as the continuity of certain rituals, particularly the Midewiwin, which were celebrated in their proper season every year since the emergence of the Ojibwa. But after examining the adaptations the western Ojibwa developed in the course of the nineteenth century, it is appropriate to remember that their perspective on their history and on their individual lives might have been quite different from that outlined in this volume. Where I, and other researchers, have pointed to ecological, economic, and human causes of change, the Ojibwa would also (or instead) have seen super-natural forces behind these things. Reverend James Settee was warned by an Ojibwa elder in 1861 that the reason the game had declined so greatly in his life-time was that European traders and sight-seers had "yearly sent home skulls of moose & deer across the big waters [i.e., showing disrespect for animal spirits] & no wonder these animals are decreasing."[3] Like the prophecies in the Interlake, such comments drive home the point that for the Ojibwa, historic change may have been perceived as being as much due to spiritual forces as to human or eco-logical ones.

While these and other perspectives may yet be fruitfully applied to the study of Ojibwa history in the West, my own perspective has departed from earlier stud-ies in significant ways. My interpretation of the history of the western Ojibwa presents challenges to established interpretations of northern plains ethnology, of the effects of participation in the fur trade on Native societies, and of the ability of Native societies to maintain their integrity in the face of multifaceted change. In particular, I have emphasized the different, yet related, Ojibwa adaptations in the West, the variety of these adaptations, and the continuities between them, an ap-proach that differs from other scholars' interpretations of the culture and history of these people.

While I show the development of these variations on the group level, I recog-nize that decisions made by individuals and families played a crucial role in this process. The decisions to spend more time hunting bison, or to live semi-permanently with Cree and Métis people, or to rely more exclusively on the fish-ery, were not made solely on the basis of climate or game populations. An entire spectrum of choices about resource use and lifeways was available to all Ojibwa in the West; human factors and individual preferences heavily influenced the particu-lar choices made by each family. These individual preferences are especially evi-dent in patterns of intermarriage and kinship and in areas such as the Qu'Appelle valley, which functioned as intermediate zones, allowing access to a wide range of resources. Ojibwa in the Qu'Appelle Valley and other such areas could have cho-sen either a bison-oriented or a fish-and-parkland-game-oriented existence, with minimal or extensive involvement in the fur trade. Instead, they developed a vari-ety of lifeways ranging from parkland-oriented to plains-oriented as well as some that emphasized different regions in different seasons. At one level, this represents a diverse and efficient use of resources; at another, it represents the role of human choice and kinship in cultural adaptation and change.

The physical and human links between cultural adaptations represented by ecozones and kinship have only recently begun to receive the scholarly attention they merit. Ethnographies and histories of Native peoples have tended to portray ecological zones and human populations as being quite separate, and to divide the northern plains into a series of well-defined boxes labelled "plains," "parkland," "forest," "Cree," "Ojibwa," "Assiniboine," with corresponding lists of identifying features or traits for the contents of each box. As ethnohistorian Susan Sharrock has noted, these boxes, or groupings, "have been viewed as islands in a static world, instead of in a framework of a realistic, dynamic interchange of persons, ideas, and material objects."[4] In classic ethnographic theory, anomalies, such as the presence of the Ojibwa, a "woodland" tribe moved to the "plains," were explained in terms of their relationship to standard categories. Thus, Skinner described the Ojibwa as being halfway between the standard woodlands and plains cultural categories, while Howard implied that they had moved completely from one box to another, during which process crucial elements of woodlands culture "gave way" to corresponding elements of plains cultures. Such interpretations stressed cultural differences and transformation and were inadequate for understanding continuity, similarities, and inter-tribal contacts. As Sharrock observes, they missed many of the most important features of human history in the northern plains.[5]

My own perspective differs from these in that what I have attempted to show in this work is that the walls between these arbitrary boxes have always been permeable, and that the human and geographic links between regions and peoples in the northern plains have played crucial roles in the human history of this entire region.[6] This has involved examining the development of a range of western Ojibwa adaptations, from the Interlake people through the plains Ojibwa. I have, as well, attempted to demonstrate the constant and intimate interaction between Ojibwa, Cree, and Métis, which shaped not only the Ojibwa but all three peoples. And yet, I also recognize that, despite this sharing, there were cores within these different societies that formed a crucial part of personal and group identity, culture, and reality. Among the Ojibwa, the maintenance of many aspects of subsistence, religion, age-gender roles, and cultural ideals contributed to this core of identity: who the Ojibwa were in the nineteenth century rested as much on continuity as on change.

Such an interpretation differs from previous studies of Ojibwa culture, particularly that of James Howard. This is not to say that these earlier studies are incorrect; far from it. But where Howard and Skinner saw cultural replacement among the Ojibwa, I see a far more complex process, which I have characterized as augmentation, or "layering": the creation of an outer layer of behaviours learned from their Cree and Métis relatives, and the retention of a larger and more crucial core of older values and behaviours that the Ojibwa brought with them when they entered the West. This several-layered structure was developed differently by Ojibwa in the various adaptations they chose in the West, but it resulted in every case in a very resilient and adaptable people.

Though the tension between continuity and change is particularly evident in the Ojibwa because of their movement between very different ecological zones and cultural traditions, it is true in another sense for all Native peoples involved in the western fur trade during the eighteenth and nineteenth centuries. Within fur-trade social history, the ethnologists' desire to identify cultural change has become the ethnohistorians' attempt to determine how long Native people remained "independent" of the fur trade, and to understand the relationship between their autonomy and cultural integrity on the one hand, and the many cultural changes wrought in Native societies by their participation in the trade on the other. Clearly, the Ojibwa – in all their adaptations – were profoundly affected by the fur trade; for many individuals, their very goals were shaped by it for decades, and their decisions about subsistence and movements revolved around it. Yet, just as clearly, these people were not "pawns in the trade, exploited, despoiled, and finally extinguished," as Harold Hickerson believed. Even during the 1860s, when they routinely exchanged furs for food during winter, they continued to find workable and creative solutions to their dilemmas. Descriptions of the Ojibwa as "d——d Rascals" and "shrewd men" indicate that they were by no means "extinguished" by the fur trade. Their close involvement in the trade, juxtaposed with their tenacity of spirit and their ability to sustain themselves throughout the nineteenth century, is a reminder that the wall between the "independence" and "dependence" boxes is, like that between cultures, quite permeable. Like the concept of "plains" and "woodlands" cultures, the states of "independence" and "dependence" might more accurately be regarded as poles on a continuum than as entirely separate states.

Ultimately, of course, the western Ojibwa were unable to prevent the destruction of fur and game populations, the loss of land, and the seizure of political control over their lives by the Canadian government. Even during the worst years of the early reserve era, though, the western Ojibwa continued to adapt and to cope. While the options from which they chose were more restricted, they were no more passive victims of history after 1870 than they had been before. Nor did they lose their sense of heritage and identity during the decades of repression and forced assimilation that followed the signing of the treaties. From forest to parkland to plains, from the first years of their expansion into the West through to the present day, the western Ojibwa have displayed a vital spirit made flexible by their willingness to adapt and strengthened by their sense of continuity with an unbroken Ojibwa heritage.

Notes

ABBREVIATIONS

PAC/NAC   Public Archives of Canada / National Archives of Canada (name changed 1992)
HBCA   Hudson's Bay Company Archives
HBC   Hudson's Bay Company
NWC   North West Company
MB   made beaver
PAM   Provincial Archives of Manitoba
SP   Selkirk Papers
CMS   Church Missionary Society

PREFACE

1 See, for example, Alanson Skinner, "The Cultural Position of the Plains Ojibway," *American Anthropologist* 16 (1914); Alanson Skinner, "Political and Ceremonial Position of the Plains Ojibway," *Anthropological Papers of the American Museum of Natural History*, vol. 2, part 6 (1914); James Howard, *The Plains Ojibwa or Bungi* (Vermilion: University of South Dakota, Anthropological Papers No. 1, 1965); and James Howard, "The Identity and Demography of the Plains-Ojibwa," *Plains Anthropologist* 6 (1961).
2 Quote: Raymond DeMallie, "Preface," Robert H. Lowie, *Indians of the Plains* (Lincoln: University of Nebraska Press, 1982), p. ix, citing Lowie, pp. 5-6. See also Skinner, "The Cultural Position of the Plains Ojibway," pp. 314-15.
3 Skinner, "The Cultural Position of the Plains Ojibway," p. 318; Howard, *The Plains Ojibwa or Bungi*, p. 3.
4 Fredrik Barth, "Introduction," *Ethnic Groups and Boundaries* (London: Allen and Unwin, 1970), pp. 10-15.
5 *Ibid.*

SYNONYMY

1 For synonymies pertaining to *Saulteaux, Ojibwa*, and variant forms, see: David Pentland's synonymy in Jack H. Steinbring, "Saulteaux of Lake Winnipeg," in *Handbook of North American Indians*, Vol. 6: *Subarctic*, ed. June Helm (Washington, D.C.: Smithsonian Institution, 1981), p. 254; Ives Goddard's synonymy in Edward Rogers, "Southeastern Ojibwa," in *Handbook of North American Indians*, vol. 15: *Northeast*, ed. Bruce Trigger, pp. 768-70; Jennifer S.H. Brown, "Northern Algonquians from Lake Superior and Hudson Bay to Manitoba in the Historical Period," in *Native Peoples: The Canadian Experience*, ed. R. Bruce Morrison and C. Roderick Wilson (Toronto: McClelland and Stewart, 1986), p. 211. See also HBCA B.3/ a/14, Albany Journal 1726; HBCA B.3/a/22, Albany Journal 1734.

2 See David Pentland's synonymy in E.S. Rogers and J. Garth Taylor, "Northern Ojibwa," in *Handbook of North American Indians*, vol. 6: *Subarctic*, ed. June Helm, p. 241.

3 Charles Bishop, "The Indian Inhabitants in Northern Ontario at the Time of Contact: Socio-Territorial Considerations," in *Approaches to Algonquian Archaeology*, ed. M. Hanna and B. Kooyman (Calgary: University of Calgary Press, 1982), p. 260.

4 Joseph Adams, Albany Journal 1733, quoted in Bishop, "The Indian Inhabitants in Northern Ontario at the Time of Contact," p. 260. See also E.E. Rich, ed., *James Isham's Observations on Hudson's Bay, 1743* (London: Hudson's Bay Record Society, 1949), p. 191.

5 "Pung'ke": Rich, *James Isham's Observations*, p. 191. On "Bungee," see also: HBCA B.51/e/1, Fort Dauphin District Report 1820, fos. 15-17; Margaret Stobie, "Backgrounds of the Dialect Called Bungi," *Historical and Scientific Society of Manitoba Transactions*, series 3, no. 24, 1967-68, p. 68; synonymy by David Pentland in Rogers and Taylor, "Northern Ojibwa," p. 241.

6 Stobie, "Backgrounds of the Dialect Called Bungi," p. 68; Pentland's synonymy in Rogers and Taylor, "Northern Ojibwa"; Victor Lytwyn, *The Fur Trade of the Little North* (Winnipeg: Rupert's Land Research Centre, 1986), pp. 58, 63, 64.

7 Elliot Coues, ed., *New Light on the Early History of the Greater North West: The Manuscript Journals of Alexander Henry* (Minneapolis: Ross and Haines, 1965), p. 533 (this source will hereinafter be referred to as Henry). It should be noted that several different terms were sometimes used on a single journal page, and they may refer to the trading affiliations of different bands: *Saulteaux* to refer to those who traded with the Canadians, and *Bungees* for those who traded with the Hudson's Bay Company. See Peter Fidler, HBCA B.22/a/21, Brandon House Journal 1818-19, 20 September 1818.

8 Howard, *The Plains Ojibwa or Bungi*, p. 9.

CHAPTER 1

1 Harold Hickerson, *The Chippewa and their Neighbors*, revised and expanded edition with Preface and Critical Review by Jennifer S.H. Brown and Laura L. Peers (Prospect Heights: Waveland Press, 1988), p. 119.

2 HBCA B.22/a/1, Brandon House Journal, 12 November 1793; HBCA B.22/a/4, Brandon House Journal 1796-97, 27 March 1797; HBCA B.22/a/5, Brandon House Journal 1797-98, 22 December 1797; HBCA B.51/a/1, Dauphin River Journal 1795-96, 17 August 1795; HBCA B.60/a/1, Edmonton House Journal 1795-96, 10 August 1795; HBCA B.235/a/1, Winnipeg Post Journal 1797-98, 26 January 1798; HBCA B.4/a/2, Fort Alexander Journal 1797-99, 14 September 1798; HBCA B.105/a/1, Lac la Pluie Journal 1793-94; Henry, p. 186, 23 August 1801; Harold Hickerson, "Journal of Charles Jean Baptiste Chaboillez, 1797-98," *Ethnohistory* 6/3, 4 (1959): 285; Edwin James, ed., *A Narrative of the Captivity and Adventures of John Tanner* (Minneapolis: Ross and Haines, 1956), p. 19 (this source will hereinafter be referred to as Tanner).

3 This early documentation is discussed in Dale Russell, *Eighteenth Century Cree and their Neighbors* (Ottawa: Canadian Museum of Civilization, Mercury Series, 1991), pp. 53-55; and Bishop, "The Indian Inhabitants of Northern Ontario at the Time of Contact," pp. 258, 263-64. On the "Ouace" see Charles Bishop, "Territorial Groups before 1821: Cree and Ojibwa," in *Handbook of North American Indians*, vol. 6: *Subarctic,* ed. June Helm, p. 160; and Lytwyn, *Fur Trade of the Little North*, p. 20n. See also Gary B. Doige, "Warfare Patterns of the Assiniboine to 1809" (M.A. thesis, University of Manitoba, 1989), who cites the 1718 reference (p. 71).

4 Doige, "Warfare Patterns of the Assiniboine to 1809," pp. 98-99, citing Johnathan Carver, 1767: "Chipeways teretories on Lake La Pluie."

5 James Bain, ed., *Travels and Adventures in Canada and the Indian Territories between the Years 1760 and 1776* (New York: Burt Franklin Press, 1969 [1901]), pp. 239-43.

6 For a review of the popularization of these theories, see Charles Bishop, "The Emergence of the Northern Ojibwa: Social and Economic Consequences," *American Ethnologist* 3/1 (1976); and Russell, *Eighteenth Century Cree and their Neighbors*, p. 1, where he cites, in particular, studies by David Mandelbaum and A.J. Ray. See also Charles Bishop, *The Northern Ojibwa and the Fur Trade: An Historical and Ecological Study* (Toronto: Holt, Rinehart and Winston, 1974), p. 314.

7 Russell, *Eighteenth Century Cree and their Neighbors*, p. 61. "Westward progression": Leigh Symms, "Identifying Prehistoric Western Algonquians: A Holistic Approach," in *Approaches to Algonquian Archaeology*, ed. M. Hanna and B. Kooyman (Calgary: University of Calgary, 1982), p. 3.

8 Adolph M. Greenberg and James Morrison, "Group Identities in the Boreal Forest: The Origin of the Northern Ojibwa," *Ethnohistory* 29/2 (1982):75-102.

9 Henry the Elder: Bain, *Travels and Adventures*, p. 240. See also Doige, "Warfare Patterns of the Assiniboine," p. 100.

10 Bishop, "Emergence of the Northern Ojibwa," pp. 44-45; Bishop, "Territorial Groups before 1821," p. 160; Harold Hickerson, *Ethnohistory of Chippewa in Central Minnesota* (New York: Garland Publishing, 1974), pp. 54, 59. See also Greenberg and Morrison, "Group Identities in the Boreal Forest," pp. 75-102.

11 Doige, "Warfare Patterns of the Assiniboine," p. 101. See also comments by Henry the Elder in Bain, *Travels and Adventures*, pp. 239-43.

12 Doige, "Warfare Patterns of the Assiniboine," p. 101.

13 Hickerson, *The Chippewa and their Neighbors*, pp. 105, 106-19.

14 See, for instance: Jennifer S.H. Brown and Laura L. Peers, "A Critical Review," in Hickerson, *The Chippewa and their Neighbors*, pp. 143-45; Tim E. Holzkamm, "Eastern Dakota Population Movements and the European Fur Trade: One More Time," *Plains Anthropologist* 28/101 (1983):225-33; Scott Hamilton, "Competition and Warfare: Functional versus Historical Explanations," *The Canadian Journal of Native Studies* 5/1 (1985):93-113; Bruce A. Cox, "Debating the 'Debatable Zone': A Re-examination of Explanations of Dakota-Algonquian Conflict," *Sociology and Anthropology Departmental Working Paper, 86-87* (Ottawa: Carleton University, 1986).

15 Thomas Vennum, *Wild Rice and the Ojibway People* (St. Paul: Minnesota Historical Society Press, 1988), p. 9.

16 Holzkamm, "Eastern Dakota Population Movements and the European Fur Trade"; Brown and Peers, "A Critical Review," pp. 143-44; Gary Anderson, *Kinsmen of Another Kind: Dakota-White Relations in the Upper Mississippi Valley, 1650-1862* (Lincoln: University of Nebraska Press, 1984), p. 47.

17 Anderson, *Kinsmen of Another Kind*; Holzkamm, "Eastern Dakota Population Movements and the European Fur Trade," pp. 231-32.

18 Harold Hickerson, "The Genesis of a Trading Post Band: The Pembina Chippewa," *Ethnohistory* 3/4 (1956):291; and see section, "Ojibwa Migration into the Prairies and Parklands, 1770-1790," this chapter.

19 See, for example: plate 14, "Prehistoric Trade," in *Historical Atlas of Canada*, vol. 1, ed. R. Cole Harris (Toronto: University of Toronto Press, 1987); and William R. Swagerty, "Indian Trade in the Trans-Mississippi West to 1870," in *Handbook of North American Indians*, vol. 4: *History of Indian-White Relations*, ed. Wilcomb Washburn (Washington, D.C.: Smithsonian Institution, 1988), pp. 351-74.

20 Abraham Rotstein, "Trade and Politics: An Institutional Approach," *Western Canadian Journal of Anthropology* 3 (1972); E.E. Rich, "Trade Habits and Economic Motivation among the Indians of North America," *Canadian Journal of Economics and Political Science* 26 (1960):35-53; Bruce White, "Give Us a Little Milk: The Social and Cultural Meanings of Gift-Giving in the Lake Superior Fur Trade," *Minnesota History* 48/2 (1982):60-71; Bruce White, "A Skilled Game of Exchange: Ojibway Fur Trade Protocol," *Minnesota History* (Summer 1987):229-40.

21 See the discussion of this issue and the references cited on it in: White, "A Skilled Game of Exchange"; and White, "Give Us a Little Milk."

22 George Hammell, "Trading in Metaphors: The Magic of Beads," in *Proceedings of the 1982 Glass Trade Bead Conference*, ed. C. Hayes III (New York: Rochester Museum and Science Center, 1982), pp. 18, 23. On items traded pre-historically, see Harris, *Historical Atlas of Canada*, vol. 1, plate 14, list of trade goods.

23 Hammell, "Trading in Metaphors," p. 25.

24 Ruth Bliss Phillips, *Patterns of Power* (Kleinberg, Ontario: The McMichael Canadian Collection, 1984), p. 29. See also Hammell, "Trading in Metaphors."

25 Hammell, "Trading in Metaphors," p. 18.

26 On the ceremonial use of trade goods, see: Henry, p. 122, 18 October 1800; Henry, p. 187, 7 September 1801. There are many other references in the archaeological literature, where cloth and other trade goods frequently occur in burials. On "Manneto menance," see: R.G. Thwaites, ed. *Early Western Travels 1746-1846*, vol. 2: *John Long's Journal 1768-1782* (Cleveland: The Arthur H. Clark Company, 1904), p. 204; and Hammell, "Trading in Metaphors," pp. 7-12. Trader George Nelson similarly stated of the Lac la Ronge Cree in 1823, "They have feasts for the dead, most commonly berries . . ." (quoted in Jennifer S.H. Brown and Robert Brightman, *The Orders of the Dreamed": George Nelson on Cree and Northern Ojibwa Religion* [Winnipeg: University of Manitoba Press, 1988], p. 102).

27 Gerald Vizenor, *The People Named the Chippewa* (Minneapolis: University of Minnesota Press, 1984), p. 24.

28 E.E. Rich, *The Fur Trade and the Northwest to 1857* (Toronto: McClelland and Stewart, 1967), pp. 102-03. See also the discussion on the origins of the "cultural amnesia" theory in Paul Thistle, *Indian-European Trade Relations in the Lower Saskatchewan River Region to 1840* (Winnipeg: University of Manitoba Press), pp. 36-39.

29 Thistle, *Indian-European Trade Relations*, pp. 36-39; Eleanor Blain, "Dependency: Charles Bishop and the Northern Ojibwa," in *Aboriginal Resource Use in Canada: Historical and Legal Aspects*, ed. Kerry Abel and Jean Friesen (Winnipeg: University of Manitoba Press, 1991).

30 Shepard Krech III, "The Development of Dependency in the Sub-Arctic" (paper presented at the Sixth North American Fur Trade Conference, Mackinac Island, fall 1991).

31 Thistle, *Indian-European Trade Relations*, pp. 36-39; Blain, "Dependency," pp. 97-100.

32 On scholars' belief in the importance of firearms, see: Bishop, *The Northern Ojibwa and the Fur Trade*; and Charles Bishop's article, "Cultural and Biological Adaptations to Deprivation: The Northern Ojibwa Case," in *Extinction and Survival in Human Populations*, ed. Charles D. Laughlin and Ivan A. Brady (New York: Columbia University Press, 1978); and Charles Bishop's review of Paul Thistle's *Indian-European Trade Relations in the Lower Saskatchewan River Region to 1840* (Winnipeg: University of Manitoba Press, 1986) in *Ethnohistory* 37/2 (Spring 1990):203-06.

33 Brian J. Given, "The Iroquois Wars and Native Arms," in *Native Peoples, Native Lands,* ed. Bruce Cox (Ottawa: Carleton University Press, 1988), pp. 3-13; Blain, "Dependency," pp. 97-100; Russell, *The Eighteenth Century Cree and their Neighbors,* p. 12; Alexander Wolfe, *Earth Elder Stories* (Saskatoon: Fifth House Press, 1988), p. 23.

34 Rindisbacher paintings showing Ojibwa with bows include: "Winter fishing on the ice of the Assynoibain and Red River. Drawn from nature in December 1821, Manitoba" (NAC Rindisbacher C-1932); and "A Savage of the Sautaux Indians on the Red River. Drawn to a twelfth part of his natural size. P.R., Manitoba, ca. 1822" (NAC Rindisbacher C-1935). Re: Ojibwa boys and their skill with bows, see: Wolfe, *Earth Elder Stories*, p. 23; Peter Grant, "The Saulteaux Indians about 1804," in *Les Bourgeois de la Compagnie du Nord-Ouest*, vol. 2, ed. L.R. Masson (New York: Antiquarian Press, Ltd., 1960), p. 324.

35 Blain, "Dependency."

36 Bellamy site: Neal Ferris, Ian Kenyon, Rosemary Prevec, and Carl Murphy, "Bellamy: A Late Historic Ojibwa Habitation," *Ontario Archaeology* 44 (1985):3-22. Cleland quote: Charles E. Cleland, "The Inland Shore Fishery of the Northern Great Lakes: Its Development and Importance in Prehistory," *American Antiquity* 47/4 (1982):781.

37 One such Native-made coat is Canadian Museum of Civilization III-X-229, Speyer collection, illustrated in Ted Brasser, *Bo'jou Neejee!: Profiles of Canadian Indian Art* (Ottawa: National Museum of Man, 1976), p. 98. On the meaning of these coats to Native people, see Dorothy Burnham, *To Please the Caribou: Painted Caribou-Skin Coats Worn by the Naskapi, Montagnais, and Cree Hunters of the Quebec-Labrador Peninsula* (Toronto: Royal Ontario Museum, 1992). On the effect of the trading captain position, see Lise C. Hansen, "Chiefs and Principal Men: A Question of Leadership in Treaty Negotiations," *Anthropologica* 29 (1987); and see the note and references on *okimahkan* in John S. Long, "Coping with Powerful People: A Hudson's Bay Company 'Boss' and the Albany River Cree, 1862-1875," *Native Studies Review* 8/1 (1992):20 (n. 65).

38 This issue is raised briefly in: Bishop's review of Thistle, *Indian-European Trade Relations in the Lower Saskatchewan River Region to 1840* in *Ethnohistory* 37/2 (Spring 1990):206; and Sylvia Van Kirk, "Toward a Feminist Perspective in Ethnohistory," *Papers of the Eighteenth Algonquian Conference*, ed. William Cowan (Ottawa: Carleton University, 1987), p. 382.

39 See, on this debate, Shepard Krech III, "Introduction," in Krech, ed., *The Subarctic Fur Trade: Native Social and Economic Adaptations* (Vancouver: University of British Columbia Press, 1984).

40 Alexander Ross, *The Red River Settlement* (Winnipeg: Helen Doherty, 1984), p. 13. See also HBCA B.159/e/1, Swan River District Report 1818-19, fo. 8: "The Sotaux are not the Aborigines of the soil but Emigrants from Canada brought in by the NorthWest Traders."

41 Alice Johnson, ed., *Saskatchewan Journals and Correspondence*, vol. 26 (London: Hudson's Bay Company Record Society, 1967), p. 6n.

42 Ross, *The Red River Settlement*, pp. 12-13. Lewis and Clark stated that the Ojibwa of Red River had been "encouraged by the British traders to hunt" there (Gary E. Moulton, ed., *The Journals of the Lewis and Clark Expedition, August 25, 1804–April 6, 1805* [Lincoln: University of Nebraska Press, 1987], p. 441). See also Harold Hickerson and Erminie Wheeler-Voegelin, *The Red Lake and Pembina Chippewa* (New York: Garland Publishing, 1974), p. 94.

43 Hickerson, "The Genesis of a Trading Post Band," p. 291. See also H. Dempsey, *Indian Tribes of Alberta*, rev. ed. (Calgary: Glenbow-Alberta Institute, 1986), p. 83.

44 Gertrude Nicks, "The Iroquois and the Fur Trade in Western Canada," in *Old Trails and New Directions*, ed. C. Judd and A.J. Ray (Toronto: University of Toronto Press, 1980), pp. 88-89.

45 For instance, see: Henry, p. 56, 21 August 1800; Henry, p. 103, 27 September 1800; Henry, p. 159, 8 December 1800.

46 Tanner, pp. 17-29. See also Hickerson, "Journal of Charles Jean Baptiste Chaboillez."

47 HBCA B.60/a/1, Edmonton Journal 1795-96, 10 August 1795; Thompson, cited in Nicks, "The Iroquois and the Fur Trade in Western Canada," p. 87.

48 Tanner, p. 20. I would like to thank John Fierst for bringing the significance of Tanner's statement to my attention.

49 Nicks, "The Iroquois and the Fur Trade in Western Canada," p. 88.

50 Fidler: A. Johnson, ed., *Saskatchewan Journals*, p. lxx; Tanner, p. 71.

51 William Warren, *History of the Ojibway Nation* (Minneapolis: Ross and Haines, 1957), p. 134.

52 "Pawns": Hickerson, *The Chippewa and their Neighbors*, p. 119.

53 Thompson: Richard Glover, ed., *David Thompson's Narrative* (Toronto: The Champlain Society, 1962), pp. 149, 208. See also: Hickerson, *Ethnohistory of Chippewa of Lake Superior*, pp. 103, 107; W.K. Lambe, ed., *The Journals and Letters of Alexander Mackenzie* (Toronto: Macmillan, 1970), pp. 106-07; and Sir Alexander Mackenzie, *Voyages from Montreal on the River St. Laurence through the Continent of North America . . .* , rpt. ed. (Toronto: Radisson Society of Canada, 1927 [1801]), pp. 63-64.

54 HBCA B.105/a/1, Rainy River Journal 1793, quoted in Lauren Ritterbush, "Documenting Environmental Adaptation on the Northern Prairies during the Fur Trade Era: The Red River Ojibwa" (paper presented to the Fur Trade Symposium of the Forty-seventh annual Plains Conference, 1989), p. 4. Evidence on the availability of game in this region is contradictory. See also George Nelson, Reminiscences 5 (Nelson Papers, Baldwin Room, Metropolitan Toronto Public Library; transcript provided by Jennifer S.H. Brown), p. 37; John Long, *Voyages and Travels of an Indian Interpreter and Trader* (Vendôme: Imprimerie des Presses Universitaires de France-Vendôme, 1968 [1791]), pp. 87, 91, 136, 144; Bishop, "The Emergence of the Northern Ojibwa," p. 143; Hickerson, *Ethnohistory of Chippewa of Lake Superior*, p. 103 (re: Ojibwa moving into northwestern tip Lake Superior in late eighteenth century); Lambe, *Journals and Letters of Alexander Mackenzie,* pp. 106-07; and Harris, *Historical Atlas of Canada*, vol. 1, plate 63 ("Depletion of Beaver").

55 Mary Black-Rogers, "Varieties of 'Starving': Semantics and Survival in the Sub-Arctic Fur Trade, 1750-1850," *Ethnohistory* 33 (1986):353-83.

56 Glover, *David Thompson's Narrative*, p. 208.

57 Lambe, *Journals and Letters of Alexander Mackenzie*, p. 103. See also Tim Holzkamm, "A Quantitative Analysis of Ojibway Sturgeon Fisheries in the Rainy River," Proceedings of the Eighteenth Algonquian Conference, ed. W. Cowan (Ottawa: Carleton University, 1987). On the availability of wild rice, particularly for fur-trade transportation routes north, west, and southwest of the tip of Lake Superior, see Lytwyn, *The Fur Trade of the Little North,* pp. 48, 50; see also George Nelson, St. Croix River Valley Journal 1802-03, typescript, p. 19, Baldwin Room, Metropolitan Toronto Public Library.

58 Mackenzie, *Voyages from Montreal*, p. 68.

59 John Macdonell, "Some Account of the Red River about 1797," in *Early Fur Trade on the Northern Plains,* ed. W.R. Wood and T. Thiessen (Norman: University of Oklahoma Press, 1985), p. 86.

60 A.J. Ray, *Indians in the Fur Trade* (Toronto: University of Toronto Press, 1983 [1974]), p. 102.

61 Glover, *David Thompson's Narrative*, p. 236. See also Ray, *Indians in the Fur Trade*, p. 105. Jody F. Decker has recently attempted to trace the diffusion of this epidemic ("Tracing Historical Diffusion Patterns: The Case of the 1780-82 Smallpox Epidemic among the Indians of Western Canada," *Native Studies Review* 4/1, 2 [1988]), but I find her use of incomplete evidence unconvincing.

62 Warren, *History of the Ojibway Nation*, p. 261.

63 Tomison in HBCA B.239/b/42, fos. 15d-16d, Matthew Cocking, York Factory August 1782 to Moose, Albany, and Churchill forts; Umfreville, quoted in John Milloy, *The Plains Cree: Trade, Diplomacy and War, 1790 to 1860* (Winnipeg: University of Manitoba Press, 1988), p. 169.

64 Warren, *History of the Ojibway Nation*, p. 261; Henry, p. 46, 19 August 1800.

65 See, for example, Dean R. Snow and Kim M. Lanphear ("European Contact and Indian Depopulation in the Northeast: The Timing of the First Epidemics," *Ethnohistory* 35/15-33 [1988]:24), who cite a sixty-seven percent to ninety-eight percent virgin soil smallpox mortality. See also C. Heidenreich, *Huronia: A History and Geography of the Huron Indians, 1600-1650* (Toronto: McClelland and Stewart, 1971), p. 97. Ann Herring's paper, "The 1918 Flu Epidemic in Manitoba Aboriginal Communities: Implications for Depopulation Theory in the Americas" (presented at the American Society for Ethnohistory meeting, Toronto, 1990), concludes that such high mortality rates were probably not uniform over the entire continent.

66 Matthew Cocking, HBCA B.239/a/42, fos. 15d-16d.

67 HBCA B.78/a/8, fo. 24d, quoted in Lytwyn, *The Fur Trade of the Little North*, p. 44.

68 Helen Tanner, ed., *Atlas of Great Lakes Indian History* (Norman: University of Oklahoma Press, 1986), p. 173.

69 Cadotte, cited in Harold Hickerson, *The Southwestern Ojibwa: An Ethnohistorical Study* (American Anthropological Association Memoir 92, vol. 64, no. 3, part 2, 1964), p. 84; HBC Gloucester House quote, cited in Bishop, *The Northern Ojibwa and the Fur Trade*, p. 321.

70 Perrault, cited in Hickerson, *The Southwestern Ojibwa*, p. 84; Warren, *History of the Ojibway Nation*, p. 262.

71 Jody L. Decker comes to the same conclusion in her wider study of this epidemic. See Decker, "'We Should Never Again be the Same People': The Diffusion and Cumulative Impact of Acute Infectious Diseases Affecting the Natives on the Northern Plains of the Western Interior of Canada, 1774-1839" (Ph.D. dissertation, York University, 1989), p. 57.

72 Nelson, Sorel Journal, p. 119; Tomison quote: HBCA B.239/a/80, 2 July 1781, cited in Decker, "'We Should Never Again be the Same People,'" p. 73.

73 On complications caused by malnutrition and lack of adequate treatment, see: Tomison, cited in Decker, "'We Should Never Again be the Same People,'" p. 73 ("Numbers died through want of food . . . for as the complaint became general there was none left . . . able to hunt"); and Paul Hackett, "The 1819-20 Measles Epidemic: Its Origin, Diffusion and Mortality Effects upon the Indians of the Petit Nord" (M.A. thesis, University of Manitoba, 1991), pp. 121-24.

74 For an account of an appeal to supernatural powers during an epidemic, and the importance placed on this, see Wolfe, *Earth Elder Stories*, p. 24.

75 On the amalgamation of survivors, see: See H. Dobyns, *Their Number become Thinned* (Knoxville: University of Tennessee, 1983), p. 311; John Taylor, "Sociocultural Effects of Epidemics on the Northern Plains, 1734-1850," *Western Canadian Journal of Anthropology* 7/4 (1977); Patricia Albers, "Pluralism on the Native Plains 1670-1870" (ms. on file at St. Paul's College Library, University of Manitoba, revised and published as "Symbiosis, Merger and War: Contrasting Forms of Intertribal Relationship among Historic Plains Indians," in *Political Economy of North American Indians*, ed. John Moore (Norman: University of Oklahoma Press, in press), ms. p. 46. Herring, "The 1918 Flu Epidemic," pp. 6-7.

76 Donald Gunn, "Peguis Vindicated," *Nor'Wester*, 28 April 1860. See also PAM MG12 A1, Archibald Papers, #780, n.d., "Draft Notes," for a similar explanation repeated "dozens of times" by Peguis.

77 Taylor, "Sociocultural Effects of Epidemics," p. 63; Carolyn Gilman, in *The Grand Portage Story* (St. Paul: Minnesota Historical Society Press, 1992), p. 64, cites Warren's *History of the Ojibway Nation*, Thistle's *Indian-European Trade Relations*, and Harold A. Innis, *The Fur Trade in Canada*, rev. ed. (Toronto: University of Toronto Press, 1984) re: the drop in the fur trade and skins being sacrificed. Peter Grant, in "The Saulteaux Indians about 1804," p. 365, also notes the custom of abandoning or giving away personal property and ceasing to trap and hunt when a death in the family had occurred. Decker, in "'We Should Never Again be the Same People,'" p. 84, notes that, while 100 canoes of Bungees came to York Factory in 1781, only 24 came in 1782.

78 Glover, *David Thompson's Narrative*, p. 237. See also Taylor, "Sociocultural Effects of Epidemics," p. 63. For similar actions resulting from spiritual advice, see Wolfe, *Earth Elder Stories*, p. 24.

79 Hickerson, "Journal of Charles Jean Baptiste Chaboillez," pp. 300, 303.

80 The question of the nature of these groups among the Ojibwa has been the subject of much debate. See the overview of this debate and references to both sides in Brown and Peers, "A Critical Review," pp. 140-42. The evidence for these groups is thin and debatable in northern Ontario; see also Edward S. Rogers and Mary Black-Rogers, "Who Were the Cranes? Groups and Group Identity Names in Northern Ontario," in *Approaches to Algonquian Archaeology* ed. Brian Kooymans and Margaret Hanna (Calgary: University of Calgary Press, 1982).

81 For the entire subsistence cycle, see Leo Waisberg, "An Ethnographic and Historical Outline of the Rainy River Ojibway," in *An Historical Synthesis of the Manitou Mounds Site on the Rainy River*, ed. W.C. Noble (manuscript report, Parks Canada, 1984); and also George Quimby, "A Year with a Chippewa Family," *Ethnohistory* 9/3 (Summer 1962):217-39. Brasser, *Bo'jou, Neejee!*, is helpful for the spiritual aspects of economic activities.

82 Tim Holzkamm, Victor Lytwyn, and Leo Waisberg, "Rainy River Sturgeon: An Ojibway Resource in the Fur Trade Economy," *The Canadian Geographer*, 32/3 (1988):194-205.

83 Hickerson, "Journal of Charles Jean Baptiste Chaboillez," p. 417.

84 See the discussion and references cited on this debate in Brown and Peers, "A Critical Review," pp. 142-43.

85 Michael Angel, "The Ojibwa-Missionary Encounter at Rainy Lake Mission, 1839-1857" (M.A. thesis, University of Manitoba, 1986), pp. 55-59; J.G. Kohl, *Kitchi-Gami: Life among the Lake Superior Ojibway* (St. Paul: Minnesota Historical Society Press, 1985), p. 43. On the Midewiwin ceremony, see: W.J. Hoffman, "The Midw'wiwin; or 'Grand Medicine Society' of the Ojibwa," Bureau of American Ethnology, Seventh Annual Report 1885-86, pp. 143-300; Christopher Vecsey, *Traditional Ojibwa Religion and its Historical Changes* (Philadelphia: American Philosophical Society, 1983); Edward Benton-Banai, *The Mishomis Book* (St. Paul: Indian Country Press, 1981).

86 On the definition of *tribe*, and problems with it, see: Morton Fried, *The Notion of Tribe* (Don Mills: Cummings Publishing Co., 1975); and Jennifer S.H. Brown, "Northern Algonquians from Lake Superior and Hudson Bay to Manitoba in the Historical Period," pp. 208-13.

87 On Ojibwa use of wild rice in the late eighteenth and early nineteenth century, see: Waisberg, "Ethnographic and Historical Outline," pp. 140-51; Thomas Vennum, *Wild Rice and the Ojibway People*; Tim Holkzamm, "Ojibway Horticulture in the Upper Mississippi and Boundary Waters," in *Actes du Dix-septième Congres des Algonquianistes*, ed. W. Cowan (Ottawa: Carleton University, 1986); Wayne Moodie, "Manomin: Historical Geographical Perspectives on the Ojibway Production of Wild Rice," in *Aboriginal Resource Use in Canada: Historical and Legal Aspects*, ed. Kerry Abel and Jean Friesen (Winnipeg: University of Manitoba Press, 1991); Lytwyn, *The Fur Trade of the Little North*, pp. 48, 50; Mackenzie, *Voyages from Montreal*, pp. 62, 67. On other summer activities, see Quimby, "Year with a Chippewa Family," pp. 230-31; Tanner, pp. 16-19; Waisberg, "Ethnographic and Historical Outline," p. 130.

88 Henry the Elder, quoted in Waisberg, "Ethnographic and Historical Outline," p. 145. See Bain, *Travels and Adventures*, pp. 239-43.

89 Quimby, "Year with a Chippewa Family"; Hickerson, "Journal of Charles Jean Baptiste Chaboillez," pp. 413-15; Waisberg, "Ethnographic and Historical Outline," p. 128.

90 Brasser, *Boujou Neejee!;* Phillips, *Patterns of Power*; David Penney, "Great Lakes Indian Art: An Introduction," in *Great Lakes Indian Art*, ed. David Penney (Detroit: Wayne State University Press, 1989), pp. 8-20.

91 Brasser, *Bou'jou Neejee!*, pp. 17-48.

CHAPTER 2

1 A. Irving Hallowell, *The Ojibwa of Berens River, Manitoba: Ethnography into History*, edited with Preface and Afterword by Jennifer S.H. Brown (Fort Worth, TX: Harcourt Brace Jovanovich College Publishers, 1992), pp. 22-24, especially map 2, p. 23.

2 Hickerson and Voegelin, *Red Lake and Pembina Chippewa*, pp. 54, 55, 56, 58. Re: bison hunting: Hickerson, "Journal of Charles Jean Baptiste Chaboillez," p. 287, 12 November 1797; HBCA B.105/a/5, 9, 10, 11, 12, cited in Lauren Ritterbush, "Culture Change and Continuity: Ethnohistoric Analysis of Ojibwa and Ottawa Adjustment to the Prairies" (Ph.D. dissertation, University of Kansas, 1990), p. 64 (re: Rainy Lake Ojibwa hunting bison). Re: sugaring commutes: see Henry, p. 170, 20 February 1801 (Red Lake and Red River Ojibwa to Red Lake for sugaring).

3 For examples of various lengths of commutes: Netnokwa and other Ottawa came from L'Arbre Croche (island in northern Lake Michigan in Michilimackinac area), some of them to visit Ojibwa relatives who may also have originated from this region. Other mentions of long-distance commuting by Ottawa: Tanner, pp. 19, 34, 45, 161; HBCA B.60/a/1, Edmonton House Journal 1795-96, 10 August 1795; HBCA B.22/a/4, Brandon House Post Journal 1795-97, 5 October 1795; HBCA B.22/a/4, Brandon House Post Journal 1797-98, 3 June 1797; HBCA B.22/a/11, Brandon House Post Journal 1803-04, 5 January and 6 March 1804. Ojibwa commutes: to Elk River and Brandon House area from Rainy Lake area, HBCA B.22/a/4, Brandon House Journal 1797-98, 11 September 1797; to Dauphin River area from Red Lake, HBCA B.51/a/1, Dauphin River 1795-96, 9 August 1795; to Interlake from "Southward of Red River," HBCA B.53/a/1, Post Doubtful 1797-98, 27, 28 September 1797; "up the Saskatchewan," met with at Cedar Lake, HBCA B.49/a/31, Cumberland House Journal 1801-02, 30 August 1801. Commutes from the Boundary Waters were especially frequent: see, for example, HBCA B. 235/a/1, Winnipeg Journal 1797-98, 26 January, 9 February 1798.

4 Hickerson, "Journal of Charles Jean Baptiste Chaboillez," pp. 270-71.

5 Ritterbush, "Documenting Environmental Adaptation," p. 6.

6 *Ibid.*, p. 8; Ritterbush, "Culture Change and Continuity," p. 77, citing Henry, Indians making sugar near Pembina post in 1801, 1802, 1803, 1808; Tanner, p. 125; HBCA B.51/e/1, Fort Dauphin District Report 1820, fo. 10.

7 Ritterbush, "Documenting Environmental Adaptation," pp. 9-11; Holzkamm, Lytwyn, and Waisberg, "Rainy River Sturgeon," p. 195.

8 Tim Holzkamm, "Ojibway Horticulture in the Upper Mississippi and Boundary Waters," in *Proceedings of the Eighteenth Algonquian Conference*, ed. William Cowan (Ottawa: Carleton University, 1987), p. 149. See also Waisberg, "Ethnographic and Historical Outline," pp. 141-42, 146. On the importance of carbohydrates as a critical component of hunter-gatherer diet, and the questioning of Lee's "original affluence" model for hunter-gatherers on the basis of the difficulty of obtaining carbohydrates, see also Fred Myers, "Critical Trends in the Study of Hunter-Gatherers," *Annual Review of Anthropology*, vol. 17, ed. Bernard Siegel (1988), p. 264.

9 Moodie, "Manomin," pp. 75-76; Ritterbush, "Documenting Environmental Adaptation," pp. 13-15.

10 In the Interlake, "Bad Governor's" band traded large quantities of rice in the years 1797 to 1801: HBCA B.4/a/2, Fort Alexander Post Journal 1797-99, HBCA B.4/a/4, Fort Alexander Post Journal 1800-01, HBCA B.236/a/1, Lake Winnipeg Journal 1796-97. The Ojibwa who traded with George Nelson also harvested rice, largely from the eastern shore of Lake Winnipeg: Nelson, Dauphin River Journal, 1810-11, 26-27 August 1810 (Broken River), and other sites mentioned in Nelson journals for 1805-11. At the Forks, see HBCA B.235/a/3 20 September to 12 October 1814 at Forks, cited in Ritterbush, "Documenting Environmental Adaptation," p. 14.

11 Early movement: Ritterbush, "Culture Change and Continuity," p. 67, citing HBCA B.105/a/5, 9, 10, 11, 12. Birchbark: Ted Brasser, "Flowers in Native American Art: A Review" (unpublished paper, copy from author), ms. p. 7, citing D.J. Lehmer, "Introduction to Middle Missouri Archaeology," Anthropology Paper 1 (Washington: National Park Service, U.S. Department of the Interior, 1971), p. 159.

12 Dale Russell, in *Eighteenth Century Western Cree and their Neighbors*, p. 115, describes Tomison's encounters with the "Mantawapowa" Indians (some of whom Tomison met returning from rice fields). A later (1788) source identifies this group as Ojibwa but does not state on what grounds (HBCA B.205/a/2, cited in Russell, p. 115). It is probable, though, that these were Ojibwa. Nicolas Jeremie claimed in 1714 that there were "Saulteurs" living around Lake Winnipegosis, but this was not based on direct observation and may have been a misinterpretation of information from Native people trading at York Factory. See: Russell, *Eighteenth Century Cree and their Neighbors*, pp. 73, 131; and also Ritterbush, "Culture Change and Continuity," pp. 22-23.

13 HBCA B.49/a/6, Cumberland House Journal 1777-78.

14 "Poor Pungee . . . hunters": HBCA B.239/b/42, fos. 15d-16d. See also Bishop, "The Emergence of the Northern Ojibwa," p. 46; Lytwyn, *The Fur Trade of the Little North*.

15 Lytwyn, *The Fur Trade of the Little North*, pp. 31-32, 149.

16 HBCA A.11/16, fo.61, Holmes and Pangman, Sturgeon River Fort, to Tomison and Longman, Hudson's House, 2 December 1779; A.I. Hallowell Papers, American Philosophical Society Library, MS coll. no. 26, p. 5. I am indebted to Jennifer S.H. Brown for sharing her copies of the Hallowell Papers with me.

17 HBCA B.49/a/13, Cumberland House Journal 1782-83, letter from William Tomison to George Hudson, 9 February 1783. See also Thistle, *Indian-European Trade Relations*, p. 65; Russell, *Eighteenth Century Cree and their Neighbours*, p. 160, quoting HBCA B.239/a/80, 10 June 1782.

18 Thistle, *Indian-European Trade Relations*, p. 66.

19 Mackenzie, *Voyages from Montreal*, p. 71.

20 HBCA B.22/a/1, Brandon House Journal 1792-93, 14 December 1792, 26 February 1793; A.S. Morton, ed., *The Journal of Duncan M'Gillivray of the North West Company at Fort George on the Saskatchewan, 1794-95* (Toronto: Macmillan Co., 1929), p. lxiii; Thistle, *Indian-European Trade Relations*, p. 71; HBCA B.148/a/1, Nipawin Journal 1794-95, 10 December 1794, 12 and 25 March 1795; Glover, *David Thompson's Narrative*, p. 149; HBCA B.51/e/1, Fort Dauphin District Report 1820, fo. 16; HBCA B.60/a/1, Edmonton House Journal 1795-96, 19 August 1795; Tanner, p. 36; Lytwyn, *The Fur Trade of the Little North*, pp. 76, 90; HBCA B.51/a/1, Dauphin River Post Journal 1795-96; John Macdonell, "Some Account of the Red River about 1797," pp. 84, 86, 87; HBCA B.213/a/6, Swan River Journal 1794-95, 16 and 18 May 1795. Lac la Biche: HBCA B.104/a/1, Lac la Biche (Greenwich House) Journal 1799-1800, 4-6 October 1799; Henry, p. 609, 7 July 1810, p. 614, 16 June 1810. Ojibwa presence at Qu'Appelle River also verified by John Macdonell, "Some Account of the Red River about 1797," p. 87.

21 HBCA B.49/a/25a, Cumberland House Journal 1793-94, 27 and 28 September 1793; HBCA B.60/a/1, Edmonton House Journal 1795-96, 19 August 1795; HBCA B.22/a/5, Brandon House Journal 1797-98, 11 September 1797.

22 Warren, *History of the Ojibway Nation*, p. 191; Christian Feest and Johanna Feest, "Ottawa," in *Handbook of North American Indians*, vol. 15: *Northeast*, ed. Bruce G. Trigger (Washington, D.C.: Smithsonian Institution, 1978), pp. 772-86.

23 Feest and Feest, "Ottawa," p. 772; Hickerson, *Central Minnesota*, p. 49. "Of Red River": Tanner, p. 16. "Found great numbers": Tanner, pp. 30-31.

24 HBCA B.60/a/1, Edmonton House Journal 1795-96; HBCA B.22/a/3, Brandon House Journal 1794-95; HBCA B.22/a/4, Brandon House Journal 1796-97; Tanner, p. 28.

25 Henry, p. 448, 11 August 1808; see also entries for 8 August and 10 May 1808; HBCA B.104/a/1, Lac la Biche (Greenwich House) Journal 1799-1800, 4-6 October 1799. It is unclear whether this represents male heads of families or the total population, although the former seems more likely.

26 Henry, "no inclination": p. 448, 8 August 1808. See also Albers, "Pluralism in the Native Plains," p. 54; HBCA B.104/a/1, Lac la Biche (Greenwich House) Journal 1799-1800, 30 September, 7 April 1800; Tanner, p. 30. Tanner's adoptive Ottawa mother, Netnokwa, illustrates the role of kin in this migration quite well. She came to Red River to visit her Ojibwa husband's kin. She wanted to return east after a time, but stayed because one of her sons refused to go.

27 HBCA B.4/a/2, Fort Alexander Journal 1797-98, 14 September 1798.

28 Morton, *Journal of Duncan M'Gillivray*, p. 18, 2 September 1794.

29 See, for example: HBCA B.60/a/1, Edmonton Journal 1795-96; Morton, *Journal of Duncan M'Gillivray*, p. 18, 2 September 1794; HBCA B.22/a/5, Brandon House Journal 1797-98, 30 January 1798; Henry, p. 275, 23 May 1805; Hickerson, "Journal of Charles Jean Baptiste Chaboillez," pp. 288, 289, 292.

30 For various statements on the importance of such "luxury" goods to the Ojibwa trade, see: HBCA B.4/a/3, Fort Alexander Journal 1799-1800, 20 May 1800; HBCA B.60/a/3, Edmonton House Journal 1797-98, 27 March 1798; Glover, *David Thompson's Narrative*, p. 156; HBCA B.22/a/1, Brandon House Journal 1793-94, 15 March 1794; Henry, p. 7, 20 July 1800 ("List of Goods for the Sauteur trade on the Red River"). Re: importance of clothes as a trade item, see also HBCA B.236/a/1, Lake Winnipeg Journal 1796-97, 10 May 1797.

31 Tomison: HBCA B.60/a/3, Edmonton House Journal 1797-98; Brandon House: HBCA B.22/a/3, Brandon House Journal 1794-95, 9 December 1794. Chaboillez: Hickerson, "Journal of Charles Jean Baptiste Chaboillez," p. 287, 12 November 1797;

32 Henry, p. 347, 21 July 1806. See Brasser, *Bo'jou, Neejee!*, p. 128, for just one such headdress, a black silk scarf covered with round trade silver brooches and fringed with trade silver tinkle cones. Eastern Great Lakes, ca. 1780 (headdress is Canadian Museum of Civilization No. III-X-245, Speyer collection). On western Ojibwa desire for silver, see N. Jaye Fredrickson, *The Covenant Chain: Indian Ceremonial and Trade Silver* (Ottawa: National Museums of Canada, 1980), pp. 43-48.

33 Glover, *David Thompson's Narrative*, p. 156. See also Peter Grant, "The Saulteaux Indians about 1804," pp. 316-19, for other descriptions of Ojibwa cloth clothing and trade silver jewellery during this period.

34 Tanner, p. 68 ("My silver ornaments, one of my guns, several blankets, and much clothing, were lost. We had been rather wealthy").

35 HBCA B.236/a/1, Lake Winnipeg Journal 1796-97, 10 May 1797; HBCA B.49/a/25a, Cumberland House Journal 1793-94, 11 January 1794.

36 David Penney, "Floral Decoration and Culture Change: An Historical Interpretation of Motivation," *American Indian Culture and Research Journal* 15/1 (1991):55-56. See also Erica Smith, "Something More than Mere Ornament: Cloth and Indian-European Relationships in the Eighteenth Century" (M.A. thesis, Universities of Winnipeg and Manitoba, 1991), pp. 116, 118.

37 Henry, p. 97, 15 September 1800; Hickerson, "Journal of Charles Jean Baptiste Chaboillez," p. 281. "As much debt as they would take": HBCA B.49/a/25, Cumberland House Journal 1793-94, 12 January 1794.

38 See, for example, HBCA B.49/a/25b, Cumberland House Journal 1793-94, 16 October 1793.

39 On this debate as a whole, see the discussion in A.J. Ray and Donald Freeman, *"Give Us Good Measure": An Economic Analysis of Relations between the Indians and the Hudson's Bay Company before 1763* (Toronto: University of Toronto Press, 1978), pp. 231-45.

40 HBCA B.49/a/25a, Cumberland House Journal 1793-94, 14 May 1794.

41 On social relationships in the fur trade, see: White, "Give Us a Little Milk"; and White, "A Skilled Game of Exchange."

42 Henry, p. 162, 25 December 1800.

43 *Ibid.*, p. 260, 1 August 1805.

44 Sylvia Van Kirk, *Many Tender Ties: Women in Fur Trade Society, 1670-1870* (Winnipeg: Watson and Dwyer, 1983), pp. 76, 80.

45 Henry, p. 163, 1 January 1801. On the advantages and disadvantages of fur-trade marriages for Native women, see also Van Kirk, *Many Tender Ties.*

46 HBCA B.22/a/5, Brandon House Journal 1797-98, 22 December 1797.

47 Ayagon references: Nelson, Reminiscences, p. 290; Jennifer S.H. Brown, "Man in His Natural State: The Indian Worlds of George Nelson," in *Rendezvous: Selected Papers of the Fourth North American Fur Trade Conference, 1981,* ed. Thomas C. Buckley (St. Paul: Minnesota Historical Society, 1984), p. 201-02. On traders being educated about Native social expectations of trade, see: White, "A Skilled Game of Exchange"; and White, "Give Us a Little Milk."

48 Henry, p. 56, 21 August 1800.

49 Tanner, p. 86.

50 George Nelson, Dauphin River Journal 1810-1811, 20 May 1810.

51 For examples, see: Brasser, *Bo'jou Neejee!*, p. 98; and *The Spirit Sings: A Catalogue of the Exhibition* (Toronto: McClelland and Stewart, 1987) pp. 74, 75. For Native re-interpretations of the meaning of such coats, see Burnham, *To Please the Caribou.*

52 Penney, "Floral Decoration and Culture Change," pp. 55-56. See also Ray, *Indians in the Fur Trade*, pp. 137-41. On the re-assessment of the status of trading captains, see: Hansen, "Chiefs and Principal Men"; and John S. Long, "Coping with Powerful People," n. 65, p. 20.

53 "Most Rascals": HBCA B.22/a/1, Brandon House Journal 1793-94, 14 December 1793. "Seldom winter": HBCA B.22/a/5, Brandon House Journal 1797-98, 11 September 1797. "Hunt nothing but Beaver": HBCA B.22/a/5, Brandon House Journal 1797-98, 11 September 1797.

54 HBCA B.22/a/5, Brandon House Journal 1797-98, 11 September 1797.

55 See, for example: HBCA B.4/a/3, Fort Alexander Journal 1799-1800, 20 May 1800; HBCA B.239/b/59, fo. 27d, letter from Angus Shaw to Joseph Colen (at Fort Augustus), 10 May 1797; HBCA B.60/a/1, Edmonton House Journal 1795-96, 20 April 1795, letter from William Tomison; HBCA B.148/a/1, Nipawin Journal 1794-95, letters from J. Bird to Magnus Twatt, 10 December 1794, 25 March 1795; HBCA B.51/a/1, Dauphin River Journal 1795-96, letter from Duncan Cameron, Partridge Crop Lake, to John Best, 16 December 1795; HBCA B.49/a/25a, Cumberland House Journal 1793-94, 11 January 1794; HBCA B.22/a/3, Brandon House Journal 1794-95, 4 December 1795.

56 Bruce Trigger, *Natives and Newcomers: Canada's "Heroic Age" Reconsidered* (Montreal: McGill-Queen's University Press, 1985), p. 193; and see pp. 183-85, 193-94. See also White, "A Skilled Game of Exchange."

57 HBCA B.60/a/2, Edmonton House Journal 1796-97, 3 May 1797; Henry, p. 6, 24 August 1800; HBCA B.51/e/1, Manitoba District Report 1820, fo. 6; Tanner, pp. 88-89.

58 HBCA B.4/a/4, Winnipeg River House (Fort Alexander) 1800-01.

59 See, for example: Henry, p. 97, 15 September 1800; HBCA B.22/a/11, Brandon House Journal 1803-04, 6 March 1804; HBCA 4/a/2, Point au Foutre Journal 1798-99, 12 March 1799; HBCA B.235/a/2, Winnipeg Post Journal 1799-1800, 1 April 1800; Henry, p. 192, 3 January 1802, and p. 196, 4 May 1802, and p. 244, 21 May 1804; HBCA B.197/a/1, Carlton House / Setting River Journal, 21 and 29 November 1798.

60 HBCA B.60/a/5, Edmonton Post Journal 1799-1800, letter from J.P. Pruden to Bird, June 1799.

61 HBCA B.22/a/9, Brandon House Journal 1801-02; Henry, p. 66, 27 August 1800; Henry, p. 59, 23 August 1800.

62 HBCA B.22/a/6, Brandon House Journal 1798-99, 29 November 1798.

63 Henry, p. 210, 13 April 1803; Henry, p. 251, 23 September 1804.

64 HBCA B.51/a/1, Dauphin River Journal 1795-96, 17 August 1795.

65 Victor Lytwyn, "'These Canadians Trade the Beaver with Them Where They Kill Them': Indian Responses to Extreme Fur Trade Competition in the Little North, 1790-1810" (paper presented at Sixth North American Fur Trade Conference, Mackinac Island, 1991). See also: HBCA B.49/a/31, Cumberland House Journal 1801-02, 7 May 1802; HBCA B.24/a/6, Buckingham House Journal 1798-99; HBCA B.197/a/1, Setting River Journal 1798-99.

66 Assiniboine River: HBCA B.22/a/1, Brandon House Journal 1793-94, 7 March 1794; Fidler: HBCA B.104/a/1, Lac la Biche Journal 1799-1800, 27 November 1799; Henry, p. 256, 1 January 1805, cited in Ritterbush, "Culture Change and Continuity," p. 122.

67 HBCA B.60/a/3, Edmonton House Journal 1797-98, 14 May 1798. See also HBCA B.104/a/1, Lac la Biche Journal 1799-1800, 30 September 1799.

68 "Mr. McKay": HBCA B.4/a/4, Winnipeg River Journal 1800-01, 11 September 1800; see also R.S. Allen, "William McKay," *Dictionary of Canadian Biography*, vol. 6 (Toronto: University of Toronto Press, 1987), pp. 464-66; "slyly": HBCA B.104/a/1, Lac la Biche Journal 1799-1800, 13 October 1799.

69 White, "Give Us a Little Milk," p. 67; Henry, p. 203, 15 September 1802.

70 Henry, p. 727; Tanner, p. 52. See also Tanner, p. 76.

71 Henry: p. 121, 18 October 1800; p. 156, 26 November 1800; p. 159, 1 December 1800; p. 168, 15 January 1801.

72 "No less than six interpreters": HBCA B.148/a/1, Nipawin Journal 1794-95, letter from James Bird to Magnus Twatt, 25 March 1795; "so drunk": HBCA B.49/a/31, Cumberland House Journal 1801-02, 7 May 1802; "tobacco in river": HBCA B.51/a/1, Dauphin River Journal 1795-96, 27 August 1795. On Ojibwa demands for alcohol, see: HBCA B.49/a/25a, Cumberland House Journal 1793-94, May 1794 (traded 220 MB for brandy over a few weeks).

73 John Webster Grant, "Missionaries and Messiahs in the Northwest," *Studies in Religion* 9/2 (1980):125-36; Helen Tanner, *Atlas of Great Lakes Indian History*, p. 48.

74 Henry, 8 May 1801, pp. 178-79. The combined supernatural and economic power of European "writings" (as in a trader's ledger book, or the Bible), surfaced again and again in these syncretic movements. See, among many other references, Peter Grant, "The Saulteaux Indians about 1804," p. 357 ("They pretend that our method of conveying our sentiments by reading and writing has originally been acquired in a dream"). Dreams, of course, are conventional Native sources of "power." Peter Grant also notes (p. 325) that the Sauteux "regard our books and writings with some degree of veneration, and allow their possessors to have some merit and, sometimes, condescend to honor them with the appellation of 'Chief' or 'Father'." See also: chapter 5, this volume, in which I discuss the 1850s Interlake prophecies; and John Long, "Manitu, Power, Books, and Wihtikow," *Native Studies Review* 3/1 (1987).

75 John Macdonell, "Some Account of the Red River (about 1797) with Extracts from his Journal 1793-95," in Masson, *Les Bourgeois de la Compagnie du Nord-Ouest*, p. 269; Tanner, p. 39; Henry: p. 59, 23 August 1800; pp. 65-66, 26 August 1800; p. 71, 29 August 1800.

76 On the Cree-Assiniboine alliance and their relations with the Sioux, see Doige, "Warfare Patterns of the Assiniboine to 1809." On war parties, see: Henry: p. 154, 18 November 1800; p. 159, 1 December 1800; p. 163, 2 and 6 January 1801; pp. 195, 197, 199, 20 March and 12 May 1802; pp. 249, 250, 19 August, 6 September 1804; p. 260, 1 August 1805; Tanner, pp. 105, 112.

77 "Swarming": HBCA B.22/a/12, Brandon House Journal 1804-05, 26 April 1805. See also HBCA B.22/a/12, Brandon House Journal 1894-05, 31 August 1804; Tanner, p. 70.

78 Henry, p. 185, 23 August 1801, and p. 190, 22-24 November 1801.

79 Tanner, pp. 31, 49, 132.

80 "Our friends": Tanner, p. 49; "brother": Tanner, p. 24.

81 Henry, p. 269, 30 October 1805.

82 Tanner, p. 31, 38; Moulton, *The Journals of the Lewis and Clark Expedition*, pp. 440-43. See also Henry, p. 185, 23 August 1801.

83 Hickerson, "Genesis of a Trading Post Band," pp. 310-11.

84 Not all Ojibwa bands had good relations with the Cree. Tanner met one band of Cree that debated whether to kill his party "on account of some old quarrel [they had] with a band of Ojibbeways" (Tanner, p. 79). Herein lies another difficulty with the concept of *tribe*: not all the members of a tribe maintain the same political alliances and enmities.

85 "Feed yourself": Tanner, p. 134. See also Henry, p. 185, 23 August 1801.

86 Albers, "Pluralism in the Native Plains," p. 41 ("local level conflict and segmentation were buffered by the kinship web").

87 Ritterbush, "Culture Change and Continuity," pp. 103-08, analyses a number of sources for Red River Ojibwa and concludes that they followed a matrilocal pattern for one or more years after marriage.

88 Ray, *Indians in the Fur Trade*, pp. 103-04, 106, 133; Milloy, *The Plains Cree*, pp. 26-29; Barth, "Introduction," in *Ethnic Groups and Boundaries*, p. 19.

89 Hugh Dempsey, *Big Bear: The End of Freedom* (Vancouver: Douglas and McIntyre, 1984), p. 17.

90 Glover, *David Thompson's Narrative*, p. 184; John Macdonell, "Some Account of the Red River about 1797," p. 88. For "conjuring and feasting," see: HBCA B.4/a/1, Point au Foutre Journal 1795-96, 8 May 1796; Tanner, p. 91; Henry, p. 182, 18 May 1802, p. 242, 16 and 18 April 1804, p. 212, 23 April 1803, p. 1977, 20, 27 May 1802.

91 Henry: pp. 197-99, 20, 27 and 28 May 1802; p. 242, 16 and 18 April 1804.

92 HBCA B.60/a/3, Edmonton Post Journal 1799-1800, letter from Peter Fidler to James Bird, 8 September 1799.

93 Henry, p. 185, 23 August 1801; p. 191, 22-24 November 1801.

94 Robert L. Bee, *Patterns and Processes: An Introduction to Anthropological Strategies for the Study of Sociocultural Change* (New York: Free Press, 1974), p. 98 ("Any ideology or activity that strengthens the group's conviction that its members are somehow better than the members of other cultures . . . can serve as a boundary-maintaining device").

95 Swagerty, "Indian Trade in the Trans-Mississippi West to 1870," pp. 351-56; W.R. Wood and T. Thiessen, *Early Fur Trade on the Northern Plains* (Norman: University of Oklahoma Press, 1985), pp. 48-69.

96 Milloy, *The Plains Cree*, pp. 55-58.

97 *Ibid.*; "war against ye Mandalls": HBCA B.22/a/3, Brandon House Journal 1794-95, 15 August 1795 (see also 26 May and 7 November). See also Glover, *David Thompson's Narrative*, p. 145.

98 Tanner, p. 38. See also: Tanner, p. 70; and Milloy, *The Plains Cree*, p. 45.

99 Henry: pp. 46-47, 19 August 1800; p. 58, 22 August 1800; p. 130, 29 October 1800.

100 Henry, p. 57, 21 August 1800. See also Henry, p. 160, December 1800, p. 94, 11 September 1800, and p. 104, 28 September 1800.

101 Charles McKenzie, "Narratives," in *Early Fur Trade on the Northern Plains*, ed. W.R. Wood and T. Thiessen (Norman: University of Oklahoma Press, 1985), p. 250.

102 Henry, p. 160, December 1800, and p. 167, 14-15 January 1801; Tanner, pp. 77, 79-80.

103 Henry, p. 244, 8 May 1804.

104 Hickerson, "Genesis of a Trading Post Band," p. 307.

105 Ritterbush, "Culture Change and Continuity," pp. 94-95.

106 "Buffalos were so numerous": Tanner, p. 44; PAM, Selkirk Papers, vol. 13, p. 4,275, 27 December 1817, Fort Douglas, Alexander Macdonell to Lord Selkirk. See also Henry, p. 46, 19 August 1800. Ritterbush, "Culture Change and Continuity," p. 70, states that their lack of horses may have impeded the early western Ojibwa in their adoption of bison hunting. I disagree with this, except insofar as the lack of horses was a handicap in competition with mounted groups.

107 According to Henry (vol. 2, pp. 614, 617), Ojibwa at Lac la Biche had horses by 1810, but these people were closely tied to freemen. There are no other references to Ojibwa in this region having horses.

108 Thompson: quoted in Hickerson, "Genesis of a Trading Post Band," p. 307; in the context of this entire speech to Thompson, this statement sounds very much like a plea for "pity," although such incidents did occur. Mackenzie: Mackenzie, *Voyages from Montreal*, p. 68.

109 Henry, p. 261, 2 August 1805.

110 Samuel W. Pond, *The Dakota or Sioux in Minnesota as They Were in 1834*, introduction by Gary C. Anderson (St. Paul: Minnesota Historical Society Press, 1986), p. 64.

111 "No horses": Glover, *David Thompson's Narrative*, p. 184; HBCA B.235/a/3, Winnipeg Journal 1815, July 1815; Tanner, p. 112, describing a war party that had a few horses but was mostly on foot; Henry, p. 250, 6 September 1804.

112 Henry, pp. 243-44, 8 May 1804. See also: Henry: p. 484, 31 August 1808; p. 286, 7 July 1806; p. 46, 19 August 1800; and Tanner, pp. 77, 112, 126.

113 David Pentland, "Metchif and Bungee: Languages of the Fur Trade" (paper read in the series "Voices of Rupert's Land," Winnipeg, 1985), p. 4.

114 "Bad medicine" and Charlo's death: Henry, pp. 167-68, 15 January 1801. Tanner, "repentance": p. 136. See also: Henry, p. 185, 23 August 1801, and p. 191, 22-24 November 1801 (trading horses for Ojibwa medicines); Tanner, p. 80 (Netnokwa fails to care for horses and they die: another indication that horses were not highly valued).

115 HBCA B.4/a/1, Point au Foutre (Fort Alexander) Journal 1795-96, 31 March, 8 April 1796.

116 Hunting bison in parkland: Henry, pp. 168-69, 19 January 1801; also p. 44, 18 August 1800, p. 57, 21 August 1800, p. 68, 28 August 1800; Tanner, p. 73, 75; Glover, *David Thompson's Narrative*, pp. 186, 208; Hickerson, "Genesis of a Trading Post Band," p. 314. Hunting bison farther out on prairie: Tanner, pp. 31, 71-75; see also Glover, *David Thompson's Narrative*, p. 184 ("As they have no Horses, and only Dogs").

117 On the game shortage in the Red River valley, see Hickerson, "Genesis of a Trading Post Band," pp. 309, 319, 320.

118 On the Ojibwa presence in this far western area, and their summer occupations and movements, see: HBCA B.104/a/1, Lac la Biche Journal, letter from Peter Fidler to James Bird, 7 October 1799; HBCA B.24/a/2, Buckingham House Journal 1793-94, 17 August 1793; HBCA B.24/a/6, Buckingham House Journal 1798-99, 5-12 July 1798; HBCA B.49/a/31, Cumberland House Journal 1801-02, 1,30 August 1801; HBCA B.60/a/1, Edmonton Journal 1795-96, 10 August 1795, 14, 16 June 1796 (also Ottawa presence). Re: the Ojibwa presence at Fort George–Buckingham House, see Lynda Gullason, "The Fort George–Buckingham House Site Plantation (1792-1800): Native-European Contact in the Fur Trade Era" (M.A. thesis, University of Alberta, 1990), pp. 46, 50-51, 59, 61, 76.

119 HBCA B.197/a/1, Carlton House / Setting River Journal 1798-99, 8 December 1798.

120 HBCA B.197/a/1, Carlton House / Setting River Journal 1798-99, 21 and 29 November, 8 December 1798; HBCA B.49/a/25a, Cumberland House Journal 1793-94, 12 and 21 December 1793; HBCA B.24/a/6, Buckingham House Journal 1798-99, 18 May, 29 June, 1, 5, 7, 8, 12 July 1798; HBCA B.60/a/4, Edmonton House Journal 1798-99, 12 and 13 August 1798; HBCA B.60/a/5, Edmonton House Journal 1799-1800, 7 August 1799.

121 HBCA B.104/a/1, Greenwich House / Lac la Biche Journal 1799-1800, 23 January, 13 October, 10 May.

122 HBCA B.60/a/5, Edmonton Journal 1799-1800, letter from J.P. Pruden to J. Bird, 17 June 1798; Lambe, *Journals and Letters of Alexander Mackenzie*, p. 113; HBCA B.60/a/1, Edmonton Journal 1795-96, 28 August 1795; Morton, *Journal of Duncan M'Gillivray*, 5 December 1794.

123 Henry, p. 44, 18 August 1800, at Forks, p. 57, 21 August 1800, p. 68, 28 August 1800, p. 251, 26 September 1804.

124 Henry, p. 40-41, 17 August 1800.

125 Tanner, pp. 71, 73, 75; Hickerson and Wheeler-Voegelin, *The Red Lake and Pembina Chippewa*, p. 39; Henry, p. 98, 16 September 1800, pp. 99, 18 September 1800; HBCA B.22/a/6, Brandon House Journal 1798-99, October-November 1798; Hickerson, "Journal of Charles Jean Baptiste Chaboillez," p. 287, 12 November 1797.

126 Tanner, pp. 119 and 225.
127 Ritterbush, "Documenting Environmental Adaptation."
128 HBCA B.22/a/5, Brandon House Journal 1797-98, 24 December to 14 March; Henry, p. 239, 18 March 1804; HBCA B.235/a/1, Winnipeg Post Journal 1797-98, 2 April 1798; HBCA B.4/a/3, Fort Alexander Journal 1799-1800, 8 February 1800; Tanner, p. 69; HBCA B.4/a/4, Fort Alexander Journal 1800-01, 15, 30 March 1801.
129 Tanner, p. 81.
130 Hickerson, "Journal of Charles Jean Baptiste Chaboillez," pp. 270-71; Tanner, p. 69.
131 Henry, p. 170, 20 February 1801; Tanner, p. 69; John Macdonell, "Some Account of the Red River about 1797," p. 81.
132 Holzkamm, Lytwyn, and Waisberg, "Rainy River Sturgeon," p. 199.
133 "Swarming": HBCA B.22/a/12, Brandon House Journal 1804-05, 25 April 1805. See also: Henry, p. 196, 4 May 1802, p. 244, 21 May 1804; Tanner, p. 76, p. 81, p. 94; HBCA B.235/a/1, Winnipeg Journal 1797-98, 27 April 1798.
134 "Killed great numbers": Tanner, p. 121; hunted elk and moose: Tanner, p. 105. See also Henry, p. 291, 9 July 1806 (re: the south end of Lake Manitoba: "At the season when swans and other birds shed their feathers, the Indians destroy great numbers by pursuing them in canoes and killing them with sticks. Eggs of all sorts they also collect in abundance, . . . even canoe-loads").
135 Citations are from: HBCA B236/a/1, Lake Winnipeg Journal 1796-97; HBCA B.51/a/1, Dauphin River Journal 1795-96; HBCA B.4/a/2, Fort Alexander Journal 1798-99; HBCA B.4/a/4, Fort Alexander Journal 1800-01; HBCA B.51/a/1, Dauphin River Journal 1795-96, 16 April 1796. See also Lytwyn, *The Fur Trade of the Little North*, pp. 76, 90. *Ogimaa* is a term for chief, boss, or anyone in authority; this term may have included trading captains as well as other kinds of leaders. John Nichols and Earl Nyholm, eds., *Ojibwewi-ikidowinan: An Ojibwe Word Resource Book* (St. Paul: Minnesota Archaeological Society), 1979.
136 Henry, p. 183, 19 May 1801. See also Black-Rogers, "Varieties of 'Starving,'" and Laura Peers, "Subsistence, Secondary Literature, and Gender Bias: The Saulteaux," in *Women of the First Nations of Canada*, ed. P. Chuchryk et al. (Winnipeg: University of Manitoba Press, in press).
137 E.g., HBCA B.49/a/25a, Cumberland House Journal 1793-94, 3 May 1794.
138 Henry, p. 97, 15 September 1800. This was a standard practice; there are many references to such gifts to women in the journals.
139 Susan Carol Rogers, "Female Forms of Power and the Myth of Male Dominance: A Model of Female/Male Interaction in Peasant Society," *American Ethnologist* 2/4 (1975):727-56. See also Eleanor Leacock, "Women's Status in Egalitarian Society," in Eleanor Leacock, *Myths of Male Dominance: Collected Essays on Women Cross-Culturally* (New York: Monthly Review Press, 1981), p. 144.
140 Tanner, p. 69, 16. See also John Macdonell, "Some Account of the Red River about 1797," p. 89.
141 Tanner, pp. 84, 94, 63.
142 For a review of recent literature on women, economics, and status, see Carol Mukhopadhyay and Patricia Higgins, "Anthropological Studies of Women's Status Revisited: 1977-1987," *Annual Review of Anthropology* 17 (1988). I accept the caveat issued by Mukhopadhyay and Higgins that non-Native, twentieth-century researchers need to be careful not to impose their own definition of "status" on other cultures.
143 Henry, p. 252, 22 October 1804. On cross-cultural interpretations of women's suicides, see: Dorothy Ayers Counts, "Fighting Back is Not the Way: Suicide and the Women of Kaliai," *American Ethnologist* (1980):332-51; and Dorothy Ayers Counts, "Female Suicide and Wife Abuse: A Cross-Cultural Perspective," *Suicide and Life-Threatening Behaviour* 17/3 (1987):194-204. Counts emphasizes that, in kin-based societies, suicide is an active form of revenge, for it places blame for the death on the woman's husband's family and makes them

responsible to her blood kin for compensating her family for her death. Furthermore, she notes that female suicides in kin-based societies often follow physical abuse by a husband. Both these conditions may have been at work in causing Ojibwa women's suicides; in the incident that provoked Henry's comment, for instance, a woman committed suicide after being beaten by her fur-trade husband.

144 June Helm, "Women's Work, Women's Art," in *Out of the North: The Subarctic Collection of the Haffenreffer Museum of Anthropology*, ed. Kate Duncan and Barbara Hail (Bristol: Haffenreffer Museum, 1989), p. 122. See also, re: women, trading captains, and women's work and status, Erica Smith, "Something More than Mere Ornament," pp. 85-87. Much research remains to be done on these interrelated questions about roles, status, and the fur trade. One wonders, for instance, whether women shared the credit when their husbands were made trading captains.

145 See the debate on this question in Leacock, "Women's Status in Egalitarian Society" pp. 169, 178.

146 Henry, p. 252, 22 October 1804.

147 Hickerson, "Journal of Charles Jean Baptiste Chaboillez," pp. 270-71; Hickerson, "Genesis of a Trading Post Band," p. 308.

148 Midewiwin locations: Tanner, p. 91; Henry, p. 242, 18 April 1804, p. 224, 27 September 1803, p. 203, 13 September 1802, p. 212, 23 April 1803, p. 197, 20 May 1802, p. 182, 18 May 1801; HBCA B.22/a/6, Brandon House Journal 1798-99, 22 September 1798; HBCA B.22/a/4, Brandon House Journal 1796-97, late August and early September. On major ceremonials as definers of group boundaries, see Susan Sharrock, "Crees, Cree-Assiniboines, and Assiniboines: Interethnic Social Organization on the Far Northern Plains," *Ethnohistory* 21/2 (1974):114.

149 Warren, *History of the Ojibway Nation*, p. 193.

150 Ritterbush, "Culture Change and Continuity," p. 5.

151 See, for instance: Tanner, pp. 37, 38, 225; Henry, p. 133, 1 November 1800; Glover, *David Thompson's Narrative*, p. 184. Ritterbush also discusses these aspects of continuity in "Culture Change and Continuity," pp. 87-99.

152 Glover, *David Thompson's Narrative*, p. 184.

153 John Macdonell, "Some Account of the Red River about 1797," p. 87.

154 Henry, p. 242, 24 April 1804. It should be noted that the bison does play a role in Ojibwa traditions, though it was far less important and was less imbued with symbolism than the bison figure among the Plains Cree, Assiniboine, or Blackfoot. See Benton-Banai, *The Mishomis Book*, pp. 40, 112-113; see also, re: the bison spirit discussed by George Nelson from his experiences with the woods Cree and Interlake Ojibwa, Brown and Brightman, *The Orders of the Dreamed*, p. 111.

155 Hickerson quote: "Journal of Charles Jean Baptiste Chaboillez," pp. 270-71. Grant quote: "The Saulteaux Indians about 1804," p. 308, 1804. See also, re: the strong thread of continuity in Ojibwa culture, Ritterbush, "Culture Change and Continuity," pp. 5, 14, 85.

CHAPTER 3

1 See, for example, Ray, *Indians in the Fur Trade*, pp. 147-56, 213; A.J. Ray, "Periodic Shortages, Native Welfare, and the Hudson's Bay Company 1670-1930," in *The Subarctic Fur Trade: Social and Economic Adaptations*, ed. Shepard Krech III (Vancouver: University of British Columbia Press, 1984); Bishop, *The Northern Ojibwa and the Fur Trade*, pp. 12-13 et passim; Gerald Friesen, *The Canadian Prairies: A History* (Toronto: University of Toronto Press, 1984), p. 130.

2 Nelson, Dauphin River Journal 1810-11, 19 February 1811; Fidler, HBCA B.22/e/1, General

Report of the Red River District 1819, fo. 12.

3 PAM SP v. 3, 2 September 1813; Tanner, pp. 147-50; Nelson, Dauphin River Journal 1810-1811, 19 February 1811; HBCA B.22/a/15, Brandon House Journal 1807-08, 11 March 1808; HBCA B.60/a/7, Edmonton House Journal 1807-08, 4 February 1808; HBCA B.49/e/1, Cumberland House District Report 1815, fo. 2. See also Ray, *Indians in the Fur Trade*, pp. 117-23.

4 HBCA B.22/a/16, Brandon House Journal 1808-09; HBCA B.22/a/18a, Brandon House Journal 1810-11; HBCA B.22/a/18b, Brandon House Journal 1811-12; HBCA B.63/a/2, Fort Ellice Journal 1812-13; Nelson, Dauphin River Journal 1807-08, 7 March 1808. For examples of the numbers of muskrats traded in these years, see: Tanner, p. 176 (killed 400 muskrats in several weeks); and HBCA B.122/a/1, Manitoba Lake Journal 1815-16, 20 September 1815 (400-500 muskrats traded in a single session).

5 HBCA B.22/e/1, Red River District Report 1819, fo. 8; HBCA B.51/e/1, Fort Dauphin District Report 1820, fo. 6.

6 Timothy Ball, "Climate Change, Droughts and their Social Impact: Central Canada, 1780-1820" (paper presented at Rupert's Land Research Centre conference, Churchill, Manitoba, 1988), p. 9. Ball notes, however, that the climate did allow successful crops at Red River between 1812 and 1816. Ball's data need to be reconciled with those of G. Herman Sprenger, whose list of dates and causes of partial and complete crop failures at Red River does not always agree with Ball's information. See G. Herman Sprenger, "The Metis Nation: Buffalo Hunting versus Agriculture in the Red River Settlement, 1810-1870," in *Native People, Native Lands*, ed. Bruce A. Cox (Ottawa: Carleton University, 1988), pp. 124-25.

7 Ball, "Climate Change," p. 5. Other evidence on unusual weather patterns for these years includes: Nelson, Dauphin River Journal 1810-11, 22 and 28 November 1810 (Indians literally starving at Dauphin River; little snow, no fish in rapids there; later in winter, "extraordinary" snow); SP v. 4, p. 1184, Macdonell to Selkirk, 25 July 1814 ("The winter was mild, and but little snow fell"); HBCA B.122/a/2, Manitoba Journal 1818-19, 29 November 1819; SP v. 21, p. 6,882, 27 May 1820, G. Garden to A. Colvile.

8 Black-Rogers, "Varieties of 'Starving.'"

9 On the relationship between measles and malnutrition, see Hackett, "The 1819-20 Measles Epidemic," pp. 124-28. Hackett observes that the epidemic seems to have hit the Red and Assiniboine River area in early summer, when fish would have been plentiful, so that malnutrition may not have been such a severe problem as it might otherwise have been.

10 On the origins of freemen, Métis and mixed-blood communities, see: Jennifer S.H. Brown, "The Métis: Genesis and Rebirth," in *Native Peoples, Native Lands*, ed. Bruce A. Cox (Ottawa: Carleton University, 1988), pp. 136-39; and essays in Jacqueline Peterson and Jennifer S.H. Brown, *The New Peoples: Being and Becoming Métis in North America* (Winnipeg: University of Manitoba Press, 1985); John E. Foster, "The Plains Métis," in *Native Peoples: The Canadian Experience*, ed. Morrison and Wilson (Toronto: McClelland and Stewart, 1986) pp. 382-88; J.E. Foster, "The Origins of the Mixed-Bloods in the Canadian West," in *Essays on Western History*, ed. L.H. Thomas (Edmonton: University of Alberta Press, 1976); Lytwyn, *The Fur Trade of the Little North*, p. 131. For references to specific mixed-blood/Native communities, see: Henry, p. 289, 9 July 1805, p. 424, 1 August 1807, p. 438, 26 July 1808; HBCA B.49/a/32b, Cumberland House Journal 1806-07, 14, 16 December 1806, 3 February, 31 March; HBCA B.49/a/32a, Cumberland House Journal 1802-03, 26 September 1802; HBCA B.122/a/1, Manitoba Lake Journal 1815-16, 18 September 1815; HBCA B.213/a/7, Swan River Journal 1817-18, 10 August 1817; HBCA B.122/e/1, Manitoba District Report, fo. 9.

11 See: George Nelson, 1825, quoted in Brown and Brightman, *The Orders of the Dreamed*, p. 12; also Lytwyn, *The Fur Trade of the Little North*, p. 125.

12 Nelson, Dauphin River Journal 1810-11; Brown and Brightman, *Orders of the Dreamed*, p. 12; SP v. 13, p. 4,275, 27 December 1817, Macdonell to Selkirk; Michael Czuboka, "St. Peter's: A Historical Study with Anthropological Observations on the Christian Aborigines of Red River, 1811-1876" (M.A. thesis, University of Manitoba, 1960), p. ii; and see sections in this and following chapters on Ojibwa relations with Métis and Swampy Cree in and around Red River and the Interlake (this volume).

13 Fidler: HBCA B.22/e/1, fo. 7. See also: HBCA B.160/a/2, Pembina Post Journal 1809-10, 16 August 1809, 13, 19 January 1810, 2 May 1810; HBCA B.160/a/4, Pembina Journal 1812-13, 24 August 1812; PAM MG1 D3, Fidler 1814-15, Fidler hiring Canadians for odd jobs; SP v. 13, p. 4,275, 27 December 1817, Macdonell to Selkirk.

14 SP v. 13, p. 4,275, 27 December 1817, Macdonell to Selkirk. See also SP v. 4, p. 1,184, 25 July 1814, Macdonell to Selkirk ("The natives and others who had not hunting horses were great sufferers"); see also discussion and references in section on Ojibwa at Red River, this chapter.

15 HBCA B. 22/a/21, Brandon House Journal 1818-19, 1 May 1819. See also HBCA B.22/e/2, Red River District Report 1819, Peter Fidler, fo. 3; HBCA B.22/a/21, Brandon House Journal 1818-19, 26 April 1819; HBCA B.22/a/18b, Brandon House Journal 1811-1812, 29 April 1812; Henry, p. 408, 3 August 1806.

16 Tanner, p. 157. See also Tanner, pp. 147-50; Hickerson, "Genesis of a Trading Post Band," pp. 301-15.

17 Tanner, pp. 147-50. "One hundred beaver" may well be an exaggeration, but the figure does express the relative abundance of the animal in this area. Henry, p. 275, 23 May 1806; these hunters were Peshauba and Washegamoishcam. Peshauba was head of the band with which Tanner spent a good deal of time.

18 Tanner, p. 147. See also R. David Edmunds, *The Shawnee Prophet* (Lincoln: University of Nebraska Press), pp. 39, 51.

19 Hickerson, "Genesis of a Trading Post Band," pp. 318, 321, 324; Milloy, *The Plains Cree*, p. 125; Tanner, p. 120; HBCA B.22/a/19, Brandon House Journal 1815-16, 26 January 1816; HBCA B.22/a/21, Brandon House Journal 1818-19, 3 June 1818; HBCA B.51/a/2, Fort Dauphin Journal 1819-20, 31 March, 3 May 1820; HBCA B.51/a/3, Fort Dauphin Journal 1820-21, 25 April 1821; SP v. 3, 17 July 1813; SP v. 4, p. 1,185, 25 July 1814, Macdonell to Selkirk; SP v. 9, p. 2,843, 16 October 1816, Selkirk to Pambrun; SP v. 16, p. 5,331, 30 August 1818, Matthey to Selkirk.

20 HBCA B.22/a/13, Brandon House Post Journal 1805-06, 22 March 1806. Fidler's talk of a peace arranged by Lewis and Clark probably refers to a conference between the explorers and the Yanktons on August 30 and 31, 1804; see James P. Ronda, *Lewis and Clark among the Indians* (Lincoln: University of Nebraska Press, 1984), pp. 24-26. Other negotiations included talks arranged by Robert Dickson in 1817 to foster HBC trade with the Sioux; see SP v. 11, p. 3,530, 7 June 1817, Fort Douglas, M. Macdonell to Selkirk.

21 Hickerson, "Genesis of a Trading Post Band"; Lauren Ritterbush, "Chippewa Exodus from Red River" (paper presented at the Forty-sixth Plains Anthropological Conference, 1988); Gregory Camp, "The Chippewa Fur Trade in the Red River Valley of the North, 1790-1830," in *The Fur Trade in North Dakota*, ed. V. Heidenreich (Bismarck: North Dakota Historical Society, 1990).

22 Ray, *Indians in the Fur Trade*, p. 168. See also HBCA B.176/a/1, Red Deer River Post Journal 1812-13, 21 January 1813 (Moose Lake Ojibwa camping at Red Deer River post); A.J. Ray, *Indian Exploitation of the Forest-Grassland Transition Zone in Western Canada, 1650-1860* (Ph.D. dissertation, University of Wisconsin, 1971), p. 205; Henry, p. 466, 21 August 1808 (Ojibwa band winters at Red Deer River); Nelson Journals, Dauphin River. The Canadian traders at Cumberland House in 1815 were said to have "a good many Bungees" trading with them (HBCA B.49/e/1, Cumberland House District Report 1815, fo. 6). See also, re: interaction between Ojibwa and Cree in the Nut Lake–Carrot River–Red Deer River–Red Earth region, David Meyer, *The Red Earth Crees, 1860-1960*, Mercury Series No. 100 (Ottawa: National Museums of Canada, 1985), pp. 36, 55, 61, 64.

23 Camp, "The Chippewa Fur Trade," p. 43; HBCA B.22/a/9 through B.22/a/12, Brandon House Journals, include mention of Turtle Mountain trade.

24 Henry, p. 612, 13 July 1810. See also Henry, p. 582, 1 February 1809, p. 584, 12 February 1809, and p. 602, 1 June 1810.

25 Henry, p. 488, 3 September 1808; Henry p. 489, 4 September 1808. See also Henry, p. 437. Other references to mixed-group camps include: John C. Ewers, *Ethnological Report on the Chippewa-Cree Tribe of the Rocky Boy Reservation* (New York: Garland Publishing, 1974), p. 150; HBCA B.49/a/32b, Cumberland House Journal 1806-07, 29 December 1806, 3 February, 31 March 1807; HBCA B.22/a/16, Brandon House Journal 1808-09; B.22/a/17, Brandon House Journal 1809-10; Hickerson and Wheeler-Voegelin, *The Red Lake and Pembina Chippewa*, p. 82.

26 Barth, "Introduction," *Ethnic Groups and Boundaries*, p. 19.

27 HBCA B.159/e/1, Swan River District Report 1818-19, fo. 9. See also Albers, "Pluralism in the Native Plains," pp. 41, 54.

28 David G. Mandelbaum, *The Plains Cree: An Ethnographic, Historical, and Comparative Study*, Canadian Plains Studies No. 9 (Regina: Canadian Plains Research Center, 1979), p. 68; see also Henry, p. 450, 11 August 1808, recalling 1799 incident: "The sagacity of the Saulteurs in tracing strong wood animals is astonishing."

29 Holzkamm, Lytwyn, and Waisberg, "Rainy River Sturgeon," p. 195.

30 Henry, p. 280, 26 June 1805; HBCA B.235/a/4, Winnipeg Post Journal 1820-21, 9, 26 December 1820; PAM MG1 B7, Reverend John West journal, 2 November 1821 (received "a good supply of fresh and dried Sturgeon" at Peguis's encampment near Netley Creek). For just a few of innumerable references to fishing, see: HBCA B.22/a/19, Brandon House Journal 1815-16, 21 May 1816; George Nelson reminiscences, v. 5, p. 24, Indian statement, "why cultivate have we not abundance of fish to eat"; also Nelson, Sorel Journal, p. 166 (Tête-au-Brochet called "Fish River"), p. 167, white fish abundant; Nelson journals 1807-08, 1808-10, almost constant Indian and European fishing; mouth of Pinawa also a fishery; Nelson, Lac du Bonnet Journal 1805-06, 5-12 September 1805, Nelson trading sturgeon.

31 Nelson, Dauphin River Journal 1810-11, 22 November 1810.

32 Moodie, "Manomin"; Ritterbush, "Culture Change and Continuity," pp. 60-62, citing Henry, 8 November 1800 (rice existed between Salt and Turtle rivers along the Red River); Nelson, Dauphin River Journal 1807-08, 1808-10, 1810-11; HBCA B.4/a/2, Fort Alexander Post Journal 1797-99; PAM MG1 D3, Fidler journal 1814-15, 20, 21, 28 September 1814 (trading rice from Indians arriving at Forks). Specific sites for ricing mentioned in the Nelson journals include "the Pi-na-wa," Chebanogan River, Broken River, and Lac du Bonnet.

33 D. Wayne Moodie, "Agriculture and the Fur Trade," in *Old Trails and New Directions*, ed. C. Judd and A.J. Ray (Toronto: University of Toronto Press, 1980), pp. 280-83. See also: D. Wayne Moodie, "Nineteenth Century Ojibwa Agricultural Sites" (paper delivered at the annual meeting of the Canadian Archaeological Association, Calgary, 1990); Wayne Moodie and Barry Kaye, "Indian Agriculture in the Fur Trade Northwest," *Prairie Forum* 11/2 (1986); Holzkamm, "Ojibwa Horticulture."

34 Tanner, p. 171; Henry, re: Netley Creek gardens 1805, p. 448, 11 August 1808; re: Netley Creek gardens 1806, p. 280, 26 June 1806; re: Pembina gardens 1804, p. 243, 4 May 1804; HBCA B.160/a/3, Pembina Post Journal 1812-13, fo. 2; HBCA B.51/e/1 1820 fo. 19: Captain Grant and others with cabins and tents; HBCA G.1/41 ("A Map of Man,ne,tow,oo,pow Lake," showing "Indian Gardens").

35 Holzkamm, "Ojibway Horticulture."

36 *Ibid.*, pp. 148-49.

37 Tanner, p. 171; Henry, p. 448, 11 August 1808 (re: Netley Creek gardens started, he claims, in 1805).

38 Ritterbush, "Culture Change and Continuity," p. 64; Henry, p. 243, 4 May 1804 (re: Pembina gardens 1804). One might also note Henry's wry comment, several days after harvesting his gardens at the Pembina River post, "XY ladies busy stealing the gleanings of my potato field" (1 November 1804, p. 252).

39 Moodie and Kaye, "Indian Agriculture in the Fur Trade Northwest," p. 175; Tanner, pp. 168, 190, 201-02. On the use of water-warmed microclimates, see: Moodie, "Nineteenth Century Ojibwa Agricultural Sites," ms. p. 7; and Waisberg, "Ethnographic and Historical Outline," p. 158.

40 HBCA B.22/a/19, Brandon House Journal 1815-16, 29 May 1816 ("The Premier and band returned to Red River to farm where they did last year"); PAM SP v. 16, p. 5,372, Fort Douglas, 12 September 1818, Captain Matthey to Lord Selkirk; Moodie and Kaye, "Indian Agriculture in the Fur Trade Northwest"; Tanner, p. 168; PAM MG7 B1, West Journal, 22 February 1823; "Diary of Nicholas Garry, Deputy-Governor of the Hudson's Bay Company from 1822-1835" (Transactions of the Royal Society of Canada, section 2, 1900), p. 135, 3 August 1821; HBCA G.1/41, Peter Fidler, "A Map of Man,ne,tow,oo,pow Lake"; HBCA B.51/a/2, Fort Dauphin Journal 1819-20, 20 May 1819, 13 September 1819.

41 HBCA B.122/e/1, Manitoba District Report, fo. 9. Like the islands in Lake of the Woods, this location may have offered a favourable microclimate for gardening.

42 Henry, p. 448, 11 August 1808; John Pritchett, *The Red River Valley, 1811-1849* (New York: Russell and Russell, 1970), p. 110. See also: Moodie and Kaye, "Indian Agriculture in the Fur Trade Northwest," pp. 174-75; and Moodie, "Agriculture and the Fur Trade," pp. 281-83.

43 See Sprenger, "The Metis Nation," pp. 120-35.

44 Ball, "Climate Change," p. 13.

45 Summer bison hunting: Henry, p. 286, 7 July 1806; Hickerson, "Genesis of a Trading Post Band," p. 314; Nelson, Dauphin River Journal 1809-10, 2 August 1810; HBCA B.176/a/1, Red Deer River Journal 1812-13, 10 September 1812; Tanner, p. 156. Winter bison hunting: see also Nelson, Dauphin River Journal 1807-08, 7 December 1807 (Ayagon has been bison hunting, then trapping). Hunting locations and other references to hunting: HBCA B.51/a/3, Fort Dauphin Journal 1820-21, 18 September 1820 and 6 February 1821; HBCA B.51/e/2, Dauphin District Report, fo. 2a; HBCA B.122/a/2, Manitoba Journal 1818-19, 21 March 1819; HBCA B.22/e/1, Red River District Report 1819, fo. 5; HBCA B.22/a/19, Brandon House Journal 1815-16, 9 February 1816. "Make a stock": HBCA B.51/a/3, Fort Dauphin Journal 1820-21, 6 February 1821.

46 Fidler, "laziness": HBCA B.22/e/1, General Report of the Red River District 1819, fo. 12; "not exerted themselves": Manitoba District Report, HBCA B.51/e/2, fo. 2; "game only": Nelson, Dauphin River Journal 1810-11, 27 April 1810. Cumberland House, "done nothing": HBCA B.49/a/32b, Cumberland House Journal 1806-07, 17 January 1807.

47 Nelson, Dauphin River Journal 1807-08, 28 March 1808.

48 *Ibid.*, 7 April 1808.

49 Charles Bishop, review of *Indian-European Trade Relations in the Lower Saskatchewan River Region to 1840* by Paul Thistle, *Ethnohistory* 37/2 (Spring 1990):205.

50 Henry, p. 268, 14 October 1805.

51 See, for example: Nelson, Dauphin River Journal 1808-10, 6-11 October and 5 November 1808; and Dauphin River Journal 1807-08, 28 March 1808.

52 Credit was discontinued at the HBC's Manitoba post in 1819-20, but until the coalition of 1821 took effect this measure had little real effect on the Ojibwa, who had numerous alternatives in the region (HBCA B.51/e/1, Manitoba District Report 1820, fo. 16).

53 On amount of credit, see: Nelson, Dauphin River Journal 1808-10, 20 September 1808, Ayagon takes 60 skins in debt, and 2 April 1810, a good hunter given twenty-five MB debt; Nelson, Dauphin River Journal 1807-08, 25 May 1808, Muffle d'Orignal's debt was thirty skins. Nelson claimed in his reminiscences to have given Ayagon 110 MB in credit one year, but I cannot

verify this in his journals (Nelson, Reminiscences 7, p. 17). See also: HBCA B.22/a/13, Brandon House Journal 1805-06, 11 May 1806; HBCA B.22/a/18b, Brandon House Journal 1811-12, 20 October 1811; HBCA B.176/a/1, Red Deer River Journal 1812-13, 19 September 1812. As figure 2 (this volume) shows, debt amounts in the Interlake at the time of coalition were between one and sixty-three MB, consistent with Nelson's figures. On amount of presents, see: HBCA B.159/a/7, Swan River (Fort Pelly) Journal 1818-19, 9 October 1818 ("customary presents of Liqr &c"); HBCA B.51/e/1, Dauphin River District Report 1820, fo. 10: trader refuses to give anything but liquor for sugar; Nelson, Dauphin River Journal 1807-08, 20 November 1807 and 29 March 1808; HBCA B.122/e/1, Manitoba District Report, fo. 9, recommending that little ammunition should be given gratis.

54 Nelson, Dauphin River Journal, 5 June 1808.

55 HBCA B.22/a/18b, Brandon House Journal 1811-12, 2 October 1811.

56 Tanner, p. 209.

57 Henry, p. 256, 1 January 1805.

58 HBCA B.22/a/18b, 16 May 1812; this may have been a mixed Cree-Ojibwa band.

59 Tanner: p. 120; Nelson: Dauphin River Journal, 30 September 1810; Peguis: HBCA B.160/a/4, Pembina Journal 1812-13, 14 October 1812.

60 Ayagon's complaint: Nelson, Dauphin River Journal 1807-08, 18 November 1807. See also: HBCA B.51/a/3, Fort Dauphin Journal 1820-21, 8 February 1821; HBCA B.122/e/1, Manitoba District Report, fo. 9; HBCA B.159/e/1, Swan River District Report 1818-19, fo. 8; HBCA B.51/e/1, Manitoba District Report, fo. 16; HBCA B.51/e/2, Manitoba District Report, fo. 2b.

61 "Never be paid": HBCA B.159/e/1, Swan River District Report 1818-19, fo. 8; "more punctual": HBCA B.51/e/1, Manitoba District Report 1820, fo. 16.

62 Nelson, Dauphin River Journal 1810-11 18, 23 September 1810; HBCA B.51/e/1, Manitoba District Report 1820, fo. 16 (credit discontinued).

63 HBCA B.51/e/1, Dauphin River District Report 1820, fo. 2. See also HBCA B.122/e/1, Manitoba District Report, fos. 8, 9.

64 Nelson, Dauphin River Journal 1810-11, 23 September 1810.

65 HBCA B.49/a/25a, Cumberland House Journal 1793-94, 11 January 1794.

66 HBCA B.51/e/1, Manitoba District Report 1820, fo. 7. Nor does one find the frequent statements in the journals about Ojibwa demand for silver jewellery after 1805 that one does before.

67 Ray, *Indians in the Fur Trade*, p. 156.

68 HBCA B.51/e/1, 1820, fo. 17a; Nelson, Dauphin River Journal 1810-11, 13 May 1810.

69 "Thievishly disposed": Henry: p. 295, 11 July 1805. See also Henry, p. 244, 8 May 1804 (band of sixty-five people with ten horses, or approximately one horse per tent). Fidler: HBCA B.235/a/3, Winnipeg Journal July 1815 (estimates 750 Ojibwa adults between Carlton House and Turtle River, with 100 horses, or approximately one horse per 7.5 adults, or one tent). "Addicted": HBCA B.22/a/21, Brandon House Journal 1818-19, 7 June 1818. "Fond of horses": HBCA B.159/e/1, Swan River District Report 1818-19, fo. 9. See also: HBCA B.22/a/10, Brandon House Journal 1817-1818, 30 July 1817; HBCA B.51/a/2, Fort Dauphin Journal 1819-20, 9 June 1819.

70 E.g., Henry, p. 286, 7 July 1806. Scholars have also noted that the corn cultivated by the western Ojibwa and Ottawa is of a Mandan strain, though they may have acquired it indirectly.

71 HBCA B.22/a/12, Brandon House Post Journal 1804-05, 27 February 1805. This trade was with Indians "from Red River," which could well have included Ojibwa. See also Milloy, *The Plains Cree*, pp. 47-58.

72 "Friendship": HBCA B.22/a/20, Brandon House Journal 1817-18, 9 November 1817; "friends": HBCA B.22/a/21, Brandon House Journal 1818-19, 23 April 1819. See also Milloy, *The Plains Cree*, pp. 57- 58, 62-64.

73 The sources used to reconstruct the following section on the Interlake include: Nelson, Dauphin River journals 1807-08, 1808-10, 1810-11, and Tête-au-Brochet 1818-19, and Nelson's Reminiscences; HBCA B.51/a/2, B.51/a/3, Fort Dauphin Journal 1819-20, 1820-21; HBCA B.51/e/1, Fort Dauphin District Report 1820; HBCA B.122/a/1, B.122/a/2, Manitoba Lake Journal 1815-16, 1818-19; HBCA B.122/e/1, Manitoba District Report; and comparative material from Tanner and Henry.

74 Nelson, Sorel Journal, p. 167.

75 HBCA B.51/a/2, Fort Dauphin Journal 1819-20, 10 December 1819.

76 HBCA B.51/e/1, Manitoba District Report 1820, fos. 10b, 18a.

77 Nelson, Dauphin River Journal 1810-11, 13 May 1810; "follow the Cree construction": HBCA B.51/e/1, fo. 5, 17.

78 HBCA B.51/e/1, Manitoba District Report 1820, fos. 10b, 18a.

79 Tanner, p. 150; Henry, p. 428, 2 April 1808; HBCA B.176/a/1, Red Deer River Journal 1812-13, 3 March 1813.

80 "1,000 roggans": HBCA B.51/e/1, Manitoba District Report 1820, fo. 10; "Cache": HBCA B.122/e/1, fo. 9b.

81 HBCA B.51/a/2, Fort Dauphin Post Journal 1819-20, 19 May 1819.

82 HBCA B.51/e/1, Manitoba District Report 1820, fo. 10b.

83 HBCA B.122/a/1, Lake Manitoba Journal 1815-16, 13 May 1816.

84 HBCA B.51/a/2, Fort Dauphin Journal 1819-20, 19 May 1820. See also: HBCA B.51/a/2, Fort Dauphin Journal 1819-20,18, 22, 29 May 1820; and HBCA B.122/e/1, Manitoba District Report, fo. 9b.

85 Nelson, Tête-au-Brochet Journal, 6, 7 June 1819.

86 HBCA B.51/e/1, Dauphin District Report 1820, fo. 10.

87 Like maple sugar, wildfowl and eggs were important seasonal food resources. Henry mentions gathering them by the canoe-load in spring and fall, and the returning flocks were a welcome sight in late spring when other game was often scarce (Henry, p. 291, 9 July 1806).

88 A note in the Fort Dauphin Journal (HBCA B.51/a/2, 1819-20, 29 May 1820) states that the old "Big Tent" was being replaced, "the former one being in a ruinous state," implying that the island had a history of use by the Ojibwa. This may have included the gardens. Nelson's statement is from his Dauphin River Journal for 1810-11, 1 June 1810; see also Nelson, Dauphin River Journal 1810-11, 14 May, 20 September ("St. Germain's women are at River Dauphine feeding upon my potatoes"), 15 October 1810. Nelson gives the Ojibwa word for "Gardening stuff (potatoes)" as *Kiht-ti-goan-ac*, and mentions Nez Corbin's liking for them (Nelson to William and Jane Nelson, 29 May 1812, George Nelson Papers, Baldwin Room, Metropolitan Toronto Reference Library).

89 Nelson, Reminiscences 5, p. 35, speaking of Little Swift Current or Dauphin River. See also HBCA B.51/e/1, Fort Dauphin District Report 1820, fos. 10b, 18a.

90 White, "A Skilled Game of Exchange"; "Indian economy": Nelson, Dauphin River Journal 1810-11, 7 February 1811.

91 Nelson, Reminiscences 5, pp. 59-60.

92 *Ibid.*, p. 34. The accuracy of these descriptions is borne out in the burial of a young adult male excavated from an eroding bank on the Red Deer River in 1966 (see David Meyer, "The Red Deer River Grave: An Historic Burial," *Napao*, 4/1 [July 1973]).

93 Tanner, p. 157 ("I lived at this time in a long lodge having two or three fires, and I occupied it in common with several other men with their families, mostly the relatives of my wife"); Nelson, in his Dauphin River journals, refers to Ojibwa men with whom he trades, and he identifies members of their families in relation to them (Hunter A's son, or wife, or nephew). See the discussion of Ojibwa family structure and marriage practices in Ritterbush, "Culture Change and Continuity," pp. 103-08. My reconstruction of the Ojibwa families trading with Nelson differs slightly from that of Jennifer S.H. Brown (see her article, "From Sorel to Lake Winnipeg:

George Nelson as an Ethnohistorical Source," in *New Dimensions in Ethnohistory: Papers of the Second Laurier Conference on Ethnohistory and Ethnology*, ed. Barry Gough and Laird Christie, Mercury Series Paper 120 [Ottawa: Canadian Museum of Civilization, 1991], pp. 166-69, and compare with Laura Peers, "An Ethnohistory of the Western Ojibwa, 1780-1830" [M.A. thesis, Universities of Winnipeg and Manitoba, 1987], p. 109).

94 Fidler: HBCA B.51/e/1, Manitoba District Report 1820, fo. 17a.
95 Fidler: *ibid*. Nelson: Journal 1803-04, quoted in Van Kirk, *Many Tender Ties*, p. 84.
96 Nelson Papers, Journal 1815, quoted in Van Kirk, *Many Tender Ties*, p. 59. This incident occurred after Nelson's first few years in the Interlake, to the east of the Interlake north of Lake Superior. I use it here only as another example of Nelson's ambiguous attitude toward Ojibwa women.
97 "Wise": Nelson, Reminiscences 5, p. 58; "wives and children's sicknesses": Nelson, Dauphin River Journal 1807-08, 30 May 1808. Nelson also wrote of hunters moving camp by canoe in early winter because there was "too much snow for the children to walk through": Nelson, Dauphin River Journal 1808-10, 13 October 1808.
98 Nelson, Dauphin River Journal 1810-11, 13 May 1810.
99 "Nearly killed": *ibid.*, 22 May 1810 (Ayagon was drunk during this incident). "Sore leg": Nelson, Dauphin River Journal 1808-10, 4 October 1808. Nelson also noted that women were forbidden from attending the ceremony during which the teachings of The Shawnee Prophet were passed on to local bands, "lest the place become contaminated" (Nelson, Reminiscences 5, p. 25).
100 HBCA B.159/e/2, Swan River District Report, 1825, fo. 2. Men did sometimes bite off each others' noses during fights, but this was not a regular punishment for adultery. See also Glover, *David Thompson's Narrative*, p. 185 (women were punished for adultery "by the husband biting off the fleshy part of the nose. . . . But this barbarous act, is very rarely inflicted but when the man is drunk").
101 Ruth Landes, *The Ojibwa Woman*, Columbia University Contributions to Anthropology No. 31 (New York: Columbia University, 1938); see the discussion on Landes in Leacock, "Women's Status in Egalitarian Society," pp. 146-50.
102 Jennifer S.H. Brown, "Afterword," in A. Irving Hallowell, *The Ojibwa of Berens River, Manitoba*, p. 114; George and Louise Spindler, "Male and Female in Four Changing Cultures," in *Personality and the Cultural Construction of Society: Papers in Honor of Melford E. Spiro*, ed. David Jordan and Marc Swartz (Tuscaloosa: University of Alabama Press, 1990), pp. 196-200.
103 Nelson, Dauphin River Journal 1807-08, 17 May 1808 (Old Muffle's wife); Nelson, Dauphin River Journal 1810-11, 22 May 1810, 4 April 1811; Nelson, Reminiscences 7, p. 24. Selected incidents of alcohol-related family violence in Henry's journals include: p. 105, 29 September 1800; p. 153, 16 November 1800; p. 156, 25 November 1800; p. 161, 28 December 1800; p. 168, 19 January 1801; p. 194, 14 March 1801; p. 197, 7 May 1801; p. 205, 5 October 1802; p. 209, 15 February 1802. Of these nine incidents from Henry, at least three involved severe injuries inflicted on women, and two involved children accidentally injured during drinking fights. See also Glover, *David Thompson's Narrative*, p. 185 (jealous husbands bite wives' noses off only when drunk).
104 On George Nelson's higher opinion of the Mashkegons, see Dauphin River Journal 1810-11, 24 October 1810 ("What difference between these people!"). See also sections in this and the following chapters on the Red River Ojibwa.
105 Edmunds, *The Shawnee Prophet*, pp. 1-41. The Shawnee Prophet's doctrines and the spread of his movement may be profitably compared to the Handsome Lake movement among the Seneca (see Anthony F.C. Wallace, *The Death and Rebirth of the Seneca* [New York: Random House, 1972]).

106 "Wild-fire": Warren, *History of the Ojibway Nation*, p. 322; "Remotest Ojibbeways": Tanner, p. 147. See also Nelson, Dauphin River Journal 1807-08, "Notes," pp. 7-10, pp. 61-64; Nelson Reminiscences 5, pp. 23-27.

107 Edmunds, *The Shawnee Prophet*, pp. 34-41.

108 Tanner, pp. 144, 146; Nelson, Dauphin River Journal 1807-08, "Notes," pp. 7, 61. See also Edmunds, *The Shawnee Prophet*, pp. 51-53.

109 Nelson, Dauphin River Journal 1807-08, "Notes," pp. 7-10, pp. 61-64; Nelson, Reminiscences 5, pp. 23-27.

110 Tanner, p. 147.

111 *Ibid.*

112 Nelson, Dauphin River Journal 1810-11, 18 August 1810.

113 *Ibid.*, 1807-08, "Notes," p. 7.

114 Nelson, Reminiscences 5, p. 24.

115 *Ibid.*, p. 26.

116 Tanner, p. 147.

117 "Imagine": HBCA B.235/a/3, Winnipeg (Red River) Journal 1814-15, 18 October 1814; see also PAM SP v. 3, 8 March 1814, Miles Macdonell to the agents of the North West Company. "Manufacture": HBCA B.235/a/3, Red River Journal (Peter Fidler diary) 1814-15, 26 July 1815.

118 "Powerful support": SP PAM MG2 M171 reel 1, 11 August 1812, Macdonell to Selkirk; also similar comment, SP v. 6, p. 1771, 11 November 1815, Statement of Miles Macdonell. See also Camp, "The Chippewa Fur Trade," p. 43, who says that some Ojibwa from the Pembina area migrated to Red River to take advantage of economic opportunities there after 1810. These sentiments are contradicted by the statement of Kawtawbetay, a "chief of Sand Lake," in 1817, who said that, "at the commencement of the settlement at Red River, some of the Indians did not like it, but at present they are all glad of its being settled" (*Statement Respecting the Earl of Selkirk's Settlement upon the Red River in North America* [Johnson Reprint Corp., 1968 (1817)], p. xxxii).

119 HBCA B.22/e/1, Brandon House District Report 1819, fo. 12; HBCA B.51/e/2, Manitoba District Report 1821, fo. 2a; HBCA B.239/a/1, fo. 35. Goods paid for produce: HBCA B.51/e/1, Manitoba District Report 1820, fo. 10b; HBCA B.51/e/2, 1821, fo. 2a.

120 "Sausey": HBCA B.122/a/1, 26 September 1815. Ritterbush, "Culture Change and Continuity," p. 62, cites Fidler, HBCA B.235/a/3, Red River Journal, 20 September to 12 October 1814, 22 canoes of Indians arrived from Lake Winnipeg and traded much rice.

121 "Avaricious": HBCA B.122/e/1, fo. 8c; "Spur": HBCA B.51/a/3, Fort Dauphin Journal 1820-21, 8 February 1821; "Presents": HBCA B.51/e/1, Manitoba District Report, fo. 16b; see also HBCA B.22/e/1, Brandon House District Report 1819, fo. 23.

122 See, for example, Henry, p. 265, 2 August 1805, and p. 291, 9 July 1806. Peguis's village at Netley Creek was the most established Ojibwa village in the West, comparable to settlements such as those at Red Lake, Leech Lake, and other locations in the Boundary Waters and Great Lakes region.

123 "Best hunters": HBCA B.160/a/4, Pembina Post Journal 1812-13, 14 October 1812. On Peguis's origins, see: Tanner, p. 150; Henry, p. 53, and p. 257, May 1805; HBCA B.22/e/1, Brandon House District Report 1819, fo. 24; Hugh Dempsey, "Peguis," *Dictionary of Canadian Biography*, vol. 9 (Toronto: University of Toronto Press, 1976), pp. 626-27, and references listed there. While several secondary sources give Peguis's community of origin as Sault Ste. Marie, this may be due to confusion over the meaning of the term *Saulteaux*. Other sources give his place of origin as Lake of the Woods, Leech Lake, or Red Lake.

124 1812: Peers, "Rich Man, Poor Man, Beggar Man, Chief: Saulteaux in the Red River Settlement, 1812-1833," in *Papers of the Eighteenth Algonquian Conference*, ed. W. Cowan (Ottawa: Carleton University, 1987); Ross, *The Red River Settlement*, pp. 20-23. "Colony Chief": SP v. 11, p. 4,197, Macdonell to Selkirk, 10 November 1817. "Highly pleased": SP v. 4, p. 1,225, Macdonell to Selkirk, 9 September 1814.

125 HBCA B.51/e/1, Manitoba District Report 1820, fo. 16b; also HBCA B.22/e/1, Brandon House (Red River) District Report 1819, fo. 23.

126 This section is taken in part from Peers, "Rich Man, Poor Man, Beggar Man, Chief: Saulteaux in the Red River Settlement, 1812-1833."

129 Macdonell ordered by Lord Selkirk to attempt to disguise the first party of settlers as traders: see SP v. 5, p. 1,621, 15 August 1815, Statement of Simon McGillivray, quoted in Pritchett, *The Red River Valley, 1811-1849*, p. 110; SP, p. 179, Instructions to Miles Macdonell; A.S. Morton, *A History of the Canadian West to 1870-71*, 2nd ed., ed. L.G. Thomas (Toronto: University of Toronto Press, 1973), p. 85. On the Ojibwa, Métis, and other Natives bartering with the settlers, see Ross, *The Red River Settlement*, pp. 21-22.

128 "Kind and generous feelings": Ross, *The Red River Settlement*, p. 23; "Yankies": SP v. 3, 31 August 1813, Macdonell to Selkirk.

129 Quarrels: Tanner, pp. 209-10. Refusing bribes: Statement of Kawtawabetay, *Statement Respecting the Earl of Selkirk's Settlement upon the Red River in North America*, p. xxxi; SP v. 5, p. 1,550, 20 June 1815, and v. 6, 22 July 1816. Drinking health of HBC: PAM MG1 D3, Peter Fidler journal, 10 June 1815.

130 HBCA B.235/a/3, Winnipeg Post Journal 1814-15, 20 June 1815.

131 MG1 D3, Fidler diary 1814-15, 25 June 1815; also SP v. 6, pp. 1,777-78, 11 November 1815, "Statement of Miles Macdonell."

132 PAM MG1 D3, Fidler diary, 24 June 1815.

133 *Ibid.,* Fidler journal, 7 June 1815, and pp. 44, 46 of the typescript of this journal, June 1815.

134 *Ibid.,* Fidler journal 1814-15, June 1815; also reported in SP v. 6, p. 1,964.

135 PAM MG1 D3, Fidler journal 1814-15, 16 July 1815.

136 Rich, *The Fur Trade and the Northwest to 1857*, p. 221; Chief Albert Edward Thompson, *Chief Peguis and His Descendants* (Winnipeg: Peguis Publishers, 1973), p. 11, citing Selkirk Papers; burial and removal reference: Thompson, *Chief Peguis and His Descendants*, p. 12; and *Statement Respecting the Earl of Selkirk's Settlement upon the Red River*, p. lvii.

137 SP v. 8, p. 2,597, 22 August 1816, Pritchard to Selkirk.

138 SP v. 10, p. 3,314, 29 March 1817.

139 HBCA B.22/a/20, Brandon House Journal 1817-18, 18 July 1817.

140 Quoted in Pritchett, *The Red River Valley*, pp. 110-11.

141 Account of Ojibwa being invited west by Crees: Gunn, "Peguis Vindicated." Cree threat: Ross, *The Red River Settlement*, p. 159; Morton, *A History of the Canadian West*, p. 198.

142 "Liberty": HBCA B.22/a/20, Brandon House Post Journal 1817-18, 18 July 1817. See also SP v. 2, 17 July 1817, S.B. Coltman to Selkirk.

143 Andrew McDermott, "Peguis Refuted," *Nor'Wester*, 28 February 1860; "The Selkirk Treaty," in Alexander Morris, *Treaties of Canada with the Indians* (Toronto: Coles Canadiana Collection [facsimile edition], 1971 [1880]), pp. 298-300. A published facsimile of the treaty map, with the "signatures" of the Native leaders, is included in Morris; the original map is HBCA E8/1, fo. 11.

144 McDermott, "Peguis Refuted."

145 SP v. 13, p. 4,275, 27 December 1817, Ft. Douglas, Alexander Macdonell to Selkirk; also SP v. 4, p. 1,184, Macdonell to Selkirk 25 July 1814, which states that the Natives did not have horses to chase bison and suffered because the Métis did, thereby driving away the herds.

146 McDermott, "Peguis Refuted." The Premier, a signator to the Selkirk Treaty, was also known as Les Grands Oreilles (HBCA B.105/a/11, Lac la Pluie Journal 1825-26, 15 May 1826: "the Old Grand Oreilles or as he was commonly called the Old Premier"; I am indebted to Leo Waisberg, of Treaty and Aboriginal Rights Research, Grand Council Treaty Number 3, for sharing his research notes on The Premier.

147 SP v. 23, p. 7,306, R. Dickson to A. Colvile, Fort Douglas, 19 June 1821.
148 Hickerson and Wheeler-Voegelin, *The Red Lake and Pembina Chippewa*, pp. 92, 100; HBCA B.51/a/2, Fort Dauphin Journal 1819-20, 4, 7, 8 June 1819; PAM SP v. 11, p. 3,530, 7 June 1817, Fort Douglas, Miles Macdonell to Selkirk, and p. 3,926, 7 August 1817, Fort Douglas, Selkirk to James Bird; PAM SP v. 13, p. 4,213, 1 December 1817, Lac des Grosses Roches, Robert Dickson to Selkirk; PAM SP v. 23, pp. 7,356-57, 30 August 1821, Robert Dickson to John Pritchard; HBCA B.22/a/20, Brandon House Journal 1817-18, 5 August 1817.
149 Sioux stealing horses: HBCA B.51/a/2, Fort Dauphin Journal 1819-20, 8 June 1819. "Very hard": PAM SP v. 13, p. 4,276, 27 December 1817, Fort Douglas, Alexander Macdonell to Selkirk. See also HBCA B.22/a/20, Brandon House Journal 1817-18, 4 December 1817.
150 Grace Lee Nute, ed., *Documents Relating to Northwest Missions 1815-1827* (St. Paul: Minnesota Historical Society, 1942), Bishop Plessis to Provencher and Dumoulin, 20 April 1818, p. 60.
151 "Savages": PAM SP v. 10, p. 3,314, 29 March 1817; "civilized life": SP v. 11, p. 3,812, 17 July 1817, Coltman to Selkirk.
152 "Seven died": Tanner, p. 257. Other references on this epidemic include: HBCA B.51/a/2, Fort Dauphin Journal 1819-20; HBCA B.60/e/3, Edmonton District Report 1819-20; Ray, *Indians in the Fur Trade*, pp. 105-13; Taylor, "Sociocultural Effects of Epidemics," p. 78; HBCA B.51/a/2, Fort Dauphin Journal 1819-20, entries for June and July; PAM MG7 B1, Reverend John West journal, 80 or 90 dead at Qu'Appelle River; HBCA B.159/a/7, Swan River Journal 1818-19, 15 February 1819; Nelson, Tête-au-Brochet Journal 1818-19; HBCA B.16/e/3, p. 26, and B.64/e/2, quoted in Lytwyn, *The Fur Trade of the Little North*, p. 155; Barry Kaye, "Birsay Village on the Assiniboine," *The Beaver* (Winter 1981):18-21. Decker ("'We Should Never Again be the Same People,'" pp. 57, 92-101) suggests that the western Ojibwa experienced a >25-percent mortality rate during this epidemic. I dispute this, however, because Decker's findings are based partially on the belief that woodland-based cultures did not store food, which does not hold true for the western Ojibwa. Hackett ("The 1819-20 Measles Epidemic") suggests a wide variation in mortality rates, depending on the season at which the epidemic struck. Since the western Ojibwa were infected in summer and early autumn (pp. 93, 95, 128), when stores of food would have been available, I suggest a mortality rate of no more than 25 percent for this group.
153 HBCA B.51/a/2, Fort Dauphin Post Journal 1819-20, 7 April 1820.
154 "Troublesome and daring": HBCA B.22/e/1, General Report of the Red River District 1819, fo. 12. Compare to Ritterbush, "Culture Change and Continuity," p. 100 ("Horse raiding does not appear to have been common among the Red River Ojibwa and Ottawa. While among many Plains Indian groups the possession of horses marked relative wealth and status, this is not readily apparent in the primary documents from Red River"). While I agree that horse raiding was not common for the entire Ojibwa population, it was becoming so for some; and the fact that these men did steal horses, without the ambivalent attitudes displayed by the Ojibwa known to Henry and Tanner, suggests that attitudes were changing and that they were beginning to assimilate the plains horse wealth-status concept.
155 "Skin tipis": Nelson, Dauphin River Journal 1810-11, 13 May 1810.
156 HBCA B.51/e/1, Manitoba District Report, fo. 17.
157 Henry, Mashquegons afraid of Ojibwa: p. 477, 26 August 1877. Nelson and medicines: HBCA B.16/a/1, p. 26, quoted in Lytwyn, *The Fur Trade of the Little North*, p. 149. "Amasingly dear": from Brown and Brightman, *The Orders of the Dreamed*, p. 218, citing Nelson's 1811 journal. See also HBCA B.49/a/32b, Cumberland House Journal 1806-07, 22 May 1807, Bungees trading for medicines; Nelson, Dauphin River Journal 1808-10, 4 October 1808: "Ayagon comes for a small keg of rum to pay Old C-fesse for medicine that he got from him to put on his sore leg, occasioned by a woman inadvertently passing over it."

158 Fidler census: HBCA B.235/a/3, Winnipeg (Red River) Post Journal 1814-15, fo. 32, July 1815. Bison hunting: On the Ojibwa situation, see: PAM SP v. 4, p. 1,184, Macdonell to Selkirk, 25 July 1814 ("the natives and others who had not been hunting horses"); PAM SP v. 3, 17 July 1813, Macdonell to Selkirk ("The Saulteaux or Bungee Indians never pounds to catch buffaloe"); HBCA B.235/a/3, Winnipeg (Red River) Post Journal 1814-15, 28 July 1814; PAM SP v. 6, p. 1,768, probably 11 November 1815, statement of Miles Macdonell; PAM SP v. 5 p. 1,494, 23 March 1815, Selkirk to Macdonell.

CHAPTER 4

1 Ray, *Indians in the Fur Trade*, pp. 195-213; Innis, *The Fur Trade in Canada*, p. 287.

2 HBCA B.115/e/1, Lesser Slave Lake District Report 1819-20, fo. 4.

3 SP v. 24, pp. 7,586-87, Simpson to Colvile, 20 May 1822.

4 Innis, *The Fur Trade in Canada*, pp. 306-07, 326-27; Ray, *Indians in the Fur Trade*, pp. 195-205. For a discussion of how these policies affected one post at which Ojibwa traded, see Olga Klimko, *The Archaeology and History of Fort Pelly I (1824-1856)* (Regina: Saskatchewan Culture and Recreation, Pastlog No. 5, 1983), pp. 24-37.

5 Innis, *The Fur Trade in Canada*, pp. 287-88, citing the SP. Sources on credit amounts include: (pre-1821) Hickerson, "Journal of Charles Jean Baptiste Chaboillez"; Henry; George Nelson Journals; HBCA B.213/d/7, Swan River Accounts 1814-15; (post-1821) HBCA B.49/z/1, Cumberland House misc.; HBCA B.159/a/ Fort Pelly Journals 1829-1838.

6 PAM CMS reel M60, Reverend David Jones journal, 6 September 1825; and see "The Transitional Ojibwa," this chapter, pages 107-12, re: the choices made by the Tolibee/Baptiste Desjarlais band.

7 Tanner, p. 172.

8 Examples of pre-1821 gratuities, including many kinds of items and more lavish quantities, include: Henry, p. 97, 15 September 1800; and Nelson, Dauphin River Journal 1808-10, 10 June 1808. Compare these with: HBCA B.159/a/12, Fort Pelly Journal 1830-31, 5 October 1830; HBCA B.159/a/11, Fort Pelly Journal 1829-30, 30 September 1829; HBCA B.4/a/5, Fort Alexander Journal 1822-23, 7 June 1822. A few posts were somewhat more generous after 1821: see HBCA B.63/d/1, Fort Ellice Accounts 1822.

9 Gerald Friesen, *The Canadian Prairies*, p. 86; Ray, *Indians in the Fur Trade*, p. 195, quoting Simpson to Governor and Committee, 31 July 1822.

10 "Grand stimulus": SP v. 24, p. 7,607, 20 May 1822, Simpson to Colvile; R. Harvey Fleming, ed., *Minutes of Council Northern Department of Rupert Land, 1821-31* (Toronto: Champlain Society, 1940), p. 24, resolution #97 of council held 8 July 1822; Ray, *Indians in the Fur Trade*, pp. 197-98.

11 HBCA B.49/e/5, Cumberland District Report 1825, fo. 1.

12 "So independent": Simpson to Governor and Committee, 31 July 1822, in Fleming, *Minutes of Council Northern Department of Rupert Land*, p. 352; Ray, *Indians in the Fur Trade*, pp. 197-98; Klimko, *Fort Pelly I*, p. 32.

13 Ray, *Indians in the Fur Trade*, pp. 199, 204; Klimko, *Fort Pelly I*, pp. 28, 32-33.

14 PAM CMS reel M60, Reverend David Jones journal, 6 September 1825.

15 HBCA B.235/a/7, Winnipeg Post Journal 1825-26, 24 March 1826.

16 For journal entries mentioning locations and effects of American competition, see: HBCA B.22/a/22, Brandon House Journal 1828-29, fo. 5; HBCA B.159/a/11, Fort Pelly Journal 1829-30, 16 December 1829; and the HBCA B.159/a/15, Fort Pelly Journal 1833-34, 11 November 1833, mentions another American firm near Fort Union "whose liberal promises . . . has turned the heads of all the plains tribes," and 17 February 1834, competition between Missouri traders

"quite a harvest for the plains tribes"; HBCA B.159/a/13, Fort Pelly Journal 1831-32, 10 June 1831, Ojibwa and Crees leave Pelly for Missouri "with a view of learning how the Indians are treated with the Americans"; HBCA B.159/a/11, Fort Pelly Journal 1829-30, 16 December 1829; HBCA B.235/a/8, Winnipeg Journal 1826-27, 1 January, 25 April 1827; HBCA B.235/a/9, Winnipeg Journal 1827-28, 30 September 1827. For secondary sources on the effects of American competition, see Innis, *The Fur Trade in Canada*, pp. 333-34; Klimko, *Fort Pelly I, 1824-1856*, pp. 30-36.

17 HBCA B. 235/a/8, Winnipeg Post Journal 1826-27, 25 April 1827.

18 HBCA B. 159/a/11, Fort Pelly Journal 1829-30, 16 December 1829. See also Klimko, *Fort Pelly I*, pp. 33-37.

19 E.E. Rich, *Hudson's Bay Company, 1670-1870*, vol. 3: *1821-1870* (Toronto: McClelland and Stewart, 1960), p. 475.

20 "Rascals": HBCA B.235/a/5, Winnipeg Journal 1822-23, 6 October 1822; "debts they never get": HBCA B. 235/a/8, Winnipeg Journal 1826-27, 3 October 1826.

21 PAM SP v. 24, p. 7,750, 8 September 1822, Bulger to Colvile, and p. 7,600, 20 May 1822, Simpson to Colvile; HBCA B.159/e/3, Swan River District Report 1828-29, fo. 1; HBCA B.235/a/8, Winnipeg Journal, 1826-27, 6 March 1827; HBCA B.235/a/5, Winnipeg Journal, 1822-23, 21 September 1822.

22 Morton, *A History of the Canadian West*, p. 658; Rich, *The Fur Trade and the Northwest to 1857*, pp. 249-50; "overrun": HBCA B.22/e/23, Brandon House District Report 1828-29, fo. 5.

23 Ray, *Indians in the Fur Trade*, p. 205. These figures are probably quite conservative, since some Métis lived as Indians with Indian relatives.

24 Ross, *The Red River Settlement*, p. 246.

25 On different prices paid to Métis and Indians, see: Ray, *Indians in the Fur Trade*, p. 205; Nicks, "The Iroquois and the Fur Trade in Western Canada," p. 95. Ross, *The Red River Settlement*, p. 269, notes Ojibwa accompanying Métis on bison hunts. Howard, *The Plains Ojibwa or Bungi*, does not distinguish between Ojibwa and Métis hunts in the Turtle Mountain area.

26 Hickerson and Wheeler-Voegelin, *The Red Lake and Pembina Chippewa*, p. 201; Ross, *The Red River Settlement*, p. 269.

27 HBCA B.115/e/1, Lesser Slave Lake District Report 1819-20, fo. 4b. I am grateful to Dr. Gertrude Nicks of the Royal Ontario Museum for sharing her research notes on the Tolibee-Desjarlais band with me. For other background information on this band at Lesser Slave Lake, see Nicks, "Native Responses to the Early Fur Trade at Lesser Slave Lake," in *Le Castor Fait Tout: Selected Papers of the Fifth North American Fur Trade Conference*, ed. Bruce G. Trigger, Toby Morantz, Louise Dechêne (Montreal: Lake St. Louis Historical Society, 1987), pp. 278-310.

28 Both quotations from HBCA B.115/e/1, Lesser Slave Lake District Report 1819-20, fo. 4b.

29 HBCA B.115/e/3, Lesser Slave Lake District Report 1821-22. See also Nicks, "Native Responses to the Early Fur Trade at Lesser Slave Lake."

30 HBCA B.115/e/1, Lesser Slave Lake District Report 1819-20, fo. 4b.

31 HBCA B.115/e/2, Lesser Slave Lake District Report 1820-21; White, "Give Us a Little Milk." "Usual fidelity": HBCA B.115/e/2, Lesser Slave Lake District Report 1820-21, fo. 4.

32 HBCA B.115/e/3, Lesser Slave Lake District Report 1821-22; HBCA B.115/a/5, Lesser Slave Lake Journal 1821-22; HBCA B.115/a/6, Lesser Slave Lake Journal 1822-23. The band may also have spent some time at Fort Vermilion: see HBCA B.224/e/1, HBCA B.115/e/4. Tolibee's promise to the trader is cited in Nicks, "The Early Fur Trade at Lesser Slave Lake," p. 305, quoting Lesser Slave Lake records for 1819.

33 HBCA B.49/a/43, Cumberland House Journal 1827-28, 31 July, 26 August, 1 and 2 October 1827. See note 45 this chapter for my reasons for believing that it was the same band at Lesser Slave Lake and Cumberland / Fort Pelly.

34 Ray, *Indians in the Fur Trade*, p. 110; Albers, "Pluralism in the Native Plains," pp. 47-48; Dobyns, *Their Number become Thinned*, p. 311; and see section on the measles epidemic in chapter 3, this volume. For a dramatic image of the effect of post closures in this region, see Harris, ed., *The Historical Atlas of Canada*, vol. 1, plate 62, insets "Trading Posts in 1821" and "Trading Posts in 1825."

35 HBCA B.22/e/3, Brandon House District Report 1828-29, fo. 4.

36 Klimko, *Fort Pelly I*, pp. 33-37; HBCA B.22/e/3, Brandon House District Report 1828-29, fo. 5.

37 General trade with settlers in and around colony: HBCA B.235/a/8, Winnipeg Journal 1826-27, 7 January, 6 and 7 March 1827; HBCA B.235/a/12, Winnipeg Journal 1828-29, 24 January 1829; HBCA B.235/e/3, Winnipeg (Red River) District Report 1826-27, fo. 3. See also Klimko, *Fort Pelly I*, pp. 27-28. HBCA B.51/e/2, Manitoba District Report 1821, fo. 2 (source of quote re: 4 shillings per pound for sugar; compare with HBCA B.239/z/1, fo. 35: usual price given was 9p. per pound); HBCA B235/a/8, Winnipeg Journal 1826-27, 6 March 1827; HBCA B.159/e/2, Swan River District Report 1828-29, fo. 1.

38 Re: muskrat trade: the Swan River district report for 1828-29 states that the 120 or so Ojibwa families in the district had for several years hunted "in the vicinity of Ft. Pelly and Manitoabun along the small lakes where the Muskrat build their lodges" (HBCA B.159/a/9, Fort Pelly Post Journal 1825-26, 24 September 1825; HBCA B.159/e/3, Swan River District [Fort Pelly] Report, 1828-29, fo. 3; HBCA B.22/e/3, Brandon House District Report 1828-29, fos. 4, 5; see also HBCA B.235/a/7, Winnipeg Post Journal 1825-26, and HBCA B.159/a/11, Fort Pelly Journal 1829-30 for muskrats, trade in general.

39 HBCA B.159/a/11, Fort Pelly Journal 1829-30, 30 September 1829.

40 HBCA B.159/a/12, Fort Pelly Journal 1830-31, 10 October 1830.

41 HBCA B.159/a/11, Fort Pelly Journal 1829-30, 10 October 1829.

42 HBCA B.159/a/10, Fort Pelly Journal 1828-29, 27 April 1829. Depending on the exact rate of exchange at Pelly that spring, such a catch would be worth between 400 and 800 MB: an enormous amount.

43 HBCA B.159/e/2, Swan River District (Fort Pelly) Report 1825, fo. 1.

44 HBCA B.159/a/12, Fort Pelly Journal 1830-31, 3 October 1830.

45 HBCA B.27a/17, Carlton Journal 1828-29, 9 September 1828, 6 canoes with a few beaver, and 22 February 1829; HBCA B.27/a/18, Carlton Journal 1829-30, 11 October 1829, in with a few beaver. While Tolibee (or Tullibee, a species of fish), was a fairly common name for Ojibwa men, there are several important clues that lead me to believe that this is the same individual first encountered at Lesser Slave Lake. At Lesser Slave Lake, Cumberland, and Fort Pelly, a number of the same band members were present, including Tolibee, Baptiste Desjarlais, and Capot Rouge; compare with the chart and names of Lesser Slave Lake band members in Nicks, "Native Responses to the Early Fur Trade at Lesser Slave Lake," pp. 290-91. At Cumberland House, a step-son of Tolibee's is noted (31 July 1827), and turns up again at Carlton in the fall of 1829 (HBCA B.27/a/18, Carlton Journal 1829-30, 12 October 1829). Tolibee is not mentioned together with Baptiste Desjarlais after the group appeared at Cumberland House in 1827, leading me to suspect that the band broke up into two groups between 1827 and 1829.

46 See, for example, HBCA B.27/a/17, Carlton House Journal 1828-29, entry for 3 March 1829, in which two Cree from Birch Hill arrived with 1,100 muskrats. See also B.60/e/8, Edmonton District Report 1824-25, fo. 2; B.27/a/19, Carlton Journal 1832-33, 28 April 1833.

47 HBCA B.27/a/18, Carlton Journal 1829-30, 12 October 1829; the Bloody Berry Hill near this site is also noted in the journals as being a good area for game hunting, reinforcing the idea of a subsistence (rather than fur-trade) orientation.

48 Some of the many references to the continuing importance of fish are found in: HBCA B.235/a/
4, Winnipeg (Red River) Post Journal 1820-21; HBCA B.235/a/8, Winnipeg (Red River) Post
Journal 1826-27; PAM MG1 B7, West Journal, 2 November 1821. Re: Saskatchewan River area
Ojibwa and their seasonal round, see: HBCA B.27/a/15, Fort Carlton Journal 1826-27; HBCA
B.27/a/17, Carlton Journal 1828-29; HBCA B.27/a/20, Carlton Journal 1833-34; HBCA B. 27/a/
22, Carlton Journal 1836-37; HBCA B.27/a/23, Carlton Journal 1838-39; HBCA B.27/a/12,
Carlton Journal 1822-23, 11 July 1822; HBCA B.159/a/17, Fort Pelly Journal 1837-38.
49 E.g., HBCA B.159/a/12, Fort Pelly Journal 1830-31, 10 October 1830 ("the Indians at the Fort
making their medicine [as they term it] and Great ceremony going on in the Lodge"). Gardens,
1821 West reference: Reverend John West, *The Substance of a Journal during a Residence at the
Red River Colony* (New York: S.R. Publishers, Ltd., Johnson Reprint Corp., 1966), p. 97;
around Fort Pelly: HBCA B.159/a/10, Fort Pelly Journal 1828-29, 16 April 1829; HBCA B.159/
a/12, Fort Pelly Journal 1830-31, 25 October 1830; HBCA B.159/a/13, Fort Pelly Journal 1831-
32, 11 May and 11 June 1832; HBCA B.159/a/15, Fort Pelly Journal 1833-34, 18, 29 April, 1
May 1834.
50 HBCA B.165/a/1, Fort Pitt Journal 1830-31, 26, 27 July 1830; HBCA B.159/a/ 13, Fort Pelly
Journal 1831-32, 3, 16 July 1831, 29 April 1832 (this last entry contains, as well as a reference
about "starving", a mention of two hunters exchanging the rum they were given for ammunition,
a measure of the difficulty of the times). See also Ray, *Indians in the Fur Trade*, pp. 220-21.
51 HBCA B.159/a/12, Fort Pelly Journal 1830-31, 11 January 1831; HBCA B.159/a/14, Fort Pelly
Journal 1832-33, 16 April 1833, referring to deaths in mid-winter. This and the following
paragraphs include material published in Laura Peers, "Changing Resource-Use Patterns of
Saulteaux Trading at Fort Pelly, 1821-70," in *Aboriginal Resource Use in Canada: Historical and
Legal Aspects*, ed. Kerry Abel and Jean Friesen (Winnipeg: University of Manitoba Press,
1991).
52 Black-Rogers, "Varieties of 'Starving,'" p. 361.
53 "The whole of the Indians": HBCA B.159/a/15, Fort Pelly Journal 1833-34, 18 April 1834. See
also: HBCA B.159/a/12, Fort Pelly Journal 1830-31, 25 October 1830; HBCA B.159/a/11, Fort
Pelly Journal 1829-30, 6 May 1830.
54 Black-Rogers, "Varieties of 'Starving,'" p. 367, quoting White, "Give Us a Little Milk."
55 HBCA B.159/a/13, Fort Pelly Journal 1831-32, 21 January, 19 February 1832.
56 HBCA Pelly Journal 1833 and 1832, 19 February, 18 May 1832.
57 *Ibid.* (the winter of 1832-33 was particularly difficult, as there was little snow to aid hunting and
the bison remained far to the south of the Saskatchewan River). See also Dempsey, *Big Bear*, pp.
15-16; HBCA B.27/a/19, Carlton House Journal 1832-33.
58 "Real starvation": HBCA B.159/a/13, Fort Pelly Journal 1831-32, 25 February 1832. See also:
HBCA B.159/a/12, Fort Pelly Journal 1830-31, 10 April 1831; HBCA B.159/a/13, Fort Pelly
Journal 1831-32, 3, 18, 30 January, 23 February 1832; HBCA B.159/a/15, Fort Pelly Journal
1833-34, 6 December 1833.
59 "Much difficulty": HBCA B.27/a/19, Carlton House Journal 1832-33, 28 April 1833. See also:
HBCA B.159/a/14, Fort Pelly Journal 1832-33, 16 April 1833; HBCA B.27/a/22, Carlton House
Journal 1836-37, 5 June 1836. Ray, *Indians in the Fur Trade*, p. 220, notes that the herds crossed
to the north side of the North Saskatchewan River in January around the Fort Pitt/Carlton area in
the 1830s, and moved south again in May and June.
60 HBCA B.159/a/13, Fort Pelly Journal 1831-32, 29 April 1832; "most valuable": HBCA B.159/a/
15, Fort Pelly Journal 1833-34, 25 December 1833, 1 May 1834; HBCA B.159/a/16, Fort Pelly
Journal 1834-35, 7 October, 15 December 1834.
61 See, for example, HBCA B.159/a/12, Fort Pelly Journal 1830-31, 10 October 1830: "the Indians
at the Fort making their medicine (as they term it) and Great ceremony going on in the Lodge."

62 HBCA B.159/a/12, Fort Pelly Journal 1830-31, 5 October 1830. See HBCA B.159/a/12, Fort Pelly Journal 1830-31, 2 May 1830, and HBCA B.159/a/11, Fort Pelly Journal 1829-30, 6 December 1829, for earlier references to Desjarlais' band around Fort Pelly.

63 HBCA B.159/a/12, Fort Pelly Journal 1830-31, 9 February 1831 (Baptiste Desjarlais's band has some 300 MB in camp, have some provisions and the bison are very near).

64 Although the Fort Pelly trader claimed there was "no want of fur" in the region, the widespread collapse of the muskrat population was not followed by higher returns in other furs, probably because of the difficulty in finding sufficient game to allow time to be spent hunting for furs.

65 HBCA B.159/a/12, Fort Pelly Journal 1830-31, 10 April 1831. See also HBCA B.159/a/14, Fort Pelly Journal 1832-33, 17, 18 October 1832, 13, 17 May 1833.

66 Quote is HBCA B.159/a/12, Fort Pelly Journal 1830-31, 12 October 1830. See also HBCA B.159/a/10, Fort Pelly Journal 1828-29, 8 February 1829, camp of forty tents Cree, Ojibwa, and Assiniboine on plains after bison; HBCA B.159/a/14, Fort Pelly Journal 1832-33, 13 May 1833; HBCA B.159/a/15, Fort Pelly Journal 1833-34, 25 December 1833; HBCA B.159/a/16, Fort Pelly Journal 1834-35, 7 October 1834; HBCA B.159/a/17, Fort Pelly Journal 1837-38, 12, 30 October 1837; HBCA B.27/a/19, Carlton House Journal 1832-33, 5 August 1832.

67 HBCA B.159/a/12, Fort Pelly Journal 1830-31, 12 October 1830; "plains Sauteaux": HBCA B.159/a/14, Fort Pelly Journal 1832-33, 17 May 1833; Tian: HBCA B.159/a/17, Fort Pelly Journal 1837-38, 12 October 1837.

68 HBCA B.159/a/13, Fort Pelly Journal 1831-32, 30 September 1831.

69 HBCA B.159/a/10, Fort Pelly Journal 1828-29, 8 February 1829. See also Sharrock, "Crees, Cree-Assiniboines, and Assiniboines," p. 110, regarding the correlation between the bison-hunting economy and multi-ethnic camps.

70 Baptiste Desjarlais: HBCA B.159/a/15, Fort Pelly Journal 1833-34, 1 May 1834; HBCA B.159/a/12, Fort Pelly Journal 1830-31, 12 January 1831. "Little or nothing": HBCA B.159/a/15, Fort Pelly Journal 1833-34, 11 May 1834. "Not exerted themselves": HBCA B.51/e/2, Manitoba District Report, 1821. The Fishing Lakes have been a productive fishing site for "plains" peoples for hundreds of years (see: Brian Smith, "The Importance of Assessing Aquatic Environments on the Northern Plains" [paper presented at the Chacmool Conference, Calgary, 1986]; and "An Ethnohistorical Evaluation of the Role of Bison and Fish in the Social Organization of Northern Plains and Parkland Native Society: 1790-1850," *Manitoba Archaeological Quarterly*, 12/1 [1988]).

71 HBCA B.27/a/17, Carlton Journal 1828-29, 23 July 1828 (quarrelled); HBCA B.27/a/17, Carlton Journal 1828-29, 1 July 1829 (re: moving); HBCA B.159/a/12, Fort Pelly Journal 1830-31, 19 March, 10, 11 April 1831; HBCA B.159/a/13, Fort Pelly Journal 1831-32, 10 June, 15 September 1831. According to Milloy (*The Plains Cree*, pp. 64-65), Assiniboine/Cree/Mandan relations between 1817 and 1823 were deteriorating but were maintained by Cree for access to Mandan horses. Milloy sees the development of a strengthened relationship among Assiniboine and Cree because of a common need for horses and a common enemy in the Mandan. Other references to Ojibwa participation in these incidents are found in HBCA B.63/a/3, Fort Ellice Journal 1822-23, 19 March 1823; HBCA B.235/a/7, Winnipeg Journal 1825-26, 22 May 1826; HBCA B.27/a/17, Carlton House Journal 1828-29, 23 July 1828. There were also several other instances of hostilities, probably unrelated to these larger alliance schemes, such as an attack on a group of Ojibwa by "Brandon House Indians" (probably either Cree or Assiniboine) in the summer of 1824 (CMS M60, David Jones journal, 17 September 1824).

72 In the summer of 1829, the Cree made "peace with the Black feet and gave their guns for which they got horses in return" (HBCA B.22/a/23, Brandon House Post Journal 1829-30, 8 November 1829; see also: Dempsey, *Big Bear*, pp. 13-14 (re: Cree-Blackfoot warfare and Black Powder's involvement in it); Hugh Dempsey, *Crowfoot: Chief of the Blackfeet* (Norman: University of Oklahoma Press, 1972), p. 12; HBCA B.159/a/12, Fort Pelly Journal 1830-31, 4 September 1830; HBCA B.159/a/16, Fort Pelly Journal 1834-35, 10 May 1835, Cree/Assiniboine war party to go against Blackfoot; Milloy, *The Plains Cree*, p. 89).

73 Camped: Dempsey, *Big Bear*, p. 11. See also HBCA B.159/a/6-17, Fort Pelly Journals 1817-38; Gregory Camp, "The Chippewa Transition from Woodland to Prairie, 1790-1820," *North Dakota History* 51/3 (1984):39-47.

74 Ray, *Indians in the Fur Trade*, p. 220; Black Powder's territory: Dempsey, *Big Bear*, p. 15. The Fort Pitt Journal also contains references to mixed groups of Ojibwa and Cree from "the Jack Lake" trading during the 1830s (e.g., HBCA B.165/a/2, Fort Pitt Journal 1831-31, 6 November 1831); these people may be Black Powder's or a similar band. According to Dale Russell, "pounding" was then a recent development among the Cree, they having not adopted it until about the late eighteenth century (see Russell, *Eighteenth Century Cree and their Neighbors*, p. 117).

75 HBCA B.159/a/12, Fort Pelly Journal 1831-32, 6 October 1831.

76 Howard, *The Plains Ojibwa or Bungi*, p. 18. George Catlin, *Illustrations of the Manners, Customs, and Condition of the North American Indians*, vol. 1, 10th ed. (London: Henry G. Bohn, 1866), p. 58, plates 35, 36.

77 Catlin, *Illustrations of the Manners, Customs, and Condition of the North American Indians*, p. 58, plates 35, 36.

78 *Ibid.*

79 Howard, *The Plains Ojibwa or Bungi*, p. 18.

80 Barbara Hail, *Hau, Kola!: The Plains Indian Collection of the Hafenreffer Museum* (Providence: Hafenreffer Museum of Anthropology, 1983), pp. 32-33. The Six's shirt looks remarkably like that worn by Wijunjon (see figure 2, *Hau, Kola!*; note the same double rosette and strip detail). On Catlin also painting the Teton Dakota that year, see Marjorie Halpin, "Introduction," in George Catlin, *Letters and Notes on the Manners, Customs, and Conditions of the North American Indians* (New York: Dover Publications, 1973), p. x. Re: Catlin's haste that summer and his variable accuracy about the decorative details of clothing, see also John C. Ewers, "George Catlin: Painter of Indians and the West," *Annual Report Smithsonian Institution 1955*, p. 498.

81 Tanner, *Atlas of Great Lakes Indian History*, pp. 98-99, map 20, "Indian Villages ca. 1810"; p. 148, map 28, "Indian Villages ca. 1830"; and p. 176, map 33, "Indian Villages ca. 1870" (Shakopee's village is noted on all three maps); see also p. 149.

82 Howard, *The Plains Ojibwa or Bungi*, p. 19 (caption for Catlin painting of The Six included in Howard). See also James Howard, *The Canadian Sioux* (Lincoln: University of Nebraska, 1984), p. 28, for the Dakota rendering of The Six's name. The Six was among the Dakota who fled to Canada in 1862; he was captured, and a photograph of him bears a certain resemblance to Catlin's portrait, although the captured man may have been the son of the man whom Catlin painted (see Alan R. Woolworth, "A Disgraceful Proceeding," *The Beaver* [Spring 1969]:57).

83 Part of the collection has been published in Christian Feest, *Indianer Nordamerikas* (Vienna: Museum für Völkerkunde, 1968); and a smaller selection in *The Spirit Sings: A Catalogue of the Exhibition*, p. 74, figures P13 (shirt) and P14 (leggings). The clothing is in the collections of the Museum für Völkerkunde, Vienna: Klinger 421 (shirt), 422 (leggings), 428, 429 (moccasins).

84 The club is illustrated and discussed in *The Spirit Sings: Artistic Traditions of Canada's First Peoples*, p. 83; it is held by the Royal Ontario Museum, accession no. 37592.

85 Dempsey, *Big Bear*, p. 15.

86 Other references to large Ojibwa and mixed Ojibwa-Cree camps: HBCA B.159/a/10, Fort Pelly Journal 1828-29, 8 February 1829 (mixed camp of 40 tents [without a pound]); Howard, in *The Plains Ojibwa or Bungi*, p. 18, states that there was a large Sun Dance encampment ca. 1835 near the North Dakota border.

87 Peter Bakker, "The Genesis of Mechif: A First Hypothesis," in *Papers of the Twenty-First Algonquian Conference*, ed. William Cowan (Ottawa: Carleton University, 1990), p. 33; Peter Erasmus, *Buffalo Days and Nights*, ed. Irene Spry (Calgary: Glenbow-Alberta Institute, 1976), p. 241.

88 Dempsey, *Big Bear*, p. 17; Ritterbush, "Culture Change and Continuity," p. 12 (inter-tribal trade and other forms of contact between ethnic groups also "accentuated differences between the two groups").

89 Howard: *The Plains Ojibwa or Bungi*, p. 3. "Fused ethnicity": Sharrock, "Crees, Cree-Assiniboines, and Assiniboines," pp.111-19.

90 Russell, *Eighteenth Century Cree and their Neighbors*, p. 218. See also Brian Smith, "The Lebret Site" (M.A. thesis, University of Saskatchewan, 1986), p. 364 ("Some Cree bands, such as the Cree-Assiniboin, were closely tied to a typical bison-oriented lifestyle centred on the Grasslands while others, such as the Calling River and Touchwood Hills people, were utilizing both the Grasslands and the Valley complexes in these areas").

91 See the overview in A.D. Fisher, "Great Plains Ethnology," in *Native Peoples: The Canadian Experience*, ed. R. Bruce Morrison and C. Roderick Wilson (Toronto: McClelland and Stewart, 1986), pp. 362-70; compare with Skinner, "The Cultural Position of the Plains Ojibway," which relies upon definitions of "plains" and "woodlands" cultures by Clark Wissler.

92 Brian Smith, "The Historical and Archaeological Evidence for the Use of Fish as an Alternative Subsistence Resource among Northern Plains Bison Hunters," in *Aboriginal Resouce Use in Canada: Historical and Legal Aspects*, ed. Kerry Abel and Jean Friesen (Winnipeg: University of Manitoba Press, 1991), p. 8 ("Due to its largeness and high visibility in Plains culture, the importance of bison has not been overrated so much as the alternative subsistence resources and their impact on Plains lifeway have been underrated"); Brian Smith, "The Lebret Site," p. 362 (distinction between parkland and plains Cree in pre-1850 period is "a matter of degree," and dependent on how closely bands conform to Wissler's list of "plains" traits: the most "plains" Cree are those most closely associated with the Assiniboine). See also Peers, "Subsistence, Secondary Literature, and Gender Bias," on the male emphasis in ethnographic descriptions of plains and parkland societies.

93 See Owen, "The Patrilocal Band: A Linguistically and Culturally Hybrid Social Unit," *American Anthropologist* 67 (1965):675-89.

94 Harriet Gorham, "Families of Mixed Descent in the Western Great Lakes Region," in *Native Peoples, Native Lands*, ed. Bruce A. Cox (Ottawa: Carleton University Press, 1988), p. 49.

95 On changes in women's labour and social position, see Alan Klein, "Political Economy of Gender," in *The Hidden Half*, ed. Patricia Albers and Beatrice Medicine (Washington, D.C.: University Press of America, 1983), pp.153, 157; Leacock, *Myths of Male Dominance*, p. 159 (women as processors and property in the fur trade). On the implications of the chase versus the pound, see Mandelbaum, *The Plains Cree*, pp. 56, 61-2, vs. Klein, "Political Economy of Gender," pp. 148-53. See also Margo Liberty, "Hell Came with Horses: Plains Indian Women in the Equestrian Era," *Montana: The Magazine of Western History* 32 (1982):10-19. Some exceptional women did become *okitcitakwe*, members of the *okitcita* society, but they did not share in all of the privileges of the male members of the society (Skinner, "The Cultural Position of the Plains Ojibway," pp. 485-86). One woman's society adopted by some bands of the plains Saulteaux did involve a war bonnet, but participation in this group did not bring greater status as was the case with men's warrior societies (Howard, *The Plains Ojibwa or Bungi*, p. 63; Skinner, "The Cultural Position of the Plains Ojibway," p. 509.)

96 This transition is seen quite clearly among the Dakota. See Kathleen Pickering, "Changes in Lakota Social Complexity" (unpublished term paper, University of Wisconsin-Madison, 1990), p. 21.

97 Howard, *The Plains Ojibwa or Bungi*, p. 18.

98 Barth, *Ethnic Groups and Boundaries*, p. 12.

99 HBCA B.235/e/1, Lower Red River District Report 1822-23. These families traded either at Fort Garry, at a sporadic HBC post near Pembina, or with the Americans near Turtle Mountain. On Black Robe's band, see CMS David Jones journal, 22 June 1824; HBCA B.235/a/6, Winnipeg (Red River) Post Journal 1824-25, 9 October 1824.

100 HBCA B.63/a/3, Fort Ellice Post Journal (Upper Red River) 1822-23, 6 June 1823; CMS reel M60, David Jones journal, 22 June 1824; HBCA B.235/a/6, Winnipeg Post Journal 1824-25, 19 June 1824; HBCA B.235/a/5, Winnipeg Post Journal 1822-23, 1 June 1823.

101 "Conveyance out": SP v. 23, p. 7,359, Pritchard to Andrew Colvile, 31 August 1821; "hostile array": SP v. 23, p. 7,355, Robert Dickson to John Pritchard, 30 August 1821; SP v. 23, p. 7,365, 4 September 1821, Allez to Colvile. See also "Diary of Nicholas Garry," p. 143, 6 August 1821 (Peguis "entreated me not to send the usual supplies to the Sieux").

102 Simpson: PAM SP v. 23, p. 7,392, 4 September 1821, Simpson to Colvile. "Not . . . expedient": Governor and Committee to Simpson, 8 March 1822, in Fleming, *Minutes of Council Northern Department of Rupert Land, 1821-31*, p. 315.

103 "Diary of Nicholas Garry," pp. 135, 143.

104 Van Kirk, *Many Tender Ties*; Van Kirk, "What if Mama is an Indian?: The Cultural Ambivalence of the Alexander Ross Family," in *The Developing West: Essays on Canadian History in Honor of Lewis H. Thomas* (Edmonton: University of Alberta Press, 1983); Gerald Friesen, *The Canadian Prairies*, pp. 95-99.

105 HBCA B.235/a/8, Winnipeg Post Journal 1826-27, 11 December 1826; HBCA B.235/a/5, Winnipeg Post Journal 1822-23, 19 October 1822.

106 Quote is from HBCA B.235/a/8, Winnipeg Post Journal 1826-27, 27 February 1827. See also: HBCA B.235/a/8, Winnipeg Post Journal 1826-27, 8, 24 January 1827; and HBCA B.235/a/7, Winnipeg Post Journal 1825-26, 30 December 1825.

107 HBCA B.235/e/1, Winnipeg District Report 1822-23, fo. 2.

108 Morton, *A History of the Canadian West*, p. 658.

109 HBCA B.235/a/12, Winnipeg Post Journal 1828-29, 24 September 1828.

110 SP v. 24, p. 7,751, 8 September 1822, A. Bulger to A. Colvile.

111 CMS A77 (M45), Cockran to Secretaries of the CMS, 25 February 1832, p. 453; CMS A85, Cockran journal 1832-33, 4 July 1833.

112 CMS A85, Cockran journal 1830-31, 2 February 1831.

113 HBCA B.235/a/12, Winnipeg Post Journal 1828-29, 31 August 1828; HBCA B.235/a/7, Winnipeg Post Journal 1825-26, 31 August, 1, 10, 14 September 1825; HBCA B.235/a/6, Winnipeg Post Journal 1824-25, 18 September 1824; West, *Substance of a Journal*, p. 68, 2 November 1821 (given dried sturgeon by Peguis's band).

114 HBCA B.235/a/5, Winnipeg Journal 1822-23, 3 October 1822; HBCA B.235/a/7, Winnipeg Journal 1825-26, 3, 24 October, 14, 18, 30 November 1825; PAM CMS M60, Reverend David Jones journal, Friday, 1 October; tobacco dram: HBCA B.235/a/13, Winnipeg Journal 1829-30, 1 January 1830; "to share": HBCA B.235/a/9, Winnipeg Journal 1827-28, 20 December 1827; see also entries for 5, 31 December 1827.

115 HBCA B.235/a/7, Winnipeg Post Journal 1825-26, 14 April 1826; HBCA B.235/a/5, Winnipeg Post Journal 1822-23, 10 March 1823; HBCA B.235/a/16, Winnipeg Post Journal 1824-25, 5 April 1825; quote, "exhausted": HBCA B.235/e/1, Lower Red River District Report 1822-23, fo. 3; spring activities: HBCA B.235/a/6, Winnipeg Journal 1824-25, 12 May, 18 June 1825; HBCA B.235/a/5, Winnipeg Journal 1822-23, 13 May 1823; HBCA B.235/a/13, Winnipeg Journal 1829-30, 7 July 1829.

116 On warfare and attempted treaties during the 1820s, see: Governor and Committee to George Simpson, 8 March 1822, in Fleming, *Minutes of Council Northern Department of Rupert Land 1821-31*, p. 315; Anderson, *Kinsmen of Another Kind*, p. 119; Hickerson and Wheeler-Voegelin, *The Red Lake and Pembina Chippewa*, p. 117-19; HBCA B.235/a/5, Winnipeg Post Journal 1822-23, 13 March, 13, 25 May 1823; HBCA B.235/a/6, Winnipeg Post Journal 1824-25, 15, 18, 24 June 1824; HBCA B.235/a/12, Winnipeg Post Journal 1828-29, 16 August 1828; HBCA B.235/a/13, Winnipeg Post Journal 1829-30, 3, 7, 20 July 1829.

117 "Roaming": CMS A77, Reverend William Cockran to Secretaries of the CMS, Red River settlement 30 July 1827; HBCA B.235/e/1, Lower Red River District Report 1822-23, fo. 3.

118 Lucille Kane, June Holmquist, and Carolyn Gilman, eds., *The Northern Expeditions of Stephen H. Long* (St. Paul: Minnesota Historical Society Press, 1978), p. 192, 18 August 1823 (re: fishing); "Diary of Nicholas Garry," p. 135, 3 August 1821 (re: corn); "beg a pipe": HBCA B.235/a/8, Winnipeg (Red River) Post Journal 1826-27, 1 August 1826 (and see entry for 5 August); HBCA B.235/a/6, Winnipeg (Red River) Journal 1824-25, 14 July 1824; HBCA B.235/a/7, Winnipeg (Red River) Journal 1825-26, 30 July, 1 August 1825.

119 HBCA B.235/e/1, Lower Red River District Report 1822-23.

120 *Ibid.*, B.235/a/6, Winnipeg Journal 1824-25; CMS, reel M60, Jones to Secretaries of the CMS, July 1827; HBCA B.235/a/7, Winnipeg Journal 1825-26, 2, 11 January 1826; Sprenger, "The Metis Nation," p. 124.

121 Decker, "'We Should Never Again be the Same People,'" p. 57, suggests a mortality rate greater than twenty-five percent for western Ojibwa in this epidemic. I disagree with her, on the basis that, since it struck in early summer, food would readily have been available, so that mortality from primary infection would not have been greatly increased by malnutrition-induced secondary infections and other complications.

122 On CMS missionization of Ojibwa in Red River, see also: Carolyn Podruchny, "Indians and Missionaries in Encounter: The Peguis Band and the Church Missionary Society At the Red River, 1820-1838" (M.A. thesis, University of Toronto, 1992).

123 See J.E. Foster, "William Cockran," *Dictionary of Canadian Biography*, vol. 9 (1976), p. 134.

124 PAM CMS A77, Cockran to Reverend E. Bickersteth, 3 August 1829.

125 West, *Substance of a Journal*, pp. 118-19.

126 *Ibid.* p. 125.

127 CMS A85, Cockran journal 1832-33, 13 September 1832, 9 April 1833. See also CMS A85, Cockran journal 1830-31, 2 February 1831.

128 PAC CMS A77, Reverend W. Cockran journal, 30 October 1828.

129 SP v. 16, p. 5,372, 12 September 1818, Capt. Matthay [sic] to Selkirk.

130 CMS A85, Cockran journal 1832-33, p. 20.

131 CMS reel M60, David Jones journal, 18 March 1825. See also: CMS reel M64, Smithurst to CMS, 2 August 1841 ("The Indians never scruple to have their children baptised, because they think no one can injure them, by conjouring"); and CMS A96, Smithurst journal 1846, 7 July 1846. See also Podruchny, "Indians and Missionaries in Encounter," pp. 48-54.

132 "Advantages": CMS A77, Cockran to Secretaries of the CMS, 30 July 1827; "begging": CMS A85, Cockran journal 1830-31, 17 October 1830. See also CMS A85, Cockran journal 1833-34, 10 September 1833.

133 West, *Substance of a Journal*, p. 103.

134 Sprenger, "The Metis Nation," pp. 120-35.

135 Guns lighter than hoes: Ross, *The Red River Settlement*, pp. 280-81. "Pointed to the plains and river": CMS A77, Cockran journal, 30 October 1828.

136 See, for example, CMS A77, reel M45, Cockran to Secretaries of the CMS, 25 February 1832, in which he estimates that thirty canoes of "Swampies" had arrived in the previous two years. See also the section on the Cree in Podruchny, "Indians and Missionaries in Encounter," pp. 33-42.

137 CMS, reel A85, Cockran journal, 28 October 1830.

138 "Conjurors": CMS, Cockran to CMS, 11 July 1836; shooting: CMS reel A85, Cockran journal 1830-31, 6 July 1831; "amalgamate": CMS A77 reel M45 Jones to CMS, 25 July 1833.

139 CMS reel M60, David Jones journal, 28 February 1826.

140 PAC CMS A77, Cockran to Secretaries of the CMS, 7 August 1828.

141 E.g., CMS reel A85, Cockran journal 1830-31, 14, 28 October 1830.

142 "Die": *ibid.*, 28 October 1830; "prosper": CMS A85, Cockran journal 1832-33, 28 August 1832.

143 CMS reel A85, Cockran journal 1830-31, 14 June 1831.
144 CMS A85, Cockran journal 1833-34, 5 February 1834 p. 40; see also West, *Substance of a Journal*, p. 117 (West claimed that the depletion of large game around Red River was "a favorable circumstance leading [the Natives] . . . to the cultivation of the soil, which would then expand their minds, and prove of vast advantage . . . in aiding their comprehension of Christianity"). Cockran's statement that the Master of Life had taken the animals away is in CMS A85, Cockran journal, 28 October 1830.
145 CMS reel A85, Cockran journal 1830-31, 31 May 1831.
146 *Ibid.*, 24 May 1831.
147 CMS A77/M45, p. 454, Cockran to Secretaries of the CMS, 25 February 1832.
148 CMS A85, Cockran journal 1834-35, 18 December 1835, p. 30. See also the incident cited in Podruchny, "Indians and Missionaries in Encounter," p. 43, in which Cockran threatened a non-Christian man whose daughter died in the 1835 influenza epidemic that more of his children might die unless he converted!
149 CMS A85, Cockran journal 1833-34, 25 September 1833.
150 *Ibid.*, 1830-31, 2 February 1831.
151 CMS A77, M45, Cockran to Secretaries of the CMS, 25 February 1832.
152 Czuboka, "St. Peter's," p. 45, citing CMS records for 1834.
153 School attendance: CMS A96, Smithurst, "Report of the CMS Station Indian Settlement Red River 1841"; CMS A96, Smithurst, 25 March and 26 October 1842, and 1842 Report of Mission Stations to CMS. "Prejudice": CMS M64, Smithurst to CMS, 15 November 1839.
154 Ross, *The Red River Settlement*, p. 13; CMS reel M64, Smithurst to CMS, 15 November 1839; J.J. Hargrave, 1871, quoted in A.I. Hallowell, "The Passing of the Midewiwin," *American Anthropologist* 38 (1936):41.
155 "Help for the sick": Martha McCarthy, *To Evangelize the Nations: Roman Catholic Missions in Manitoba 1818-1870* (Papers in Manitoba History Report No. 2, Manitoba Culture, Heritage and Recreation, Historic Resources, 1990), p. 78 (see also pp. 75-86); Ross, *The Red River Settlement*, pp. 286-87; Leo Waisberg and Marie-Ange Beaudry, "Manitou Mounds: Historical Evaluation of the Mission Lot," in *A Historical Synthesis of the Manitou Mounds Site on the Rainy River* (Manuscript report, Parks Canada, 1984), p. 10.
156 PAM SP v. 24, p. 7,587, 20 May 1822, Red River, George Simpson to Andrew Colvile.

CHAPTER 5

1 "Saved": Ray, *Indians in the Fur Trade*, p. 190. See also: HBCA B.159/a/17, Fort Pelly Journal 1837-38, 20 September 1837; Dempsey, *Big Bear*, p. 16.
2 HBCA B.159/a/17, Fort Pelly Journal 1837-38, 30 October, 2 November 1837; Dempsey, *Big Bear*, p. 16.
3 Dempsey, *Big Bear*, p. 17, states that the Blackfoot were harder hit than the Cree. Milloy, *The Plains Cree*, p. 71, also expresses this opinion. Decker, "'We Should Never Again be the Same People,'" p. 57, contradicts this, giving a mortality figure greater than fifty percent for Cree as well as Blackfoot. More detailed studies of this epidemic that are better grounded in the cultural history of the region than Decker's are required for certain estimates.
4 Albers, "Pluralism in the Native Plains," pp. 46-48.
5 Dempsey, *Big Bear*, p. 16.
6 H.Y. Hind, *Narrative of the Red River Exploring Expedition of 1857-58* (New York: Greenwood Press Publishers, 1969), vol. 2, p. 121.
7 Hind, *Narrative of the Red River Exploring Expedition*, p. 311; Dempsey, *Big Bear*, p. 17; CMS A95, Settee to CMS, 14 September 1857. Ray, *Indians in the Fur Trade*, pp. 182-87, reaches slightly different conclusions regarding population movements, though his general pattern matches mine.

8 HBCA B.159/a/18, Fort Pelly Journal 1853-54; Fort Pelly Journal 1855-57, Fort Pelly Journal 1852-53 (microfilm copy of this journal consulted at HBCA and cited by kind permission of the Lake of the Woods Museum).

9 Two hundred tents: Fort Pelly Journal 1855-57, 7 July 1856. Finlayson sketch: HBCA E.12/5, fo. 73. On fishing, see Brian Smith, "The Historical and Archaeological Evidence for the Use of Fish."

10 Rudolph F. Kurz, *Journal of Rudolph Friederich Kurz*, ed. J.N.B. Hewitt, trans. Myrtis Jarrell, Bureau of American Ethnology Bulletin 115 (Washington: Smithsonian Institution, 1937), pp. 84-85; Mandelbaum, *The Plains Cree*, pp. 52, 55, 77; Ewers, *Ethnological Report on the Chippewa-Cree Tribe of the Rocky Boy Reservation*, p. 64; CMS A95, Charles Pratt journal 1852-53, 25 August 1852.

11 Quotations given are from Fort Pelly Journal 1852-53, 8 December 1852, and Fort Pelly Journal 1855-57, 21 January 1856. See also CMS A95, Pratt to Bishop of Rupert's Land, 21 February 1856 (on Christmas Day of 1855, Charles Pratt met four camps of Ojibwa and Cree on the plains). Other Guard Post references: Isaac Cowie, *The Company of Adventurers: A Narrative of Seven Years in the Service of the Hudson's Bay Company . . .* (Toronto: William Briggs, 1913), p. 419; HBCA B.62/a/1, Guard Post/Egg Lake Journal 1853-54, 20, 27 November 1853. Annual cycle references: Dempsey, *Big Bear*, pp. 32-37; Mandelbaum, *The Plains Cree*, p. 77.

12 Dempsey, *Big Bear*, pp. 36, 26.

13 Howard, "The Identity and Demography of the Plains-Ojibwa," p. 171.

14 Paul Kane, *Wanderings of an Artist among the Indians of North America* (Edmonton: M.G. Hurtig Ltd., 1968), p. 86. I wish to note again that while, for purposes of analyzing change and continuity among the Saulteaux, I have focused on plains aspects of Cree culture as a foil, even "plains" Cree culture contained a strong parkland component, and the Cree moved readily across ecological zones.

15 David W. Penney and Janet Stouffer, "Horse Imagery in Native American Art," in *Great Lakes Indian Art*, ed. David W. Penney (Detroit: Wayne State University Press, 1989), p. 44; Mandelbaum, *The Plains Cree*, p. 63.

16 Dempsey, *Big Bear*, pp. 18-19; CMS A95, Charles Pratt journal at Fort Pelly 1859-60, 11 June 1859. It should be pointed out here that Ojibwa also continued to trade horses: see, for example, Fort Pelly Journal 1855-57, 25 April 1856.

17 Dempsey, *Big Bear*, pp. 22-25.

18 Skinner, "Political and Ceremonial Organizations of the Plains Ojibway," pp. 482-93; Howard, *The Plains Ojibwa or Bungi*, pp. 21, 60-65.

19 Dempsey, *Big Bear*, pp. 23, 28.

20 The Kane portrait of Black Powder, held by the Royal Ontario Museum, bears the accession number ROM 946.15.54.

21 Kurz, *Journal*, plate 21; and see Kurz, *Journal*, pp. 84-85.

22 *Ibid.*, p. 85. In a footnote to this (p. 85, n. 25), Kurz notes that the clothing received on that occasion was "for the most part . . . gay-colored military coats of red, blue, or green cloth and shirts of soft white deerskin, either laced or richly embroidered with colors."

23 Ted J. Brasser, "Backrest Banners among the Plains Cree and Plains Ojibwa," *American Indian Art Magazine* (Winter 1984). The banner is Glenbow Museum cat. no. AP-1525.

24 *Ibid.*, "Backrest Banners," p. 56; Skinner, "Political and Ceremonial Organizations of the Plains Ojibway," p. 488; and Howard, *The Plains Ojibwa or Bungi*, p. 24 (a bison-caller or poundmaker who "carried a flag or banner of red strouding to signal the buffalo"). Howard (*The Plains Ojibwa of Bungi*, pp. 51-52), also discusses other horned headdresses, of which he says the Bungi were very fond.

25 HBCA B.159/a/12, Fort Pelly Journal 1831-32, 6 October 1831.

26 Dempsey, *Big Bear*, pp. 25, 84.

27 Hind, *Narrative of the Red River Exploring Expedition*, vol. 2, pp. 145-46. See also Henry, pp. 511-12 (states that Cree did not have clans).

28 See, for instance, Fort Pelly Journal 1852-53, 5 September 1852; HBCA B.63/a/4, Fort Ellice Journal 1858-59, 12 September 1858; Hugh Dempsey, ed., *The Rundle Journals 1840-48* (Calgary: Historical Society of Alberta and the Glenbow-Alberta Institute, 1977), p. 50; CMS A95, Settee Journal 1855-56, Shoal River, 20 August 1855.

29 These objects are in the collection of the British Museum, accession numbers 2252 (board) and 2223 (drum). The board is illustrated in *The Spirit Sings: A Catalogue of the Exhibition*, p. 88. I would also like to acknowledge personal communication with Dr. Jonathan King, Assistant Keeper, Department of Ethnology, British Museum. The wooden board is believed to have been used as a mnemonic device during the Wabano ceremony, although it is also similar to one depicted by Rindisbacher in his painting of a Chippewa scalp dance. See illustration and discussion in Ted Brasser, "By the Power of their Dreams: Artistic Traditions of the Northern Plains," *The Spirit Sings: Artistic Traditions of Canada's First Peoples* (Toronto: McClelland and Stewart, 1987), pp. 129-30.

30 "Wreak havoc": Dempsey, *Big Bear*, p. 21; "treat the sick": Mandelbaum, *The Plains Cree*, p. 165. This challenges Howard's statement that the Plains Ojibwa developed a different "psychology" and were less concerned with "magic power" than their Ojibwa relatives and ancestors (Howard, "Identity and Demography of the Plains-Ojibwa," p. 172). Howard's statement stemmed from his belief in the total cultural replacement among these people, which I am also challenging.

31 Mandelbaum, *The Plains Cree*, p. 164-65.

32 Dempsey, *The Rundle Journals*, p. 50, entry for 17 January 1841.

33 Rindisbacher: "A family from the Tribe of the wild Sautaux Indians, on the Red River" (PAC C-1935) and "Chippewa Mode of Travelling in the Spring and Summer," West Point Military Museum; Finlayson, "Souteaux Family in the Plains," HBCA E.12/5, fo. 73. These images depict the straps themselves or the straight-cut, decorated neckline typical of such dresses; Rindisbacher's may also depict the separate sleeves used with such dresses. The Kurz illustration is in Kurz, *Journals*, pp. 84-85, plates 21 (lower), 23 (upper). The woman shown in the strap dress in plate 23 is Ojibwa (or "Sauteuse," as marked on the original sketch), which matches the date July 27, 1851, beside her, when a group of Red River Ojibwa departed from Ft. Berthold (p. 85). This identical dress does re-occur in another Kurz sketch as "Cree," however; see "Cree Indians and Whites in the chief trader's office, Ft. Union," Gilcrease Institute of American History and Art, cat. no. 1326.1093 and published in Swagerty, "Indian Trade in the Trans-Mississippi West to 1870," p. 370.

34 Catlin's portrait of Kay-a-gis-gis (National Museum of American Art, Smithsonian Institution, cat. no. 1988.66.183) is illustrated in Karlis Karklins, *Trade Ornament Usage among the Native Peoples of Canada: A Source Book* (Ottawa: Parks Service, 1992), p. 123.

35 See also Kurz, *Journals*, p. 156, on the older style of Cree women's dresses ("The Cree woman's garment is like that of the Sauteurs women; i.e., shoulders and arms bare, skirt held up by means of bands or straps. When the weather is cold they put on sleeves that are knotted together in the back at the nape of the neck and on the breast"). See also Hail, *Hau, Kola!*, pp. 88-89; Henry, pp. 514-15; and Mandelbaum, *The Plains Cree*, p. 83, on types of Cree dresses.

36 See, for example, *The Spirit Sings: A Catalogue of the Exhibition*, p. 61, fig. W 108, an Ojibwa medicine doll ("Visually, the reduction of the body to a triangular torso and simplified tubular limbs is a sculptural analogue to the pictographic outlines of Midewiwin scrolls and song boards"). See also the designs on the Royal Ontario Museum war club, thought to be consistent with "an early Western Great Lakes Ojibwa origin" (p. 83, fig. P 53).

37 Manitoba Museum of Man and Nature, Kane/Allen collection, #H4-41-25. I would like to express my gratitude to Dr. Katherine Pettipas, Curator, Department of Native Ethnology, for permission to examine and photograph objects from this collection.

38 Erica Smith, "Something More than Mere Ornament," pp. 85-87; Penney, "Floral Decoration and Culture Change," p. 54 ("If clothing design is functionally related to personal and social identities, innovations . . . must be tied to changes in such identities among American Indians").

39 The seminal interpretations of this process of ethnic "mixture" and genesis are found in: Albers, "Pluralism on the Native Plains," pp. 47-48; and Sharrock, "Crees, Cree-Assiniboines, and Assiniboines."

40 One Ojibwa elder stated that, when his ancestor first arrived at what is now Sakimay reserve, "He could see all kinds of buffaloes. . . . There were all kinds of elk on the other side of the hill." Later in his narrative, the elder mentioned harvesting fish, rabbits, ducks, and partridge in this area (Koozma Tarasoff, *Persistent Ceremonialism: The Plains Cree and Saulteaux*, Canadian Ethnology Service, Mercury Series No. 69 [Ottawa: National Museums of Canada, 1980], pp. 174-77).

41 On the use of this region by both Ojibwa and Cree, see: Mandelbaum, *The Plains Cree*, p. 77 (re: the Cree use of this area); CMS A97, Stagg journal 1856 to January 1857, 25 December 1857, notes an Ojibwa camp of twenty tents seven miles from Fort Pelly; CMS A95, Pratt to Reverend A. Cowley, 21 February 1855, notes that on Christmas day 1855 there were four camps of Cree and Ojibwa in the plains near the Qu'Appelle Lakes; Fort Pelly Journal 1855-56, 21 January 1856, notes a large camp of Ojibwa in the midst of the bison at Devil's Lake; HBCA B.159/a/18, Fort Pelly Journal 1853-54, 27 April 1854 (Ojibwa come in to post from the Touchwood Hills after the winter); CMS A95, Pratt journal 1855-56 at Pelly, 15 September 1855 and 6 October, Ojibwa at Touchwood Hills and Qu'Appelle Lakes.

42 CMS A95, Pratt journal 1856-57, 22 November (Ojibwa wintering at Qu'Appelle Lake); Glenbow Archives M1531, "Journal of Daily Occurrences at Fort Qu'Appelle Lake, 1857-58," collected by A.S. Morton (mentions Ojibwa wintering in Qu'Appelle Lakes district; also some arrive from the plains with pemmican, 22 September, 5 October); Fort Pelly Journal 1855-57, 7 July, mentions a camp of 200 tents of Cree and Ojibwa in the middle of the bison, about four days from the Touchwood Hills post.

43 CMS A95, Pratt journal 1859-60, 22 May at Little Touchwood Hills, Ojibwa and Cree planting gardens, 17 June 1859.

44 Brian Smith, "The Historical and Archaeological Evidence for the Use of Fish," p. 45.

45 Hind, *Narrative of the Canadian Red River Exploring Expedition*, p. 311.

46 See Brian Smith, "The Lebret Site," p. 364 ("Some Cree bands, such as the Cree-Assiniboin, were closely tied to a typical bison-oriented lifestyle centred on the Grasslands while others, such as the Calling River and Touchwood Hills people, were utilizing both the Grasslands and the Valley complexes in these areas").

47 Mandelbaum, *The Plains Cree*, pp. 76, 92.

48 Earth Elder's band, for instance, which was based at Strawberry Lake, kept south of the Qu'Appelle River and ranged south to Buffalo Lodge and west to the Cypress Hills (see Wolfe, *Earth Elder Stories*, pp. 22-23).

49 CMS A95, Pratt journal 1855-56, 14 October at Qu'Appelle Lakes. Collections of western Ojibwa artifacts examined included those at the Royal Ontario Museum, the Manitoba Museum of Man and Nature, the Glenbow-Alberta Institute, the Alberta Provincial Museum, and the Canadian Museum of Civilization. See also Tarasoff, *Persistent Ceremonialism*.

50 Mandelbaum, *The Plains Cree*, p. 165; see also Mandelbaum, pp. 313, 212-214; Alanson Skinner, "Notes on the Plains Cree," *American Anthropologist* 16 (1914):77-78.

51 Hind, *Narrative of the Canadian Red River Exploring Expedition*, pp. 108-09, 179; HBCA B.159/a/18, Fort Pelly Journal 1853-54, 27 November 1853, 24 February 1854 (bison in Touchwood Hills).

52 Ray, *Indians in the Fur Trade*, pp. 212-13; Dempsey, *Big Bear*, p. 16; Milloy, *The Plains Cree*, pp.104-05.

53 Milloy, *The Plains Cree*, pp. 103-18; Hind, *Narrative of the Canadian Red River Exploring Expedition*, p. 108.

54 Fort Pelly Journal 1855-57, 7 July 1856; CMS A95, Pratt journal 1859-60, 30 July 1859.

55 Hickerson and Wheeler-Voegelin, *The Red Lake and Pembina Chippewa*, p. 174; Hind, *Narrative of the Canadian Red River Exploring Expedition*, p. 179; E.E. Rich, ed., *London Correspondence Inward from Eden Colvile, 1849-52* (London: Hudson's Bay Record Society, 1956), p. xxxvi.

56 "Threats and lectures": Hind, *Narrative of the Canadian Red River Exploring Expedition*, pp. 334, 360. See also: Cowie, *Company of Adventurers*, p. 334; John L. Tobias, "Canada's Subjugation of the Plains Cree," *Canadian Historical Review* 64/4 (1983):523; Milloy, *The Plains Cree*, p. 108.

57 Hind, *Narrative of the Canadian Red River Exploring Expedition*, p. 108; Hickerson and Wheeler-Voegelin, *The Red Lake and Pembina Chippewa*, p. 156.

58 Ray, *Indians in the Fur Trade*, p. 205-06.

59 Ewers, *Ethnological Report on the Chippewa-Cree Tribe of the Rocky Boy Reservation*, p. 68; Ross, *The Red River Settlement*, p. 269; Kane, *Wanderings of an Artist*, pp. 55-56 (as a result of Sioux attacks, "the Saulteaux do not venture to hunt in the plains except in company with the half-breeds"); Hickerson and Wheeler-Voegelin, *The Red Lake and Pembina Chippewa*, p. 201; Howard, *The Plains Ojibwa or Bungi*, p. 10 (Métis usually acted with the full-bloods at Turtle Mountain).

60 Kurz, *Journals*, pp. 84-85; Ewers, *Ethnological Report on the Chippewa Cree Tribe of the Rocky Boy Reservation*, p. 64, quoting Kurz (this was a trading party as well).

61 Gregory Camp, "The Turtle Mountain Plains-Chippewa and Métis, 1797-1935" (Ph.D. dissertation, University of New Mexico, 1987), pp. 73-74.

62 Ewers, *Ethnological Report on the Chippewa-Cree Tribe*, p. 60; Hickerson and Wheeler-Voegelin, *The Red Lake and Pembina Chippewa*, p. 143.

63 E.g., Kane, *Wanderings of an Artist*, p. 55.

64 Hickerson and Wheeler-Voegelin, *The Red Lake and Pembina Chippewa*, pp.168-69 (driving herd away), and pp.137, 165; Ross, *The Red River Settlement*, pp. 269-71, 324-30.

65 Some of the material in this section on Red River is taken from Laura Peers, "The Saulteaux, Red River, and the Forks, 1770-1870" (paper presented at the "Focus On the Forks" conference, Winnipeg, 1991).

66 Ross, *The Red River Settlement*, pp. 331-32; Kane, *Wanderings of an Artist*, p. 49; CMS A96, Smithurst journal, 1845-46, entries 1, 2 September; PAM MG2 C38, Peter Garrioch journal, typescript, pp. 54-55 (Sioux party was The Burnt Ground and his young men). Some of the details of this incident are unclear. Garrioch claims that the Sioux was shot by "a Soutoux of the Upper Catholic Missouri" rather than a local Ojibwa. Smithurst, on the other hand, claims that the Sioux delegation was attacked by several hundred local Ojibwa, and that he himself spoke to Peguis afterwards about giving the murderer up (which contradicts Ross), implying that the shooting was by one of Peguis's band. (CMS A78, Smithurst journal, August 1845 to March 1846, 1, 2 September 1845). Other conflicts between Red River Ojibwa and Sioux are recorded in 1842 and 1844; this last was probably unrelated to the 1844 incident, which led to the hanging (CMS A96, Smithurst journal, 7 July 1842; CMS A96, Smithurst journal August 1843-February 1844, 15 September 1844).

67 Ross, *The Red River Settlement*, p. 331.

68 *Ibid.*, p. 160.

69 Cited in Morton, "Introduction," *London Correspondence Inward from Eden Colvile*, ed. E.E. Rich (London: Hudson's Bay Record Society, 1956), p. xiv; see also map of Red River in Gerald Friesen, *The Canadian Prairies.*

70 Cited in Morton, "Introduction," *London Correspondence Inward from Eden Colvile, 1849-52*, p. xxi.

71 HBCA B.239/z/10, fo. 45.

72 Jean Friesen, "Grant Me Wherewith to Make My Living" (unpublished research report for Treaty and Aboriginal Rights Research [TARR] of Manitoba, 1985), pp. 4-5.

73 Ross, *The Red River Settlement*, p. 330; H.J. Warre, "Fort Garry, June 7-16, 1845," plate 10, in Warre, *Overland to Oregon in 1845: Impressions of a Journey across North America*, ed. Madeleine Major-Fregeau (Ottawa: Public Archives of Canada, 1976), p. 23.

74 John McDougall, account of conversation with Thomas Truthwaite, *Winnipeg Free Press*, 30 April 1909, quoted in Jean Friesen, "Grant Me Wherewith to Make My Living," pp. 49-50.

75 Penney, "Floral Decoration and Culture Change," p. 61. Penney gives several examples of clothing style employed "as a symbol of mediation between Indians and whites" and "for calculated political effect," and notes that clothing style was re-assessed by Native peoples over the eighteenth and nineteenth centuries "in light of continuing pressures by whites – missionaries who wanted to convert them, authorities who wanted to control them, neighbors who were afraid of them" (p. 62).

76 HBCA B.239/n/1, Lower Red River District Returns 1841-61.

77 Holzkamm, Lytwyn, and Waisberg, "Rainy River Sturgeon," pp. 200-01.

78 Bison hunt: CMS A96 Smithurst, "Report of the Indian Settlement Station R.R. etc. 1843" (most students in plains with parents). Fishery: CMS A96, Smithurst journal August 1842-February 1843, 11 January 1843; CMS A96, Smithurst journal, 10 July 1842; CMS A96, Smithurst journal August 1845 to March 1846, 24 October, 30 November, 14 December 1845; CMS A97, Smithurst journal August 1847 to August 1848, 19 September 1847; CMS A96, Smithurst journal 1839-40, 2 March 1840; Morton, "Introduction," *London Correspondence Inward from Eden Colvile*, p. xiii.

79 Dempsey, "Peguis," p. 626, states that Peguis was baptised in 1840. CMS A96, Smithurst journal 1843-44, 24 December 1843, notes that Peguis wanted to be admitted as a communicant, which he had desired for three years.

80 CMS PAM M64, Smithurst to CMS, 2 November 1840. See also: CMS A96, Smithurst journal 1843-44; CMS A96 Smithurst journal, August 1842 to February 1843; CMS A97, Smithurst journal 1847-48; CMS A96, "Report of the Indian Settlement Station R.R. etc. 1843."

81 CMS A96, Smithurst, "Report of the Indian Settlement Station R.R. etc. 1843."

82 CMS A96, Smithurst journal, 4 May 1842; see also entry for 11 May.

83 "Best clothes": CMS A97, Smithurst, 1843 Missions Report, section on Red River. Rabbitskin clothing: CMS A96, Smithurst journal August 1843-1844, 19 February 1844.

84 McCarthy, *To Evangelize the Nations*, p. 90. See also Camp, "The Turtle Mountain Plains-Chippewas and Metis, 1797-1935," pp. 89-92.

85 McCarthy, *To Evangelize the Nations*, pp. 87, 88.

86 *Ibid.*, pp. 88, 90.

87 "Persuaded": Reverend A.C. Garrioch, *First Furrows: A History of the Early Settlement of the Red River Country* (Winnipeg: Stock Co. Ltd., 1923), p. 92; see also p. 94. Hind, *Narrative of the Canadian Red River Exploring Expedition*, vol. 1, pp. 204-05, states that the inhabitants of this settlement were "Plain and Swampy Crees and half-breeds." Like Baie St. Paul before it, more research is needed on this community.

88 Garrioch, *First Furrows*, pp. 95-97. Pachetoo seems to have been the same individual as Kissoway, an Ojibwa (or Métis) trader (PAM MG 12 A1, Archibald Papers, no. 784, n.d., "Draft Notes," implies that Pachetoo and Kasisheway, "a half-breed trader," are the same individual). MG12 B2, Morris K no. 153, 8 July 1876, Morris to the Minister of the Interior, mentions a "Kassowayis," a Saulteaux trader, brother to Yellow Quill; and John E. Foster, "The Saulteaux and the Numbered Treaties: An Aboriginal Rights Position?" in *The Spirit of the Alberta Indian*

Treaties, ed. Richard Price (Edmonton: Pica Pica Press, 1987 [1979]), pp. 168-69, notes that Kissoway, "the noted Saulteau free trader," was a brother of The Gambler and was also involved in treaty negotiations with Yellow Quill's band. These are likely all the same individual. Some confusion is introduced by John Neufeld's article "Picheito, Manitoba's Last Saulteaux-Cree war chief" (Indian Record 48 [2], 1985, pp.19-20), which claims that Pachetoo was the son of John Tanner, and was also known as "Gambler Tanner." Pachetoo seems to have had both Ojibwa and Métis connections; it is uncertain how he would have identified himself.

89 Hind, *Narrative of the Canadian Red River Exploring Expedition*, p. 283, quoted in Brian Smith, "The Lebret Site," p. 289.

90 CMS A96, Smithurst journal, 13 May 1840.

91 HBCA B.239/z/10, "Indian Population of Sundry Districts," "Saulteaux Attached to New Fort Garry, 1838"; CMS A96, Smithurst, Report of CMS Station, Indian settlement, Red River, 1 August 1841.

92 Kane, *Wanderings of An Artist*, p. 69. The dog feast does not appear in Kane's origina log (Stark Museum of Art, no. 11.85/4).

93 CMS (PAM M64), Smithurst to CMS, 2 August 1841; CMS A96, Smithurst journal August to November 1846, 7 July 1846. See also the references to Ojibwa notions of baptism in chapter 4 (this volume).

94 CMS A97 Stagg journal, 20 June 1854.

95 Mink prices: HBCA B.63/d/3, Upper Red River Accounts 1850, fo. 50; HBCA B.159/z/1, Swan River misc. 1858-59, fos. 24d-25. Muskrat prices: HBCA B.63/d/3, Upper Red River Accounts 1850, fo. 50; HBCA B.159/z/1, Swan River misc. 1858-59, fos. 24d-25; *Nor'Wester* 28 December 1859, p. 3. Prices may have been slightly different at Manitoba Post, but not much.

96 Fur prices: see HBCA B.239/h/2, District Returns 1842-68. Free traders: CMS A97, Stagg Journals 1854 to late 1850s.

97 Dissatisfaction: HBCA B.159/a/17, Fort Pelly Journal 1837-38, 17 February 1838. The missionaries themselves gave out some clothing, but it is uncertain how much they gave and whether what they did give was useful for winter in the region. See also David F. Aberle and George E. Simpson, "Cultural Deprivation and Millenial Movements: A Discussion," in *Cultural and Social Anthropology: Selected Readings*, ed. Peter B. Hammond (New York: Macmillan Co., 1965).

98 Sugar: CMS A97, Stagg journal 1854, Fairford Mission, 14 March. Gardening: CMS A95, Settee journal 1855-56, trip through Lake Winnipeg, entry for 13 October 1855; CMS A95, Settee journal 1856-57, 6 October 1856. Hunting: CMS A97, Stagg journal, January 1857 to April 1858, 12, 14, 21 February 1857, 25 January 1858. Fishing: CMS A97, Stagg journal, January 1857 to April 1858, Fairford Mission, 6, 14 November 1857; CMS A95 Settee journal 1856-57, Fairford mission, autumn fishery at "Kesiscachwaness," Little Swift Current River; CMS A97, Stagg journal 1855-56, Fairford, 18 August, 22 September 1855; Belcourt to Bishop of Quebec, *Notice sur les missions du diocese de Quebec* no. 4, January 1842 (Quebec: Frechette et Cie.), letter dated 9 November 1840, p. 5. Eggs, waterfowl: Kane, *Wanderings of An Artist*, pp. 70, 73; Belcourt to Bishop, *Notice sur les missions*, letter dated 9 November 1840, p. 5.

99 Cumberland House: CMS A96, Mr. H. Budd's Answers to Questions Relative to His Mission, 1841, p. 20. Elsewhere, see CMS (PAM M64), Smithurst to CMS, 22 December 1843; Belcourt to Bishop of Quebec, 9 November 1840, in *Notice sur les missions*, p. 5; Hind, *Narrative of the Canadian Red River Exploring Expedition*, vol. 1, pp. 119, 490, vol. 2, p. 27, 31 (including 1857 references).

100 Bishop, "Cultural and Biological Adaptations to Deprivation," p. 209.

101 *Ibid.*, p. 221, citing Rogers (the eighty-eight moose taken in a season by the Weagamow Lake Ojibwa in 1958-59 produced over 35,000 pounds of meat, while 7,500 hare produced only 11,200 pounds).

102 See, for instance, Aberle and Simpson, "Cultural Deprivation and Millenial Movements"; and the early literature on Melanesian cargo cults, especially Peter Worsley, *The Trumpet Shall Sound: A Study of Cargo Cults in Melanesia*, 2nd, augmented edition (New York: Schocken Books, 1968). For a recent re-assessment of such interpretations, see John D. Kelly and Martha Kaplan, "History, Structure, and Ritual," *Annual Review of Anthropology* 19 (1990):129-36.

103 Christopher Hanks, "The Swampy Cree and the Hudson's Bay Company at Oxford House," *Ethnohistory* 29/2 (1982):109.

104 Mary Black (Rogers), "Ojibwa Power Belief Systems," in *The Anthropology of Power*, ed. R.D. Fogelson and R.N. Adams (New York: Academic Press, 1977), p. 145.

105 "Nearly all": CMS A97, Annual Letter, Stagg to CMS, 25 August 1857. See also McCarthy, *To Evangelize the Nations*, p. 106.

106 CMS A86, Reverend Cowley to Reverend Davies, 17 July 1846 (re: ceremonial activities around the Partridge Crop); CMS A95, Settee journal 1856-57, 17 September, 6 October 1856; CMS A97, Stagg journal, January 1857 to April 1858, Fairford, 25 October 1857; CMS A95, Stagg journal 1855-56, Fairford, 13 September 1855; "ridiculous practices": Belcourt to Bishop of Quebec, 9 November 1840, pp. 6-9, 11, *Notice sur les missions*. Kane, in *Wanderings of an Artist*, pp. 47-48, describes what was likely a Midewiwin lodge and ceremony in progress at Fort Alexander, 11 June 1846; and see Hallowell, "The Passing of the Midewiwin in the Lake Winnipeg Region," pp. 32-51. According to Hallowell, Midewiwin ceremonies were held at Garden Island until the 1870s (pp. 37-38); at Black Island, until at least 1932 (pp. 44-45); Dog Head, until late century (p. 46); Jack Head, same (p. 47); Berens River until ca. 1870 (pp. 48-49).

107 CMS A97, Stagg journal 1855-56, Fairford, 19 February 1856.

108 *Ibid.*, Stagg journal 1859-60, 17 October 1859. See also John Webster Grant, *Moon of Wintertime: Missionaries and the Indians of Canada in Encounter since 1534* (Toronto: University of Toronto Press, 1984), p. 134 (re: conflict between Native and Missionary authority in mission situations, and the resultant frustration among converts).

109 CMS A97, Stagg journal, Fairford, January 1857–April 1858, 13 March 1858; CMS A97, Stagg journal 1859-60, Fairford, 17 October 1859.

110 CMS A97, Stagg journal, January 1857–April 1858, Fairford, 25 October 1857; CMS A95, Stagg journal 1855-56, Fairford, 13 September 1855.

111 Rabbitskin as warm as cloth: CMS A97, Stagg journal 1855-56, Fairford Mission, 12 August 1855. The missionary perspective on rabbitskin clothing is expressed in CMS A96, Smithurst journal 1843-44, Indian Settlement Red River, 19 February 1844, in which a Saulteaux is said to look "like a wild beast" in his fur robes. On Native versus European clothing and its political meaning, see Penney, "Floral Decoration and Culture Change," pp. 60-62.

112 CMS A97, Stagg journal, Fairford, June 1859–June 1860, 28 October; see also entries for 20 and 23 November. There is no evidence that Christianity was seen in this situation as another type of medicine society, other than the syncretic belief in the healing and protective powers of Christian rituals and ritual objects, as has been suggested as a possible response to missionization (see George Hammell, "Strawberries, Floating Islands, and Rabbit Captains: Mythical Realities and European Contact in the Northeast During the Sixteenth and Seventeenth Centuries," *Journal of Canadian Studies* 21/4 [1986-87]:89).

113 Other Ojibwa from as far away as the Rocky Mountains and Red Lake visited the Catholic mission in the 1840s to learn more about Christian beliefs and powers (cited in McCarthy, *To Evangelize the Nations*, pp. 82, 84, 103).

114 CMS A97, Stagg journal, Fairford, 7 December 1854; see similar incident in CMS A97, Stagg journal, Fairford, 16 November 1855. Interestingly, this syncretic use of Christian power occurred at a fishery. At Rainy River, the Ojibwa worried that the fish would leave the fishery if a Christian mission were established there (Waisberg and Beaudry, *Manitou Mounds*, p. 34).

115 Father Edouard Darveau, 1843, cited in McCarthy, *To Evangelize the Nations*, p. 109.
116 Tissot, quoted in McCarthy, *To Evangelize the Nations*, p. 119; statement to Darveau quoted in McCarthy, *To Evangelize the Nations*, p. 108. See also Agasgokat's "double-barelled gun" metaphor, in McCarthy, *To Evangelize the Nations*, p.109.
117 "God will rain": CMS A95, James Settee journal 1855-56, 14 June 1856, near Berens House; CMS A97, Stagg journal 1855-56, Fairford, 19 February 1856; Stagg journal, Fairford, 1856-57, 5 August 1856. Similar prophecies were recorded by Cowley in 1850 in which it was said that "[the Indians] are henceforth to receive supplies from the clouds that all the white people are to die, and that the Indians are to be in affluent circumstances" (CMS A86, Cowley journal 1849-50, 15 June 1850).
118 Jennifer S.H. Brown, "Abishabis," *Dictionary of Canadian Biography*, vol. 7 (Toronto: University of Toronto Press, 1988), pp. 3-4; Jennifer S.H. Brown, "The Track to Heaven: The Hudson's Bay Cree Religious Movement of 1842-43," *Papers of the Thirteenth Algonquian Conference*, ed. William Cowan (Ottawa: Carleton University, 1982), pp. 53-63; John Webster Grant, "Missionaries and Messiahs," pp. 125-36.
119 John Webster Grant, *Moon of Wintertime*, pp. 129, 134.
120 CMS A85, Cockran journal, 28 October 1830.
121 On the fates of the ceremonial leaders, see: CMS A86, Cowley journal 1850-51, 28 February 1851, and CMS A97, Stagg journal 1856-57, 16 and 23 November 1856; cited in "Fairford Mission," research report on file with Manitoba Historical Resources. Hind, *Narrative of the Canadian Red River Exploring Expedition*, vol. 2, pp. 36-37.
122 John Webster Grant has observed that other such prophecies have been agents of "revitalization rather than merely of adaptation or of stubborn resistance" (*Moon of Wintertime*, p. 132). See also Hammell, "Strawberries, Floating Islands, and Rabbit Captains," p. 85, and pp. 84, 86, 89.
123 John S. Long, "*Manitu*, Power, Books, and *Wihtikow*," p. 2.
124 Fort Pelly Journal 1847-48, 10 May 1848; HBCA B.27/a/23, Fort Carlton Journal 1838-39.
125 CMS A97, Stagg to CMS, 25 August 1857; CMS A96, Smithurst journal 1843; Dempsey, *The Rundle Journals*, p. 50, entry for 17 January 1841; John Webseter Grant, *Moon of Wintertime*, p. 102. Belcourt's success at Duck Bay is described in McCarthy, *To Evangelize the Nations*, pp. 102, 104; the threat to his life is mentioned in Belcourt to Bishop of Quebec, 9 November 1840, *Notice sur les missions*, p. 4.
126 "Presents": CMS A96, Smithurst to CMS, 1 August 1845. "Prejudices": CMS A95, Settee journal 1855-56, 13 April 1856. "Obstinate": CMS A95, Pratt journal 1859-60, 29 May 1860.
127 "Keep off": CMS A95, Settee journal 1854-55, 18 May 1855. Weir: CMS A95, Settee journal, 4 August 1860. Pratt at Pelly Journal 1859-60, 11 June (re: horses stolen), 12 November 1859. "Go back": CMS A95, Pratt journal, Fort Pelly, 12 August 1851.
128 Midewiwin locations: CMS A95, Pratt journal 1855-56, 14 October 1855, at Qu'Appelle Lake; Fort Pelly Journal 1852-53, 5 September 1852; HBCA B.63/a/4, Fort Ellice Journal 1858, 12 September; Dempsey, *The Rundle Journals*, p. 50. Other ceremonies: CMS A95, Settee journal 1855-56, Shoal River, 20 August 1855; Dempsey, *Big Bear*, pp. 25, 84.
129 "Spoilt saucy": Fort Pelly Journal 1855-57, 2 February 1856. "Prosperity": CMS A95, Settee journal 1855-56, 2 April 1856. "Independent": CMS A96, Smithurst, Report of the CMS Station at Fort Ellice, 1843.
130 Fort Pelly Journals 1852-53, 1855-57; HBCA B.159/a/18, Fort Pelly Journal 1853-54; CMS A95, Settee journal 1854-55; HBCA B.2/a/1, Fort-à-la-Corne Journal 1851-52, and HBCA B.2/a/2, Fort-à-la-Corne Journal 1852-53; Ray, "Indian Exploitation of the Forest-Grassland Transition Zone in Western Canada 1650-1860," p. 239.
131 Sugar: Fort Pelly Journal 1852-53, 3 April 1853. Gardens: CMS A95, Settee journal, Swan River, 25 April 1865 (Coté's garden about fifteen miles from Pelly; another garden at the "Crow-stand").

132 "Pitched off": HBCA B.159/a/18, Fort Pelly Journal 1853-54, 5 May 1854. Moose kills: Fort Pelly Journals 1852-53 and 1853-54. Moose hides traded: HBCA B.159/d/37b, Fort Pelly Accounts 1844 (curiously, Pelly accounts for the early 1850s do not show all the moose that are mentioned in the journals). "Staff of life": Peter Grant, "The Saulteaux Indians about 1804," p. 341. Parts of the following paragraphs are adapted from Peers, "Changing Resource-Use Patterns of Saulteaux Trading at Fort Pelly, 1821-70."

133 HBCA B.239/h/2 (759 large elk and deer hides were traded in 1843, as well as 3,000 buffalo robes; these figures were exceeded only by the Saskatchewan District returns).

134 Horse stolen: CMS A95, Pratt journal 1859-60, 11 June. Bison-hunting areas: HBCA B.159/a/ 18, Fort Pelly Journal 1853-54, 27 November 1853, 24 February 1854; CMS A95, Pratt journal 1856-57, 3 October, 18 November 1856. Moving to plains/Touchwood Hills in winter: Fort Pelly Journal 1855-57, 2-5 December 1856; Ray, *Indians in the Fur Trade,* pp. 220-21.

135 Ray, *Indians in the Fur Trade*, p. 224; Fort Pelly Journal 1852-53, 27, 28 December 1852; Fort Pelly Journal 1855-57, 2-5 December 1856; HBCA B.159/a/19, Fort Pelly Journal 1853-54, 19 November 1853, 22 March 1854.

136 Fort Pelly Journal 1852-53, 22 March 1853. Long, "*Manitu,* Power, Books, and *Wihtikow,*" p. 13.

137 Fort Pelly Journal 1855-57, 4 December 1856.

138 Ray, *Indians in the Fur Trade*, p. 222; Bishop, "Cultural and Biological Adaptations to Deprivation," p. 221; "some claim": HBCA B.159/a/13, Fort Pelly Journal 1831-32, 19 February 1832. See also Cowie, *Company of Adventurers*, p. 419.

139 Gerald Friesen, *The Canadian Prairies*, p.130; Ray, *Indians in the Fur Trade*, p. 224 (HBC supplying provisions to prevent Indians from going after bison in mid-winter). One might also add to this debate Patricia Shifferd's conclusion that, for the Wisconsin Chippewa after 1850, "The increasing importance of cash over barter did not . . . result in any fundamental economic or cultural discontinuity" ("A Study in Economic Change, the Chippewa of Northern Wisconsin," *Western Canadian Journal of Anthropology* 6/4 (1976):16).

140 "Considerably more than": Fort Pelly Journal 1847-48, 10 January 1848. "Empty stores": Fort Pelly Journal 1847-48, 11 May 1848. Debts: Fort Pelly Journal 1852-53, 20 September 1852; Fort Pelly Journal 1855-57, 24 March, 10 April 1856; HBCA B.159/a/18, Fort Pelly Journal 1853-54, 20 February 1854. Even during the bad winter of 1855-56, Young Stutterie paid three debts over the winter (Fort Pelly Journal 1855-56, 5, 24 March 1856). See also Ray, *Indians in the Fur Trade*, pp. 220-24.

141 Gerald Friesen, *The Canadian Prairies*, pp. 100-01.

142 Innis, *The Fur Trade in Canada*, p. 331; Morton, "Introduction," in *Correspondence Inward from Eden Colvile*, p. lxxxii.

143 HBCA B.159/a/18, Fort Pelly Journal 1853-54; CMS A97, Stagg Journal 1854- 55, 1855-56, 1856-57, 1857-58; Irene Spry, "The Transition from a Nomadic to a Settled Economy in Western Canada, 1856-95," *Transactions of the Royal Society of Canada*, vol. 6, series 4, June 1968, section 2, p. 188.

144 "Anxious": HBCA B.159/a/18. Fort Pelly Journal 1853-54, 10 October 1853; see also HBCA B.62/a/1, Guard Post (Egg Lake), 12 November 1853. Refuse to pay debts: Fort Pelly Journal 1852-53, 8 December 1852; Fort Pelly Journal 1855-1857, 21 January 1856. Refused to sell at tariff: HBCA B.62/a/1, Guard Post Journal 1853, 20 November.

145 CMS A95, Settee Journal 1854-55, 25 October 1854; Fort Pelly Journal 1855-1857, 2 February 1856.

146 "Customary gratuity": Fort Pelly Journal 1855-1857, 11 April 1856; Saucy Fellow: Fort Pelly Journal, 20 September 1856 (doesn't say how much he got for this meat). See also: Fort Pelly Journal 1855-57, 11 April, 14 August, 20 September 1856; Fort Pelly Journal 1852-53, 18, 20, 25 September 1852, 12 April 1853; HBCA B.159/a/18, Fort Pelly Journal 1853-54, 2 December 1853; CMS A95, Settee journal, Pelly, 23 April 1861 (Coté murders a man during a drinking bout).

147 "Row with Saulteaux Indians": Fort Pelly Journal 1852-53, 25 September 1852; see also HBCA B.159/a/18, Fort Pelly Journal 1853-54, 22 August 1853.
148 Camp, "The Turtle Mountain Plains-Chippewas and Metis," pp. 74-75, quoting speech of Green Setting Feather. General references on Turtle Mountain in this era: Hickerson and Wheeler-Voegelin, *The Red Lake and Pembina Chippewa*, pp. 165, 150-51; Camp, "The Turtle Mountain Plains-Chippewas and Metis."
149 Camp, "The Turtle Mountain Plains-Chippewas and Metis," pp. 85-86, 95.
150 Gregory Camp, "Working Out their own Salvation: The Allotment of Land in Severalty and the Turtle Mountain Chippewa Band, 1870-1920," *American Indian Culture and Research Journal* 14/2 (1990):21.

CHAPTER 6

1 Richard Huyda, *Camera in the Interior: H.L. Hime, Photographer* (Toronto: Coach House Press, 1975), plates 28, 29.
2 Huyda, *Camera in the Interior*, plates 30, 31. On the Point Douglas graveyard, see: Henry, p. 46, August 1800 ("the old graves, of which there are many"); McDermott, "Peguis Refuted"; and John West, cited in Rodger Guinn, *The Red-Assiniboine Junction: A Land Use and Structural History* (Parks Canada: Manuscript and Record Series No. 355, 1980), p. 25, who noted in August 1821 that Ojibwa were burying their dead at the Forks with grave goods.
3 Hind, *Narrative of the Canadian Red River Exploring Expedition*, vol. 1, p. 202, and vol. 2, p. 123; "Indian Incantations," *Nor'Wester,* 14 June 1860; Hallowell, "The Passing of the Midewiwin," pp. 41-42; CMS A95, Settee journal, Scanterbury, 1868-69, 14 December 1868 referring to Netley Creek Indians.
4 These items are in the Canadian Museum of Civilization, nos. V-X-243, collected by Dr. Robert Bell in 1879. Documentation on these artifacts includes a mention of guns being fired during the ceremony and offerings being made to Pakuk, or Bony Spectre, the spirit to whom the ceremony is dedicated. Howard, *The Plains Ojibwa or Bungi*, p. 88, notes that "Miniature bows and arrows . . . are still a common offering for children to make to Paguk or Bony Spectre in the Trade dance ceremony." See also discussion and references in *The Plains Ojibwa or Bungi*, pp. 112-14; Brown and Brightman, *Orders of the Dreamed*, p. 111; Nick Johnson, "Bits of Dough, Twigs of Fire," in *Stone, Bones and Skin* (ArtsCanada, December 1973/January 1974), pp. 61-69; and Hind, *Narrative of the Canadian Red River Exploring Expedition*, vol. 1, p. 403.
5 Flood: Walter Traill, *In Rupert's Land: Memoirs of Walter Traill*, ed. Mae Atwood (Toronto: McClelland and Stewart, 1970), p. 38. "Refractory": Hind, *Narrative of the Canadian Red River Exploring Expedition*, p. 281.
6 Huyda, *Camera in the Interior*, plate 15; Traill, *In Rupert's Land*, p. 141.
7 Minutes of Council of Assiniboia meeting, 30 May 1865, in E.H. Oliver, ed., *The Canadian North-West – Its Early Development and Legislative Records: Minutes of the Council of the Red River Colony*, vol. 1 (Ottawa: Government Printing Bureau, 1914), p. 555.
8 Jean Friesen, "Grant Me Wherewith to Make My Living," p. 17; Traill, *In Rupert's Land*, p. 39.
9 Traill, *In Rupert's Land*, p. 43.
10 CMS A97, Stagg journal, Fairford 1859-60, 24 September, 3, 7, 25 October, 14 November; CMS A95, Settee journal, Scanterbury, November 1867, March 1868; Hind, *Narrative of the Canadian Red River Exploring Expedition*, vol. 1, pp. 124, 490, vol. 2, pp. 27, 31 (Garden Island).
11 CMS A95, Settee journal, Scanterbury, 1868-69 (incident at Jack Head, 23 September, and winter and spring at Scanterbury); CMS A97, Stagg journal 1859-60, Fairford, 16 October 1859.

12 "Thunderbird": CMS A95, Settee journal, Scanterbury, 1868-69, 1 July 1868; "run about": CMS A97, Stagg to CMS, 24 August 1860. The *Nor'Wester* also reported a *Windigo* killing at Jack Head in 1860, but this is not confirmed by any of the missionaries in the region ("Heartless Murder," 28 March 1860, and "Horrible Case of Cannibalism," 14 June 1860). Hind, *Narrative of the Canadian Red River Exploring Expedition*, vol. 2, pp. 36-37, notes some fifteen houses of converts at Fairford in the late 1850s.

13 Traill, *In Rupert's Land*, p. 54, 1867 (herds are usually three days' travel from Fort Qu'Appelle, but [p. 57] Touchwood Hills are no longer good for bison); HBCA B.63/a/8, Fort Ellice Journal 1864-65, 16 September 1864 (bison are near Fort Ellice, but by 4 November are far away on plains); Ray, *Indians in the Fur Trade*, p. 223 (Touchwood Hills the northernmost point where bison abundant in mid-winter after late 1850s, and by late 1860s are found only south of the Qu'Appelle River); Cowie, *Company of Adventurers*, p. 187, says people winter "near the herds" at Turtle or Moose Mountain; James Southesk, Earl of Carnegie, *Saskatchewan and the Rocky Mountains: A Diary and Narrative of Travel, Sports, and Adventure . . .* (Toronto: James Campbell, 1875), p. 59, 2 July 1859, mentions a group of Ojibwa waiting at Fort Qu'Appelle for the rest of their band before going to the plains with "the main body of their tribe"; Erasmus, *Buffalo Days and Nights*, p. 213.

14 Captain John Palliser, *Papers Relative to the Exploration by Captain Palliser . . .* (London: Eyre and Spottiswode, 1859), p. 14.

15 Skinner, "Political and Ceremonial Organizations of the Plains Ojibway," pp. 491-92; Hime photo, "The Prairie Looking West," in Huyda, *Camera in the Interior*, plate 44. See also Cowie, *Company of Adventurers*, p. 305 (re: late 1860s); Traill, *In Rupert's Land*, pp. 86-87 (re: 1867); CMS A95, Settee journal, Fort Pelly, 19 May, 12 July 1861; CMS A95, Pratt journal 1859-60, 30 July; Dempsey, *Big Bear*, p. 26; Hugh Dempsey, *Red Crow: Warrior Chief* (Lincoln: University of Nebraska Press, 1980), pp. 29-80; Cowie, *Company of Adventurers*, p. 305.

16 Hind, *Narrative of the Canadian Red River Exploring Expedition*, pp. 360, 334; CMS A95, Settee to CMS, 6 February 1862; Sharrock, "Crees, Cree-Assiniboines, and Assiniboines," p. 113. See also: Tobias, "Subjugation," p. 523; Spry, "Transition"; Traill, *In Rupert's Land*, p. 166; Cowie, *Company of Adventurers*, p. 445.

17 Traill Papers, Glenbow Archives, "1866? summer."

18 Cowie reference in Sharrock, "Crees, Cree-Assiniboines, and Assiniboines," pp. 112-14; Traill Papers, Glenbow Archives, "1866? Summer"; Tobias, "Subjugation," p. 523.

19 Hind, *Narrative of the Canadian Red River Exploring Expedition*, p. 121. John Milloy, "Our Country: Significance of the Buffalo Resource for a Plains Cree Sense of Territory," in *Aboriginal Resource Use in Canada: Historical and Legal Aspects*, ed. Kerry Abel and Jean Friesen (Winnipeg: University of Manitoba Press, 1991), p. 65. See also Mandelbaum, *The Plains Cree*, p. 68.

20 Traill Papers, Glenbow Archives, "1866? Summer" (re: camp of about 300 tents Crees, Saulteaux, Assiniboines near Cypress Hills). See also Sharrock, "Crees, Cree-Assiniboines, and Assiniboines," pp. 113-14.

21 Erasmus, *Buffalo Days and Nights*, p. 241. Hind, *Narrative of the Canadian Red River Exploring Expedition*, pp. 323-24 ("An Ojibwa remains always an Ojibwa, and Swampy Cree a Swampy Cree, in the eyes of the haughty and independent children of the prairies [the Cree]"). See also Hind, *Narrative of the Canadian Red River Exploring Expedition*, p.122.

22 Morris, *Treaties of Canada with the Indians*, p. 174.

23 Skinner, "The Cultural Position of the Plains Ojibway," and "Political and Ceremonial Organizations of the Plains Ojibway"; Howard, *The Plains Ojibwa or Bungi*. Some eastern bands of Ojibwa and Menomini did adopt a formal policing body, who controlled the wild-rice harvest, comparable to the role of the *okitcitak* among the western Ojibwa (Skinner, "The Plains Ojibway," pp. 498-99).

24 Skinner, "Political and Ceremonial Organization of the Plains Ojibway," p. 509; Howard, *The Plains Ojibwa or Bungi*, pp. 62, 63, 104.
25 Skinner, "Political and Ceremonial Organization of the Plains Ojibway," pp. 484, 490; Penney and Stouffer, "Horse Imagery in Native American Art," pp. 40-51.
26 Headdress: Royal Ontario Museum no. HK 469, Morris collection (collected ca. 1900-14); and see Howard, *The Plains Ojibwa or Bungi*, p. 63 ("The chiefs, councilors, and members of the *okitsita* were exempted from all camp work").
27 Skinner, "Political and Ceremonial Organization of the Plains Ojibway," p. 488.
28 Southesk, *Saskatchewan and the Rocky Mountains*, 2 July 1859, p. 60; Hail, *Hau, Kola!*, pp. 88-89; Mandelbaum, *The Plains Cree*, p. 272. Howard claims that Plains Ojibwa women did adopt northern plains-style dresses after 1850, but gives no concrete evidence of this (*The Plains-Ojibwa or Bungi*, [1965], p. 50).
29 Southesk, *Saskatchewan and the Rocky Mountains*, p. 61.
30 Hail, *Hau, Kola!*, p. 71. The shirt is Hafenreffer Museum cat. no. 77-17.
31 Hail, in *Hau, Kola!*, cites a similar shirt in Howard, *The Plains Ojibwa or Bungi*, plate 13, worn by a Turtle Mountain chief. The Royal Ontario Museum shirt is no. HK 585, Morris collection (bequest of Edmund Morris, son of Alexander Morris).
32 CMS A95, Settee journal, Fort Pelly 1861-62, 26 May 1861.
33 "Best customers": Traill, *In Rupert's Land*, pp. 129-30. See also: Kenneth Tyler, "Paskwaw," *Dictionary of Canadian Biography*, vol. 11 (Toronto: University of Toronto Press, 1982), pp. 674-75 (said to live around Leech Lake, Saskatchewan, with a band of Plains Saulteaux); HBCA B.159/a/1, Fort Pelly Returns 1861, fos. 266, 266d; W.H. Long, ed., *Fort Pelly Journal of Daily Occurrences, 1863* (Regina: Transcribed and published by the Regina Archaeological Society, 1987), pp. 88, 94.
34 Traill, *In Rupert's Land*, pp. 131-32; Pasqua tent, Glenbow Museum no. P1014-2409 (documentation on the Pasqua tent notes, "Old Pasqua was told by a young bison that if he painted these designs on his tipi he would always have many bison").
35 Shortage of provisions: Traill, *In Rupert's Land*, p. 122; "rich in furs," p. 138. See also W.H. Long, *Fort Pelly Journal of Daily Occurrences*, 14 December 1863, 10 February 1864; Cowie, *Company of Adventurers*, p. 362 ("furred animals were abundant in the hunting grounds of the Fort Pelly Indians" in 1868-69).
36 Erasmus, *Buffalo Days and Nights*, pp. 190-91; compare with HBCA B.49/d/102, Fur Prices, Fort-à-la-Corne, 1869. Monetary conversion between currencies is difficult for the nineteenth century. Figures range from a value of 1 pound sterling = $4.44, $4.86, $5.30 (personal communication, W.R. Swagerty, University of Idaho, W. Brown, University of Winnipeg); A.B. McCullough, *Money and Exchange in Canada to 1900* (Toronto: Dundurn Press, 1984), p. 292. Innis, *The Fur Trade in Canada*, p. 331, gives the American Fur Co. price for fisher in 1857 as $2, and the Hudson's Bay Company price 2/.
37 HBC Posts: CMS A95, Settee journal January-February 1865, 7 February; CMS A95, Settee journal, Fort Pelly, 2, 9 February, 22 March 1861; HBCA B.60/e/9, Saskatchewan District Report 1862. Free traders: Cowie, *Company of Adventurers*, p. 362; Traill, *In Rupert's Land*, p. 100; HBCA B.2/a/5, Fort-à-la-Corne 1868, 5 December; W.H. Long, *Fort Pelly Journal of Daily Occurrences*, 30 November 1863, p. 20.
38 HBCA B.2/d/2, Fort-à-la-Corne 1864-67 (notation inside front cover of book).
39 See Traill, *In Rupert's Land*; W.H. Long, *Fort Pelly Journal of Daily Occurrences*; HBCA B.63/a/6, Fort Ellice Journal 1862-63; Ray, *Indians in the Fur Trade*, p. 224.
40 See, for example, W.H. Long, *Fort Pelly Journal of Daily Occurrences*, 14 November 1863.
41 *Ibid.* ("unable to Kill Moose," p. 16; trading rum for pemmican, 28 December 1863, p. 34; see also entries for 21 January, 10 February 1864); HBCA B.63/a/10, Fort Ellice Journal 1868-69, 26 February 1869; Traill Papers, Glenbow Archives, Walter Traill to Mrs. C.P. Traill (postscript), Fort Ellice, 2 January 1868.

42 "Exchanged the autonomy": Gerald Friesen, *The Canadian Prairies*, p. 130; Traill, *In Rupert's Land*, p. 143. See also Ray, *Indians in the Fur Trade*, pp. 224-25. W.H. Long, *Fort Pelly Journal of Daily Occurrences*, gives constant examples of Ojibwa purchasing and trading for pemmican as well.

43 W.H. Long, *Fort Pelly Journal of Daily Occurrences*, 20 November 1863; Traill Papers, Glenbow Museum, Fort Ellice diary typescript, p. 3, 8 August 1864 (many ducks; "plenty of Elk Moose & Antelopes here in Winter," and mention of a productive weir [although Hudson's Bay Company station men prevented Indians from using it]). "Teeming": Traill, *In Rupert's Land*, p. 134; see also p. 81 ("The Indians get plenty of fish from the barriers they place in the [Qu'Appelle and area] lakes"). Gardens: Hind, *Narrative of the Canadian Red River Exploring Expedition*, vol. 1, p. 432.

44 W.H. Long, *Fort Pelly Journal of Daily Occurrences*, 28 January 1864 (trading 88 rabbits for pemmican), and p. 48, 1 February 1864; "luckily numerous": 14 Dec 1863, p. 27.

45 Cowie, *Company of Adventurers*, p. 362.

46 HBCA B.159/a/13, Fort Pelly Journal 1831-32, 19 February 1832.

47 W.H. Long, *Fort Pelly Journal of Daily Occurrences*, 30 January 1864.

48 Traill, *In Rupert's Land*, pp. 122, 126.

49 *Ibid.* (re: Ft. Qu'Appelle), pp. 65-66 (all prices up by at least 1d. for fresh and dried meat, pemmican, fowl, and rabbits); re: Riding Mountain: pp. 126, 132-34.

50 "d——d Rascals": HBCA B.2/d/2, Fort-à-la-Corne Accounts 1864-67; "very difficult to deal with": Traill, *In Rupert's Land*, p. 146.

51 Foster, "The Saulteaux and the Numbered Treaties." Some of the plains Ojibwa, of course, were caught in the same dilemma as the plains Cree during the treaty negotiations, but most Ojibwa were somewhat better off.

52 CMS A95, Settee journal, Fort Pelly, 9 January 1862, 14 June 1863. See also Erasmus, *Buffalo Days and Nights*, p. 190.

53 CMS A95, Settee journal, Fort Pelly, 22 June, 18 August 1861.

54 *Ibid.*, at Shoal River, 25 July 1863.

55 HBCA B.63/a/4, Fort Ellice Post Journal 1858-59, 12 September 1859; CMS A95, Settee journal, Fort Pelly, 8 October 1861, 8 May 1862; Traill Papers, Glenbow Archives (Fort Ellice, 8 August 1864, detailed description of lodge, dog feast, offerings, and "shooting").

56 Conversions: Gabriel Coté was an early convert; Settee converted Nasuhwung, a medicine man and husband of a "noted conjuror" (CMS A95, Settee journal, Fort Pelly, 8 May 1862). Thomas Manitou Keesik: Cowie, *Company of Adventurers*, p. 368.

57 CMS A95, Settee journal, Fort Pelly, 11 April 1860.

58 Hind, *Narrative of the Canadian Red River Exploring Expedition*, vol. 2, p. 176; "Indian Manifesto," *Nor'Wester*, 15 April 1861.

59 Hind, *Narrative of the Canadian Red River Exploring Expedition*, vol. 2, pp. 173-75.

60 *Ibid.*, p. 176; McDermott, "Peguis Refuted." See also: Donald Gunn, "The Land Controversy," *Nor'Wester*, 28 June 1860; and Jean Friesen, "Grant Me Wherewith to Make My Living."

61 This and the following several paragraphs are adapted from Peers, "The Saulteaux, Red River, and the Forks, 1770-1870" (paper presented at the "Focus on the Forks" conference, Winnipeg, spring 1991).

62 Anderson, *Kinsmen of Another Kind*, pp. 255-60; Peter Douglas Elias, *The Dakota of the Canadian Northwest: Lessons for Survival* (Winnipeg: University of Manitoba Press, 1988), pp. 16-17.

63 Anderson, *Kinsmen of Another Kind*, pp. 261-20; Elias, *The Dakota of the Canadian Northwest*, pp. 20-21.

64 Elias, *The Dakota of the Canadian Northwest*, pp. 21-22. Other Dakota bands had already crossed the border by then and were settling in the Turtle Mountain and Souris River valley (pp. 20-21). See also Morris, *Treaties of Canada with the Indians*, pp. 276-84.

65 Council of Assiniboia meeting: Oliver, *The Canadian Northwest*, pp. 511-17, 532-33; Elias, *The Dakota of the Canadian Northwest*, p. 27.

66 "A lot of trouble": Howard, *The Canadian Sioux*, p. 43. Ogimauwinini account in Skinner, "Plains-Ojibway," p. 485. This account suggests that the presence of the Sioux may have kept many war customs alive for the Ojibwa through the last decades of the nineteenth century. It also challenges somewhat Elias's claim that the Ojibwa distinguished between refugee and enemy bands of Sioux.

67 Morris, *Treaties of Canada with the Indians*, p. 278; Elias, *The Dakota of the Canadian Northwest*, pp. 27, 29.

68 Elias, *The Dakota of the Canadian Northwest*, p. 29; Oliver, *The Canadian Northwest*, pp. 566-67 (re: Meeting of the Governor and Council of Assiniboia, 23 June 1866). Dakota account of ceremony: Howard, *The Canadian Sioux*, pp. 43-44.

69 "Resentment": Cowie, *Company of Adventurers*, p. 446 (referring to "refugee Yankton Sioux under White Cap and Standing Buffalo, who had been hunting north of the line and trading at Fort Ellice for a number of years," and writing of delegates from Sitting Bull's band of Sioux who came to ask for refuge in the 1870s). "Industrious": Cowie, *Company of Adventurers*, pp. 187-88. See also: HBCA B.63/a/10, Fort Ellice Journal 1868-69, 25 November 1868 (there are Sioux in the Moose Mountains and about Fort Ellice, trapping); Traill, *In Rupert's Land*, p. 166, were many Sioux at and around Fort Ellice in 1869, and p. 88, Sioux raid on Fort Qu'Appelle horses.

70 Traill Papers, Glenbow Archives, letter from Fort Ellice, 8 August 1864.

71 That the Ojibwa in the Red River area knew of these things is suggested by Palliser, who stated that the Saskatchewan Indians were aware of treaties in the American plains, that they were concerned for the future, and that they were "opposed to the country becoming settled up like the Red River, which many have seen and all have heard of" (Palliser, *Further Papers Relative to the Exploration of British North America* [London: Eyre and Spottiswoode, 1859], p. 48).

72 Gerald Friesen, *The Canadian Prairies*, p. 133, quoting Cowie, *Company of Adventurers*.

73 PAM MG12 B1, Morris (Lieutenant-Governor's) Collection, 24 August 1873, Edward McKay to Morris.

74 Coté incident: CMS A95, Settee journal, Fort Pelly, 3 September 1860. See also CMS A95, Settee journal, Fort Pelly, 16 July 1861 (HBC trying to prohibit sale of liquor in Pelly region, hopes free traders will follow example).

75 CMS A97, Stagg to CMS, Fairford Mission, 24 August 1860.

76 CMS A95, Settee journal, Swan Lake, 16 November 1863.

77 CMS A97, Stagg to CMS, Fairford Mission, 24 August 1860.

78 CMS A95, Settee journal, Scanterbury, 27 July, 14 August, 2 September 1868.

79 CMS A95, Settee to CMS, 25 November 1868; "fish belong to Indians": Cowie, *Company of Adventurers*, p. 419.

80 Thompson, *Chief Peguis and His Descendants*, p. 36; Morris, *Treaties of Canada with the Indians*, pp. 26-27; Jean Friesen, "Grant Me Wherewith to Make My Living," pp. 65-66. Ojibwa far away from Red River were disturbed by the events of 1869-70. According to Isaac Cowie, *Company of Adventurers*, p. 398, Ojibwa from Egg and Nut Lakes refused to trade their furs because they were upset by rumours from Red River.

81 Quoted in Jean Friesen, "Grant Me Wherewith to Make My Living," p. 65.

82 Tobias, "Canada's Subjugation of the Plains Cree," p. 520; and he cites Morris, *Treaties of Canada with the Indians*, p. 37 (uneasiness among settlers "arising partly from the often-repeated demands of the Indians for a treaty with themselves, and partly from the fact that certain settlers in the neighborhood of Portage la Prairie and other parts of the Province, had been warned by the Indians not to cut wood or otherwise take possession of the lands upon which they were squatting").

83 Jean Friesen, "Grant Me Wherewith to Make My Living," pp. 67-68.

84 Morris, *Treaties of Canada with the Indians*, p. 31.

85 Quotation and data from Jean Friesen, "Grant Me Wherewith to Make My Living," in *Aboriginal Resource Use in Canada: Historical and Legal Aspects*, ed. Kerry Abel and Jean Friesen (Winnipeg: University of Manitoba Press, 1991), p.143. See also Morris, *Treaties of Canada with the Indians*, p. 29.

86 NAC RG 10 v. 3,604, file 2,553, R#C10104, Petition from St. Peter's Saulteaux and Cree to Governor General of Canada, 15 October 1873. See also: Jean Friesen, "Grant Me Wherewith to Make My Living"; Thompson, *Chief Peguis and His Descendants*, pp. 38-46; and the "Report of St. Peter's Indian Reserve Commission 1911," Manitoba Legislative Library.

87 Foster, "The Saulteaux and the Numbered Treaties," pp. 165-67.

88 George McDougall to Lieutenant-Governor A. Morris, 23 October 1875, in Morris, *Treaties of Canada with the Indians*, p. 174. McDougall was a long-time missionary among the plains Cree and other western tribes.

89 PAM MG12 B1, Morris Collection, #524, Robert Bell to Alexander Morris, 14 October 1873; PAM MG12 B1, Morris Letterbook K, #370, 4 December 1876, Morris to Minister of the Interior.

90 PAM, MG12 B1, Morris Collection, #1247, 20 April 1876 (signed Little Child, Little Black Bear, Blade Bone, Ne-ca-ta-ne-kau).

91 Sarah Carter, *Lost Harvests: Prairie Indian Reserve Farmers and Government Policy* (Montreal: McGill-Queen's, 1990). See also Shifferd, "A Study in Economic Change: The Chippewa of Northern Wisconsin, 1854-1900," *Western Canadian Journal of Anthropology* 6/4 (1976), who concludes that Chippewa in this region were able to adjust to enormous economic, social, and political changes in the latter half of the nineteenth century without suffering "massive social breakdown."

CONCLUSION

1 James, *A Narrative of the Captivity and Adventures of John Tanner*; Tarasoff, *Persistent Ceremonialism*; Wolfe, *Earth Elder Stories*.

2 Quoted in Bee, *Patterns and Processes*, p. 198.

3 CMS A95 Settee journal, Fort Pelly, 6 December 1861. See also Dempsey, *Big Bear*, pp. 37-38 (re: the Native interpretation of the removal of a meteorite).

4 Susan Sharrock, "Preface," *Western Canadian Journal of Anthropology* 7/4 (1977):1.

5 See: Ritterbush, "Culture Change and Continuity," p. 153; and Sharrock, "Preface."

6 In doing so, I have followed the example set by A.J. Ray, who, in *Indians in the Fur Trade*, examined interactions within a broad region. Ritterbush, in "Culture Change and Continuity," p. 16, also notes the importance of environmental and human links in the northern plains, and their prominent absence from classic ethnographies.

References Cited

PRIMARY SOURCES: ARCHIVAL

Hudson's Bay Company Archives, Winnipeg (HBCA)

B.2/a Fort-à-la-Corne Journals
B.3/a Fort Albany Journals
B.4/a Fort Alexander Post Journals
B.22/a Brandon House Journals
B.22/e Brandon House / Red River District Reports
B.24/a Buckingham House Journals
B.27/a Fort Carlton Journals
B.27/e Carlton District Reports
B.49/a Cumberland House Journals
B.49/e Cumberland District Reports
B.51/a Fort Dauphin Journals
B.51/e Fort Dauphin District Reports
B.53/a Post Doubtful Journal
B.60/a Edmonton Journals
B.60/e Edmonton District Reports
B.62/a Egg Lake Journals
B.63/a Fort Ellice Journals
B.104/a Lac la Biche Journals
B.115/a Lesser Slave Lake Journals
B.115/e Lesser Slave Lake District Reports
B.122/a Lake Manitoba Post Journals (Big Point House, Manitoba House)
B.148/a Nipawin Journals
B.159/a Fort Pelly Journals
B.159/e Fort Pelly / Swan River District Reports
B.160/a Pembina Post Journals
B.165/a Fort Pitt Journals
B.176/a Red Deer River Post Journals
B.197/a Setting River / Carlton House Journals
B.213/a Swan River Journals

B.235/a Winnipeg (Red River) Post Journals
B.236/a Lake Winnipeg Post Journal
Fort Pelly Journals for 1847-48, 1852-53, and 1855-1857 were consulted on microfilm at the HBCA and are quoted here by kind permission of the Lake of the Woods Museum.

Provincial Archives of Manitoba (PAM)

PAM MG1 D3, Peter Fidler, "Journal at the Red River Settlement 1814-15."
PAM MG2 C38, Peter Garrioch Journal 1843-47
PAM MG12 A1, Archibald Papers
Selkirk Papers (SP), microfilm copy
Morris Papers
Church Missionary Society Papers (CMS), microfilm copy
Nor'Wester, microfilm copy
"Report of St. Peter's Indian Reserve Commission 1911," Manitoba Legislative Library.

Glenbow-Alberta Institute, Archives

M1531, "Journal of Daily Occurrences at Fort Qu'Appelle Lake, 1857-58" collected by A.S. Morton
Traill Papers.
Baldwin Room, Metropolitan Toronto Reference Library
George Nelson Papers. Transcripts kindly provided by Dr. Jennifer S.H. Brown, University of Winnipeg.

PRIMARY SOURCES: PUBLISHED

Bain, James, ed. *Travels and Adventures in Canada and the Indian Territories between the Years 1760 and 1776.* 1901. Reprinted, New York: Burt Franklin Press, 1969.
Cameron, Duncan. "The Nipigon Country." In *Les Bourgeois de la Compagnie du Nord-Ouest.* Vol. 2, ed. L.R. Masson. New York: Antiquarian Press, Ltd., 1960.
Catlin, George. *Illustrations of the Manners, Customs, and Condition of the North American Indians.* 2 vols. 10th edn. London: Henry G. Bohn, 1866.
Chaboillez, Charles: see Hickerson, Harold, ed.
Coues, Elliot, ed. *New Light on the Early History of the Greater North West: The Manuscript Journals of Alexander Henry.* Minneapolis: Ross and Haines, 1965.
Cowie, Isaac. *The Company of Adventurers: A Narrative of Seven Years in the Service of the Hudson's Bay Company. . . .* Toronto: William Briggs, 1913.
Dempsey, Hugh, ed. *The Rundle Journals 1840-48.* Calgary: Historical Society of Alberta and the Glenbow-Alberta Institute, 1977.
"Diary of Nicholas Garry, Deputy-Governor of the Hudson's Bay Company from 1822-1835." *Transactions of the Royal Society of Canada.* Section 2, 1900.
Erasmus, Peter. *Buffalo Days and Nights,* ed. Irene Spry. Calgary: Glenbow- Alberta Institute, 1976.
Fleming, R. Harvey, ed. *Minutes of Council Northern Department of Rupert Land, 1821-31.* Toronto: Champlain Society, 1940.
Glover, Richard, ed. *David Thompson's Narrative.* Vol. 40. Toronto: The Champlain Society, 1962.
Grant, Peter. "The Saulteaux Indians about 1804." In *Les Bourgeois de la Compagnie du Nord-Ouest.* Vol. 2, ed. L.R. Masson. New York: Antiquarian Press, Ltd., 1960.
Henry, Alexander (Younger): see Coues, Elliot, ed.

Hickerson, Harold, ed. "Journal of Charles Jean Baptiste Chaboillez, 1797-98." *Ethnohistory* 6/3, 4 (1959).

Hind, H.Y. *Narrative of the Red River Exploring Expedition of 1857-58.* New York: Greenwood Press Publishers, 1969.

James, Edwin, ed. *A Narrative of the Captivity and Adventures of John Tanner.* Minneapolis: Ross and Haines, 1956.

Johnson, Alice, ed. *Saskatchewan Journals and Correspondence.* Vol. 26. London: Hudson's Bay Company Record Society, 1967.

Kane, Lucille, June Holmquist, and Carolyn Gilman, eds. *The Northern Expeditions of Stephen H. Long.* St. Paul: Minnesota Historical Society Press, 1978.

Kane, Paul. *Wanderings of an Artist among the Indians of North America.* Edmonton: M.G. Hurtig Ltd., 1968.

Kurz, Rudolph F. *Journal of Rudolph Friederich Kurz.*, ed. J.N.B. Hewitt, trans. Myrtis Jarrell. Bureau of American Ethnology Bulletin 115. Washington, D.C.: Smithsonian Institution, 1937.

Lambe, W.K., ed. *The Journals and Letters of Alexander Mackenzie.* Toronto: Macmillan, 1970.

Long, John. *Voyages and Travels of an Indian Interpreter and Trader.* 1791. Reprinted, Vendôme: Imprimerie des Presses Universitaires de France-Vendôme, 1968.

Long, W.H., ed. *Fort Pelly Journal of Daily Occurrences 1863.* Regina: Transcribed and published by the Regina Archaeological Society, 1987.

Macdonell, John. "Some Account of the Red River about 1797." In *Early Fur Trade on the Northern Plains*, ed. W.R. Wood and T. Thiessen. Norman: University of Oklahoma Press, 1985.

——. "Some Account of the Red River (about 1797) with Extracts from his Journal 1793-95." In *Les Bourgeous de la Compagnie du Nord-Ouest*, ed. L.R. Masson. New York: Antiquarian Press Ltd., 1960.

Mackenzie, Sir Alexander. *Voyages from Montreal on the River St. Laurence through the Continent of North America. . .* 1801. Reprinted, Toronto: Radisson Society of Canada, 1927.

McKenzie, Charles. "Narratives." In *In Early Fur Trade on the Northern Plains*, ed. W.R. Wood and T. Thiessen. Norman: University of Oklahoma Press, 1985.

Morton, A.S. *The Journal of Duncan M'Gillivray of the North West Company at Fort George on the Saskatchewan, 1794-95.* Toronto: Macmillan, 1929.

Moulton, Gary E., ed. *The Journals of the Lewis and Clark Expedition, August 25, 1804–April 6, 1805.* Lincoln: University of Nebraska Press, 1987.

Notice sur les missions du diocese de Quebec. No. 4. Quebec: Frechette et Cie, January 1842.

Nute, Grace Lee, ed. *Documents Relating to Northwest Missions 1815-1827.* St. Paul: Minnesota Historical Society, 1942.

Oliver, E.H., ed. *The Canadian North-West – Its Early Development and Legislative Records: Minutes of the Council of the Red River Colony.* Vol. 1. Ottawa: Government Printing Bureau, 1914.

Palliser, Captain John. *Papers Relative to the Exploration by Captain Palliser . . .* London: Eyre and Spottiswode, 1859.

——. *Further Papers Relative to the Exploration of British North America.* London: Eyre and Spottiswoode, 1859.

Pond, Samuel W. *The Dakota or Sioux in Minnesota as They Were in 1834.* 1908. Reprinted, St. Paul: Minnesota Historical Society Press, 1986.

Rich, E.E., ed. *James Isham's Observations on Hudson's Bay, 1743.* London: Hudson's Bay Record Society, 1949.

——, ed. *London Correspondence Inward from Eden Colvile 1849-52.* London: Hudson's Bay Record Society, 1956.

Southesk, James, Earl of Carnegie. *Saskatchewan and the Rocky Mountains: A Diary and Narrative of Travel, Sports, and Adventure . . .* Toronto: James Campbell, 1875.

Statement Respecting the Earl of Selkirk's Settlement upon the Red River in North America. 1817. Reprinted, Johnson Reprint Corp., 1968.

Tanner, John: see James, Edwin, ed.

Thwaites, R.G., ed. *Early Western Travels 1746-1846.* Vol. 2, *John Long's Journal 1768-1782.* Cleveland: The Arthur H. Clark Company, 1904.

Traill, Walter. *In Rupert's Land: Memoirs of Walter Traill,* ed. Mae Atwood. Toronto: McClelland and Stewart, 1970.

Warre, H.J. *Overland to Oregon in 1845: Impressions of a Journey across North America,* ed. Madeleine Major-Fregeau. Ottawa: Public Archives of Canada, 1976.

West, Reverend John. *The Substance of a Journal during a Residence at the Red River Colony.* New York: S.R. Publishers, Ltd., Johnson Reprint Corp., 1966.

SECONDARY SOURCES

Aberle, David F., and George E. Simpson. "Cultural Deprivation and Millenial Movements: A Discussion." In *Cultural and Social Anthropology: Selected Readings,* ed. Peter Hammond. New York: Macmillan, 1965.

Albers, Patricia. "Pluralism on the Native Plains 1670-1870." Ms. on file at St. Paul's College Library, University of Manitoba. Substantially revised and published as "Symbiosis, Merger and War: Contrasting Forms of Intertribal Relationship among Historic Plains Indians." In *Political Economy of North American Indians,* ed. John Moore. Norman: University of Oklahoma Press, in press.

Allen, R.S. "William McKay." In *Dictionary of Canadian Biography,* ed. Francess Halpenny. Vol. 6. Toronto: University of Toronto Press, 1987.

Anderson, Gary. *Kinsmen of Another Kind: Dakota-White Relations in the Upper Mississippi Valley, 1650-1862.* Lincoln: University of Nebraska Press, 1984.

Angel, Michael. "The Ojibwa-Missionary Encounter at Rainy Lake Mission, 1839-1857." M.A. thesis, University of Manitoba, 1986.

Bakker, Peter. "The Genesis of Mechif: A First Hypothesis." In *Papers of the Twenty-First Algonquian Conference,* ed. William Cowan. Ottawa: Carleton University, 1990.

Ball, Timothy. "Climate Change, Droughts and their Social Impact: Central Canada, 1780-1820." Paper presented at Rupert's Land Research Centre conference, Churchill, Manitoba, 1988.

Barth, Fredrik. *Ethnic Groups and Boundaries.* London: Allen and Unwin, 1970.

Bee, Robert L. *Patterns and Processes: An Introduction to Anthropological Strategies for the Study of Sociocultural Change.* New York: Free Press, 1974.

Benton-Banai, Edward. *The Mishomis Book: The Voice of the Ojibway.* St. Paul: Indian Country Press, 1981.

Bishop, Charles. "The Indian Inhabitants in Northern Ontario at the Time of Contact: Socio-Territorial Considerations." In *Approaches to Algonquian Archaeology,* ed. M. Hanna and B. Kooyman. Calgary: University of Calgary Press, 1982.

_____. "Territorial Groups before 1821: Cree and Ojibwa." In *Handbook of North American Indians,* Vol. 6, *Subarctic,* ed. J. Helm. Washington, D.C.: Smithsonian Institution, 1981.

_____. "Cultural and Biological Adaptations to Deprivation: The Northern Ojibwa Case." In *Extinction and Survival of Human Populations,* ed. Charles Laughlin Jr. and Ivan Brady. New York: Columbia University Press, 1978.

_____. *The Northern Ojibwa and the Fur Trade: An Historical and Ecological Study.* Toronto: Holt, Rinehart and Winston of Canada, Ltd., 1974.

_____. "The Emergence of the Northern Ojibwa: Social and Economic Consequences." *American Ethnologist* 3/1 (1976).

_____. Review of *Indian-European Trade Relations in the Lower Saskatchewan River Region to 1840*, by Paul Thistle. *Ethnohistory* 37/2 (spring 1990).

Black-Rogers, Mary. "Varieties of 'Starving': Semantics and Survival in the Sub-Arctic Fur Trade, 1750-1850." *Ethnohistory* 33/4 (1986).

Black (Rogers), Mary. "Ojibwa Power Belief Systems." In *The Anthropology of Power*, ed. R.D. Fogelson and R.N. Adams. New York: Academic Press, 1977.

Blain, Eleanor. "Dependency: Charles Bishop and the Northern Ojibwa." In *Aboriginal Resource Use in Canada: Historical and Legal Aspects*, ed. Kerry Abel and Jean Friesen. Winnipeg: University of Manitoba Press, 1991.

Brasser, Ted. *Bou'jou Neejee!: Profiles of Canadian Indian Art*. Ottawa: National Museum of Man, 1976.

_____. "Backrest Banners among the Plains Cree and Plains Ojibwa." *American Indian Art Magazine* (winter 1984).

_____. "Flowers in Native American Art: A Review." Paper, copy from author, 1990.

_____. "By the Power of their Dreams: Artistic Traditions of the Northern Plains." In *The Spirit Sings: Artistic Traditions of Canada's First Peoples*. Toronto: McClelland and Stewart, 1987.

Brown, Jennifer S.H. "Afterword." In *The Ojibwa of Berens River, Manitoba: Ethnography into History*, ed. A. Irving Hallowell. Toronto: Harcourt Brace Jovanovich College Publishers, 1992.

_____. "The Métis: Genesis and Rebirth." In *Native Peoples, Native Lands*, ed. Bruce A. Cox. Ottawa: Carleton University, 1988.

_____. "Abishabis." In *Dictionary of Canadian Biography*, ed. Francess Halpenny. Vol. 7. Toronto: University of Toronto Press, 1988.

_____. "The Track to Heaven: The Hudson's Bay Cree Religious Movement of 1842-43." In *Papers of the Thirteenth Algonquian Conference*, ed. William Cowan. Ottawa: Carleton University, 1982.

_____. "Northern Algonquians from Lake Superior and Hudson Bay to Manitoba in the Historic Period." In *Native Peoples: The Canadian Experience*, ed. R. Bruce Morrison and C. Roderick Wilson. Toronto: McClelland and Stewart, 1986.

_____. *Strangers in Blood: Fur Trade Company Families in Indian Country*. Vancouver: University of British Columbia Press, 1980.

_____. "Man in His Natural State: The Indian Worlds of George Nelson." In *Rendezvous: Selected Papers of the Fourth North American Fur Trade Conference*, 1981, ed. Thomas C. Buckley. St. Paul: Minnesota Historical Society, 1984.

_____. "From Sorel to Lake Winnipeg: George Nelson as an Ethnohistorical Source." In *New Dimensions in Ethnohistory: Papers of the Second Laurier Conference on Ethnohistory and Ethnology*, ed. Barry Gough and Laird Christie. Mercury Series No. 120. Ottawa: Canadian Museum of Civilization, 1991.

Brown, Jennifer S.H., and Robert Brightman. *"The Orders of the Dreamed": George Nelson on Cree and Northern Ojibwa Religion and Myth, 1823*. Winnipeg: University of Manitoba Press, 1988.

Burnham, Dorothy. *To Please the Caribou: Painted Caribou-Skin Coats Worn by the Naskapi, Montagnais, and Cree Hunters of the Quebec-Labrador Peninsula*. Toronto: Royal Ontario Museum, 1992.

Camp, Gregory. "Working Out their own Salvation: The Allotment of Land in Severalty and the Turtle Mountain Chippewa Band, 1870-1920." *American Indian Culture and Research Journal* 14/2 (1990).

_____. "The Chippewa Transition from Woodland to Prairie, 1790-1820." *North Dakota History* 51/3 (1984).

_____. "The Chippewa Fur Trade in the Red River Valley of the North, 1790-1830." In *The Fur Trade in North Dakota*, ed. Virginia Heidenreich. Bismarck: North Dakota Historical Society, 1990.

_____. "The Turtle Mountain Plains-Chippewa and Métis, 1797-1935." Ph.D. dissertation, University of New Mexico, 1987.

Carter, Sarah. *Lost Harvests: Prairie Indian Reserve Farmers and Government Policy*. Montreal: McGill-Queen's University Press, 1990.

Cleland, Charles E. "The Inland Shore Fishery of the Northern Great Lakes: Its Development and Importance in Prehistory." *American Antiquity* 47/4 (1982).

Counts, Dorothy Ayers. "Fighting Back is Not the Way: Suicide and the Women of Kaliai." *American Ethnologist* 7/2 (1980).

_____. "Female Suicide and Wife Abuse: A Cross-Cultural Perspective." *Suicide and Life-Threatening Behavior* 17/3 (1987). Cox, Bruce A. "Debating the 'Debatable Zone': A Re-examination of Explanations of Dakota-Algonquian Conflict." *Sociology and Anthropology Departmental Working Paper, 86-87.* Ottawa: Carleton University, 1986.

Czuboka, Michael. "St. Peter's: A Historical Study with Anthropological Observations on the Christian Aborigines of Red River, 1811-1876." M.A. thesis, University of Manitoba, 1960.

Decker, Jody F. "'We Should Never Again Be the Same People': The Diffusion and Cumulative Impact of Acute Infectious Diseases Affecting the Natives on the Northern Plains of the Western Interior of Canada, 1774-1839." Ph.D. dissertation, York University, 1989.

_____. "Tracing Historical Diffusion Patterns: The Case of the 1780-82 Smallpox Epidemic among the Indians of Western Canada." *Native Studies Review* 4/1-2 (1988).

DeMallie, Raymond. Preface to *Indians of the Plains*, by Robert H. Lowie. Lincoln: University of Nebraska Press, 1982.

Dempsey, Hugh. *Crowfoot: Chief of the Blackfeet*. Norman: University of Oklahoma Press, 1972.

_____. *Indian Tribes of Alberta*. Rev. ed. Calgary: Glenbow-Alberta Institute, 1986.

_____. "Peguis." In *Dictionary of Canadian Biography*, ed. Francess Halpenny. Vol. 9. Toronto: University of Toronto Press, 1976.

_____. *Big Bear: The End of Freedom*. Vancouver: Douglas and McIntyre, 1984.

_____. *Red Crow: Warrior Chief*. Lincoln: University of Nebraska Press, 1980.

Dobyns, H. *Their Number become Thinned*. Knoxville: University of Tennessee Press, 1983.

Doige, Gary B. "Warfare Patterns of the Assiniboine to 1809." M.A. thesis, University of Manitoba, 1989.

Edmunds, R. David. *The Shawnee Prophet*. Lincoln: University of Nebraska Press, 1983.

Elias, Peter Douglas. *The Dakota of the Canadian Northwest: Lessons for Survival*. Winnipeg: University of Manitoba Press, 1988.

Ewers, John C. "George Catlin: Painter of Indians and the West." *Annual Report.* Smithsonian Institution 1955.

_____. *Ethnological Report on the Chippewa Cree Tribe of the Rocky Boy Reservation*. New York: Garland Publishing, 1974.

Feest, Christian. *Indianer Nordamerikas*. Vienna: Museum für Völkerkunde, 1968.

Feest, Christian, and Johanna Feest. "Ottawa." In *Handbook of North American Indians*. Vol. 15, *Northeast*, ed. Bruce Trigger. Washington, D.C.: Smithsonian Institution, 1978.

Ferris, Neal, et al. "Bellamy: A Late Historic Ojibwa Habitation." *Ontario Archaeology* 44 (1985).

Fisher, A.D. "Great Plains Ethnology." In *Native Peoples: The Canadian Experience*, ed. R. Bruce Morrison and C. Roderick Wilson. Toronto: McClelland and Stewart, 1986.

Foster, John E. "William Cockran." In *Dictionary of Canadian Biography*, ed. Francess Halpenny, Vol. 9. Toronto: University of Toronto Press, 1976.

_____. "The Origins of the Mixed-Bloods in the Canadian West." In *Essays on Western History*, ed. L.H. Thomas. Edmonton: University of Alberta Press, 1976.

_____. "The Saulteaux and the Numbered Treaties: An Aboriginal Rights Position?" In *The Spirit of the Alberta Indian Treaties*, ed. Richard Price. 1979. Reprinted, Edmonton: Pica Pica Press, 1987.

_____. "The Plains Métis." In *Native Peoples: The Canadian Experience*, ed. R. Bruce Morrison and C. Roderick Wilson. Toronto: McClelland and Stewart, 1986.

Fredrickson, N. Jaye. *The Covenant Chain: Indian Ceremonial and Trade Silver*. Ottawa: National Museums of Canada, 1980.

Fried, Morton. *The Notion of Tribe*. Don Mills: Cummings Publishing Co., 1975.

Friesen, Jean. "Grant Me Wherewith to Make my Living." In *Aboriginal Resource Use in Canada: Historical and Legal Aspects*, ed. Kerry Abel and Jean Friesen. Winnipeg: University of Manitoba Press, 1991.

_____. "Grant Me Wherewith to Make my Living." Research report for Treaty and Aboriginal Rights Research of Manitoba, 1985.

Friesen, Gerald. *The Canadian Prairies: A History*. Toronto: University of Toronto Press, 1984.

Garrioch, Reverend A.C. *First Furrows: A History of the Early Settlement of the Red River Country*. Winnipeg: Stock Co. Ltd., 1923.

Gilman, Carolyn. *The Grand Portage Story*. St. Paul: Minnesota Historical Society Press, 1992.

Given, Brian J. "The Iroquois Wars and Native Arms." In *Native Peoples, Native Lands*, ed. Bruce A. Cox. Ottawa: Carleton University Press, 1988.

Goddard, Ives. "Synonymy." In Edward Rogers, "Southeastern Ojibwa," *Handbook of North American Indians*. Vol. 15, *Northeast*, ed. Bruce Trigger. Washington, D.C.: Smithsonian Institution, 1978.

Gorham, Harriet. "Families of Mixed Descent in the Western Great Lakes Region." In *Native Peoples, Native Lands*, ed. Bruce A. Cox. Ottawa: Carleton University Press, 1988.

Grant, John Webster. "Missionaries and Messiahs in the Northwest." *Studies in Religion* 9/2 (1980).

_____. *Moon of Wintertime: Missionaries and the Indians of Canada in Encounter since 1534*. Toronto: University of Toronto Press, 1984.

Greenberg, Adolph, and Jim Morrison. "Group Identities in the Boreal Forest: The Origin of the Northern Ojibwa." *Ethnohistory* 29 (1982).

Guinn, Rodger. *The Red-Assiniboine Junction: A Land Use and Structural History*. Parks Canada: Manuscript and Record Series No. 355, 1980.

Gullason, Lynda. "The Fort George-Buckingham House Site Plantation (1792-1800): Native-European Contact in the Fur Trade Era." M.A. thesis, University of Alberta, 1990.

Hackett, F.J. Paul. "The 1819-20 Measles Epidemic: Its Origin, Diffusion and Mortality Effects upon the Indians of the Petit Nord." M.A. thesis, University of Manitoba, 1991.

Hail, Barbara. *Hau, Kola!: The Plains Indian Collection of the Haffenreffer Museum*. Providence: Haffenreffer Museum of Anthropology, 1983.

Hail, Barbara A., and Kate C. Duncan. *Out of the North: The Subarctic Collection of the Haffenreffer Museum of Anthropology*. Bristol, RI: Brown University, 1989.

Hallowell, A.I. "Ojibwa Ontology and World View." In *Teachings from the American Earth*, ed. Dennis Tedlock and Barbara Tedlock. Toronto: George J. McCleod, 1975.

_____. "The Passing of the Midewiwin in the Lake Winnipeg Region." *American Anthropologist* 38 (1936).

_____. *The Ojibwa of Berens River, Manitoba: Ethnography into History*, edited with preface and afterword by Jennifer S.H. Brown. Fort Worth, TX: Harcourt Brace Jovanovich College Publishers, 1992.

Halpin, Marjorie. Introduction to *Letters and Notes on the Manners, Customs, and Conditions of the North American Indians*, by George Catlin. New York: Dover Publications, 1973.

Hamell, George. "Trading in Metaphors: The Magic of Beads." In *Proceedings of the 1982 Glass Trade Bead Conference*, ed. C. Hayes III. New York: Rochester Museum and Science Center, 1982.

_____. "Strawberries, Floating Islands, and Rabbit Captains: Mythical Realities and European Contact in the Northeast during the Sixteenth and Seventeenth Centuries." *Journal of Canadian Studies* 21/4 (1986-87).

Hamilton, Scott. "Competition and Warfare: Functional versus Historical Explanations." *The Canadian Journal of Native Studies* 5/1 (1985).

Hanks, Christopher. "The Swampy Cree and the Hudson's Bay Company at Oxford House." *Ethnohistory* 29/2 (1982).

Hansen, Lise C. "Chiefs and Principal Men: A Question of Leadership in Treaty Negotiations." *Anthropologica* 29 (1987).

Harris, R. Cole, ed. *Historical Atlas of Canada*. Vol. 1, *From the Beginning to 1800*. Toronto: University of Toronto Press, 1987.

Heidenreich, Conrad. *Huronia: A History and Geography of the Huron Indians 1600-1650*. Toronto: McClelland and Stewart, 1971.

Helm, J.. "Women's Work, Women's Art." In *Out of the North: The Subarctic Collection of the Haffenreffer Museum of Anthropology*, ed. Kate Duncan and Barbara Hail. Bristol: Haffenreffer Museum, 1989.

Herring, Ann. "The 1918 Flu Epidemic in Manitoba Aboriginal Communities: Implications for Depopulation Theory in the Americas." Paper presented at the American Society for Ethnohistory Meeting, Toronto, 1990.

Hickerson, Harold. *The Chippewa and their Neighbors: A Study in Ethnohistory*. Rev. ed., with foreword and critical review by Jennifer S.H. Brown and Laura L. Peers. Prospect Heights: Waveland Press, 1988.

_____. *Ethnohistory of Chippewa in Central Minnesota*. New York: Garland Publishing, 1974.

_____. *The Southwestern Ojibwa: An Ethnohistorical Study*. American Anthropological Association Memoir 92, vol. 63, no. 3, part 2, 1964.

_____. *Ethnohistory of Chippewa of Lake Superior*. New York: Garland Publishing, 1974.

_____. "The Genesis of a Trading Post Band: The Pembina Chippewa." *Ethnohistory* 3/4 (fall 1956).

Hickerson, Harold, and Erminie Wheeler-Voegelin. *The Red Lake and Pembina Chippewa*. New York: Garland Publishing, 1974.

Hoffman, W.J. "The Midw'wiwin; or 'Grand Medicine Society' of the Ojibwa." *Bureau of American Ethnology, Seventh Annual Report 1885-86*.

Holzkamm, Tim E. "Eastern Dakota Population Movements and the European Fur Trade: One More Time." *Plains Anthropologist* 28/101 (1983).

_____. "Ojibwa Horticulture in the Upper Mississippi and Boundary Waters." In *Actes du Dix-Septième Congres des Algonquinistes*, ed. William Cowan. Ottawa: Carleton University, 1986.

_____. "A Quantitative Analysis of Ojibway Sturgeon Fisheries in the Rainy River." In *Proceedings of the Eighteenth Algonquian Conference*, ed. William Cowan. Ottawa: Carleton University, 1987.

Holzkamm, Tim E., Victor P. Lytwyn, and Leo G. Waisberg. "Rainy River Sturgeon: An Ojibway Resource in the Fur Trade Economy." *The Canadian Geographer* 32/3 (1988).

Howard, James. *The Plains Ojibwa or Bungi*. Vermilion: University of South Dakota, Anthropological Papers No. 1, 1965.

_____. "The Identity and Demography of the Plains-Ojibwa." *Plains Anthropologist* 6 (1961).

_____. *The Canadian Sioux*. Lincoln: University of Nebraska, 1984.

Huyda, Richard. *Camera in the Interior: H.L. Hime, Photographer*. Toronto: Coach House Press, 1975.

Innis, Harold A. *The Fur Trade in Canada*. Rev. ed. Toronto: University of Toronto Press, 1984.

Johnson, Nick. "Bits of Dough, Twigs of Fire." In *ArtsCanada – Stone, Bones and Skin: Ritual and Shamanic Art* (December 1973 / January 1974).

Karklins, Karlis. *Trade Ornament Usage among the Native Peoples of Canada: A Source Book.* Ottawa: Parks Service, 1992.

Kaye, Barry. "Birsay Village on the Assiniboine." *The Beaver* (winter 1981).

Kelly, John D., and Martha Kaplan. "History, Structure, and Ritual." *Annual Reviews of Anthropology* 19 (1990).

Klein, Alan. "Political Economy of Gender." In *The Hidden Half*, ed. Patricia Albers and Beatrice Medicine. Washington, D.C.: University Press of America, 1983.

Klimko, Olga. *The Archaeology and History of Fort Pelly 1 (1824-1856).* Regina: Saskatchewan Culture and Recreation, Pastlog No. 5, 1983.

Kohl, J.G. *Kitchi-Gami: Life among the Lake Superior Ojibway.* 1860. Reprinted, St. Paul: Minnesota Historical Society Press, 1985.

Krech, Shepard III. "The Development of Dependency in the Sub-Arctic." Paper presented at the Sixth North American Fur Trade Conference, Mackinac Island, fall 1991.

Krech, Shepard III, ed. *The Subarctic Fur Trade: Native Social and Economic Adaptations.* Vancouver: University of British Columbia Press, 1984.

Landes, Ruth. *The Ojibwa Woman.* New York: Columbia University Contributions to Anthropology No. 31, 1938.

Leacock, Eleanor Burke. "Women's Status in Egalitarian Society." In *Myths of Male Dominance: Collected Essays on Women Cross-Culturally.* New York: Monthly Review Press, 1981.

Liberty, Margo. "Hell Came with Horses: Plains Indian Women in the Equestrian Era." *Montana: The Magazine of Western History* 32 (1982).

Long, John S. "*Manitu*, Power, Books, and *Wihtikow.*" *Native Studies Review* 3/1 (1987).

_____. "Coping with Powerful People: A Hudson's Bay Company 'Boss' and the Albany River Cree, 1862-1875." *Native Studies Review* 8/1 (1992).

Lytwyn, Victor. *The Fur Trade of the Little North.* Winnipeg: Rupert's Land Research Centre, 1986.

_____. "'These Canadians Trade the Beaver with them Where they Kill Them': Indian Responses to Extreme Fur Trade Competition in the Little North, 1790-1810." Paper presented at the Sixth North American Fur Trade Conference, Mackinac Island, fall 1991.

Mandelbaum, David G. *The Plains Cree: An Ethnographic, Historical, and Comparative Study.* Canadian Plains Studies No. 9. Regina: Canadian Plains Research Centre, 1979.

McCarthy, Martha. *To Evangelize the Nations: Roman Catholic Missions in Manitoba 1818-1870.* Papers in Manitoba History, Report No. 2, Manitoba Culture, Heritage and Recreation, Historic Resources, 1990.

McCullough, A.B. *Money and Exchange in Canada to 1900.* Toronto: Dundurn Press, 1984.

Meyer, David. "The Red Deer River Grave: An Historic Burial." *Napao* 4/1 (July 1973).

_____. *The Red Earth Crees*, 1860-1960. National Museum of Man Mercury Series No. 100. Ottawa: National Museums of Canada, 1985.

Milloy, John. "Our Country: Significance of the Buffalo Resource for a Plains Cree Sense of Territory." In *Aboriginal Resource Use in Canada: Historical and Legal Aspects*, ed. Kerry Abel and Jean Friesen. Winnipeg: University of Manitoba Press, 1991.

_____. *The Plains Cree: Trade, Diplomacy and War, 1790 to 1860.* Winnipeg: University of Manitoba Press, 1988.

Moodie, D. Wayne. "Manomin: Historical Geographical Perspectives on the Ojibway Production of Wild Rice." In *Aboriginal Resource Use in Canada*, ed. Kerry Abel and Jean Friesen. Winnipeg: University of Manitoba Press, 1991.

_____. "Nineteenth Century Ojibwa Agricultural Sites." Paper presented at the annual meeting of the Canadian Archaeological Association, Calgary, 1990.

_____. "Agriculture and the Fur Trade." In *Old Trails and New Directions*, ed. C. Judd and A.J. Ray. Toronto: University of Toronto Press, 1980.

Moodie, D. Wayne, and Barry Kaye. "Indian Agriculture in the Fur Trade Northwest." *Prairie Forum* 11/2 (1986).

Morris, Alexander. *Treaties of Canada with the Indians*. 1880. Facsimile reprint, Toronto: Coles Canadiana Collection, 1971.

Morton, A.S. *A History of the Canadian West to 1870-71*, ed. L.G. Thomas. 2d ed. Toronto: University of Toronto Press, 1973.

Morton, W.L. Introduction to *London Correspondence Inward from Eden Colvile 1849-52*, ed. E.E. Rich. London: Hudson's Bay Record Society, 1956.

Moulton, Gary, ed. *The Journals of the Lewis and Clark Expedition, August 25, 1804–April 6, 1805.* Lincoln: University of Nebraska Press, 1987.

Mukhopadhyay, Carol, and Patricia Higgins. "Anthropological Studies of Women's Status Revisited: 1977-1987." *Annual Review of Anthropology* 17 (1988).

Myers, Fred. "Critical Trends in the Study of Hunter-Gatherers." *Annual Review of Anthropology* 17 (1988).

Neufeld, Peter Lorenz. "How the Saulteaux-Cree Were Driven Out of Riding Mountain Park." *Indian Record* 44/3 (1985).

_____. "Picheito, Manitoba's Last Saulteaux-Cree War Chief." *Indian Record* 48/2 (1985).

Nichols, John, and Earl Nyholm, eds. *Ojibwewi-ikidowinan: An Ojibwe Word Resource Book*. St. Paul: Minnesota Archaeological Society, 1979.

Nicks, Gertrude. "The Iroquois and the Fur Trade in Western Canada." In *Old Trails and New Directions*, ed. C. Judd and A.J. Ray. Toronto: University of Toronto Press, 1980.

_____. "Native Responses to the Early Fur Trade at Lesser Slave Lake." In *Le Castor Fait Tout: Selected Papers of the Fifth North American Fur Trade Conference*, ed. Bruce G. Trigger, Toby Morantz, and Louise Dechêne. Montreal: Lake St. Louis Historical Society, 1987.

Owen, Roger C. "The Patrilocal Band: A Linguistically and Culturally Hybrid Social Unit." *American Anthropologist* 67 (1965).

Peers, Laura. "Rich Man, Poor Man, Beggar Man, Chief: Saulteaux in the Red River Settlement, 1812-1833." In *Papers of of the Eighteenth Algonquian Conference*, ed. William Cowan. Ottawa: Carleton University, 1987.

_____. "An Ethnohistory of the Western Ojibwa, 1780-1830." M.A. thesis, Universities of Winnipeg and Manitoba, 1987.

_____. "Changing Resource Use Patterns of Saulteaux Trading at Fort Pelly, 1821 to 1870." In *Aboriginal Resource Use in Canada: Historical and Legal Aspects*, ed. Kerry Abel and Jean Friesen. Winnipeg: University of Manitoba Press, 1991.

_____. "The Saulteaux, Red River, and the Forks, 1770-1870." Paper presented at "Focus on the Forks," Winnipeg, April 1991.

_____. "Subsistence, Secondary Literature and Gender Bias: The Saulteaux." In *Women of the First Nations of Canada.*, ed. Patricia Chuchryk, et al. Winnipeg: University of Manitoba Press, in press.

Penney, David W. "Floral Decoration and Culture Change: An Historical Interpretation of Motivation." *American Indian Culture and Research Journal* 15/1 (1991).

_____. "Great Lakes Indian Art: An Introduction." In *Great Lakes Indian Art*, ed. David W. Penney. Detroit: Wayne State University Press, 1989.

Penney, David W., and Janet Stouffer. "Horse Imagery in Native American Art." In *Great Lakes Indian Art*, ed. David W. Penney. Detroit: Wayne State University Press, 1989.

Pentland, David. "Synonymy." In Jack H. Steinbring, "Saulteaux of Lake Winnipeg," *Handbook of North American Indians*. Vol. 6, *Subarctic*, ed. J. Helm. Washington, D.C.: Smithsonian Institution, 1981.

_____. "Synonymy." In E.S. Rogers and J. Garth Taylor, "Northern Ojibwa." *Handbook of North American Indians*. Vol. 6, *Subarctic*, ed. J. Helm. Washington, D.C.: Smithsonian Institution, 1981.

_____. "Metchif and Bungee: Languages of the Fur Trade." Paper read in the series "Voices of Rupert's Land," Winnipeg, 1985.

Peterson, Jacqueline. "Many Roads to Red River: Métis Genesis in the Great Lakes Region, 1680-1815." In *The New Peoples: Being and Becoming Métis in North America*, ed. Jacqueline Peterson and Jennifer S.H. Brown. Winnipeg: University of Manitoba Press, 1985.

Peterson, Jacqueline, and Jennifer S.H. Brown, eds. *The New Peoples: Being and Becoming Métis in North America*. Winnipeg: University of Manitoba Press, 1985.

Phillips, Ruth Bliss. *Patterns of Power*. Kleinberg, Ontario: The McMichael Canadian Collection, 1984.

Pickering, Kathleen. "Changes in Lakota Social Complexity." Term paper, University of Wisconsin-Madison, 1990.

Podruchny, Carolyn. "Indians and Missionaries in Encounter: The Peguis Band and the Church Missionary Society at the Red River, 1820-1838." M.A. thesis, University of Toronto, 1992.

Pritchett, John. *The Red River Valley, 1811-1849*. New York: Russell and Russell, 1970.

Quimby, George. "A Year with a Chippewa Family." *Ethnohistory* 9/3 (summer 1962).

Ray, A.J. "Indian Exploitation of the Forest-Grassland Transition Zone in Western Canada, 1650-1860." Ph.D. dissertation, University of Wisconsin, 1971.

_____. "Periodic Shortages, Native Welfare, and the Hudson's Bay Company 1670-1930." In *The Subarctic Fur Trade: Social and Economic Adaptations*, ed. Shepard Krech III. Vancouver: University of British Columbia Press, 1984.

_____. *Indians in the Fur Trade*. 1974. Reprint, Toronto: University of Toronto Press, 1983.

Ray, A.J., and Donald Freeman. *"Give Us Good Measure": An Economic Analysis of Relations between the Indians and the Hudson's Bay Company Before 1763*. Toronto: University of Toronto Press, 1978.

Rich, E.E. "Trade Habits and Economic Motivation among the Indians of North America." *Canadian Journal of Economics and Political Science*. 26 (1960).

_____. *Hudson's Bay Company 1670-1870*. Vol. 3, *1821-1870*. Toronto: McClelland and Stewart, 1960.

_____. *The Fur Trade and the Northwest to 1857*. Toronto: McClelland and Stewart, 1967.

Ritterbush, Lauren. "Culture Change and Continuity: Ethnohistoric Analysis of Ojibwa and Ottawa Adjustment to the Prairies." Ph.D. dissertation, University of Kansas, 1990.

_____. "Documenting Environmental Adaptation on the Northern Prairies during the Fur Trade Era: The Red River Ojibwa." Paper presented to the Fur Trade Symposium of the Forty-seventh Annual Plains Conference, 1989.

_____. "Chippewa Exodus from Red River?" Paper presented at the Forty-sixth Plains Anthropological Conference, 1988.

Ronda, James P. *Lewis and Clark among the Indians*. Lincoln: University of Nebraska Press, 1984.

Rogers, Edward. "Southeastern Ojibwa." In *Handbook of North American Indians*. Vol. 15, *Northeast*, ed. Bruce G. Trigger. Washington, D.C.: Smithsonian Institution, 1978.

Rogers, Edward S., and J. Garth Taylor. "Northern Ojibwa." In *Handbook of North American Indians*. Vol. 6, *Subarctic*, ed. J. Helm. Washington, D.C.: Smithsonian Institution, 1981.

Rogers, Edward S., and Mary Black-Rogers. "Who Were the Cranes? Groups and Group Identity Names in Northern Ontario." In *Approaches to Algonquian Archaeology*, ed. Brian Kooymans and Margaret Hanna. Calgary: University of Calgary, 1982.

Rogers, Susan Carol. "Female Forms of Power and the Myth of Male Dominance: A Model of Female/Male Interaction in Peasant Society." *American Ethnologist* 2/4 (1975).

Ross, Alexander. *The Red River Settlement: Its Rise, Progress, and Present State*. 1856. Facsimile reprint, Winnipeg: Helen Doherty, 1984.

Rotstein, A. "Trade and Politics: An Institutional Approach." *Western Canadian Journal of Anthropology* 3 (1972).

Russell, Dale. *Eighteenth Century Cree and their Neighbors*. Mercury Series. Ottawa: Canadian Museum of Civilization, 1991.

Sharrock, Susan. Preface to *Western Canadian Journal of Anthropology* 7/4 (1977).
_____. "Crees, Cree-Assiniboines, and Assiniboines: Interethnic Social Organization on the Far Northern Plains." *Ethnohistory* 21/2 (spring 1974).
Shifferd, Patricia. "A Study in Economic Change: The Chippewa of Northern Wisconsin, 1854-1900." *Western Canadian Journal of Anthropology* 6/4 (1976).
Skinner, Alanson. "Political and Ceremonial Organizations of the Plains Ojibway." *Anthropological Papers of the American Museum of Natural History*, vol. 11, part 6 (1914).
_____. "The Cultural Position of the Plains Ojibway." *American Anthropologist* 16 (1914).
_____. "Notes on the Plains Cree." *American Anthropologist* 16 (1914).
Smith, Brian. "The Historical and Archaeological Evidence for the Use of Fish as an Alternative Subsistence Resource among Northern Plains Bison Hunters." In *Aboriginal Resource Use in Canada: Historical and Legal Aspects*, ed. Kerry Abel and Jean Friesen. Winnipeg: University of Manitoba Press, 1991.
_____. "An Ethnohistorical Evaluation of the Role of Bison and Fish in the Social Organization of Northern Plains and Parkland Native Society: 1790-1850." *Manitoba Archaeological Quarterly* 12/1 (1988).
_____. "The Lebret Site." M.A. thesis, University of Saskatchewan, 1986.
_____. "The Importance of Assessing Aquatic Environments on the Northern Plains." Paper presented at the Chacmool Conference, Calgary, 1986.
Smith, Erica. "Something More than Mere Ornament: Cloth and Indian-European Relationships in the Eighteenth Century." M.A. thesis, Universities of Winnipeg and Manitoba, 1991.
Snow, Dean R., and Kim M. Lanphear. "European Contact and Indian Depopulation in the Northeast: The Timing of the First Epidemics." *Ethnohistory* 35 (1988).
Sprenger, G.H. "The Métis Nation: Buffalo Hunting versus Agriculture in the Red River Settlement, 1810-70." In *Native People Native Lands*, ed. Bruce A. Cox. Ottawa: Carleton University, 1988.
Spindler, George, and Louise Spindler. "Male and Female in Four Changing Cultures." In *Personality and the Cultural Construction of Society: Papers in Honor of Melford E. Spiro*, ed. David Jordan and Marc Swartz. Tuscaloosa: University of Alabama Press, 1990.
The Spirit Sings: A Catalogue of the Exhibition. Toronto: McClelland and Stewart, 1987.
The Spirit Sings: Artistic Traditions of Canada's First Peoples. Toronto: McClelland and Stewart, 1987.
Spry, Irene. "The Transition from a Nomadic to a Settled Economy in Western Canada, 1856-95." *Transactions of the Royal Society of Canada*, vol. 6, series 4, section 2, June 1968.
Steinbring, Jack H. "Saulteaux of Lake Winnipeg." In *Handbook of North American Indians*. Vol. 6, *Subarctic*, ed. J. Helm. Washington, D.C.: Smithsonian Institution, 1981.
Stobie, Margaret. "Backgrounds of the Dialect Called Bungi." *Historical and Scientific Society of Manitoba Transactions.*, series 3, no. 24, 1967-68.
Swagerty, William R. "Indian Trade in the Trans-Mississippi West to 1870." In *Handbook of North American Indians*. Vol. 4, *History of Indian-White Relations*, ed. Wilcomb Washburn. Washington, D.C.: Smithsonian Institution, 1988.
Syms, E.L. "Identifying Prehistoric Western Algonquians: A Holistic Approach." In *Approaches to Algonquian Archaeology*, ed. M. Hanna and B. Kooyman. Calgary: University of Calgary Press, 1982.
Tanner, Helen, ed. *Atlas of Great Lakes Indian History*. Norman: University of Oklahoma Press, 1986.
Tarasoff, Koozma. *Persistent Ceremonialism: The Plains Cree and Saulteaux*. Canadian Ethnology Service, Mercury Series No. 69. Ottawa: National Museums of Canada, 1980.
Taylor, John. "Sociocultural Effects of Epidemics on the Northern Plains, 1734-1850." *Western Canadian Journal of Anthropology* 7/4 (1977).

Thompson, Chief Albert Edward. *Chief Peguis and His Descendants*. Winnipeg: Peguis Publishers, 1973.

Thistle, Paul. *Indian-European Trade Relations in the Lower Saskatchewan River Region to 1840*. Winnipeg: University of Manitoba Press, 1986.

Tobias, John L. "Canada's Subjugation of the Plains Cree." *Canadian Historical Review* 64/4 (1983).

Trigger, Bruce. *Natives and Newcomers: Canada's "Heroic Age" Reconsidered*. Montreal: McGill University Press, 1985.

Tyler, Kenneth. "Paskwaw." *Dictionary of Canadian Biography*, ed. Francess Halpenny. Vol. 11. Toronto: University of Toronto Press, 1982.

Van Kirk, Sylvia. *"Many Tender Ties": Women in Fur Trade Society, 1670-1870*. Winnipeg: Watson and Dwyer, 1983.

_____. "What if Mama is an Indian? The Cultural Ambivalence of the Alexander Ross Family." In *The Developing West: Essays on Canadian History in Honor of Lewis H. Thomas*. Edmonton: University of Alberta Press, 1983.

_____. "Toward a Feminist Perspective in Ethnohistory." In *Papers of the Eighteenth Algonquian Conference*, ed. William Cowan. Ottawa: Carleton University, 1987.

Vecsey, Christopher. *Traditional Ojibwa Religion and its Historical Changes*. Philadelphia: American Philosophical Society, 1983.

Vennum, Thomas. *Wild Rice and the Ojibway People*. St. Paul: Minnesota Historical Society Press, 1988.

Vizenor, Gerald. *The People Named the Chippewa*. Minneapolis: University of Minnesota Press, 1984.

Waisberg, Leo. "An Ethnographic and Historical Outline of the Rainy River Ojibway." In *An Historical Synthesis of the Manitou Mounds Site on the Rainy River*, ed. W.C. Noble. Manuscript report, Parks Canada, 1984.

Waisberg, Leo, and Marie-Ange Beaudry. *Manitou Mounds: Historical Evaluation of the Mission Lot*. Manuscript report, Parks Canada, 1984.

Wallace, Anthony F.C. *The Death and Rebirth of the Seneca*. New York: Random House, 1972.

Warren, William. *History of the Ojibway Nation*. Minneapolis: Ross and Haines, 1957.

White, Bruce. "Give us a Little Milk: The Social and Cultural Meanings of Gift-Giving in the Lake Superior Fur Trade." *Minnesota History* 48/2 (1982).

_____. "A Skilled Game of Exchange: Ojibway Fur Trade Protocol." *Minnesota History* 50/6 (1987).

Winterhalder, Bruce. "Boreal Foraging Strategies." In *Boreal Forest Adaptations: The Northern Algonquians*, ed. A. Theodore Steegman Jr. New York: Plenum Press, 1983.

Wolfe, Alexander. *Earth Elder Stories*. Saskatoon: Fifth House Press, 1988.

Wood, W. Raymond, and Thomas D. Thiessen, eds. *Early Fur Trade on the Northern Plains*. Norman: University of Oklahoma Press, 1985.

Woolworth, Alan R. "A Disgraceful Proceeding." *The Beaver* (spring 1969).

Worsley, Peter. *The Trumpet Shall Sound: A Study of Cargo Cults in Melanesia*. 2d, augmented ed. New York: Schocken Books, 1968.

Index

Abishabis (Cree), prophecies of 171
Adams, Joseph xvi
age and power 57
agricultural settlement of the West 197-98
agriculture. SEE farming; gardens and
    gardening
alcohol 82, 85, 101-02, 178, 201
    cultural meanings of 41-43
    and violence 42-43, 85, 201
alliance 34-35, 125
    Ojibwa concepts of 89-90
amnesia, cultural. SEE cultural amnesia
Anishinabe xvii
Anishinabeg xv
Assiniboine (aboriginal people) 4-5, 18-19
Athabasca War 74
Ayagon (Interlake Ojibwa man) 74, 75, 80
    and alcohol 85
    relations of with George Nelson 36, 82
    treatment of women by 84, 85

Bad Governor (Matchi Huggemaw) 55-56
Baie St. Paul 138
Barth, Frederik
    on free will 208
Barth, Karl
    on ethnicity ix
Battle of Oldman River 201
bear spirit and power 149
beaver, decline in numbers of 39, 64
Belcourt, Father George 138, 161, 162, 165,
    174

Big Bear 142
    ethnic identity of 119-20, 144-46
Bird, James 125
Bishop, Charles
    on Northern Ontario Ojibwa 165
bison 50-51, 72
    ban on hunting of 90
    decrease in numbers of 109, 154-57, 186
    increased use of 96, 110, 114
    Métis control of hunt 48, 66, 67, 104, 186
Black Coat (Ojibwa leader) 93, 94
The Black Duck (Midewiwin leader) 168
The Black Man (Ojibwa leader) 88, 91
Black Powder, Mukatai (Ojibwa leader) 115,
    139, 142, 144-45, 146, 146 ill.
Black Robe (Ojibwa leader) 124
Black-Rogers, Mary
    on starving 17
Blue Robe. SEE Black Coat
Bourgeault, Henri 149
bows and arrows 11-12
Brasser, Ted
    on Ojibwa-Cree relations 148
Brown, Jennifer S.H.
    on male and female subcultures 85
Budd, Reverend Henry
    on food resources of Interlake 165
Bulger, Andrew 126
bungee xvi
Bungi xvii
burials 21, 182-83

Cadotte, J.B.
  on smallpox epidemic 19
Cameron, Duncan 74
Carter, Sarah
  on Treaties 205
Catlin, George 116-18
Chaboillez, Charles Jean Baptiste 15, 32, 33
change, cultural 121-22, 209, 210
  and cultural continuity xi-xii, 95-97, 210-11
  emergence of plains cultures 78, 115
  opportunism in 138-39
  in response to environment 22, 51, 95-96,
    109-10, 130, 152-53
  in response to fur trade 11-14, 13, 31, 39-41,
    43, 73-76, 106-07, 193-94, 211
  women's roles in 35-36, 45, 80, 121-22, 139,
    150
changes and adaptations 51-53, 59-61, 95-97
  in clothing 25-26, 37, 77, 146, 148, 189-93
  in economic activities 39, 64-65, 70-71, 73,
    95-96, 108-10, 113, 143-44
  in ethnic identities 49, 114, 115, 119-20,
    121-122, 145
  in gender ideology 58, 121-22, 121-23, 145,
    151, 188-89
  in house construction 77, 80, 96
  in male status symbols 12-13, 36-37, 148,
    151
  in religious practice 148-49
  in social organization 96-97
  in technology 36-37
  in use of horses 77-79
  in wealth ideology 36-37, 58-59, 86-87
  SEE ALSO change, cultural; continuity and
    preservation; syncretism
Charlo (Ojibwa man)
  and horse raiding 47-48, 50
Chippewa xv, xvii
The Chippeway Frenchmen (trading company)
  16
choice, human, and decision making 209
Christianity
  Ojibwa views on 132-38, 160-63, 167-69,
    174, 185-86, 196, 197
clans (descent groups) 22
Clear Weather (Ojibwa man) 179
Cleland, Charles
  on European technology 12
climate change, effects of 72, 165
  on Ojibwa 65, 81, 95-96, 109-10, 130

cloth and clothing
  changes in 25-26, 37, 77, 148, 189-93
  cultural meanings of 12-13, 25-26, 33, 37,
    77, 159-60, 161
  as historical evidence 116-19
  preservation of design in 149-51, 189
Cochrane, Archdeacon 184
Cocking, Matthew
  on smallpox epidemic 19
Cockran, Reverend William 131-36 passim,
    167, 172
colours, cultural meanings of 9-10, 26, 77
communities
  fusion of 20-21, 67, 69, 96
  locations of 3-6, 50-53, 59, 102, 115, 124,
    142, 155, 173-75, 187
communities, multi-ethnic 31-32, 49, 144-45,
    148
  boundary maintenance in 120, 187-88
  genesis of 20-21, 67, 69, 96, 114, 115, 142,
    187
"commuting"
  to Boundary Waters 51, 59
  theory of westward expansion 28
continuity, cultural 52-55, 59-61, 96-97, 120-
    21, 123, 185
  and change 138-39, 210-11
  role of Midewiwin in 175
  roles of women in 189-91
continuity and preservation. SEE ALSO
    revitalization
  of canoe technology 60, 154, 182
  of clothing design 149-51, 189
  of east-west Ojibwa relations 51
  of economic activities 60-61, 96-97, 126-30,
    135, 183, 184
  of ethnic identities 77, 97, 120-21, 123, 149,
    188
  of house construction 18, 60, 77, 80, 182
  of religious beliefs and practice 59-60, 60-
    61, 135-37, 148-49, 154, 162-63, 182-84,
    196-97
  of social structures 148-49, 154
  of value system 50, 60-61, 96
corn 46, 70, 71, 128-29
Coté, Gabriel 176, 178, 201
Cowley, Reverend Abraham 167, 171
credit and debt 75, 76-79 100-01, 125-26
  effect of horse acquisition on 78-79
  Ojibwa concepts of 33-34
  Ojibwa use of 37-38, 75

Cree 18-19, 47-48, 133-34, 159
  adoption of Midewiwin by 153
  at Cypress Hills 187, 201, 205
  land claims of 93
  relations with Ojibwa 39, 44, 66-67, 93, 120,
    133-34, 155, 188
  westward movement of 4-5, 142
Crow (tribe) 46
cultural amnesia, theory of 10-11
cultural borrowing 12, 49, 50
  in multi-ethnic communities 120, 153-54
culture areas, concept of x-xi, 153-54
Cypress Hills 201, 205

Dakota Sioux
  migration to Red River 199-201
  synonymy of xvii-xviii
  trade with Hudson's Bay Company 94, 124
Dakota War of 1862 199
"debatable zone" 6-7, 15
debt. SEE credit and debt
Dempsey, Hugh
  on Ojibwa spirituality 45
Department of Indian Affairs
  and Treaties 205-06
dependency 10-12, 77, 195
  meaning of term 8, 13-14
Desjarlais, Baptiste, Nishicabo (Métis man)
    104-06, 112, 114, 139
destitute, meanings of 101
Dickson, Robert 94
disease, responses to 20-21
Doige, Gary
  on Ojibwa-Dakota warfare 6
dreams and dreaming 43, 86, 171
  in nativism 172

Echeepoes xvi
economic activities 15, 22-25, 32, 79-81, 143-
    44, 195
  changes in 64-65, 65, 73, 109, 110, 113
  continuity and preservation of 60-61, 135,
    184
  of North Saskatchewan River Ojibwa 52-53
  of Red River valley Ojibwa 53-55, 126-30
economic conditions
  and responses to Christianity 175
environment
  as agent for change 22, 51, 72, 95-96, 110,
    152-53, 165
  influence of in human history 209-10

Erasmus, Peter
  on ethnic attitudes of Cree 120, 188
ethnic identities xi-xii, 49
  clothing and 159-60
  cultural change and 121-22
  emergence and maintenance of xi-xii, 20-21,
    49, 60-61, 96, 97, 114, 115, 119-20, 185,
    188
  gender and 121-22
  influences on 210
  Ojibwa concepts of 24
  personal 119-20, 145, 193
  resource ownership and 44-45
  spirituality and 97
  syncretism in plains cultures 151-52
  SEE ALSO communities, multi-ethnic
Evans, Reverend James 167, 171
execution of Ojibwa man 158
external relations
  Blackfoot-Cree 115, 142
external relations, Ojibwa 34, 44-45, 52, 188
  with Assiniboine 44
  with Blackfoot 24, 32
  changes in 79, 142, 154-56
  with Cree 39, 44, 66-67, 93, 114-15, 120,
    133-34, 154-55, 187
  with Dakota 6, 43, 94, 124
  with Europeans 90, 91, 124-26, 130-33, 203-
    04
  with French traders 16
  with Ottawa (aboriginal people) 31
  SEE ALSO war(s) and warfare

Fairford (Midewiwin leader) 185
family 22, 83. SEE ALSO kinship
farming 133-37. SEE ALSO gardens and
    gardening
  missionary views on 133
  Ojibwa views on 133-37
Fidler, Peter xvi, 40
  census of Ojibwa 97
  on Ojibwa expansion 14
  on Ojibwa-French trader relations 16
firearms
  Cree-Mandan trade in 78
  role of in Native economies 11-12
fish and fishing 22-23, 24, 70, 128-20
  in "debatable zone" 6
  rights restricted by governments 204
Fontaine, Philip ix

food, cultural meanings of 176-77
food resources 6-7, 22-24, 28-29, 50-51, 54-55,
        69-72, 81-82, 143-44, 160, 175-76, 185
    competition for 7, 45
    of "debatable zone" 6-7
    effect of climate change on 165
    of Interlake 81-82, 163-67
    of Red River valley 17-18, 28-29, 160
    scarcity of 17, 194-95
Foster, John
    on aggressive negotiations of Ojibwa 205
free traders 65, 66
French and Indian War 7
French Canada Indians xvi
Friesen, Jean
    on meaning of treaties to Ojibwa 204
fur resources of Interlake 163-64
fur trade 11-14, 31, 41-43
    competition in 14, 39-41, 53, 73-76, 103-04,
        108, 177-78
    effects of on Ojibwa 14-16, 39-41, 43, 53,
        193-94, 211
    Native perceptions of 8
    Ojibwa power in 16, 32-34, 39-40, 176
    women in 13, 35-36, 45, 125
fur-trade companies
    American 103, 108
    mergers of 66, 99
    relations with Ojibwa 16, 73-75
    as relief agencies 110, 195, 196
    SEE ALSO Hudson's Bay Company; North
        West Company

game resources 24-25
    decline in 17, 194
    as factor in Ojibwa expansion 17-18
gardens and gardening 29, 70-71, 81-82, 110,
        128-29, 133, 134-35, 185, 196
    commercial 72, 80
gatherings, communal 22-24, 71, 114
    of Interlake 81
    and maintenance of ethnic identities 60
    reasons for 23, 46, 54-55, 81, 167-68
gender
    creation of masculinity 58, 189
    and cultural change 121-12, 151
    and ethnicity 121-22
    missionary concepts of 134-35
    in plains cultures 122-23, 145, 151, 188-91
gifts and gift giving
    cultural meanings of 34, 36, 105

Goodwin, Mr. (Hudson's Bay Company trader)
    reputation for power of 50
Grant, Peter
    on moose 175
Green Setting Feather (Ojibwa leader) 156
Gros Ventres. SEE Minnetarees
guardians, spirit 25

Hail, Barbara
    on continuity of clothing styles and design
        191
Hallowell, A. Irving
    on Ojibwa expansion 28
Hammell, George
    on cultural meanings of colours and metals
        9-10
Helm, June
    on women's public status 58
Henry, Alexander, the Elder
    on family 22
    on location of Ojibwa villages 4
Henry, Alexander, the Younger xvi
    on fur-trade marriages 35
    unable to influence Ojibwa 15
Heron, Francis 107-08
Herring, Ann
    on responses to epidemics 20-21
Hickerson, Harold
    on Ojibwa expansion 6-7, 14, 28, 68
    on relations with Assiniboine 44
    on use of horses 48, 49, 59
Hillyer, Reverend Charles 174
Hime, H.L.
    photographic records of 181-82
Hind Expedition 141, 181
    on ethnic identities 188
history, written 146-51
    interpretations of xii, 207-09
    sources for xii, 27, 116-19, 207-08
Holzkamm, Tim
    on wild rice 29
horse-raiding complex 47-48, 50, 78
horses 48-49
    cultural meanings of 48-51, 145
    Ojibwa desire for 77-79
    Ojibwa possession of 47-51
    trade in 46-47, 78, 114-15
house construction 23, 182
    changes in 18, 60, 77, 80, 96

Howard, James xvii, 118, 120
  on emergence of plains Ojibwa 116
  on western Ojibwa x
Hudson's Bay Company 39
  challenged by Métis 176
  manipulated by Ojibwa 16, 39-40, 74-76,
    176
  parliamentary investigation of 201-02
  posts of 100, 102, 108
  records of 27
  reforms of 100-03
  relations with Ojibwa 73-74, 92
  as relief agency 110, 195, 196
  hunting and gathering 24-25, 73
  hunting rights, restrictions on 204

Indian settlement. SEE St. Peter's
individuals
  roles of in historical events 209
Innis, Harold Adams
  on Indians after 1821 99
Iroquois
  contracts of with Montreal traders 15
Isham, James xvi

The Jackfish (Ojibwa)
  band of requests relief 110-11
Jacobs, Reverend Peter 167
Jones, Reverend David 131, 132, 134, 167

Kay-a-gis-gis 151
Keesik, Thomas Manitou 197
Kennedy, Robert 105, 138
kinship 22, 114
  creation of 24, 34-36, 82
  obligations of 36, 45, 195
Klinger, Joseph 118
Krech, Shepard, III
  on dependence 11
Kurz, Rudolf 146-47, 151

La Vérendrye 4
  on Ojibwa expansion 5
land claims and transfers
  Cree 93
  Métis 198-99
  Ojibwa 92-94, 126, 179, 198-99, 201, 204
language and rhetoric
  Ojibwa use of 101, 102, 111, 176
  and power 50, 119-20

leadership, Ojibwa 139
Les Grand Oreilles (Ojibwa leader)
  land claims of 94
Long, John S.
  definition of starving 176
Lower Fort Garry
  establishment of 157
Lytwyn, Victor
  on effects of competition on Natives 40

Macdonell, John
  describes Red River valley 18
  on Ojibwa spiritual power 46
Macdonell, Miles xvi
Mackenzie, Alexander
  describes Red River valley 18
  on reasons for Ojibwa expansion 17
Man that Gives the War Whoop (Cree chief)
    145
Manatawapowa 30
Mandan
  trade in horses 78, 114-15
Mandan-Hidatsa
  and corn trade 46
  trade fairs of 29-30, 46-47
  and horse trade 46-47
Mandelbaum, David
  on Ojibwa reputation for spiritual power 149
Manitoba Indian Brotherhood ix
marriage 35-36, 45, 83, 125
material culture
  changes in 9-13, 43, 59-61, 146-48
  collections and collecting of 115-16, 118-19
  continuity and preservation of 154, 182, 184,
    189
  cultural meanings of 9-10, 12, 162
  as historical evidence 116-19, 146-48
  spiritual power in 25-26
Maymiutch (Ojibwa man) 36
McDermott, Andrew 198
McDougall, Reverend George
  on Cree fear of Ojibwa spiritual power 188
  on Ojibwa 205
McGillivray, Duncan 32
McKay, John
  on reasons for Ojibwa expansion 17
McKay, Terry 187
measles 65-66, 95, 107
medicine, spiritual. SEE power, spiritual

men
  status of 17, 58, 122-23
  work of 22, 54
Mercredi, Ovide ix
Métis
  control of bison hunt by 48, 66, 67, 104, 186
  emergence as ethnic community 63
  harassment of settlers by 91
  land claims of 198-99
  locations of 155
  numbers of 104
  resistance of 177, 203
  westward expansion of 155
Midewiwin 23-24, 54, 81, 112, 148-49
  Cree adoption of 153
  and Ojibwa reputation for spiritual power
    45-46
  role of in cultural continuity 24, 54-55, 59-
    60, 167-69, 172, 175, 183-84
  role of in ethnic identity 59-60, 146
millenarianism 170-73
Milloy, John
  on Cree interest in Ojibwa spiritual power
    187
  on inter-group relations 47
Minnetarees 19, 47
missionaries 94-95, 130-33
  attitudes of to Ojibwa 131, 132
  conversion campaigns of 167, 168-69, 172-
    73
  Ojibwa attitudes to 196
mobility, Ojibwa 38, 50-52, 59
Monsoni 4
Morris, Alexander 205
Muchekeewis 161
muskrat 108-09, 112-13

Nakawawuck Indians xvi
nakawininiok xvii
names and naming
  kinship terms for Europeans 35, 36, 82
  power of xviii
  synonymy of Dakota Sioux xvii-xviii
  synonymy of Ojibwa ix, xv-xviii
nativism 43, 68, 85-87, 170-73, 202
  in Interlake 167, 170-73
Nelson, George 15, 75, 79
  relations with Ayagon 36, 82
  on smallpox epidemic 20
  on suicide 20

Netnokwa (Tanner's Ottawa mother) 31, 36, 42,
  57
Nicks, Gertrude
  on traders' roles in Ojibwa expansion 15, 16
Nolin, Angelique 138
North West Company 14, 16, 39, 66, 91
Noyons, Jacques de 4
Nut Lake banner 148

Oachiapoia xvi
Ochippeways xvi
ocipwe xvi
odawag 31
Ogeebois xvi
Ogimauwinini (Ojibwa elder)
  on Dakota people 200
Ojibwa
  expansion of 3-7, 28-32 passim, 43, 67-68,
    142; and "commuting" theory 28; and
    "debatable zone" 6-7; reasons for 14-18,
    30-31, 50
  synonymy xv-xvii, 5
Ojibwa, Cypress Hills
  request for aid 205
Ojibwa, Dauphin River 79-83
Ojibwa, Interlake 55-56, 81-82, 163-73, 177,
  185-86
Ojibwa, North Saskatchewan River 51-53
Ojibawa, Northern Ontario 165-66
Ojibwa, Plains 79, 112-23, 142-44, 148-54, 188
  emergence of 113-15, 119, 148, 151-54
Ojibwa, Portage la Prairie 161-62
Ojibwa, Red River 53-55, 67, 123-29, 130-33,
  157-61, 185, 203
  numbers of 124, 158-59
  relocation southward of 67
Ojibwa, Transitional Zone 107-12, 173-79
  numbers of 107
Ojibwa, Turtle Mountain
  loss of lands of 179
Ojibwa, Western
  emergence of ix, 3
  historiography of x-xi
  reliance of on bison 50-51
  ties with eastern Ojibwa 29
Ojibwa-Ottawa kin group 15, 21
Ojibway xv, xvii
ornamentation
  cultural meanings of 9-10, 26, 32-33

Ottawa (aboriginal people) 31-32, 71
  westward move of 15
Ottawa-Ojibwa kin group 31
Ouace (Ojibwa clan) 4
Outchibouec xv, xvi
ownership
  of resources 54, 80
  of territories 54

Pachetoo
  prosperity of 162
Pakuk (supernatural being) 184
Palliser Expedition 141
  information gathered by 181
Pasqua
  ethnic identity of 193
Peguis (Ojibwa leader) 75, 89-90, 91, 93, 134,
  139
  conversion of 160-61
  land claims of 94
  location of band of 124
  and Red River land transfers 126
  use of clothing symbolism 159-60
  views on farming 133, 135-37
  views on land and resource rights 198
  views on missionaries 131-32
  views on polygamy 133
pemmican 72
  ban on export of 90
Penney, David
  on cultural meanings of cloth and clothing
    33, 37
Perrault, J.B.
  on smallpox epidemic 19-20
Phillips, Ruth
  on clothing, ornamentation and power 9
plains cultures x, 121, 144, 145
  ethnic identities in 151-52
  gender in 122-23, 145, 151, 189
  origins of 49-50, 79
  syncretism in 151-52
political organization, Ojibwa 24
polygamy 83, 133
potatoes 70
poverty
  cultural meanings of 166-67
  resulting from epidemics 21

power, spiritual 10, 25-26, 45-46, 97, 134, 149,
  188
  of clothing 9-10
  of language 50, 119-20
  of names xviii
  of women 84-85
  of writing 171
power, political
  growth of European 184-85
  of Ojibwa in fur trade 16, 39-40
Pratt, Reverend Charles 174
The Premier (Ojibwa man)
  signs Selkirk Treaty 93
The Premier's son (Ojibwa)
  claims access to bison grounds 93
Prince, Henry 203
profit, concepts of 38
prophets and prophecies 43, 67-68, 85-87, 170-
  73
  syncretic elements in 172
  SEE ALSO Tabashaw; Tenskwatawa
prosperity, Ojibwa 32-33, 59, 82-83, 162, 177
protests, Métis, 176, 177, 203
protests, Ojibwa
  of post closings 100, 102
  of Selkirk Treaty 126
pung'ke xvi

racism
  in Hudson's Bay Company hierarchy 177
Ramsey, Alexander 179
Ray, Arthur J.
  on dependency 77
  on Natives after 1821 99
  on Ojibwa manipulation of traders 176
  on seasonal movements of Ojibwa and Cree
    68-69
  on starving 176
reciprocity. SEE sharing and reciprocity
Red River settlement
  census at, 1871 202-03
  establishment of 88
  and flood, 1826 130
  land transfers at 92, 93
  as market for Natives' products 88-90, 108,
    126
  as Ojibwa communications centre 124
  Ojibwa expectations of 89-90
Red River valley
  descriptions of 18
  numbers at 123-24

religious beliefs and practice 23, 25, 54-55
    changes in 148
    continuity of 59-61, 183, 196-97, 182-84,
      197
    male orientation of plains 189
    revitalization of 87, 170-73
    syncretism in 151-53, 153-54, 163, 169, 183,
      197
resources
    competition for 64-67
    ownership of 54, 80
rice, wild 22, 24, 28, 29, 70, 81-82
    cultivation of 70
    in "debatable zone" 6-7
Ritterbush, Lauren
    on cultural continuity of Red River valley
      Ojibwa 54
    on Ojibwa at Pembina 68
Rogers, Susan
    on women's power in families 56-57
Ross, Alexander
    on Ojibwa expansion 14
Russell, Dale
    on Cree and Assiniboine migrations 5
    on Ojibwa movements 30
    on plain cultures 120-21

Saucy Fellow (Ojibwa man)
    and alcohol 178
Saulteaux xv, xvi, xvii
Saulteur xv, xvii
Sayer, Guillaume, trial of 177
Sayos (Big Bear's Ojibwa wife) 148
schools, missionary 131, 137-38
seasonal round, Ojibwa 22-25, 52-55, 68-69,
    80-82, 107, 126-30, 142-44, 160
Select Committee of House of Commons, 1857
    201-02
Selkirk, Lord 72
Selkirk reserve
    loss of 204-05
Selkirk Treaty, 1817 92-93, 198
    Ojibwa protests about 126
    and quit rent 124
Semple, Governor 91
Settee, Reverend James 168, 171, 174, 185,
    197, 202
    on Cree adoption of Ojibwa customs 193

settlers, European 63
    dependence of on Natives 88
    harassment by Métis and North West
      Company 91
    Ojibwa responses to 156-57
    views on Ojibwa 157
Seven Oaks incident 91
Shaking Tent 23, 46, 81, 172
Shakopee (Dakota chief). SEE The Six
sharing and reciprocity
    cultural meanings of 8-9
Sharrock, Susan
    on multi-ethnic families 120
Shaw-gwaw-goo-sink (Ottawa man)
    introduces maize cultivation 71
Simpson, George 134, 138, 161
    bans alcohol 101-02
    ends trade with Sioux 124
    reforms of 100-03
    views on Indians 99-100
Sioux
    trade with Hudson's Bay Company 94, 124
Sisseton (Dakota Sioux band)
    peacemaking attempt of 94
The Six 117, 117 ill.
    identification of 116-18
The Six, wife of 117, 117 ill.
Skinner, Alanson
    on western Ojibwa x
smallpox 18-21, 21, 115, 141-42, 201
Smithurst, Reverend 132, 161
    on fur and food resources of Interlake 165
    reputation for conjuring 162-63
social organization 22, 24, 52
    changes in 13
    continuity and preservation of 148-49
    syncretism in 148
sororate 83
Sotos xvi
Southesk, Earl of 189
spirits, guardian 25
spirituality. SEE power, spiritual
St. Peter's 157, 162
Stagg, Reverend William 163, 167, 168, 171,
    202
    criticized by Fairford 185
starvation 109, 111
    winter increase in 194-95
starving, meanings of 17, 56, 65, 101, 109-10,
    111, 176

sugar 22, 28-29, 54, 80-81, 108
  ownership of trees 80
suicide 20
  among women 57
Sun Dance 96, 113-14, 145, 148-49, 188
Sutherland, George 88
syllabic writing
  invention of 171
syncretism
  in clothing styles and design 189-93
  in nativistic prophecies 172
  in plains cultures 149, 151-52
  in religious beliefs and practice 151-53, 163,
    167, 169-70, 172-73, 184, 197
  in social organization 148-49

Tabashaw (Ojibwa leader) 36, 88
  dreams and revelations of 43, 86, 171
Tanner, John 15, 16, 31, 44, 75
  on family 22
  and horse raiding 47-48, 50
  narrative of xii
  on Ojibwa expansion 16
  protests fur-trade monopoly 100
Taw-ga-we-ninne (Tanner's Ojibwa father) 31
technology, European
  cultural meanings of 12
  Native views on 10, 11
Tenskwatawa (The Shawnee Prophet) 67-68,
    85-86, 171
territories
  ownership of 54
  shifts in 142
Thirst Dance. SEE Sun Dance
Thistle, Paul
  on cultural amnesia 11
Thompson, David 15-16
  on Ojibwa spiritual power 45-46
  on prosperity of Ojibwa 32-33, 59
  on reasons for Ojibwa expansion 17
  on smallpox epidemic 18-19
Tian (Ojibwa man) 114, 142
Todd, William
  and vaccination 141
Tolibee (Ojibwa man) 104-06, 109, 112, 139
Tomison, William
  on smallpox epidemic 19
  on suicide 20

trade
  as agent of change 43-44
  and alliance 34-36, 46
  and American firms 102-04
  cultural meanings of 8-9, 12, 33-38, 106-07
  in horses 46-47, 78, 114-15
  in "medicine" 46
  Ojibwa strategies in 16, 39-40, 74-76, 176
  reasons for 8-10, 13, 32-34, 37-38
  seasons for 23, 24, 54, 128, 129
  SEE ALSO fur trade
Trade Dance 184
trade fairs
  of Mandan-Hidatsa 29-30, 46-47
trade goods
  in burials 21
  cultural meanings of 9-10, 12
  desired by Ojibwa 32-33, 40, 77
trading captains 37, 108
  cultural meanings of 12-13, 36-37
  decrease in numbers of 101
  and male status 58
  traders' manipulation of 37
trading posts
  locations of 100, 102, 108, 164, 173, 194
Traill, Walter
  fear of Dakota 200-01
trapping 15, 24-25
  decline in 73, 109
  increase in 113
travel and transportation, water 30
treaties
  Ojibwa perception of 24, 92-93, 204
Treaty Number 1 (Stone Fort Treaty) 203
Treaty Number 2 205
Treaty Number 4 205
Trigger, Bruce
  on concepts of profit 38
Turtle Mountain treaty, 1851 179
Twin Wolverine 148

Umfreville, Edward
  on smallpox epidemic 19

vaccination 141
value system Ojibwa
  continuity in 96
  revitalization of 87
Vennum, Thomas
  on war over food resources 7

Vieux Collier (Ojibwa man) 36
violence
    alcohol and 85
    in fur trade 41, 42
Vizenor, Gerald
    on Ojibwa spirituality 10

Wabano 46
war club, Western Ojibwa 119, 119 ill.
Warren, William
    on Ojibwa-French trader relations 16
    on smallpox epidemic 18-19
war(s) and warfare 145, 201
    as agent of change 43-44
    invitations to 81
    reasons for 6-7, 44, 78, 154, 186, 189
    use of horses in 48-49
    Blackfoot-Cree 115, 142, 186
    Cree-Mandan 79, 114-15
    Dakota War of 1862 199
    Mandan-Minnetaree 47
    Métis-Sioux 157
    Ojibwa-Blackfoot 32
    Ojibwa-Dakota 5-6, 39, 200
    Ojibwa-Mandan 47, 114-15
    Ojibwa-Métis 128-29, 156
    Ojibwa-Sioux 43-44, 48-49, 67, 68, 94, 104,
        128, 156, 157-58
    Sioux 47
wealth
    accumulation of male 58-59
    changing attitudes to 12, 36-37, 58-59
    cultural meanings of 32-33, 58-59, 166-67
    emergence of individualized 58-59
    redistribution of by captains 36
    SEE ALSO poverty; prosperity

West, Reverend John 131, 167
    views on gardening 109
    views on polygamy 133
White, Bruce
    on concepts of profit 38
    on cultural meanings of gifts 105
    on reciprocity as storage 82
whooping cough 65-66, 95, 107, 130
Wisiniw (Ojibwa leader) 111-12, 139
women
    in fur trade 35-36
    and male wealth 58-59
    ownership of resources by 54, 80
    in plains cultures 188-90
    power of 56-57, 84-85
    roles of in cultural change 35-36, 80, 139
    roles of in cultural continuity 121-22, 189-91
    status and value of 13, 56-59, 58-60, 84-85,
        122-23
    and suicide 57
    work of 22, 23, 25, 54, 56, 71, 83, 143
women, Cree
    changes in clothing styles of 150
woodland cultures x
work, sexual division of 21, 56, 80. SEE ALSO
    women, work of
world views, Ojibwa
    continuity and preservation of 59-61, 148-49
    revitalization of 170-73
    syncretism in 170, 172-73
writing, power of 171

XY Company
    merger with North West Company 66

Yanktonai (Dakota Sioux band)
    peacemaking attempt of 94
Yellow Quill's band
    attitude to settlers 203